An Anthology

MORAL FICTION

Edited by

Joe David Bellamy

fiction international

For my mother
Beulah Zutavern Bellamy
"Toad"
and for
John Sullivan

"The Camel, the Lion, the Leopard, the Crow, and the Jackal," from the book *Kalila and Dimna* by Ramsay Wood.
Copyright © 1980 by Ramsay Wood. Reprinted by permission of Alfred A. Knopf, Inc.

"The Heavenly Animal," from *Black Tickets* by Jayne Anne Phillips.
Copyright © 1979 by Jayne Anne Phillips. Reprinted by permission of Delacorte/Seymour Lawrence.

"The Lost Tribe," from *The Gasoline Wars* by Jean Thompson.
Copyright © 1979 by Jean Thompson. Reprinted by permission of the University of Illinois Press.

Library of Congress number: 80-67335
ISBN 0-931362-02-4

Printed in the United States of America
First Edition

This project is supported by a grant from the National Endowment for the Arts in Washington, D.C., a Federal agency.

fiction international, St. Lawrence University, Canton, N.Y. 13617

Contents

A Writers' Forum on Moral Fiction

Contributors were asked to respond to John Gardner's controversial book, On Moral Fiction, *or to offer their own reflections on moral fiction—however they might care to define it—as it relates to the present condition of the art of fiction writing in the United States or in the world-at-large.*

When I watch Monday night football I wish that Howard Cosell would stop belaboring the obvious. I wish that he wouldn't practice his bits of sportscaster one-up-man-ship, and I wish he wouldn't treat his own insights as if they arrived from the mouth of the oracle. Still, now and then, I learn something from Howard. Compared to the millions who hate him, I'm almost a fan. I feel the same way about John Gardner's *On Moral Fiction.*

Because Gardner's anger is honest and wholesome, the criticism of his contemporaries never descends to mere vindictiveness and gossip. He simply knows what he likes and why he likes it and is ready to share his beliefs. His straightforward sincerity mingled with his certitude make it difficult to detach oneself from his opinions.... It seems almost rude to reject truths offered with such enthusiasm and good intention; but when Gardner moves from the general to the specific, it is sometimes as easy to say no to him as it is to the missionary on the street corner. When he tries to ground his argument in the framework of aesthetic theory, he is solemnly tedious....

When Gardner is making the grandiose claims of art in simple language, he is most eloquent. "Art asserts and reasserts those values which hold off dissolution...rediscovers, generation by generation what is necessary to humanness." He knows that often writers settle for the tricks of style, and that critics tend to fall into the bureaucracy of their diction. His indignation and the general truths he represents should shake us even when the specifics of his argument do not.

— Max Apple

Modern fiction and modern physics share at least one belief concerning their respective activities—that the world cannot be described except metaphorically. And just as physics has always been moral only insofar as it has measured the known limits of the physical universe, fiction has been moral only insofar as it has measured the known limits of language. But the technology of language, our access to it, has shifted from time to time and place to place, and it goes on shifting, often radically and always unpredictably (the technology of language is created by what we can hear and speak, what we can make our metaphors from). As a consequence, a consequence with a moral dimension, our knowledge of the limits of language must shift. Or else we lie. To continue the analogy, witness the effect of the discovery of the telescope on the known limits of the physical universe, or the effect of the discovery of the microscope. And recall the righteous indignation of those who had grown comfortable with the old limits. Mr. Gardner's essay and agitation should be read from that perspective, lest his fiction be misread.

— **Russell Banks**

I happen to believe that just as an excellent teacher is likely to teach well no matter what pedagogical theory he suffers from, so a gifted writer is likely to rise above what he takes to be his aesthetic principles, not to mention what *others* take to be his aesthetic principles. Indeed, I believe that a truly splendid specimen in whatever aesthetic mode will pull critical ideology along behind it, like an ocean liner trailing seagulls.

— **John Barth**

On Moral Fiction is more media event than philosophical inquiry, a work of high fashion, another vote for the conservative consensus, the book's real issues displaced and disguised. As far as I can tell, an odd mixture of self-contempt and self-assertion is its deepest impulse, anti-intellectualism and anti-estheticism merely its superficial occasion. Why make serious discussion about the unserious. Gardner's own work at its best is too radical for his own church. Trust the tale, not the teller.

In a period of moral and esthetic stultification, of economic censorship and rampant educated illiteracy, the job of moral fiction, in my view, is to make large demands on the reader, to create experiences that trouble his most cherished preconceptions, that allow him no easy gratifications, that extend his intelligence and enlarge his capacity to feel, that enable the reader to see only if he is willing to open his eyes.

—**Jonathan Baumbach**

"Morality"—selflessness, or at least the voluntary subjugation to a code of behavior—might well be considered an unnatural act. This would seem to be the message of Darwin and Freud (however they might regret it) and this line of thought is certainly in keeping with the sociobiologists.

Morality in fiction, then, would seem to be an examination of an unhealthy impulse towards self-denial and eventual suicide. The moral vision opposes the natural order, seeks to subvert it and call its survivors to account. I assume that most of us—writers, readers, reflective, introspective and introverted sorts—fear the survivors among us and desire their annihilation. We certainly do not honor them for their raw talent; we'd rather identify with their victims. Fiction, like psychoanalysis, can be a palliative; either an attempt to accommodate us to the brute reality—or a subtle persuasion to go over and join the other side. These last two categories might be called "amoral" and "immoral" fiction, in that they do not combat evil and do not advance the good.

The question, to me, is precisely the degree to which morality is a challenge to nature and, in challenging nature, deserves our uncritical adherence. We all know the trash that results from an uncritical acceptance of a "moralistic" (as distinct from a "moral") vision; I don't wish to get into the sophistry of defining the "good" for anybody—it seems to me that morality has become another charming artifact, a congenial character trait, a glimmering but always-receding harmony. Its animating power (for fiction-writers) resides in its elusiveness; I would suggest that one encounters the moral vision in contemporary fiction in much the same way one encounters a mythic structure. In other words, morality is a narrative force, an older and (I hope) trustier tool than psychology for the plotting of inevitability. It is imbedded in story, in action, in plot; it is an inevitable component in man's thought, just as myth and psychology are. But to extract it from the fundament of fiction is to treat it as allegory. The only morality I can trust is that which is discovered in the working out of action—the morality that is proper to a particular action—and there is no guarantee that the moral vision in a particular work is not going to be squinted or less than 20-20. Unlike Gardner, I think we can talk of fragmented moral visions just as we might talk of broken mythic patterns and of deliberate disharmonies, and not be talking of inferior works of art.

Morality implies only this to me: a certain negative capability, an ability to anticipate legitimate challenges to its ancient authority, and sympathy for losers in the struggle. The clash between an aspiration for ethical hierarchy, the perceived moral structure, and the apparently brutal, "natural" one, is the grand tragic theme throughout all of literature. And the shaping dilemma (keeping the conflict from resulting in utter chaos) is the central artistic preoccupation—how much "nature" (in the naturalistic sense, or journalistic model) to trust; how much external order and manipulation to impose. My instinct is to trust the story and free the moral within.

My point is only this: morality is a great and enduring myth, it is the lone universal myth (as in my initial definition) out of which spring all notions of religion, ethics, conscience, duty and neurosis. I do not advocate its neglect. I would not care to live in a world in which that myth was no longer operative. But I'm not so certain, not so certain as Mr. Gardner, that it's driving us to greater heights than our genes are.

— **Clark Blaise**

I am a beast. I learned this long ago. Any number of times I have put a shirt and shoes on my ape and we have walked among men and no one noticed until we opened our mouths—and it wasn't so much what we said that disturbed them as it was our shifty eyes, our canines when we grinned, our breath. How could *I* write Moral Fiction? I couldn't even if a man stood with a gun at my head ready to drill me at the first glimmer of immorality. In fact, the mere words "Moral Fiction" whisk me back 30 years and I see myself sneaking out of Sunday evening services at the Logan Street Baptist Church in Mt. Vernon, Illinois, to spend some time in the back of Rev. Pierce's Hudson with his daughter, Sandy. We used to play a game. Sandy would say, "Now, Bump, you bad boy, don't you get another hard on," and she would shake her finger at it. Or clasping her hands she would plead, "*Please* don't get another hard on," while tears, in the light of the moon, ran down her cheeks. . . .

Back to Moral Fiction. I cannot write it. It is against my nature. I'm not at home in the House of Intellect or, just up the street, the House of Morality. I'm more at home in that old hotel downtown with Villon, Genet, Celine, Kerouac, Bukowski, John Bennett. I don't want to improve people with my writing. I'm always amazed, in fact, when I meet people who have read and liked something of mine—mainly I'm surprised that they are bona fide *people* and not beasts in disguise.

Though I have gone my separate way and not stirred up much trouble, the long arm of Moral Fiction has reached out and touched me with its pallid hand. Moral Fiction himself was the fiction judge of the *Kansas Quarterly*/Kansas Arts Council Awards for 1978, and he gave my story second prize. (First prize went to "The Gallant," a fine story by Eugene Garber, an old friend of mine and classmate from the Writers Workshop at Iowa.) I had/have no gripes, but Moral Fiction's comments (from *Kansas Quarterly,* Vol. 10, No. 1, Winter 1978) are worth passing on, for in them I detect the faintest taint of ape breath.

> I give second prize, somewhat grudgingly, to Jerry Bumpus's "A Morning in Arcadia" (*Kansas Quarterly,* Vol. 9, No. 3, Summer 1977). The story wears its learning with a beautiful indifference (the love of Greek athletes and philosophers reduced to

silly homosexuality in a dingy room); it wastes not a word, not an image; it convinces me against my will. Though the story is slight, it does not pretend to be more than it is and is a good deal more than it advertises.

But I suffer from a blind prejudice in the case of Bumpus's story. I think the story is terrific, though I know it's not. It's not profound, the characterization hardly exists, and I know stories about homosexuality are inherently trivial (besides, I tend to hate homosexuals). I could argue that Bumpus can lay down a line of prose in a way that puts everyone else in this collection to shame; he's professional in a way no one else here is— his sentences have the authority of a Zen painting or a Mozart transition; but I don't really think I like the story for those reasons. I admire the fact that the oral sex scene is absolutely tasteful, I admire the accurate, idiotic dialogue, I admire the original way in which Bumpus creates suspense—I know nothing quite like it—but none of this, I think explains why I, who ought to hate this story (virtually meaningless, immoral, characterless, virtually plotless, in many ways unpoetic, also at least mildly pornographic) should find this story a pleasure to read and, after a month, memorable.

So much for standards.

— **Jerry Bumpus**

At the center of the current debate about "moral fiction" is a simple semantic confusion between the adjective "moral" and the noun "moral."

My own feeling about what I do when I am writing fiction—and like Kant, I'm inclined to make a categorical imperative out of it—is that I am creating a world, or worlds, that will sustain within an aesthetic framework the contradictions that in real life threaten to divide us. I believe this is a moral thing to do. I also believe it is a more fundamental good than any particular moral that can be explicitly stated in *fiction*. To work toward this larger vision is to exercise the capacity for love, which among humans is an act of the imagination.

Most fiction at any time will of course deliver *a* moral; it is easier to write that way than to conceive with full sympathy views of the world that contradict one's own. It is also easier to read this kind of fiction. As readers, we like to have our prejudices confirmed or even challenged, since either is easier than embracing doubt or paradox. But this is why time so often overturns contemporary literary judgment, after the need for a particular homily has passed. We also like to feel that what we are reading is profound or insightful, and it is easier to believe that a book is profound or insightful when the book plainly announces to us, I am profound and insightful and here is my moral to prove it. Finally, it is harder—simply, requires more work of us—to read a book that defies, sometimes, it is true, against the writer's wishes, easy moralistic summation.

I think that in significant measure the recent cry for "moral fiction" is prompted by the fashion among writers for characters who are one-dimensional, or cartoons, and plots that are elaborate puzzles. I have nothing against (though also nothing for) puzzles, but this deliberate thinning of characterization worries me, as what I've written here so far should indicate. If a novel is, or can be, a vessel for containing eternally in peace points of view eternally at variance, then the characters in that novel—and I include structure as a "character," it being the closest thing to the writer's voice and point of view—the characters must be sturdy representatives of those points of view. How important this is! Fiction is the root civilizing act. It is how the world is made inhabited; it is how we move beyond solipsism; it is a way to other minds. We tell each other stories, you and I, and if we tell them convincingly enough, those who listen are enabled to imagine that we exist. The flesh puts on the word.

— **Kelly Cherry**

Morality in fiction is a matter of artistic integrity. The writer must make significance, not plead it or borrow it. In our time the danger lies in confusing significance with surface dazzle.

Since everyone assumes that any modernist (or contemporary modernist) work of fiction is literature and therefore probably significant, and since so many readers judge a work solely by the sophistication of its surface, the writer can fool himself into shirking the difficult, heartbreaking task of structuring a work of art—on the grounds that art is imitation (all of a sudden) and a slapdash fiction imitates a troubled world.

— **Annie Dillard**

John Gardner is full of shit. I've read three of his books and nothing, nothing, nothing whatever lingers in the mind.

— **Frederick Exley**

"Only bad art is immoral," Ezra Pound often said. Or better yet, Samuel Beckett on Proust: "Proust is completely detached from all moral considerations. There is no right and wrong in Proust nor in his world. (Except possibly in those passages dealing with the war, when for a space he

ceases to be an artist and raises his voice with the plebs, mob, rabble, canaille). Tragedy is not concerned with human justice. Tragedy is the statement of an expiation, but not the miserable expiation of a codified breach
of a local arrangement, organized by the knaves for the fools."
   One always argues for a "moral fiction" out of despair, out of insecurity,
and from an anemic awareness of social and political illness. It is a strictly
humanist (at one time one said Bourgeois) point of view which excludes all
books that (presumably) depict a bad way of life, for instance the works of
the Marquis de Sade, Huysmans, D. H. Lawrence, Marcel Proust, Henry
Miller, Samuel Beckett, Jean Genet, and many others, including of course
all the so-called Postmodern fictioneers—all those, in other words, who in
the interest of moral security have been taxed with decadence and immorality and thereby placed out of reach of young girls of good families.
   This has always been the position totalitarian systems must assume in
order to survive in the context of their own twisted morality. It is an old
historical truth—historical trick rather—of the ruling class to brush aside,
exclude, censure, burn even, on moral grounds, those books which do not
conform to its idea of morality and therefore are found detrimental to its
moral good health. But of course this can only be done by negating aesthetic value, by deliberately failing to distinguish good art from bad art,
and by raising one's voice with the plebs, mob, rabble, canaille.

                                                        — Raymond Federman

   I've thought quite a lot about the whole issue of "moral fiction," but I
keep coming back to the same question (and position): Why should fiction
take a stance or offer answers or absolutes when experience never does? I
think that fiction simply shows us human beings faced with moral dilem-
mas and choices. One alternative is not clearly good and another bad,
though often one may seem better or worse than the other. And often
characters, like people, make poor choices. Error can be morally "instruc-
tive," too.
   Could we not have a moral fiction whose purpose is to help us be less
uncertain and afraid in a world of moral ambiguities?

                                                        — Malcolm Glass

   If, in his *On Moral Fiction,* John Gardner's biases are not unexpected, his
careless reasoning and indifferent writing are. I for one am glad that his
book is no better than it is, because it reads, finally, like a species of literary McCarthyism; and living as we are in a time characterized by recession,
contraction, suspicion, displaced anger, I would not want to see Gardner's

ungenerous assertions take root.

I will not argue with Gardner's insistence that too much of today's "innovative writing" is taken up with the "elaboration of texture" for its own sake; and that this is in part due to the extreme difficulty in presenting "truth" unmediated. Moral lassitude, cynicism, and a profitable pandering to decadent popular taste are other reasons, according to Gardner, for the excessive reliance on technical dexterity.

However, with these propositions (and with others, more subjective, about the spirit of our age) Gardner seeks to buttress his contention that artists must revitalize their moral relationship with the world. The mischief in this formulation is Gardner's definition of moral. Although he devotes a good many sentences to the virtues of pluralism, Gardner does not accept the notion that artistic excellence is various. Not at all: John Irving is good, John Barth is not good; John Fowles is splendid, Thomas Pynchon is meretricious. Irving and Fowles are of course "moral," in that they present in their writings a "benevolent vision of the possible which can inspire virtue." How do we discern bad (immoral) art? Gardner would have us believe that though it comes in several guises, the immoral "is always basically creepy [sic]; that is its first and most identifying sign."

Here, as elsewhere, Gardner immodestly equates the accidental circumstances that have contributed to his own temperament with a categorical imperative: If it feels "creepy," it is not merely immoral for John Gardner, but for civilized readers universally.

Ruskin, in his *Modern Painters* (III), erected a hierarchy of moral-esthetic values in which even as "a peach is nobler than a hawthorn berry," so is a representation of a Pietá nobler than a landscape. The American W. D. Howells, around the turn of the century, maintained that the writer's moral obligation was to concentrate on the "smiling aspects of life." In our own time Yvor Winters seized every opportunity to demonstrate his version of moral exegesis. And of course we have had the brittlely elegant declarations of Eliot. Although from this distance these well-known dutch uncles display as many rents as flourishes, none paraded his biases with so little regard for consistency as does Gardner.

If, Gardner writes, the artist "can find no pleasure in what happy human beings have found good for centuries (children and dogs, God, peace, wealth, comfort, love, hope, and faith)—then it is safe to hazard that he has not made a serious effort to sympathize and understand..." The above acquisitions, then, represent the preconditions for a sympathetic understanding. But sympathy for whom? Surely not for those who are most visibly lacking John Gardner's dogs and wealth and comfort: the impoverished, the afflicted.

Gardner's selective morality is disagreeably transparent on this point. Despite his several allusions to the Tolstoy of "What is Art?", Gardner's God has nothing in common with Tolstoy's Christ-as-Paraclete. Gardner in fact admonishes us *not* to give sustained attention to the afflicted and despairing (he calls them "freaks"), because "to worship the unique, the unaccountable and freaky, is—if we're consistent—to give up the right to say to our children, 'Be good.' " (The operative word here is "worship"; need one worship someone to be sympathetically aware of his unfortunate circumstances?) Consequently, *The Death of Bessie Smith* is a failure because it "hints of the unhealthy fascination with ugliness and pain that will later become Albee trademarks." What we "get from" Diane Arbus is "a forced message of helplessness and despair...neurotic concern." And Beckett, "brilliantly dramatized" as his despair is, does not succeed in inspiring his audience with a "tragic recognition," but merely provokes them to "laugh with the recollection, 'I remember one time when *I* felt as miserable as that.' "

Gardner's tone in this passage is of the balanced, principled intellectual-as-citizen; but peek in beneath the loose-fitting mask and you will see that the lips are rigidly compressed and that the intense stare is mistrustful, splenetic. So that it is unsettling but not surprising to run head-on into the pious certitude which, though it comes much later in his argument, is evidently the keystone of Gardner's uncharitable assertions about the afflicted: "What a careful study of freaks reveals is that they're all alike."

Is that so? And are we to believe that Gardner himself has made this "careful study"? The depressing truth is that Gardner's God (God and good and moral are equated throughout his book), far from resembling Tolstoy's Jesus, appraises with the calculating glint of the Mathers or of J. P. Morgan: a secure investment rather than an emblem of disinterested love. Hence: "Morality means nothing more than doing what is unselfish, helpful, kind, and noble-hearted...*with at least a reasonable expectation that in the long run as well as the short we won't be sorry for what we've done.*" (My emphasis.)

Just as Gardner degrades Tolstoy's morality by aligning it with his own, so does he commend William Blake evidently without having noticed that Blake's "morality" is to his own approximately as Jesus' morality was to the Pharisees. Loath as he is to mucking about with "freaks," can Gardner have approved of these impassioned (and representative) lines from the "Enion's Complaint" section of *The Four Zoas*?

> It is an easy thing to triumph in the summer's sun
> And in the vintage & to sing on the waggon loaded
>   with corn.
> It is an easy thing to talk of patience to the afflicted,
> To speak the laws of prudence to the houseless wanderer...
>
> Then the groan & the dolor are quite forgotten, & the
>   slave grinding at the mill,
> And the captive in chains, & the poor in prison...

It is an easy thing to rejoice in the tents of prosperity:
Thus could I sing & thus rejoice: but it is not so with me.

Such disgust and abhorrence as Gardner has demonstrated throughout
his argument (while apparently trying partially to obscure it), bellies up into this crescendo near the close: "The bad is an obstruction of the light, a
competitor against good, a filth and a pestilence that must be driven out.
Every chance composition purposely or accidentally backs a lie.... Every
nonsense artist, destructionist, or painter of bruised entrails on a field of
burning red is a plague carrier, a usurper of space that belongs to the sons
of God... Let a state of total war be declared."

I come now to my own version of "morality," which has been implicit
in my assessment of Gardner's, and which to certain readers will doubtless
sound no less sentimental.

As in the years on either side of the "Great Depression," it seems to me
vital that artists *who have the inclination* should re-acquaint themselves
with the afflicted living among us. Even Gardnerites would concede that
certain classes of citizens are scarcely visible even in our ripest times.
When, though, a harsh economic reality (not to mention other contributing factors) turns ripe to sere, there comes a foul wind. This wind is gust-
ing now; its constituents are self-absorption, rekindled resentments, de-
flected anger, scapegoating... Already it has left a vast human detritus in
its wake, principally impoverished non-white Americans, the anonymously
indigent, the emotionally tormented (John Gardner calls them "freaks";
John Connolly would call them "losers.") These humans lack articulate
advocates.

I am not here recommending a specific political posture. Nor am I suggesting that writers take up the broadsword of the Muckrakers, of Lincoln
Steffens, of Michael Gold (which is not to derogate the validity of straight-
ahead social-art). I am merely reflecting (as a writer to writers) on a humanistic option which will not compromise the integrity of our work;
which indeed will enrich it.

In certain instances it may still be possible artistically to revalidate social "truths" unmediated by technical complexity, but it is at this stage extremely difficult. Let us continue to write textured prose (applications can
be made to other genres), and to draw from the entire range of pertinent
technical advancements—but with a concern for the afflicted at or near
the work's moral center; it is this which I am advocating.

It might seem that to render this humanistic concern in oblique ways
would be to obscure it; that, moreover, the very souls who figure prominently in our works will be unable to comprehend them. This is not entirely so: the obscure—but engaged—will, after close readings and sufficient
time, yield its meanings (or at least resonate meaningfully), and certain of
these meanings (or resonances) will filter through to those people who are

not themselves equipped to unearth them. Obscure or no, a moral concern for the needy is imbued with a remedial energy. At the very least it is as a tree to shelter those whom that theocrat Gardner would cast out.

—Harold Jaffe

Things we'd all better look out for (together with particular irritant for each piece of grand wisdom):

1. Mistaking myth (a human invention) for God's will (*On Moral Fiction*)

2. Mistaking neurosis for fiction (virtually any book by Thomas Berger)

3. Mistaking the craft of writing for coldly logical market analysis (March issue of Ozark Airlines *Flightime* magazine, on the Writers Workshop)

4. Mistaking a work of literature for a 50-word summary of moral truth (Paramount Films educational catalogue, in which Hemingway's *Islands in the Stream* is cut down to 38 minutes of screen time and three sentences of synopsized "meaning")

5. Mistaking superannuated critics, whose goals are to become part of history themselves, for real writers (just about any critical book in America, it seems, including books by the author of this bitch-list)

6. Mistaking the product of art for the process of art (any critical approach, for example, which thinks fiction is story, narrative, puppetry, whatnot)

7. Mistaking the saleable products of Hollywood and Academia for the art of one's time (any mailbox full of junkmail, any day—the one quality these advertised items have in common, it seems, is that they are all *moral narratives*. . .and herein lies the problem).

— Jerome Klinkowitz

I believe that, if we are lucky, we have three great pleasures in life, the pleasure of a fine meal (my memories, which are life-long on this subject, go back to certain wines—usually French—and to certain dinners, usually fish, for some reason, but once fresh-made pasta with truffles); the pleasure of having sex with someone who means a lot to us, when we have the patience and inclination to spend a long time at it; and the aesthetic pleasure, which some take in art or music, I in literature, on those occasions when we have some great work in our hands, and are fully attuned to it. Most people are able to partake to some degree of all three of these supreme kinds of pleasure, but I am elitist enough to think the better our health, our character, our sophistication, our education, the more keenly we savor them.

I can't think of anything less necessary than someone asserting that these things—the sharpest pleasures in our lives—are somehow meaningless unless they have a "moral" dimension: the food must build strong bodies, the sex must be for procreation, and the literature must build a better world. What could be more middle-brow? However many times the Puritans burn down our theaters for being filled with lies, we spontaneously regrow them. Joy is proof against the wettest blanket. Joy is the most moral thing we possess.

— **Norman Lavers**

I own a copy of *On Moral Fiction.* I own copies of lots of books I don't guess I'm ever going to get the will to read. They're maybe wonderful or awful or so-so. But I don't suppose it'll happen that I'll find out which one I think they are. Still, it's a comfort to have them up there on these more or less terrific bookshelves I've got. Because there's no telling when one of your kids is going to go wrong and ask for something off. You can see how a generous father wouldn't want to get himself caught short. Who knows what dippy directions your kids are going to find their interests running in? I mean, it's maybe in the cards for me that one or more of them's liable to come by the depressing opinion that Morality belongs to be a fit subject under the general topic of Art—or, worse, to put the question the other way around. Either way, I hope not—but who can tell? A father prays, is all—but is there any depending?

Look, I don't want to count on anything. The way I see it, it's a risky habit, expecting.

On the other hand, it'd be really swell if the day comes when a kid of mine gives me the chance to get up there and reach down *The Wreckage of Agathon,* say. Or *The King's Indian. Jason and Medea.* Or, best of all, *Grendel.* Which are books that when it comes to John Gardner I think Heaven Itself had a hand in.

I guess I can see how every artist would like to have that kind of help. But I imagine there's no counting on it, not on a regular basis, anyhow. What I guess he can pretty regularly depend on is no help at all. But you take a fellow that's had the luck to have it, you can see how he'd get jittery when it quit. A person'll do some silly things when Heaven drops him flat after a stretch of Its abundant connivance. You can see how he'll likely stop at nothing to gain Its favor again. He's bound to try some stunt to propitiate the gods, maybe even look around him for a preoccupied citizen or three, some poor sap who's minding his own business and you can sneak up on and wallop him one and incinerate the shit out of him by way

of human sacrifice, going the whole oblation one better by jumping in the
fire yourself.

— **Gordon Lish**

   I believe that fiction ought to clarify life, ought to let us observe images
of ourselves in action so that we may be (as well as entertained) *moved,*
made more aware, motivated to examine how we act (what counts in the
course of things) and how we can make better choices. Which is not at all
the same as saying fiction's primary purpose is to instruct. It is to reveal. I
remember something Phil Levine said once—he said: I mean, you can't lie
to your brother on the phone and then expect to sit down and write a
good poem. The point I take from that being: the moral level of a piece of
writing comes from the artist's indelible angle on the world. I don't think
any of us are really indifferent to the relative goodness of our characters—
aren't we always, even in fictions where they are doomed, cheering for
them to do the right thing?—which may be another way of saying, aren't
we inside our characters and doesn't it hurt when they screw up again and
again?
   As for the fiction I read, first I think it's fair to say there have always
been junky books around and we're not talking about them. We're talking
about literature, stories worthy of preserving, stories which matter. Or
claim to. There are two kinds of writing which trouble me, I must admit,
though I don't know as I'd cast the problem into moral terms. There are,
first, the second wave metafictions. It strikes me that it's one thing to
move through our traditional forms and then with a strong sense of having
encountered a limitation, go beyond it. It's quite another to come along
later and see only the new forms and to copy them. The first seems like an
authentic sort of process, one indigenous to the nature of art. The second
seems like graduate school stuff. I'm sure there's a terrific hole in this argument, but the fact remains, when I finish a piece of fiction (reading) I
want to feel that I'm a little bigger for having invested my time in it. I want
more than cleverness—for clever I do double-crostics. So that's one sort,
the literary game-show variety. The other is the miniature, which I suspect
might be couched in "moral" terms, though that would be pushing the
point. I'm thinking of the *New Yorker* stories, the bad ones. I read one
the other day that really amazed me. I didn't know so little could go on
in a story. It makes me nervous to read this stuff—being as I am, in the
process of understanding the marketing of fiction, and of an inclination
to blame myself for my failures. The miniature story seems to sell very
well and the bottom line is: don't touch on anything important. Gives me
the willies.
   Fortunately, I'm happy with a lot that I read. Here are some novels I've

read in the past year, all of which I think are well done craft-wise, moving emotionally, and moral in the sense that they show people making choices and being responsible for the consequences of the choices, and further in the sense that, as I mentioned earlier, they compel me to examine my own carrying-on. First, *Garp*—read it three times; *A Bend in the River*; Toni Morrison's *Sula* and *Song of Solomon*; Leslie Silko's amazing, overlooked book, *Ceremony*; Jim Welch's *Loney; As I Lay Dying*; Sheila Ballantyne's *Norma Jean the Termite Queen*; Andre Dubus' two story collections; and so on.

So, I guess, to summarize a bit, there may be something in Gardner's remarks that needed saying and from which we can have a good talking out of things. But personally, I find a wealth of fine writing every trip to the library or the bookstore down the street. I feel no sense of impoverishment with regard to the literature of my time. Again, there's always junk and readers have always had to discriminate.

— **David Long**

Because I've only skipped the light fantastic through Gardner's book (though I think I catch its drift). I'll not respond to the book's arguments but to the general question of "moral fiction." I can speak only of my own response to the works (let's stick to fiction) I love and admire and of the main thrust of my own work.

All the fiction I've read and written is, to some degree, concerned with morality, and that includes conventional and individualistic morality. But whether I am reading or writing, what animates me most forcibly is a different kind of moral question that derives from this precept: the act of creativity is in itself a moral act. To give the raw materials of one's perceptions a relatively new perspective and shape so that others may experience them emotionally, imaginatively, and intellectually—above all esthetically—is an act of the highest moral order, because the achievement (not necessarily the motive) is impersonal, fixed in neither time nor place, neither in one transitory social, political, religious, philosophical, or subjective configuration nor another. I am thinking, of course, of those elements in a fiction that are finally transcendent, that do not, finally, derive their energy from the details of a particular society or the principles of a particular moral scheme.

Whatever the artist's intentions, whether they be infused with morality or amorality, the fiction that emerges out of the processes of the imagination, fused with the processes of the emotions and the intellect, has an independent existence, and to the degree that it is a work of art, I respond fully to it, and do not feel I need to experience *in* it or carry away *from* it the author's or "mankind's" moral vision. Every fiction I admire has moral implications, and I respond to them, but I am motivated to re-read, re-experience that fiction only as it is an esthetically charged work that discharges its electricity every time I return to it, long, long after its moral implications have fully satisfied whatever craving for moral edification I may have. I am consciously aware of the moral implications of my own fiction, but I much more consciously strive to give it esthetic force and permanence, and that is what I hope readers most intensely experience.

— **David Madden**

I read Gardner, and I believe that the only thing that would meet his criteria would be a story about a middle-class, suburban family in which the husband/father loses his job...things go from bad to worse...the wife-mother decides to commit suicide rather than give in to the advances of the banker who has offered to burn the mortgage in return for a little head...finally in the last pages a fairy rides in on a Harley and makes everything right and dull again.

— **James Ashbrook Perkins**

As Flannery O'Connor reminds us in her *Letters* (*The Habit of Being,* edited by S. Fitzgerald), "James said the morality of a work of fiction depended on the *felt life* that was in it, and St. Thomas said that art didn't require rectitude of the appetite." Freedom cannot be simply conceived; it is a mystery as strange as love. A definition of "moral fiction" is certainly allowable and may be useful to the writer composing it, but definitions by nature are limited and open to interpretation and will not serve artists in any general way.

We move in the mystery served by language but not *of* language—a mystery the writer can hope to deepen.

— **Jayne Anne Phillips**

The crux of the moral fiction issue is not morality, but the role of content. The deemphasis of content which Gardner decries is the literary equivalent of a trend which pervades modern life. Life has more and more apparatus and texture, less and less final product. The writer whose story is about getting it written is the soulmate of the government bureaucrat whose job is to facilitate, coordinate, and motivate. I have spent a good many years trying to understand why writers and critics would wish to squeeze content out of literature, but the only answer I can offer is that, like most political leaders and very many ordinary citizens, they behave the way they do because they cannot make heads nor tails out of the substance of life.

Take the structuralists. The central tenet of structuralism is that individual human beings are an improper measure of things. The source of literary structuralism was a nation physically and morally humiliated in war. The emotional thrust of structuralism is a counter-attack against people who can *act,* act *meaningfully* and act *morally,* by people who can't. Structuralism as literary criticism is really little more than formalism: it puts the real stuff of life at an unnecessary remove while emphasizing increasingly arcane concepts of pattern. Structuralism as a lifestyle is the administrative principle which delivers your mail. It is the guiding principle of all government service functions (though not of the IRS, which the government perceives as substantive and critical to its survival).

I have noticed an astonishing and melancholy phenomenon in recent years among literary intellectuals of all kinds, and especially among members of university English faculties. If you wish to shock a group of English professors out of their minds at a dinner party, the level of shock, say, that one might expect from advocacy of genocide or preemptive nuclear war, it is necessary only to speak as if you assume that life is a serious (if often funny) business, and that there are substantive and important decisions for individual human beings to make.

Another melancholy fact which I have come to observe is that few members of college English faculties care to spend much off-duty time discussing anything having to do with the contents of a book. Leading topics are real estate, home repairs, sports (especially, for some reason, basketball and boxing), restaurants, and departmental scandals, estimable subjects all, but somewhat incomplete as a total definition of human existence. Structuralism offers itself as a metaphor for the academic critic because it accurately describes his relationship to his job and his discipline. A pragmatic instinct tells him that what he finds in novels, stories, and plays is not critical to either his job or his life. His attitude puts me in mind of a piece of proverbial folk wisdom GIs used to ascribe to the Vietnamese: if you can't eat it, drink it, screw it, or take shelter under it, the hell with it. So much for literature.

I like to think that this is Gardner's major quarrel, too, rather than any more specific and prescriptive definition of morality. At any rate, I share his concern and his judgment that John Fowles' *Daniel Martin* is an important and seminal work which points the way back to the right track. *Daniel Martin* is about the sort of subject—an important and very complicated life decision—that fiction should either be directly about or at least leave us better prepared to make. If literature does not do this—if it does not deepen and reinforce the best parts of us as teachers, readers, and writers—I cannot imagine what is *is* good for. Not, at any rate, now, when sex and television place instant amusement at everyone's fingertips. Yes, fiction needs to be *about* something. The antithesis of content, as Gardner correctly argues, is not style, but emptiness.

— **James Park Sloan**

Susan Sontag's remarks from "On Style" seem especially apropos: "Art is connected with morality, I should argue. One way that it is so connected is that art may yield moral *pleasure*; but the moral pleasure peculiar to art is not the pleasure of approving of acts or disapproving of them. The moral pleasure in art, as well as the moral service that art performs, consists in the intelligent gratification of consciousness."

— **Anon.**

If Mr. Gardner is sincere about his reflections on "moral fiction" and is not simply giving us a turn or two from the repertoire of the comedy team of Bouvard and Pécuchet, I must vote with M. Rimbaud who, in another context, growled: "La morale est la faiblesse de la cervelle."

— **Gilbert Sorrentino**

Gardner's campaign in favor of what he calls "moral fiction" seems to be strictly for the public—a sort of advertisement for himself. That's his privilege, but I don't know of any of his fellow writers who takes him seriously, and I think the best thing to do with Gardner on this issue is ignore him. The public reception given his book is related to conglomerate publishing's effort to bolster its waning literary prestige. This is not to say there is no relation between morality and fiction. On the contrary, a strong argument could be made that, given the state of the art and the state of the culture, all "realistic" fiction is immoral.

— **Ronald Sukenick**

I have not read Mr. Gardner's book, so cannot address whatever points he makes. I am sure that my acquaintance with his ideas as summarized by *The New York Times* some time ago is inadequate; but I do admire anyone who can coin a phrase that becomes current, like "objective correlative" or "the me generation." I have always taken fiction's morality to be its truth, its will toward truth, from accuracy in minor factual matters to fidelity in matters of form and style to the author's intimate intuition and sense of things. No two people have quite the same sense of things; momentous authors of modernism are those—Joyce, Proust, Kafka—who persuade us they have followed their sense of things to an ultimate of strangeness and fullness. Any effort of individual truth-seeking and -stating of course will involve refusals: a refusal to imitate exactly one's mighty forebears, a refusal to be as "nice" as one's family and loved ones would prefer, a refusal to heed the pious strictures and fulminating vocabulary of literary critics, however obviously intelligent and honorable, including demands to write "moral fiction" in any sense but that I have tried to describe.

— **John Updike**

One of the joys I take in *On Moral Fiction* derives from its author's credentials. If John Gardner were only an academic, few, even among academics, would pay much heed. But the author of excellent fictions as diverse as *Grendel* and *October Light* commands the attention of everyone seriously concerned with literary values. It is extremely gratifying to me to see the public statement of *On Moral Fiction* made by a man who has earned his forum with credentials both academic and literary.

On Moral Fiction is a conservative statement, one I hope will be taken to heart, if not by the generations of writers and writing teachers devoted to the laissez-faire excess of the now-remote 1960's and 1970's, then by the generation now in the making in academia. What Gardner knows—and what has either been forgotten by many, or was never learned by some to begin with—is that all art is conservative, and that literary art is especially so, since language is the most conservative formal human behavior of all. If it were otherwise, if language were as amenable to change as, for example, industrial technology or the rules governing organized sports, there would be no art because there would be no culture, no morally understood, shared human experience, without which art is impossible.

Gardner will be accused of advocating didacticism, but only by those who prefer to understand "morality" in the narrowest socio-political sense. That literature (hence, fiction) is moral (created to the end of the moral interpretation, definition, and critique of human experience in our culture), that it must be *moral* in this sense to be *literature,* ought to be understood as axiomatic by anyone with any serious pretension to art. If a fiction is not moral, then it is trivial, whatever the glitter of its facility or the fashion of its reference. To take but one school of contrary thought, literature as "play," I would contend that is the sum of it—play—and whatever the level of skill of *play* (as with organized sport), it is unworthy of the serious interest and attention of serious people.

I suspect the most agitated response to *On Moral Fiction* will come from writers who parade themselves as "experimentalists," but Gardner's remarks should not discourage anyone self-consciously engaged with the genre's formal tradition, and I hope he *does* dishearten (since it is probably impossible to discourage them) merely glib practitioners. Easy experiment in fiction, the ignorant or willful disregard or defiance of conventions forged in the genre's tradition, is, I sincerely hope, as dead as the decades of the sixties and seventies—would that the morally indifferent and corrupt experimentation of our society's technocrats were as doomed! John Gardner's fiction, of course, redeems the concept of experiment from the debasement effected by writers who have confused ephemeral politics and superficial sociology (programatic or instinctive *Angst*) with literature. At their worst, they have been responsible for driving away legions of readers who might have become the audience whose absence we all lament; at their best, they have given a spurious legitimacy to the formal fallacy that argues fiction and reality are indistinguishable.

I applaud Gardner's book, and thank him for it, hoping and trusting it will continue to be discussed by all who care about fiction. In closing, I would recommend two other books I think reinforce what this fine writer has to say. One is "old," Wayne C. Booth's *The Rhetoric of Fiction* (University of Chicago Press, 1961), the other new, Gerald Graff's *Literature Against Itself* (University of Chicago Press, 1979). And I applaud *fiction international* for its attention to *On Moral Fiction*, and thank its editor for inviting me to participate in this forum.

— **Gordon Weaver**

Before I say anything about John Gardner and morality I must tell you that he has called me, in the *New York Times Book Review*, that repository of Revealed Truth, a "mushy" writer who is not a serious novelist. If you want to go on reading this, then, consider the source.

I read *On Moral Fiction* some time ago, and my first reaction was that here was further proof of my theory that writers always say they write what they don't write. Or perhaps it is just "modernist" writers who can safely say that they are actually moralists and that their creations celebrate the good. As for John Gardner, his critical reputation is based upon his modernist, academically fashionable tendencies. *Grendel* is a single interesting idea, *The Sunlight Dialogues* his Ph.D dissertation at the University of Iowa; *The Life and Times of Chaucer* is evidently someone else's Ph.D dissertation. I haven't read *October Light* or *Freddie's Book*, but from the reviews I gather that here, too, are the usual modernist gimmicks, the cool temperatures of the graduate seminar, the very qualities he seems to condemn in his rivals.

My second reaction had to do with my continuing wonder about the true sources of passion in the literary world. John Barth recently referred to *On Moral Fiction* as "literary kneecapping." I have to agree (I still limp a little bit, myself, from John Gardner's territorial instincts) and I'm afraid we must take the book, in spite of some possibly legitimate issues it raises and ultimately evades, as another glimpse of the nether regions of literature where ego, undisciplined by art, throws jealous tantrums.

— **Thomas Williams**

Morality isn't simply an artistic consideration, something that can be controlled creatively. Fiction writing is an imaginative act; perhaps living one's life is, too. It's very difficult for me to separate the moral demands of the two. It would be like trying to dream with a different sensibility, a different set of ethics. One's real values, one's real politics, whatever they are, spill over into work as they do into dreams. Only the metaphor changes.

— **Hilma Wolitzer**

While I think fiction at its best does center around some moral issue, I think a far better word for this private process is integrity. Because: I think this process is by nature private..., no more apparent to the reader than the crossed out words and handwritten late insertions on an early draft.

And I don't think it has anything to do with providing role models, who are the invention not of artists but of politicians. When I was a freshman in college, hopelessly destined for impractical pursuits but not quite ready to devastate my parents and so enrolled in an education course or two (this was of course in the days when parents all believed that any daughter who had no husband at eighteen could at least still get a teacher's license), I once spent an entire week in a classroom where the subject of discussion was teachers and smoking. This was the instructor's conclusion: while it is permissible that a teacher puff in private, he ought not have a pack of Winstons bulging in his pocket because students are impressionable and a teacher is a *role model.* Well, I dropped out, disappointed my parents, and began to write fiction, feeling privileged to be amused when, years later, we all found out that Pat Nixon was sneaking cigarettes in a White House closet because the First Lady too was a role model. These are trivial examples to be sure, not what Gardner had in mind. Nevertheless, though his morality may be on a grand scale, to put it on any scale at all strikes me to include this at its bottom. The idea that fiction should hold up examples of behavior is for me too reminiscent of that awful classroom. I *detest* any notion that fiction *must* inspire us. In one of my workshops, a student I had not yet got to once suggested that another student, whose material was essentially "redneck," have his characters say "black" instead of "nigger." My feminists are violent when the worksheet contains stories about passive women or chauvinistic men; my Christians turn pale when characters start to cuss. They and Gardner may disagree on what a role model is, but, by *prescribing* that literature provide any, they all join the deplorable ranks of the censor.

There is no art without freedom. In order to have the kind of integrity that enables the writer to discover moral issues and tell what *he* sees to be the truth about them, fiction must be *amoral*. When it pretends by nature to be anything else, I think it becomes something less than art, something more like propaganda. I don't care how good the cause is; propaganda is not art as long as it is conscious of being propaganda, and no matter what highfalutin terms Gardner puts it in, he is essentially suggesting that we write moral propaganda. He's worse than irresponsible; he's a traitor to the essential freedom of art.

So much for his aesthetics. On craft: Flannery O'Connor says that some people "have the notion that you read the story and then climb out of it into the meaning, but for the fiction writer himself the whole story is the meaning, because it is an experience, not an abstraction." The kind of writer who would have his southern redneck characters say "black" in order to satisfy his own conscience is dealing in abstraction when he might say what he wants to say far better if he concentrated on the experience. I think only a very unskilled writer expects that his cart of moral baggage can pull a drag-assed horse.

— **Lee Zacharias**

The Camel, the Lion, the Leopard, the Crow, and the Jackal*

Ramsay Wood

'There was once a remote road which twisted through some mountains and skirted along a ridgeline above a wooded valley wherein a lion ruled as king. Among his advisers were three crafty creatures who fed off his leavings, namely, an elderly leopard, a jackal, and a crow.

Now this particular lion—a powerful hunter—wished to be considered honourable and just. He never neglected his duty of providing for those weaker than himself. He developed a keen sense of justice and always sought to do the right thing, even in a crisis.

One morning a long caravan of camels passed along the road and kicked up a huge cloud of dust that hovered for hours over the lion's valley. And when the tinkling of their bells had finally receded in the distance towards the world of men, a young, pitiful straggler could be seen flopped down on the rocky verge. He was exhausted and wide-eyed from fear at his aban-donment, his owner—one of the caravan's merchants—having shared out his load among some other camels and left this weak, stumbling one be-

---

* from *Kalila and Dimna: Selected Fables of Bidpai* or *A Mirror for Princes*—a modern retelling by Ramsay Wood from the great Eastern and Sufi classic that is the predecessor to all our fables from Aesop to LaFontaine to Uncle Remus. This is a major, self-contained section of the *Tales of Bidpai,* which originally appeared in Sanskrit approximately 1700 years ago.

hind. For a long time he lay stretched out along the ground, breathing heavily, hardly able to move. At length, however, he managed to stagger to his feet and, with an even looser-jointed amble than is normal for his kind, careened down in a drunken manner from the roadside to the much cooler forest below.

This young camel was leaning against a tree, wondering where to find some chewy grass to eat, when the lion suddenly appeared. Expecting nothing but to be devoured, he attempted to save his life by humbly making the only offer he could.

"Help me, O Powerful and Tawny One—help me, please," he cried out. "I am weak and utterly alone. Lend me thy mighty protection so that when I am recovered, I can repay you with devoted service."

The lion immediately took pity on this feeble one-humper, the likes of which he had never seen before. His patriarchal instincts to offer refuge were fully aroused.

"What manner of beast are you?" he asked. "And what is it you think you might be able to do for me?" He paused to look inquisitively into the camel's huge brown eyes while the latter quivered at being so near what he supposed was the brink of death. The lion noticed his fear and moved back a pace.

"Not that it matters," he said soothingly. "You don't have to bargain with me for my protection. I don't believe that I should limit myself to performing only those acts which are directly in my own interest. I was just curious to know what you might have in mind. I'll help you in any case—whether or not you can do anything for me."

"Th-thank you, you're v-very k-k-kind," stammered the camel. "I can see th-th-that someone as strong as you are has little n-need for someone as weak as I." He paused briefly to collect himself and then continued with greater confidence.

"I am a beast of burden, Sir—a humper of goods for men, a vegetarian called camel. Yesterday in the mountains I was eating some bright green thornberries which I was too young to recognize as poisonous. When my master caught me, he beat me, and the other camels—even my mother—called me fool, but already it was too late. My sickness began as sharp blats of pain which grew like those rough gusts of wind that precede the desert sandstorm. I fainted briefly and could move no more when the final whirlwind struck deep within my guts; they transferred my load and left me on the road above. Now I stand feebly before you. What I can do for you is uncertain, for I am as ignorant of your habits as you are of mine. But I can tell you this: no one will be more devoted to you for the kindness you have shown in simply listening. I thank you as one living beast to another. Do with me as you wish." He bowed his head and knelt, but the lion begged him to rise.

"This forest and its surrounding fields are my realm and I am lion, King of Beasts," he said. "You are welcome here and have my personal guarantee of safety. No one will dare molest you, therefore go about your business in peace. Come—let me show you to a nearby meadow where you may feed and a stream from which to drink."

And so, in next to no time, the camel recovered his health and grew sleek and fat-humped. Most of his days were spent eating, resting, and socializing with other friendly animals in the territory. Aside from infrequent errands requested by the lion, the camel had no duties to perform. Everything proceeded as smoothly as dew down a leaf until one day the lion was wounded by a huge bull elephant during a hunting expedition. By the time he limped back to his den, he was weak from loss of blood. There was nothing to do except rest and hope that somehow he would survive. Like any other wild animal he fasted for several days, concentrating his strength. His eyes grew bright and his stare intense. He let his mind drift blankly down the flow of time, for he could feel that inner calm increased proportionally to his detachment. Meanwhile his dependents—the crow, the leopard, and the jackal—grew very hungry indeed. The lion eventually noticed their condition and took pity on them.

"Look," he said, coming out of his restorative reverie. "Just because I'm incapacitated doesn't mean you three have to mope about half-starving. Surely old leopard here is able to hunt up a few tidbits to keep you going until I've recovered my strength."

The crow rustled his wings and shot a quick glance to jackal's briefly lifted eyes. They both knew that leopard, however beautiful the rosettes that still dappled his splendid coat, was simply no longer an efficient hunter. Oh, he *tried* for several days after lion's rather pointed suggestion, but ...well, he couldn't *really* make a go of it. There were a few scrawny guineafowl, the odd anteater or skinny monkey—but nothing you could really call a meal, especially once it was shared among three. Slowly but surely, the leopard, the crow, and the jackal began to waste away. And things hardly improved when lion announced he wished to break his fast; now their slim pickings had to be shared with him as well, and as king he naturally enjoyed first choice. It was not long, therefore, before leopard called a private meeting with crow and jackal.

"I must mention," he said, "something which has been on my mind for many days. Here we are struggling to survive while among us that wretched camel thrives. Where is the justice in this situation? He is not even of our fraternity, being an eater of vegetation rather than meat. He is, in short, but an overfed stranger who, however pleasant a personality, contributes very little to our community. What say we kill and eat him? He's so big and fat that, even after subtracting His Majesty's share, there'll be enough of him to keep us going for more than a week."

"The idea is excellent," commented jackal drily, "and hunger pleads much in its favour. However, I am afraid you are forgetting that our noble

leader, like a good many creatures of power, is rather enchanted with the
concept of projecting a clean image to posterity. It is simply inconceiv-
able for him to view himself outside a role of the most unsullied honor.
Surely you remember his promise of protection to our delicious-looking
friend? History would judge him odious if he now retreated from his
word. Certainly he will veto your suggestion, and you would be an utter
fool, in my opinion, to believe otherwise."

"Why, you snotty little carrion crawler," hissed leopard. "Have you
got a better idea, then?" he snarled, leering forward ominously, fangs
bared.

"Now, now!" crow cawed loudly. "Come, come, gentlebeasts," he said.
"It does us no good to argue among ourselves—none whatsoever." He ruf-
fled his feathers, shook himself smooth, and hopped from one foot to the
other in a bouncy little dance that distracted their attention.

"It so happens," he said, once he'd settled down between them, "that I
may well be able to reconcile your different attitudes. It won't be easy,
but with your permission I am prepared to try. The highly nutritional potential of leopard's idea cannot be denied, and yet, to be sure, jackal is absolutely correct with his assumption about the king's most likely response.
But what if the unsavoury fact of camel's death is packaged and delivered
in such a way as to be acceptable to lion? It's all a question of proper presentation. If you're prepared to wait here peacefully for a while, I shall fly
immediately to the king and try to sugarcoat this pill. What say you, then?
Are we agreed? No more bickering while I'm away?"

"Yes, yes," said leopard and jackal in unison. They well knew crow was
the cleverest in presenting anything to lion. "We agree."

"All right, then," said crow, "see you soon," and he launched himself
into the air and flapped over to King Lion's den. Putting on a starved and
meagre look, he made a profound reverence and, puffing ever so slightly
with pretended exertion, said: "May it please Your Majesty to hear me a
few words?"

The lion had been dozing, but was filled with expectancy at seeing the
crow, for it had become this black bird's routine to wing over on those occasions when leopard made a kill. "Oh, my belly—be prepared; good news,
by God's will," he said to himself. And to crow he said, "Say on, Master
Corvo," for such was his name. "Speak what is in your mind. How goes
the hunt? What is the menu today?"

Blushing like a black dog, crow set a good face on the matter and answered boldly (for he knew what was likely to come). "Sire, I'm afraid our
claws are bare and, as it were, the menu is blank. Old leopard is not the
hunter he once was, and as a result we're almost famished to death. He
simply lacks the speed to catch what he could in his youth. And as he
weakens with each day that passes, so do things go from bad to worse.
Thus, Your Majesty, I cannot report meat for today. Leopard missed his

pounce upon a young piglet which jackal and I were helping him to stalk. However, despite this unwelcome news, Your Majesty's three servants have put their heads together and found a remedy for our strife, and, if your Majesty will but give them leave, have contrived how we shall enjoy a feast."

"A feast, you say? How? What's your idea?"

"Well, and here I hesitate, Sire, for I know that what I am about to suggest will deeply sting Your Majesty's heart. I proceed, nevertheless, for it is sincerely what we advise." Crow paused to take a deep breath, and, looking bashfully away from the lion's gaze, continued.

"To put it bluntly, Sire, we want you to condone the death of camel for the sake of Your Majesty's life. He is round, plump, fat, and full as an egg. Dead he will serve Your Majesty better than alive."

"What?" roared the lion, and with a front paw thumped the ground in outrage. "You dare to suggest that I break a solemn promise? You vile bundle of stinking feathers—get out of my sight before I tear you to pieces!" He began a mock lunge forward, but his wound froze him with a jolt of pain.

"Hoouuu! Aww!" he quavered, and, screwing up his face in agony, gingerly lay back down. Crow obediently retreated a few steps and braced himself for another flow of hot words.

"If it weren't for that damned elephant you'd probably be dead by now," grumbled lion after he'd opened his eyes. "You miserable beast of wickedness. I ought to—"

"With respect, Your Highness," interrupted crow. "Without 'that damned elephant' we would have no problem, and I never would have made my suggestion. As it stands, 'that damned elephant' is likely to prove the death of both of us, not to mention many others."

"Bird, shut your beak!" snarled the lion. "Say what you will, nothing in your faithless sophistry will ever lead me to violate my word. You can heap up shallow pretexts and cunning fallacies into the most splendid edifice of treacherous argument, yet never will I enter in your evil trap! Can you not see what you are asking? Am I to snatch back the gift of safety? Rescind my hospitality to creatures in distress? Camel has never in the slightest degree excited anyone's displeasure, and yet now, prodded by selfish hunger, you see him as a meal and not a friend! Oh, leave me, leave me; I weary of this game."

"And if I leave, Your Majesty, then soon we both shall leave this wretched scene by death, and after we are starved away, what then of poor friend camel? Your kingdom gone and chaos reigning, who will save him from marauders bound to come? Camel will lie dead and stripped of flesh by hunting wolves or slavering jungle dogs, or even, dare I say it, another lion who holds no promise like your own. What then, O King? Throw our lives away, yes—camel, jackal, leopard, and I are but your slaves—but keep your own. My Liege, I beg you from the knees of my heart, keep your own life or dissolution follows, especially for gentle camel and all other creatures in your land."

"I will not do it!" declared the lion emphatically. "No matter how you build your words, I will not allow you to kill camel!"

"Kill, Your Majesty? Did I say kill? Caww, now at last I see what has trapped Your Majesty in the goodness of his royal heart. No, Sire, killing is not the way; we are not taking a life, it is being donated! Please let me prove this to Your Majesty. Camel will come here with all of us and Your Majesty will hear him volunteer his death. I promise what I say is true. Leopard, jackal, camel, and I have decided Your Majesty's survival precedes our own: we are ready, as it were, to be destroyed for our own safety. Hence my visit. I only wished to warn Your Majesty of the nature of our business when we come."

"Get out of here," lion said quietly, "and this time I mean it." He bowed his great head in fatigue and anguish, and after a long sigh added: "Your trim tale has put me in a foul temper and I want to be alone."

"Certainly, Your Majesty," said crow as he withdrew. "I apologize for upsetting you. Please forgive me." Crow flew quickly to the other two and found them asleep on the ground.

"Wake up, wake up!" he cried, and when they did he told them all that had passed in conversation with the lion.

"So if you'll follow me in my plans," he said at the end of his report, "I'll tell you how we go. Are we three now agreed? Are you two with me?"

Leopard and jackal looked briefly at each other and then nodded their heads.

"Affirmative," said leopard.

"Ditto," said jackal.

"Good," said the crow, and he strutted about between them for a moment, seemingly lost in deliberation.

"Okay," he said at length. "Here's how it's going to go. Jackal, in a minute I want you to fetch our fat morsel. Tell him The King is starving, and that in duty to his Majesty we three propose to go and surrender ourselves up as food to prolong his royal days. Tell him it's merely a formality, but we wondered if he would care to accompany us by way of expressing gratitude for our lives of peace and plenty under good lion's reign. Got it?"

"Yes," said jackal. "I understand."

"Fine," said crow, "that's great. I'm sure you'll succeed very easily. But now hear me out. Come closer, for this part of the plan is for your ears only."

Leopard and jackal huddled forward with crow, and all anyone outside their circle could hear was whisper, whisper, whisper. Soon jackal shot off

to find camel, and it was not long before the four beasts together made
their way to the king.

"Your Majesty," said crow to the exhausted lion, "we your servants are
most powerfully moved by the sight of Your Majesty so greatly weakened.
It deeply ails us that Your Majesty's most precious life might perish from
famine and, though I am miserable at how little-worthy I can offer Your
Majesty, yet with willing mind I present this feeble body. Take and feed,
My Lord, of this my poor and simple carcass; die not for hunger—make me
a meal. The consequence to public good of Your Majesty's best health out-
weighs my puny life." And here he waddled humbly forward to prostrate
himself at lion's feet and stretched out his neck, lying still as death.

The leopard no sooner saw the crow flat on the ground than he slinked
smoothly up and gave the bird a kick in the tailfeathers. Crow, giving a
loud caw of pain, fluttered off to one side, looking very annoyed.

"Crowmeat for a king?" leopard asked. "Why, nothing could be worse
for anyone, Your Majesty. That filthy fowl is hardly fit for worms: eat
him and you'll feel worse, not better. And look here, Your Majesty: you
need a meal, not a mouthful of dry bones and feathers. Have some real
meat, then, Sire—eat me!" And leopard followed crow's ceremony and
lay upon the ground before the king, offered his neck and waited.

"Wait a minute, wait a minute," yapped jackal, stepping forward. "This
will not do, Your Majesty; his flesh will prove tough as old tree trunks,
and impossible to digest. I have as much true sense of duty as I hope does
any loyal subject. Hear me, then, when I say that, though I am smaller, my
youth makes me more tender. Bite leopard to break your teeth, but if you
want flesh for food—bite me!" And here he too lay down while leopard
hissed from short retreat.

"Caw!" shouted crow as he hopped down from a rock and pranced up.
"No way, Your Majesty, no way! You can't consume dogsbody; it's not
safe. More tender than leopard, yes—I grant you. But fit for lions? Never! Jackal flesh stinks to high heaven; and even fresh it is putrid." Jackal
swung his head around and glared sideways at crow in a most annoyed manner.

All this scene stirred camel's emotions into suggestible confusion. The
dynamics of group pressure tugged him steadily towards conformity. He
did not wish to be left out of the action any more than he wished to dis-
please the lion. So he felt it perfectly safe and only good manners to plod
forward once jackal had moved aside.

"With respect, Your Majesty," he began, "but I am many times larger
than all these other three combined. And my flesh is neither foul nor
tough, but in fact by many considered delicate and sweet. None of the
earlier objections apply in my case; I am truly many meals fit for a king.
Please, Your Majesty, save your life: eat me up and suck my bones!" And
likewise he lay upon the ground and stretched his neck towards lion.

Contrary to expectation, however, after a brief pause crow was heard to say: "You know, I think he's right. Don't you?"

"Yes," said leopard as he sprang, "camel flesh is dainty." And he sank his gripping claws deep in camel's neck and tore open his throat before that poor beast had a chance to breathe another word. Jackal and crow rushed in to lend some helpful nips and pecks—and all this while, of course, lion looked the other way.'

Thief

Robley Wilson, Jr.

He is waiting at the airline ticket counter when he first notices the young woman. She has glossy black hair pulled tightly into a knot at the back of her head—the man imagines it loosed and cascading to the small of her back —and carries over the shoulder of her leather coat a heavy black purse. She wears black boots of soft leather. He struggles to see her face—she is ahead of him in line—but it is not until she has bought her ticket and turns to walk away that he realizes her beauty, which is pale and dark-eyed and full-mouthed, and which quickens his heartbeat. She seems aware that he is staring at her and lowers her gaze abruptly.

The airline clerk interrupts. The man gives up looking at the woman— he thinks she may be about twenty-five—and buys a round-trip, coach class ticket to an eastern city.

His flight leaves in an hour. To kill time, the man steps into one of the airport cocktail bars and orders a scotch and water. While he sips it he watches the flow of travelers through the terminal—including a remarkable number, he thinks, of unattached pretty women dressed in fashion magazine clothes—until he catches sight of the black-haired girl in the leather coat. She is standing near a Travelers Aid counter, deep in conversation with a second girl, a blonde in a cloth coat trimmed with gray fur. He wants somehow to attract the brunette's attention, to invite her to have a drink with him before her own flight leaves for wherever she is traveling, but even though he believes for a moment she is looking his way he cannot catch her eye from out of the shadows of the bar. In another instant the two women separate; neither of their directions is toward him. He orders a second scotch and water.

When next he sees her he is buying a magazine to read during the flight and becomes aware that someone is jostling him. At first he is startled that anyone would be so close as to touch him, but when he sees who it is he musters a smile.

"Busy place," he says.

She looks up at him—Is she blushing?—and an odd grimace crosses her mouth and vanishes. She moves away from him and joins the crowds in the terminal.

The man is at the counter with his magazine, but when he reaches into his back pocket for his wallet the pocket is empty. *Where could I have lost it?* he thinks. His mind begins enumerating the credit cards, the currency, the membership and identification cards; his stomach churns with something very like fear. *The girl who was so near to me,* he thinks—and all at once he understands that she has picked his pocket.

What is he to do? He still has his ticket, safely tucked inside his suitcoat —he reaches into the jacket to feel the envelope, to make sure. He can take the flight, call someone to pick him up at his destination—since he cannot even afford bus fare—conduct his business and fly home. But in the meantime he will have to do something about the lost credit cards—call home, have his wife get the numbers out of the top desk drawer, phone the card companies—so difficult a process, the whole thing suffocating. What shall he do?

First: Find a policeman, tell what has happened, describe the young woman; damn her, he thinks, for seeming to be attentive to him, to let herself stand so close to him, to blush prettily when he spoke—and all the time she wanted only to steal from him. And her blush was not shyness but the anxiety of being caught; that was most disturbing of all. *Damned deceitful creatures.* He will spare the policeman the details—just tell what she has done, what is in the wallet. He grits his teeth. He will probably never see his wallet again.

He is trying to decide if he should save time by talking to a guard near the x-ray machines when he is appalled—and elated—to see the black-haired girl. (*Ebony-Tressed Thief,* the newspapers will say.) She is seated against a front window of the terminal, taxis and private cars moving sluggishly beyond her in the gathering darkness; she seems engrossed in a book. A seat beside her is empty, and the man occupies it.

"I've been looking for you," he says.

She glances at him with no sort of recognition. "I don't know you," she says.

"Sure you do."

She sighs and puts the book aside. "Is this all you characters think about—picking up girls like we were stray animals? What do you think I am?"

"You lifted my wallet," he says. He is pleased to have said "lifted," thinking it sounds more worldly than *stole* or *took* or even *ripped off.*

"I beg your pardon?" the girl says.

"I know you did—at the magazine counter. If you'll just give it back, we can forget the whole thing. If you don't, then I'll hand you over to the police."

She studies him, her face serious. "All right," she says. She pulls the black bag onto her lap, reaches into it and draws out a wallet.

He takes it from her. "Wait a minute," he says. "This isn't mine."

The girl runs; he bolts after her. It is like a scene in a movie—bystanders scattering, the girl zig-zagging to avoid collisions, the sound of his own breathing reminding him how old he is—until he hears a woman's voice behind him:

"Stop, thief! Stop that man!"

Ahead of him the brunette disappears around a corner and in the same moment a young man in a marine uniform puts out a foot to trip him up. He falls hard, banging knee and elbow on the tile floor of the terminal, but manages to hang on to the wallet which is not his.

The wallet is a woman's, fat with money and credit cards from places like Sak's and Peck & Peck and Lord & Taylor, and it belongs to the blonde in the fur-trimmed coat—the blonde he has earlier seen in conversation with the criminal brunette. She, too, is breathless, as is the policeman with her.

"That's him," the blonde girl says. "He lifted my billfold."

It occurs to the man that he cannot even prove his own identity to the policeman.

*

Two weeks later—the embarrassment and rage have diminished, the family lawyer has been paid, the confusion in his household has receded—the wallet turns up without explanation in one morning's mail. It is intact, no money is missing, all the cards are in place. Though he is relieved, the man thinks that for the rest of his life he will feel guilty around policemen, and ashamed in the presence of women.

Eat Your Grief, Cora Dance

Harold Jaffe

Osiris

killed in his own living room. Curled bleeding on his carpet. The police cut away the swatch of carpet where the body lay. As evidence. Months later his widow lives in the same three-room apartment, the gruesome rug cutout still in her living room. Her landlord insists he isn't responsible for replacing the carpet.

Osiris the listless one

killed man was disabled, black. His widow is "low-rent" housing development, Flushing, NY

According to Plutarch, "Osiris' body was washed up upon the Syrian shore at Byblos. The chest containing the body was cast up into a tree which grew around it. Isis obtained possession of the tree."

black. City agencies exist, are charged to redress these grievances. Their phone numbers are in the directory under "City..."

Unable to revive Osiris wholly, Isis contrived to revive him sufficiently to be able to conceive a son by him. Horus.

widow's name is Dance. She says: My Floyd fought in two wars for this country. Our baby died in stillbirth while he was fighting in Korea. Now ...this.

Another version has Horus emerging whole out of his mother's menstrual discharge. Are we referring here to Horus or to the goddess Hathor? Osiris is, in any case, the key. Osiris if you can't locate them under "City," try "State," though I am certain they they are under "City." What is it you want, Mrs. . . .Dance?

Is the sufferer with all life, but at the same time he is the source of revival. He is plant growth and animal growth. Dead, he is yet the growing motive for all living things. He may be seen then as our first anarchist.

yes, the carpeting. Money as well? That's liable to be complicated. Your husband was gainfully employed? He was disabled. The carpeting is frankly between you and your landlord. The money

Chomsky cites Rudolph Rocker's definition of anarchism as opposing not only the "exploitation of man" but the "dominion of man over man." As for distinguishing anarchism from "socialism," the true anarchist steadfastly refuses to render to the state what is properly the individual's. In this respect anarchism might be regarded (in Chomsky's words) as the "libertarian wing of socialism."

killed in his own living room. His bad leg dangling, the rest of him curled like a child, bleeding. His hip pocket and wallet severed from his trousers with the same knife that stabbed him multiple times (seventeen, according to the police report). A police technician cut away the swatch of bloody carpeting for further analysis. Cora

If Osiris is our first anarchist, surely Horus must be our first royalist. Lifting up out of the menstrual waste he straddles his birth. From the vast reaches of heaven, in the realm of pure fire, he is the God-falcon who yet draws sustenance from the low: in mountain and desert, in primordial slime. Horus/Osiris. Systole, diastole.

Dance thumbs through the telephone directory. She walks to the supermarket. Observe the dislocated gait. Childless greyhaired black widow-lady. Her husband's insurance policy contained no provision for "crime-related demise."

O functionary, yours is a pauper spirit. You are white and your calling is to pronounce on the fate of Cora Dance. (Is this not how you would put it? Consider): function in accord with station. The gracile attendant sets the pink princely child on the water lily. If the lily were vertebrate it would experience an exquisite gravity. This figure is obviously drawn from royalty, and yet we allude to an essential hierarchy: indeed the metaphor is adapted (loosely) from the "Egyptian Book of the Dead." There are cognate passages in the Buddhist "Dhammapada," in Aristotle's "Ethics". . .

small fucking consolation.

. . .We haven't quite framed the thought. Bakunin was a promethean figure, was he not? Initially. Bakunin's anarchism was a "No! in thunder!" to exploitation, to structure imposed from the top, to any delimitation of individual rights. A Melvillian presence. And like Melville he ended finally

by compromising not with the "system," but in accord with the Tao, with the nature of systems. There being no other "way" (double meaning intended). Are we thinking here of Bakunin or Kropotkin? Or of the German Stirner? Never mind, the principle holds.

the police have a suspect, black kid from the neighborhood. Name of Ditts. Didn't admit it. Not yet. Motive? We're working on that. Dope money probably. Boogie money.

Our stance is clinical, phenomenological. What else can it reasonably be? Observe that dead catbird on the lawn. Watch now how the dahlias bloom. Woman is fundament. Eat your grief, Cora Dance. As for

as it turned out Ditts had an air-tight alibi. Was shooting up in some tenement basement. Fresh tracks and some other junkie confirm. Lock their ass up for breaking and entering. No right being on that property, not theirs.

Consolation, Blofeld in his recent study of Taoism refers to " 'dragon veins,' invisible lines running down from the sky into the mountains and along the earth, whose function is rather similar to that of psychic channels within the body, as in Yoga..." These "dragon veins" are faith. Faith in what is (faith in "what seems" is something else, truly), in spite of personal grief. Those who have this faith—and blacks are not excluded—will find their dope, so to speak, in Jesus, Buddha, Zoroaster, whatever.

a neighbor managed to get hold of one of Cora Dance's relatives in Tupelo, Mississippi, and yesterday a grand niece bussed up to New York and will be staying with Widow Dance so that she won't be alone. This same neighbor is trying to raise money on the block to replace Cora Dance's living room carpet. Since the landlord refuses to budge on this.

A homely instance, an emblem: We read the other day of a young nursing mother from Wales who attempted to suckle a baby bat (Eumops perotis), starving for want of insects this cold summer. Of course the creature died; though not before infecting the young mother, so that she could no longer suckle her true child. This was Wales, U.K., of the planet Earth, you understand, and not Cockayne or Erewhon. Cora's got to take her

turning the pages of the telephone directory with unsteady fingers, Cora Dance unexpectedly recalls something from her youth in Tupelo, Mississippi: a Choctaw Indian family: father, wife, two children, all in tatters, gazing in through a store window at a floor-model radio for sale, gazing with their faces up against the glass, with an expression that...she couldn't then describe. Somehow she feels she understands it now, this expression. Understands now forty-odd years later north of

Lumps. Like the rest of us.

Mississippi.

Rock & Roll Heaven

T. Coraghessan Boyle

for Griff Stevens

I died and went to rock & roll heaven. It looked like Houston Street. This can't be rock & roll heaven, I thought.

A fat black man in a dirty white suit was sitting on a suitcase toodling on a saxophone. Other black men were lying on the sidewalk. They were asleep. I decided to ask the fat black man if this was rock & roll heaven. "This rock & roll heaven?" I said.

He stopped toodling. The saxophone was like a buttercup in his big black hands. "No, this be-bop heaven," he said. "You want two blocks down."

I passed a knishery on the way. The sign said: Yonah Shimmel, 97 Years In Business. I hadn't eaten since I'd died. The smell of hot knishes was a siren song to a man who has no qualms about mixing metaphors. I stepped in. It was dark, but non-threatening. After all, this was heaven.

Two men in open-to-the-navel shirts were sitting on a table, making music. One of them had an acoustic guitar, the other had a mouthharp. What they were playing sounded a lot like rock & roll. "Hey," I said, "that rock & roll you're playing?"

The man with the mouthharp stopped sawing the instrument across his lips. His hair was ringlets, his eyes were blue. "Where's your ear, man? This is blue-eyed blues." He pulled a second mouthharp from a glass of water and shot through a series of high stops, sucking and puffing. Music filled the room.

I took a table in back and rested my axe against a chair. The waiter was bald. I ordered a kasha knish and homemade yogurt. The waiter held the steaming knish in his hands and sang "Lassù in cielo" from *Rigoletto.*

"I had the impression this was blue-eyed blues heaven," I said.

"This ain't my neighborhood," the waiter said. "I live over on the other . side of town. In opera heaven."

The next block was choked with organ grinders and dancing monkeys. I was confused. I stopped to listen to a thick-eared man in a Pinocchio hat. He ground out a rendition of *The Dance of the Sugar-Plum Fairy* while his monkey executed a tricky series of glissades and entrechats. When it was over the man handed me a quarter. I put in in the monkey's cup. "Tank-a-you," the man said.

I followed my ears. They took me through reggae heaven, disco heaven, punk heaven and mariachi heaven. In punk heaven people were cutting themselves with razor blades and amplifying air-raid sounds. There was dancing in the streets in mariachi heaven.

I heard a sound like thunder in the distance. It could have been rock & roll. I hurried toward it. Three blocks down I turned a corner and found myself in St. Celia's Square. All the buildings round the square had organ pipes, bronze like the sun, instead of chimneys. In the middle of the square, just under the statue, a man in a periwig sat at an organ. His fingers made mountains quake, his feet toppled buildings in distant parts of the city. No one had to tell me. I was in toccata & fugue heaven.

In showtune heaven I met Frieda. She was wearing a peasant blouse, chamois jumper and patent-leather shoes.

I'd just turned down a street of sand-blasted brownstones, dejected, axe under arm, when a man in a ducktail haircut came bounding up to me. He vaulted a fire hydrant and a phalanx of parking meters. His mouth was open. "I'm the luckiest guy in the world!" he sang. Shutters opened up and down the block. Faces leaned from them. "He's the luckiest guy in the world!" they howled. He spread his arms and threw his head back. "In love with the love-liest girl!" The faces retreated coyly, but reappeared on the upbeat to shriek, "He's in love with the loveliest girl!"

"I don't mean to be a wet blanket," I said, "but I'm really not all that interested in your private ecstasies or the state of your soul. Not that I have anything against ecstasy per se, but the fact is I'm trying to get to rock & roll heaven."

"Rock & roll heaven?" he warbled interrogatively.

"Rock & roll heaven?" the faces returned.

He planted his feet and swelled himself with a titanic breath of air.

"Neverrrrrrrrr," he began.

"Neverrrrrrrrr," echoed the faces.

"Hearrrrrrd...of it!"

"He's never heard of it!" sang the voices on high.

I sat down on my sturdy masonite axe case and buried my face in my hands. When I looked up, the street was deserted and Frieda stood before me. Her cheeks were stuffed with cotton, her hair was in braids.

"Looks like you stumbled into the wrong heaven," she said.

"I'm looking for rock & roll heaven," I said.

She held out her hand.

Frieda was not in costume. Actually she lived in polka heaven, but worked musicals on the side. Her outfit pretty much restricted her to *Fiddler on the Roof* and revivals of *Heidi.* She took me home with her.

Frieda's father weighed three hundred pounds. He was wearing lederhosen and a cap with a tassel. He played accordion. Frieda's mother played tuba. Neighbors roasted chestnuts, kartoffels and bratwurst, raised steins of black beer and stamped over the floorboards of the tiny apartment. I danced with Frieda. She took me into a corner and held a wet sausage to my lips. Then she drew the cotton from her cheeks and kissed me. It was all very gemütlich. And yet it wasn't rock & roll.

Frieda's directions led me straight to rock & roll heaven by way of turkey-in-the-straw heaven and bossa nova heaven. Rock & roll heaven looked a lot like the Felt Forum. There were lines of people outside. The people were drinking white port from the bottle and smoking dope. Some of them were hawking tickets. I heard the strains of *Jumpin' Jack Flash* and knew I was home.

I pushed through the crowd with my axe held high. A man in a *Vita Brevis, Ars Longa* T-shirt stopped me at the gate. "Where you think you're going?" he said.

"Inside," I said.

His hair was like plant life. He was big enough to break the backs of normal people like breadsticks. "Oh, yeah?" he said. "Well let me tell you something: I don't recognize you."

I unhoused my axe, plugged it into one of the hundreds of amps stacked up round the gate, and gave him a dose of *Treetorn Boogie* from our last album.

He folded his arms. "Still don't recognize you," he said.

"Lead guitar with The Toads."

"Never heard of them."

I was stunned. "Never heard of us? We cut eleven albums for Electra. Cover of the *Rolling Stone,* coast-to-coast TV. When I split up with Krista I got 20,000 letters in one day."

"Sorry." He struck a match on his bicep and lit a cigarette.

I lashed into *Serengetti Serenade,* our big single. The chords mounted like leapfrogging thunderstorms. I played the savannah, the spring of the springbok, the roar of the lion. I played the heat of midday, the solitude of the baobab, the deathscream of the hyena. I played my heart out.

He was laughing. "You couldn't even make session man around here, brother," he said. "I mean this is rock & roll *heaven.* We got the King here. And everybody else you ever heard of. What do you think, we let just any hack off the street in here?"

I stretched my axe on the blacktop like a crucified christ. Feedback hissed through the amp. Inside they were playing *Rock & Roll Never Forgets.* I turned my back on the gate and made my way through the crowd, wondering how long it would take to learn tuba.

Sin

Joyce Carol Oates

"Hello?" says Marya uncertainly. "Are you awake—?"

He is sitting up, propped against oversized pillows in his cranked-up hospital bed; reading a book—or pretending to—as if he had no notion of the time and of the fact that the school bus must have stopped down on the highway some minutes ago. (It was ten minutes late today.) It is Monday, and Marya comes to visit on Mondays and Thursdays, never on the weekend when the room is likely to be crowded with people she can't stand. Father Shearing—Cliff Shearing—is so popular a priest, or anyway was, all sorts of unwelcome visitors show up in his hospital room during the most convenient hours, and of course Marya refuses even to greet him from the doorway on such occasions. Sometimes she fails to visit him on Mondays and Thursdays too, for reasons she cannot explain: she deliberately misses the 3:15 bus at school, and hides in one of the girls' lavatories, crying softly and angrily, whispering, You're such a fool, Marya, you're so ugly, what the hell kind of game is this, do you think you can fool *him*: and when she does return to Father Shearing's room on the third floor of St. Joseph's he smiles forgivingly at her, and squeezes her hand a little harder, never uttering a word of reproach. And a hot sullen shameful blush spreads across her face, distressing, and extremely pleasurable.

But Marya has not missed a visit for weeks now. Today she fidgeted during her afternoon classes, and sat by herself on the noisy schoolbus, and snapped at the bus driver to let her out at the Sunoco station—it's Monday, I visit the hospital on Mondays, she said—and when she ran across the debris-littered vacant lot beside the Sunoco station, and climbed the hill behind St. Joseph's, her muscular legs strained to carry her even faster, and her shoulders and neck were tense with expectation. Again the asphalt parking lot, half-filled with cars, and the heavy rear door of the hospital, again the sharp odor of disinfectant and floor polish and old wood, which she inhaled gratefully. One of the nuns greeted her with a smile and Marya nodded curtly and murmured something, hurrying past—she *isn't* rude, she can't help herself, the strong cheekbones of her moonshaped face and her dark, thick eyebrows which grow straight, without an arch, give to even her most neutral expression a sullen, censorious cast; and she knows she is ugly; and, at five feet nine inches, far too tall for her age. (She will be sixteen in three weeks, the day after Easter.) When she first began to visit Father Shearing, after his operation many weeks ago, the nuns were openly irritated with her, and one of them—tall, busty Sister Margaret—scolded her for running on the stairs; but now everyone knows that she is Father Shearing's special friend, she is the girl who takes dictation for him, and brings him an armload of books twice a week. So they respect her. Most of them dislike her—she can see *that*—but they respect her, and would not dare scold her as if she were a child. Though Marya's curt unsmiling manner gives no indication, she is halfway fond of the nuns—there is something about their long black skirts that appeals to her, the very ungainliness, perhaps, the old-fashioned and slightly comic formality; and the gentle clattering of the rosaries at their waists; and their dazzling white starched headpieces, which Marya knows are absurdly impractical. The nuns are special women, rather like herself.

Today she ran up the stairs, her long hair flying, and hurried breathless down the corridor, half-knowing how she would appear to him (child-like, eager, innocent, hopeful): in certain of her dreams she rushes to him, like this, and tells him that his doctor has allowed *her* to bring him the good news. The most recent tests.... The laboratory analysis.... They've stopped it spreading, she whispers.

Pausing in the doorway she sees two things: there are no other visitors, thank God; and Father Shearing looks no worse than he did last Thursday.

"Hello?" she says, rapping lightly on the opened door. "Are you awake...?"

"Marya," he says, smiling wanly, and lifting his good arm to wave her in, "what a welcome surprise, come here, you're alone, are you?—come right here. You brought the books—?"

He shakes her hand, squeezing it hard, in a robust adult gesture that would be embarrassing in anyone else, and Marya sets the books down on his bedside table, making room. (What a clutter! Books, carelessly folded newspapers, his wristwatch, a scummy glass of liquid, a pink hyacinth in a dime-store plastic pot that has begun to curl for lack of water, a plain black rosary, his breviary. One of his parishioners gave him a handsome little red radio which he never uses.) As always they chatter: Marya is girlish and breathless, Father Shearing is jocular, even a little loud, asking her about the weather—her health—her classes at the high school—"and how are things at home," he will invariably ask, not minding, or not noticing, how evasive Marya's replies are. His voice is hoarser than she recalls, the pupils of his eyes are dilated, his welcoming smile is perhaps too wide, too strained...so that knife-sharp creases appear in the skin beside his mouth. His face is papery-white. The bones show prominently on his high cheeks, and his nose looks longer and more pointed, and oddly white, waxen-white, at its very tip. Tiny sores at the corners of his mouth. His eyelids reddened, flakes of skin in the lashes, the skinny neck, the bony shoulders beneath the oversized hospital gown, the sickly-sweet airlessness, the odor of his breath.... "I slept fairly well last night," Father Shearing says, leafing through one of the books. "My rib—you know one of my ribs cracked? —from coughing—but it's mending now. Though I must have told you this last week...."

Marya says, "I'm glad it's getting better," in a faint voice.

She can't decide: *does* he look thinner, are his eyes really so dilated, or is she imagining it? You wouldn't know, seeing this pale skinny young-old man with the mocking lines about his mouth, that Father Shearing—"Cliff" Shearing—had been playing baseball the summer before, with the older boys, lithe and quick and audacious in dark trousers and a dark turtleneck sweater, and that he had had the power, simply by raying his smile in one direction or another, of lavishing grace wherever he chose.... He's only thirty-four years old, people said, when he was hospitalized for his first operation, but their incredulity, like Marya's, had less to do with his age than with his personality: for no one was so alive as Father Shearing, no one could be so sharp-witted and funny one moment and so serious, so profound, the next. Is he going to die, Marya asked in a slow uninflected voice, before she became angry, and refused to talk to anyone about him. Before she realized what bad luck it was, and how stupid of her, to say the word *die* aloud.

He is almost boyishly pleased with one of the books Marya has brought, *The Religious Dimension in Hegel's Thought* by a Jesuit named McNeil, for which Marya is grateful—the damn thing caused her a great deal of trouble for not only is it dismayingly heavy but the head librarian at the Invernere Public Library was reluctant to order it from the larger library at Vanderpoel, and kept asking Marya, suspiciously, if that title was *really* the one she wanted. (Of course Marya would never tell Father Shearing, even by way of a droll self-mocking anecdote, about the difficulties she had, for he would immediately choose someone else to do his errands for him— there are innumerable friends of his, there are innumerable helpful parishioners, or at any rate there *had* been, at the start of his illness.) While he reads aloud a passage, squinting, bringing his face close to the page, shifting his voice into a playful register, Marya takes off her jacket (odd, he has forgotten to tell her to do so) and looks covertly about the room. Any new presents? The poor man has had forced upon him a tide of get-well cards and potted flowers and bedroom slippers and robes, one of them made of cashmere, and obviously very expensive; there are a handsewn quilt, innumerable boxes of home-baked cookies, homemade candy and jams, the radio, the handsome Swiss watch, and many books and magazines, most of which he hasn't troubled to read. (Not simply because his eyes often ache, but because he hasn't any interest in them—in their level of intelligence.) Across the sill of the single broad window potted tulips, gloxinia, mums, daffodils, jonquils, and even an enormous Easter lily are ranged, giving off warring scents, too weak to combat the pervading odor of medicinal sourness. It must be in the sheets, Marya thinks, in the blanket, in the pillows and stiff starched pillowcases.... There is a small wicker basket of painted Easter eggs on the floor, and the pile of magazines on the table seems to have grown, so Marya reasons that visitors have come over the weekend. And another tin—the third—of English toffees. (Take all you want, Marya, take them home to your brothers and sisters, *I'm* certainly not going to eat them, Father Shearing will say. But Marya will decline his offer politely. She cannot trust herself with sweet things in her pockets, she might eat them ravenously as soon as she leaves the hospital, littering the parking lot with the gold foil wrappers, her mouth watering and her fingers trembling absurdly. No thank you, she tells Father Shearing, with dignity, you can save them for your other visitors.)

Whitehead's *Adventures of Ideas.* Teilhard de Chardin's *How I Believe.* Montcheuil's essays. Rahner's *The Christian Commitment.* Marcel's *The Mystery of Being.* The McNeil study of Hegel. Father Shearing leafs through them all, eagerly, and Marya wonders if she should help him—at least hold the books in place—for his left arm is practically useless now. But if he wants her aid he will request it. As he has indicated, in the past. Since his hospitalization Father Shearing is—well, he is less *himself*; a mysterious person emerges, from time to time, quickly irritated, short-tempered, susceptible to small hurts and insults. The mother of one of Marya's s classmates drew his wrath when she went to help him swing his tray in place, and Marya was present when one of the nuns, bullying in a motherly way, inspired him to a hilarious but upsetting five-minute speech—a little monologue, really, a sort of comic monologue, in which Father Shearing imitated the high squeaky voice of a very young child or a moron. Yes Sister, yes Sister, he kept saying cravenly. Oh *yes* Sister. Please don't spank.

Father Shearing thinks well of himself, people used to say, before his illness. And long before Marya began visiting him, long before she became his "assistant" (the word, the lovely word, is *his*), it was observed that Marya and Father Shearing were "two of a kind."

For many months, for more than a year, Marya has brought her doubts to Father Shearing. And he has listened to her, and talked with her, never impatiently; he seems to have recognized in her—despite her brusque shyness, her habit of stumbling over her words or trailing off into silence—an intelligence rare in his parish, rare even in this remote part of the world. Often Marya has wanted to break into tears and say that of course she believes in God—she believes in Christ—if *he* believes it must be true—she's an idiot to doubt. For she senses how very much he wants her to say such words. I believe, I do believe, now I see, now I understand. (Marya has yet to be confirmed in her faith. Which makes her even more of an oddity in church, shuffling up for communion, her head bowed and her dark eyes shining beneath those thick straight stern brows.) At the same time she senses that there is a certain rhythm, a certain hidden protocol, to their conversations. She cannot quite grasp it but thinks at times, half-amused, half-contemptuous, that her doubts are in a way like her virginity. (Though more significant than her virginity.) The struggle for Marya's soul, for her absolute conviction, is like a struggle for her virginity: she will surrender, certainly she will surrender, but not too quickly, not without resistance and even defiance. The other week Father Shearing paused to explain a point in the essay he was dictating to her, a point that had to do with God as Pure Act, containing no potency, and Marya had concentrated upon his words, frowning, and picking at her teeth with a fingernail, and though she had been nodding as he spoke she finally interrupted to say, Yes, yes, I understand, but I don't *believe*; if you tell me Japan exists and you've been there I can agree, I can understand, but I don't believe it, not really, the word "Japan" doesn't mean a damn thing, it's just a word or a shape on the map, I can't feel anything about it because I haven't been there myself, it doesn't have as much reality as—as—as this watch of yours here. And she picked the watch up, for emphasis, for she could not help herself sometimes—her demonstrativeness, her clumsy boldness, her impulsive gestures that brought, hours later, waves of hot embarrassment flooding over her! She seized the watch and gave it a shake and Father Shearing appeared to smile as if vastly amused. (It was no accident, Marya's snatching up of the watch. For it was the only present Father Shearing had received that she coveted. A costly watch, the gift of a wealthy parishioner, its workings so compact that the watch seemed hardly thicker than a silver dollar: Marya had been present when Father Shearing had for some reason pried the back open to show a twelve-year-old boy the intricate wheels and cogs and springs, and the thing had seemed to her a miracle. But the human brain is far more complex, Father Shearing had said, in the gay expansive voice the drugs sometimes brought forth, and the soul—well, you can imagine the *soul!*—is far more complex still. The boy exchanged a glance with Marya, an uneasy or embarrassed glance, but Marya refused to meet his eye. When Father Shearing talked in that way he *did* embarrass her, but at the same time her face burned with pride in him and all his words. For no one she knew, absolutely no one, talked as he did: no one ever spoke of God or Christ or the soul: it was as if Father Shearing addressed her in another language, far more beautiful, more mesmerizing, than her own. And it wasn't altogether true that she might doubt the existence of Japan though he had visited it—if he had, and if he described it to her, she *would* have believed.

Marya is seated with Father Shearing's notebook on her lap, ready to begin dictation (first they do letters, then they work on his long essay) when Sister Mary Margaret enters the room. She is a big, high-colored, fussy woman in her late fifties, no friend of Marya's but at least not hostile to her; she has brought Father Shearing a pill (large and white, Marya sees covertly, with an instinct of shame) which he must take in her presence. So he takes it, managing a neutral smile. The nun cannot then leave the room: of course she must fuss about, snapping on the overhead light, straightening Marya's high school jacket which has been tossed down on a chair, making innocuous remarks which Father Shearing acknowledges with amiable grunts. When she leans over to smell the lily, exclaiming at its beauty, Marya and Father Shearing cannot resist exchanging a glance—it is almost as funny a moment as the time one of Father Shearing's visitors, Mrs. Caitlan, rattled on and on about something or other and happened to say *alter ecca.* For Sister Margaret is a broad-hipped woman, and her girlish enthusiasm for the lily is not only overdone but appears rather forced.

Marya grins, ducking her head. She will not giggle because that would embarrass Father Shearing. How droll, how marvelous, these accidental moments of understanding—for it seems that Father Shearing and Marya often require another person in the room with them, a foil, to point up their kinship. You're two of a kind, Marya's step-mother once said, in a spiteful voice.

*   *   *

Marya, comes the voice, *Marya,* and she wakes suddenly because her heart has stopped.

A violent thump, and it stops. But then it begins again, rapidly.

Beating beating beating, as if a frightened bird were flapping its wings in her chest.

She wakes in the middle of the night, in her sweat-drenched sheets, and sometimes if she is quick enough, and sits up at once, raising her elbows from her sides, the erratic heartbeat slows to normal immediately. Otherwise it will continue in its light breathless flutter, beating beating beating, and her throat and mouth will go dry in panic. Oh dear God no, please no, no, she prays, though even at this terrible time a voice assures her that prayer is hopeless: there is no God.

She has been dreaming about something that slips away, something with a human presence; but very small, and liquid; turned to liquid; slipping away across the surface of a table...or a long low smooth counter....

(She has glimpsed, once, a very long time ago, in the Invemere County Morgue, a table used for autopsies. A table that is really a sink. Made of porcelain. With long shallow grooves. And a drain at its foot.)

When her heartbeat slows she sits in the dark, trying to catch her breath. Her nightgown sticks to her sides. Within minutes it turns cold, and she begins to shiver; but she can't get up to change it for fear of waking her sister, whose sleep she has already disturbed. Her panic turns to resentment and then to anger. Across the nighttime miles—across the five miles between her home and St. Joseph's Hospital—her spirit flies, to accost Father Shearing in his bed. You're not really going to die, she screams, what kind of a game are you playing, haven't you wrung enough pity out of us, what the hell do you want—!

Three years ago when Clifford Shearing first came to Invemere, from Port Oriskany, it was noted how certain of the young women gathered around him—it was noted how he laughed with them, and held their gaze, his dark eyes slitted with knowledge. He was audacious and playful, he knew exactly what to say, and when to be silent, he *knew* them, and took an obvious delight in their discomfort. The former parish priest had been an elderly pot-bellied man with a perpetually beery breath; it was said that he frequently belched in confession, and even while administering holy communion. And here was Father Shearing, looking even younger than thirty-one, with his dark curly hair and his beautifully modulated voice, and of course everyone fell in love with him...even the married sister of one of Marya's friends at school, seven months pregnant, and given to spells of furious helpless weeping. And Marya had thought in contempt: How crude, how obvious, *he* isn't impressed with such idiocy.

When she wakes in the night after that dream she sees again his sly grinning face, his priest's cassock, the curve of his shoulder and arm, and she hears again his hearty flirtatious laughter. It *is* a game. His very being is a game. He wants to tease, to vex, to provoke. What do you want from me, Marya shouts, you know you aren't going to die—why are you *pretending*?

Once, shortly after his operation, when he was still heavily drugged, he spoke to her and two or three other visitors about Christ as a butterfly...a yellow butterfly...and there was a web, a spider's web, something about a web.... His words came slowly, as if from a great distance. Though each was precisely enunciated it was somehow difficult to grasp. Christ, a yellow butterfly, a giant spider's web.... Father Shearing had smiled at them with a drunkard's kindly unfocussed affection. (That night Marya had written a poem—had tried to write a poem—about the experience. But Father Shearing was at its center, not Christ. He, and not Christ, was the butterfly struggling at the center of the spider's web.)

But what sort of *game* is it, Marya wanted to know.

She takes down his words. Which come a great deal slower than they did in the past; though still, from time to time, there are odd little rushes. *Maréchal challenging St. Thomas... Karl Barth on Hegel: a great question mark, a great disappointment, yet perhaps also a great promise.... As Küng has said, we must see in the ontic perspective the God-world-happening grounded not only in speculative necessity, but in God's free grace....* Marya has taken down eleven pages of notes so far for Father Shearing's essay, which is titled "The Paradox-God: Where Does He Dwell?" As a young seminarian Father Shearing published essays in journals like *Thomist Quarterly, Renascence, Thought,* and *The Journal of Metaphysics,* none of which is to be found in the Invemere Public Library. (Father Shearing has lent Marya his copies and she has tried, she has tried very hard, to read the essays. But their meaning eludes her. The words coil and writhe, always about to emerge into clarity; but then they recede again, and she is left trembling with self-loathing. How ignorant she is, how limited, she is lucky he doesn't quiz her, he might reconsider his friendship with her, and find another assistant...!) He had been accepted by the Princeton philosophy department as a doctoral candidate at about the time his "sickness" became obvious.

(Of course he had known about it earlier. He had half-known. For months his secret prayer had been for the return of his health: the disappearance of certain symptoms: how childish, how selfish, as he wryly confessed, for him to have begged Christ to do his worrying for him! Instead of going to a doctor as he had known he should Father Shearing had pushed off his obligations on Christ. Sometimes sin defines itself with a terrible clarity, Father Shearing told Marya, speaking in that slow drugged certain voice that intimidated her; sometimes you see—you *feel*—precisely what sin is. And never afterward are you altogether innocent.)

...If humanity tries to reach God through the discipline of the intellect, the God that awaits is Aristotle's God...the unmoved mover, the self-thinking thought, pure act, a God to whom creation has no meaning, individuals cannot matter.... A God beyond measurement who is wholly God and yet not God-as-man: for God-as-man is Christ, and Christ only, in the mystery of the Incarnation. Our perspective must then be violently altered if we are to break free of....

Father Shearing pauses, and lets his head fall back on the pillow. He is gaunt; he is skeletal; Marya gazes upon him pitilessly, hardening herself so that she will not ask if something is wrong. (For he is tired. Merely resting. There is no need, there is no need, for her to become alarmed.) At the start of the essay, long ago, he had been enthusiastic, and the drugs at that time had given him a curious gaiety, so that he could speak for minutes in long beautifully shaped sentences that flowed gracefully into paragraphs. Writing them down Marya had marveled at their fluidity, their effortless structure. This and this and this. And that. An argument, points made one by one, a summing-up, another argument, another passage, the words transcribed in the notebook in her careful hand, immensely gratifying. She did not entirely grasp the logic of what she wrote but she felt its rightness, in its very rhythms. The hum of an engine, the quiet faultless ticking of a watch, the precision of the heart's beat. She could hear, she could feel. There was no margin for doubt. ...Sometimes he spoke so excitedly and so rapidly that she could not keep up with him, and she had to ask him to repeat himself, pretending not to hear the sharp intake of his breath, or to see the irritated little twitches of his fingers. But in the end the words were transcribed with great care, and none was lost, and she had flushed with pride at his gratitude.

He had even squeezed her hand once, hard, as she was about to leave, though Sister Margaret hovered in the corridor (it was the end of visiting hours); he had said in a hoarse, urgent voice, I don't know what I would do without you, Marya, there's no one else in this terrible corner of the world I want near.

He can hold a pen but he can't write. His handwriting is all wriggly, the words are illegible. Perhaps by now he can't even hold a pen.

Marya is staring at his face, at his heavy eyelids with their bluish cast. The creases that bracket his mouth are harsher than ever; his skin is dead-white. She notes the thin bruised arms that protrude from the white sleeves. Hardly a man's arms now; more like a child's. Long-boned, like her own. But less muscular than her own. Dotted with ugly black scabs. How has it happened, what sort of miracle is it...? The flesh falling away week by week. The cheekbones protruding, the nose growing longer. For a while his lips were peeling and had to be kept greasy with ointment. Twin strips of hair had fallen out at his temples, as if someone had gone at him with an electric razor, to disfigure him. Fortunately the hair had grown back—less curly than before, and much thinner, but at least it had grown back.

One of his ribs had cracked, the consequence of a coughing spell.

It seems hard to believe, Marya said slowly, when she heard.

If only they would let him alone, perhaps he could gain back his strength. But he is scheduled for radiation therapy. They wheel him down to another part of the hospital, once or twice a week. There are transfusions and injections as well. And of course they are always drawing out samples of his blood to see what has gone wrong.

"Father Shearing...?"

In recent weeks he has fallen asleep in her presence several times. His eyelids drooped, his lower lip sagged, his breathing grew coarser until Marya teased herself by imagining she could hear the start of the death rattle. ...Marya, you bitch, she whispered to herself. She pinched the inside of her forearm until her eyes smarted with tears.

"Father Shearing, should I.... Do you want...." she says.

He opens his eyes. He blinks rapidly. A thread of bright saliva appears on his chin and with a deft movement of his fingers he wipes it off. "Was I asleep?" he says, surprised. "I don't think I was asleep but something came toward me... Well. Do you want to continue, or are you tired?" Marya hunches over the notebook, waiting. She *is* tired, of course. Her shoulders and arms still ache from carrying those books, and when she leaves the hospital she will have to catch a bus downtown to Main Street, and then she will have to catch a Greyhound bus out to her home, and she won't be home until after six. Helping her step-mother with supper, then clean-up afterward, and then her homework...though maybe she will postpone her homework until the morning.... She holds the pen ready, waiting for him to begin. Should she reread what he has dictated? *Our perspective must then be violently altered if we are to break free of....*

But Father Shearing says in a sudden flat voice, "I don't think we'll do any more today."

Marya looks anxiously at him. He is staring at the foot of his bed, at the chipped enamel railing, and for a long moment he seems unaware of her.

"Did you bring anything of your own," he asks. He clears his throat, and speaks more forcibly. "...Anything of your own. Your poems. Those little poems."

Marya has been scribbling poem-fragments all day, during her classes. Embarrassing little snatches of words, lines that go nowhere, images that are baffling and unclear. She has wanted very much to read them to Father Shearing for he always praises her, he always encourages her, and though it is a fairly obvious and even perfunctory sort of "encouragement" she is grateful nonetheless. But now she hesitates, her fingers have gone cold and numb, it is far too much trouble to leaf through her own notebook; she is suddenly very exhausted. She too could sleep.... She could crawl up beside Father Shearing and lay her head on his pillow and close her eyes and sleep, and sleep....

"Didn't you bring anything?" he asks. Each of his words is enunciated clearly, and he is blinking and holding his eyes wide open as if to strengthen his vision. "I'm disappointed, Marya. After that hopeless twaddle of my own it might have been refreshing...it might have been stimulating...."

"They're no good," Marya says.

"What isn't? Your poems?"

"...Not even poems," she says.

"What? I can't hear you."

Marya is blushing; she can feel her cheeks darkening with heavy sullen blood.

"I'm disappointed," Father Shearing says. A corner of his mouth lifts upward, wryly, to show that he is teasing; he is provoking; but in the next instant his face sags. "You don't trust me. You don't want to share anything with me. Because you're going to outlive me and you think...you think.... Well, it's a rotten investment."

Marya is too shocked to protest. She drops the pen and it clatters to the floor at her feet.

"It *is* a rotten investment," Father Shearing says amiably. "For clearly I'm a foregone conclusion. I'm a syllogism whose outcome is obvious, given its first premise. After all. *You* know. Everyone else knows, they knew from the start, so they're being cautious—they're staying away—who knows, dying might be infectious—these things aren't well understood. Poor Marya! Looking at me like that! You should grab one of these pillows and press it over my face. Shut me up. Be a good thing."

Marya laughs, to show that she understands his joking.

"I'm disappointed you didn't bring along a poem," he says.

"You don't want to hear any goddam old...goddam old idiot *poem*," Marya whispers. She gropes about for the pen and locates it just under the bed. "I should leave and you could sleep before supper."

"Plenty of time for sleep," Father Shearing says irritably. "Don't tell *me*. ...You know, they said it was pea-sized. No larger. And they scooped it all out. And more beside. And sewed me up, and pumped fresh bright blood into me, and then a little while later they said it wasn't gone after all .... Like ink spilled in water. Poison in the blood. Swimming around, looking for a place to seed. That's what they call it—*seeding*. It's a hard word. I mean, inside your skull. Skull and liver. You don't like to think of things *seeding* there. But you could write a poem about it someday. Long afterward. Is that what you're thinking? No?"

Marya says nothing. She is ready to spring to her feet. She needs only to grab her jacket, and her purse and books, and then she can retreat, mumbling goodbye. Goodbye and goodnight and I'll see you again on Thursday.

"If you won't read a poem then recite one," Father Shearing says.

Marya laughs harshly. But obeys. In a self-conscious breathy voice she says: *"The thought of God—I mean God-in-thought— The moon-sliver eclipsing the sun."* As soon as the words are uttered, however, she knows how inane they are: they don't mean a single thing.

Father Shearing lets his head fall back on the pillow again. But his eyes aren't closed; he is watching her.

"That isn't a love poem," he says. "Those others— There were some, a while back, that were different."

Marya says nothing. She knows he is teasing her but she refuses to respond.

"Weren't there?" he asks, his voice rising. "—A while back."

Marya mumbles something.

"What? I can't hear."

"I threw them away," Marya says curtly.

Her answer seems to offend him. He watches her in silence, his chapped lips slightly parted. The pupils of his eyes *are* dilated. And there are soft shadowy bruises beneath his eyes, sunk far into the flesh.

Isn't it a pity, people said when they first heard. The hospitalization, the immediate operation, the recovery in intensive care. They were reverent, they were astonished. Of course they were frightened as well but their fear was not articulated.

Marya had said bluntly, *He'll* be all right.

In Father Shearing there was a kind of shadowless light. It was all play, all energy, thin as a knife-blade, airy as milkweed fluff. He was *there* of course in his tall narrow-shouldered body yet his presence was insubstantial as a candle flame. And when he laughed he threw his head back, showing his even white teeth, the tendons of his neck standing out boldly. His laughter was spontaneous and loud, and sometimes a little puzzling. He was cruel, people said. When they failed to understand him. When they failed to evoke his love.

Now he is saying in a flat tired voice, ". . .really had something to say. To make. Up to a week or so ago I thought, well, *still* there was time. If I concentrated it, abbreviated it. Then maybe later someone would.... It's in the nature of what we do, it's in the nature of thought, someone building upon someone else.... Ladder-rungs. It should give me pleasure to.... But I can't help but.... Ten years might not have been enough, though, I can't be sure. The hell of it is you *can't* be sure. . . ."

Noises in the corridor, the elevator's doors opening with a pneumatic hiss; the creaking of a cart. Voices, footsteps. Are visitors about to enter the doorway of 307...? Marya holds herself stiff.

Down in the parking lot—a car's engine racing.

But Father Shearing does not hear. No one enters the room and he continues to stare at Marya, the fingers of his good hand twitching. She sees how long they are; how slender and pale. The nails have grown out unevenly and have been trimmed in a quick blunt fashion, almost straight across.

"So you won't read me a poem...." Father Shearing says with mock aggression.

Marya is about to protest that she *has* read—she has recited—a poem; but Father Shearing continues, now lolling his head from side to side as if he were greatly restless, and restrained only by the bed: ". . .not in the least afraid. Slanderous. Too much gossip anyway, a place like this. What's death but a.... Well, if you wrote it on the blackboard. Block letters. No fear, but disappointment. Now yes—*yes*—I can agree with you there. Disappointment. The shade flapping up to the ceiling but outside the window a brick wall. I've seen that. Marya, little Marya, thinking her secret thoughts. You're an orphan like me. You once said. But I wasn't closely listening. Can you hear me? Can you come a little closer?"

"I should be leaving," Marya says faintly, falsely, "there's the bus downtown, and the Greyhound...."

"What? I can't seem to hear," Father Shearing says with an angry laugh.

"Are you leaving? Come here, though, first. Before one of the nurses walks in.... Those notes, you can throw them out when you leave, better tear them up first just in case. Don't have mercy. Marya? Come here?"

She stands, and steps forward. A tightrope walker suddenly. One step and then another, and another. Small frightened steps. And then she is close beside him, her thigh pressing against the side of the bed. She is very nervous; she imagines she can hear the watch's ticking.

Father Shearing takes her hand. His fingers are surprisingly warm, and dry; it is Marya's hand that is limply cold. "I wanted.... I only wanted ...." he says. But his words are blurred now, as if he were speaking underwater; or in a dream; and dream-like too are the noises in the corridor that rise and fade. "I only wanted," Father Shearing says helplessly, "I wanted ...everything."

Marya stares in silence. She feels a queer bright smile distorting her face.

Father Shearing says, more softly, "Would you touch me? Before you leave. Would you? Is it too late?"

Her smile is a smile of terror, calmly distorting her face.

He pulls her hand down, he presses it against his groin, or what must be his groin, beneath the bedclothes. All the while he is staring helplessly at her. His lips drawn back from his teeth, but not in a smile; in an expression of grief she has never seen before. "...too late? Marya? Before you...."

He makes a movement, then, to draw back the covers, and in that instant Marya jerks away. She seizes her jacket, her purse and books, she can barely hear his voice beyond the wild thudding of her heart, and then she is in the corridor running, and on the stairs, and a nun in the company of a man in a business suit is saying angrily, Please don't run on the stairs, you must know better—

When news came of Father Shearing's death, not long after Marya's birthday, she did not cry. She had not cried, that April afternoon; and she did not cry afterward. Nor did she attend his funeral.

They asked her why—why she had stopped visiting him so suddenly, why she refused to go to the funeral, though everyone went. And wept, too: for he had been a much-loved priest. Despite his young age, and his penchant for sarcasm.

Marya was sullen, even rude in her replies. Her face heated with shame as she said, I do what I want to do.

He had willed the wristwatch to *her.* And only when it was actually given to her, wrapped in tissue in a candy box, handed over by the housekeeper in the rectory, did she think in a panic—Now I'm going to cry, now I'm going to break down.

But there was too much bustle in the room. The housekeeper, two other priests, visitors, her brother awkward in his soiled clothes, and eager to leave, eager to drive back home.... She did not cry even then, though her heart filled with the sense of her sin, her terrible guilt, for she knew she did not deserve the watch, and she knew she would accept it just the same.

The Heavenly Animal

Jayne Anne Phillips

Jancy's father always wanted to fix her car. Every time she came home for a visit, he called her at her mother's house and asked about the car with a second sentence.

Well, he'd say, How are you?

Fine, I'm fine.

And how's the car? Have any trouble?

He became incensed if Jancy's mother answered. He slammed the receiver down and broke the connection. They always knew who it was by the stutter of silence, then the violent click. He lived alone in a house ten blocks away.

Often, he would drive by and see Jancy's car before she'd even taken her coat off. He stopped his aging black Ford on the sloping street and honked two tentative blasts. He hadn't come inside her mother's house since the divorce five years ago. He wouldn't even step on the grass of the block-shaped lawn. This time Jancy saw his car from the bathroom window. She cursed and pulled her pants up. She walked outside and the heavy car door swung open. Her father wore a wool hat with a turned-up brim and small gray feather. Jancy loved the feather.

Hi, she said.

Well, hi there. When did you get in?

About five minutes ago.

Have any trouble?

She got into the car. The black interior was very clean and the empty litter bag hung from the radio knob. Jancy thought she could smell its new plastic mingling with the odor of his cigar. She leaned over and kissed him.

Thank god, she thought, he looks better.

He pointed to her car. What the hell did you do to the chrome along the side there? he said.

Trying to park, Jancy said. Got in a tight spot.

Her father shook his head and grimaced. He held the butt of the cigar with his thumb and forefinger. Jancy saw the flat chewed softness of the butt where he held it in his mouth, and the stain on his lips where it touched.

Jesus, Honey, he said.

Can't win them all.

But you got to win some of them, he said. That car's got to last you a long time.

It will, Jancy said. It's a good car. Like a tank. I could drive that car through the fiery pits of hell and come out smelling like a rose.

Well. Everything you do to it takes money to fix. And I just don't have it.

Don't want it fixed, Jancy said. Works fine without the chrome.

He never asked her at first how long she was going to stay. For the past few years she'd come home between school terms. Or from far-flung towns up East, out West. Sometimes during her visits she left to see friends. He would rant close to her face, breathing hard.

Why in God's name would you go to Washington, D.C.? Nothing there but niggers. And what the hell do you want in New York? You're going to wear out your car. You've driven that car thirty thousand miles in one year—Why? What the hell for?

The people I care about are far apart. I don't get many chances to see them.

Jesus Christ, you come home and off you go.

I'll be back in four days.

That's not the goddamn point. You'll get yourself crippled up in a car wreck running around like this. Then where will you be?

Jancy would sigh and feel herself harden.

I won't stay in one place all my life out of fear I'll get crippled if I move, she'd say.

Well I understand that, but *Jesus.*

His breathing would grow quiet. He rubbed his fingers and twisted the gold Masonic ring he wore in place of a wedding band.

Honey, he'd say. You got to *think* of these things.

And they would both sit staring.

Down the street Jancy saw red stop signs and the lawns of churches. Today he was in a good mood. Today he was just glad to see her. And he didn't know she was going to see Michael. Or was she?

What do you think? he said. Do you want to go out for lunch tomorrow? I go down to the Catholic church there, they have a senior citizen's meal. Pretty good food.

Jancy smiled. Do you remember when you stopped buying Listerine, she asked, because you found out a Catholic owned the company?

She could tell he didn't remember, but he grinned.

Hell, he said. Damn Catholics own everything.

He was sixty-seven. Tiny blood vessels in his cheeks had burst. There was that redness in his skin, and the blue of shadows, gauntness of the weight loss a year ago. His skin got softer, his eyelids translucent as crepe. His eyelashes were very short and reddish. The flesh drooped under his heavy brows. As a young man, he'd been almost sloe-eyed. Bedroom eyes, her mother called them. Now his eyes receded in the mysterious colors of his face.

OK, Jancy said. Lunch.

She got out of the car and bent to look in at him through the open window.

Hey, she said. You look pretty snappy in that hat.

Tonight her mother would leave after supper for Ohio. Jancy would be alone in the house and she would stare at the telephone. She tore lettuce while her mother broiled the steaks.

I don't know why you want to drive all the way up there at night, Jancy said. Why don't you leave in the morning?

I can make better time at night, her mother said. And besides, the wedding is in two days. Your aunt wanted me to come last week. It's not every day her only daughter gets married, and since you refuse to go to weddings...

She paused. They heard the meat crackle in the oven.

I'm sorry to leave when you've just gotten here. I thought you'd be here two weeks ago, and we'd have some time before I left. But you'll be here when I get back.

Jancy looked intently into the salad bowl.

Jancy? asked her mother. Why are you so late getting here? Why didn't you write?

I was just busy . . . finishing the term, packing, subletting the apartment—

You could have phoned.

I didn't want to. I hate calling long-distance. It makes me feel lost, listening to all that static.

That's ridiculous, her mother said. Let's get this table cleared off. I don't know why you always come in and dump everything on the first available spot.

Because I believe in instant relief, Jancy said.

—books, backpack, maps, your purse—

She reached for the books and Jancy's leather purse fell to the floor. Its contents spilled and rolled. She bent to retrieve the mess before Jancy could stop her, picking up small plastic bottles of pills.

What are these? she said. What are you doing with all these pills?

I cleaned out my medicine cabinet and threw all the bottles in my purse. They're pills I've had for years—

Don't you think you better throw them away? You might forget what you're taking.

They're all labeled, Jancy said.

Her mother glanced down.

Dalmane, she said. What's Dalmane?

A sleeping pill.

Why would you need sleeping pills?

Because I have trouble sleeping. Why do you think?

Since when?

I don't know. A long time. Off and on. Will you cut it out with the third degree?

Why can't you sleep?

Because I dream my mother is relentlessly asking me questions.

It's Michael. Michael's thrown you for a loop.

Jancy threw the bottles in her purse and stood up quickly. No, she said, Or yes. We're both upset right now.

He certainly is. You're lucky to be rid of him.

I don't want to be rid of him.

He'll drive you crazy if you're not careful. He's got a screw loose and you know it.

You liked him, Jancy said. You liked him so much it made me angry.

Yes, I liked him. But not after this whole mess started. Calling you cruel because he couldn't have things his way. If he was so in love it would have lasted. Cruel. There's not a cruel bone in your body.

I should never have told you he said those things.

They were silent. Jancy smelled the meat cooking.

Why shouldn't you tell me? her mother asked quietly. If you can't talk to your mother, who can you talk to?

Oh Christ, Jancy said. Nobody. I'm hungry. Let's eat and change the subject.

They sat down over full plates. There was steak when Jancy or her brothers came home. Their mother saved it for weeks, months, in the freezer. The meat sizzled on Jancy's plate and she tried to eat. She looked up. The lines in her mother's face seemed deeper than before, grown in. And she was so thin, so perfectly groomed. Earrings. Creased pants. Silk scarves. A bath at the same time every morning while the *Today* show played the news. At night she rubbed the calluses off her heels carefully with a pumice stone.

She looked at Jancy. What are you doing tomorrow? she asked.

Having lunch at the Catholic church, Jancy said.

That ought to be good. Canned peaches and weepy mashed potatoes. Your father is something. Of course he doesn't speak to me on the street, but I see him drive by here in that black car. Every day. Watching for one of you to come home.

Jancy said nothing.

He looks terrible, her mother said.

He looks better than he did, said Jancy.

That's not saying much. He looked horrible for months. Thinner and thinner, like a walking death. I'd see him downtown. He went to the pool hall every day, always by himself. He never did have any friends.

He did, Jancy said. He told me. In the war.

I don't know. I didn't meet him till after that, when he was nearly forty. By then he never seemed to belong—

I remember that weekend you went away and he moved out, Jancy said. He never belonged in this house. The house he built had such big rooms.

Did you know that house is for sale again? her mother asked. It's changed hands several times.

I didn't know, Jancy said. Let's not talk about it.

Her mother sighed. All right, she said. Let's talk about washing these dishes. I really have to get started.

Mom, Jancy said, I might call Michael.

What for? He's five states away and that's where he ought to be.

I may go up there.

Oh, Jancy.

I have to. I can't just let it end here.

Her mother was silent. They heard a gentle thunder.

Clouding up, Jancy said. You may have rain. Need help with your bags?

The car's already packed.

Well, Jancy said.

Her mother collected maps, parcels, a large white-ribboned present. Jancy heard her moving around and thought of waking at night in the house her father had built, the house in the country. There would be the cornered light from the bathroom in the hall. Her father would walk slowly past in slippers and robe to adjust the furnace. The motor would kick in and grunt its soft hum several times a night. Half asleep, Jancy knew her father was awake. The furnace. They must have been winter nights.

Can you grab this? her mother asked.

Jancy took the present. I'll walk you out, she said.

No, just give it to me. There, I've got it.

Jancy smiled. Her mother took her hand.

You're gutsy, she said. You'll be OK.

Good, said Jancy. It's always great to be OK.

Give me a hug.

Jancy embraced her. How often did someone hold her? Her hair smelled fragrant and dark.

Jancy left the lights off. She took a sleeping pill and lay down on the living room couch. Rain splattered the windows. She imagined her father standing by the dining room table. When he moved out he had talked to her brothers about guns.

One rifle goes, he'd said. One stays. Which do you want?

Jancy remembered cigarette smoke in the room, how it curled between their faces.

It don't make any difference to me, he said. But this one's the best for rabbit.

He fingered change far down in his trouser pockets. One brother asked the other which he wanted. The other said it didn't matter, didn't matter. Finally the youngest took the gun and climbed the steps to his room. Their father walked into the kitchen, murmuring, It'll kill rabbits and birds. And if you go after deer, just use slugs.

Jancy heard water dripping. How long had it gone on? Rain was coming down the chimney. She got up and closed the flue, mopped up the rain with a towel. The pills didn't work anymore. What would she do all night? She was afraid of this house, afraid of all the houses in this town. After midnight they were silent and blank. They seemed abandoned.

She looked at the telephone. She picked up the receiver.

Michael? she said.

She dialed his number. The receiver clicked and snapped.

What number are you calling please?

He's gone, thought Jancy.

Hello? What number—

Jancy repeated the numerals.

That number has been disconnected. There's a new number. Shall I ring it for you?

The plastic dial of the princess phone was transparent and yellowed with light.

Ma'am? Shall I ring it?

Yes, Jancy said.

No one home.

Jancy took a bottle of whiskey off the shelf. She would drink enough to make her sleep. The rain had stopped and the house was still. Light from streetlamps fell through the windows. Jancy watched the deserted town. Heavy elms loomed over the sidewalks. Limbs of trees rose and fell on a night breeze. Their shadows moved on the lit-up surface of the street.

A black car glided by.

Jancy stepped back from the window. Taillights blinked red as the car turned corners and passed away soundlessly.

She picked up the phone and dialed. She lay in the cramped hallway while the purr of a connection stopped and started. How did it sound there, ringing in the dark? Loud and empty.

Hello?

His voice, soft. When they lived together, he used to stand looking out the window at the alley late at night. He was naked and perfect. He watched the Midwestern alleys roll across eight city blocks paved in old brick. Telephone poles stood weathered and alone. Their drooping wires glistened, humming one note. He gripped the wooden frame of the window and stood looking, centaur, quiet, his flanks whitened in moonlight.

Jancy, he said now. It's you, isn't it.

Jancy wore a skirt and sat in the living room. Her father would pull up outside. She would see him lean to watch the door of the house, his head inclined toward her. His car shining and just washed. His hat. His cigar. His baggy pants bought at the same store downtown for thirty years.

Jancy walked outside to watch for him. She didn't want to jump when the horn sounded. And it suddenly hurt her that her father was always waiting.

Did he know their old house was being sold again? He had contracted the labor and built it himself. He had designed the heating system, radiant heat piped under the floors so the wooden parquet was always warm. He had raised the ceiling of the living room fifteen inches so that the crown of her mother's inherited antique bookcase would fit into it. He was a road builder, but those last few years, when Jancy was a teen-ager, he'd had a series of bad jobs—selling bulldozers, cars, insurance—After they'd moved he stopped working altogether . . .

The horn sounded suddenly close and shocked her.

Jancy?

Now why did you do that? I'm standing right here, aren't I?

Are you asleep?

No, I just didn't hear you pull up. But you didn't have to blare that horn at me. It's loud enough to wake the dead.

Well, he said, I thought you needed waking, standing there staring into space like a knothead.

Right, said Jancy. She got into the car and he was still smiling. She laughed in spite of herself.

I'm a little early, he said. They don't open at the church till noon. Do you want to go for a drive?

Where to?

We could drive out the falls road, he said.

That would take them past the old house. The hedges and trees would be larger than Jancy could believe, lush with new leaves, and rippling. Her father had planted them all.

I don't think so, said Jancy.

The house is for sale.

I know.

Dumbest thing I ever did was to let your mother talk me into selling that house.

I don't want to hear about my mother.

I'll hate her for the rest of my life for breaking up our family, he said, his breathing grown heavy. He scowled and touched the ridges in the steering wheel.

Jancy leaned back in the seat and watched clouds through the tinted windshield. Remember when you built roads? she asked.

He waited a moment, then looked over at her and pushed his hat back. I built a lot of them around here, he said, but the state don't keep them up anymore. They closed the graveyard road.

He'd taught her how to drive on that road, a narrow unpainted blacktop that wound under train trestles and through the cemetery. He said if she could drive on that road she could drive anywhere. He made her go that way, cutting across a blind curve up the sudden hill of the entrance, past the carved pillars with their lopsided lamps. This way, he'd said, and she'd pulled off onto a gravel path that turned sharply along the crest of a hill. Tombstones were scattered in the lumpy grass. Far below Jancy saw the graveyard road looping west by the river, on through woods to the country towns of Volga and Coalton and Mud Lick.

Stop here, her father directed. He nodded at a patch of ground. There we are, he said, this is where we'll be.

Jancy was sixteen; she'd stared at him and gripped the steering wheel.

All right, he'd said. Back up. Let's see how you do going backward.

Now her father started his black Ford and they passed the clipped lawns of houses. He drove slowly, his cigar in his mouth.

What will they have to eat at the church? Jancy asked.

Oh, he said. They publish a menu in the paper. Meat loaf today. Fifty cents a person over sixty. Not bad food. Cooks used to work up at the junior high. But we don't have to go there. We can go to a restaurant if you want.

No, I'd rather go where you usually go. But are you sure I'm allowed?

Certainly. You're my guest. A dollar for guests.

They pulled into the church parking lot. The doors of the rec center were closed. They sat in the car and waited. Jancy remembered dances held in this building, how she was thirteen and came here to dance with the high school boys. They had danced until they were wet with sweat, then stepped outside into the winter air. Girls stood by the lighted door and shivered while the boys smoked cigarettes, squinting into vaporous trails of smoke rings.

What about your car? asked her father.

What about it?

I'm going to take it up to Smitty's and have him go over it.

No. Doesn't need it. The car is fine. I had it checked—

I've made arrangements with Smitty for today. He's got room and we better—

But the last time he fixed it, one of the sparkplugs flew out while I was driving on the interstate—

Don't you be taking off on Smitty, her father said. He's done us a lot of good work on that car. I'm trying to help you. You don't want my help, why just let me know and I'll bow out anytime.

Jancy sighed. Her father held his hat in his lap and traced the faint lines of the wood plaid with his fingers.

I appreciate your help, she said. But I don't know if Smitty—

He might have made a mistake that one time, her father said. But he usually does real good by us.

Volkswagen buses of old people began to pull up. Drivers opened the double doors of the vans and rolled up a set of mobile steps. Old ladies appeared with their blond canes and black-netted pillbox hats. They stepped out one after another, smiling and peeking about.

Where are the old men? Jancy asked.

I think they die off quicker, her father said. These same old dames have been coming here ever since I have. They just keep moving.

*   *   *

Inside were long rows of Formica tables. Eight or nine elderly people sat at each. There were rows of empty chairs. Women with a cashbox between them sat beside the door. Jancy's father put his arm around Jancy's waist and patted her.

This is my daughter, he said.

Well, isn't she pretty? said one of the cashiers. The women nodded and smiled.

Jancy signed the guest book. Under 'address' she wrote 'at large.' Her father was waiting at one of the tables. He had pulled a chair out for her and was standing behind it, waiting to seat her. The women were watching them, like the circling nurses that day at the hospital. Her father lay in bed, his arms so thin that his elbows seemed too large.

This is my daughter, he'd said to the nurses. She came all the way from California to see me.

Isn't that nice, they said. Is she married?

Hell no, her father had laughed. She's married to me.

Now Jancy felt the chair press up behind her legs and she sat down. Her father took his hat off and nodded at people across the table. She saw that his eyes were alight.

Aren't you going to have to get yourself a summer hat? she asked.

I reckon so, he said. I just can't find one I like.

Behind the waist-high counter, Jancy saw the fat cooks spooning peaches onto plates from metal cans. They were big women, their hair netted in silver nets, faces round and flushed from the ovens. They passed out cafeteria trays premolded for portions.

I used to eat out of those trays in grade school, Jancy said. Are they going to make us sing 'God Is Great?'

No, her father said. But go ahead if it makes you feel better.

He chuckled. The last time they'd eaten together was last December. Michael had come home with Jancy and they'd gone out to lunch with her father at the Elks Club. Afterward he had held Michael's coat for him and eased it onto his shoulders. He'd never done that for anyone but his sons. Later he'd asked her, Are you going to marry this man?

Jancy? Aren't you going to eat? Her father was leaning close to her, pointing at her plate.

What? Oh. I ate a big breakfast. Here, you eat the rest of mine.

You should eat, said her father. Your face looks thin. Have you lost weight?

Maybe a little.

You run around too much. If you'd stay in one place for a while you'd gain a little weight and look better.

Jancy picked up her fork and put it down. Her father had always made her uneasy. He went into rages, especially in the car. If he couldn't pass or the car in front slowed suddenly for a turn, he'd turn red and curse— Goddammit, you son of a bitch, he'd say. That's right, you chucklehead— That word 'chucklehead' was his utmost brand of contempt. He said it stressing the first syllable, fuming like a mad bull.

Jancy? You finished? Ready to go?

Her father pushed his plate away and sat watching her, touching the rim of his empty glass with a finger. She couldn't answer him. She knew that she would leave to see Michael. When she told her father, he would shake his head and stammer as he tried to talk. She got up and started for the door.

Jancy's father burned a coal fire past mid-May. He picked up a poker and stabbed at white embers clinging to the grate. Flakes of ash drifted into the room.

How long will you be up there? he asked.

I don't know, she said.

Christ Almighty. What are you doing? If this thing between you and him is over, just forget it. Why go chasing up there after him? Let him come here, he knows where you are.

I don't have a place for him to stay.

Why couldn't he stay up at the house with you and your mother?

Because we don't want to stay with my mother.

He clenched his fists and glowered into the fire. He shook his head.

I know you're an adult, he said. But goddammit, Jancy, it's not right. I don't care what you say. It's not right and it won't come to no good.

It already *has* come to good, Jancy said. She looked at him until he broke their gaze.

Why don't you give it up? he said. Give it up and marry him.

Give what up?

All this running around you're doing. Jesus, Honey, you can't do this all your life. Aren't you twenty-five this summer? I won't be here forever. What's going to happen to you?

I don't know, Jancy said. How can I know?

He leaned forward, elbows on knees, and clasped his hands. You need a family, he said. No one will ever help you but your family.

Maybe not, said Jancy.

She thought of the drive. Moving up the East Coast to Michael. She would arrive and sit in the car, waiting to stop trembling, waiting for twelve hours of hot road and radio talk to go away. She would want Michael so much and she would be afraid to go into the house.

She looked up at her father.

I have to do this, she said.

What time are you leaving?

Five A.M.

Does your mother know you're going?

I told her I might.

Well. Come down by and we'll hose off the car.

No, you don't need to get up that early.

I'm always awake by then, he said.

Her father was sitting outside on the porch swing as she drove up. He motioned her to pull into the yard under the buckeye tree. The sky had begun to lighten. The stars were gone. The air was chill, misted. He wore a woolen shirt and the hat with the feather nearly hidden in the brim. Before Jancy could get out of the car he picked up the garden hose and twisted the brass nozzle. Water streamed over the windshield. Jancy watched his wavering form as the water broke and runneled. He held the cigar between his teeth and sprayed the bumpers, the headlights, the long sides of the car. He sprayed each tire, walking, revolving, his hand on his hip, the hat pulled low. His face was gentle and gaunt. He would get sicker. Jancy touched her eyes, her mouth. A resignation welled up like tears. He was there and then he was made of moving lines as water flew into the glass. The water stopped slowly.

Jancy got out of the car and they stood looking up at a sky toned the coral of flesh.

It's a long way, he said. You'll get there while it's light?

Yes, Jancy said. Don't worry.

The car sat dripping and poised.

It looks good, Jancy said. I'm taking off in style.

She got in and rolled the window down. Her father came close.

Turn the motor on, he said, then nodded, satisfied at the growl of the engine. Above them the buckeye spread out green and heavy.

When are the buckeyes ripe? Jancy asked.

Not till August.

Can you eat them?

Nope, her father laughed. Buckeyes don't do a thing, don't have a use in the world.

He bent down and kissed her.

Take your time, he said. Go easy.

She drove fast the first few hours. The sun looked like the moon, dim, layered over. Morning fog burned off slowly. Maryland mountains were thick and dipped in pockets of fog. Woods stretched on both sides of the road. Sometimes from an overpass Jancy saw straggled neon lights still burning in a small town. No cars on the highway; she was alone, she ate up the empty ribbon of the road.

She drove up over a rise and suddenly, looming out of the mist, the deer was there. She saw the sexual lines of its head and long neck. It moved into her, lifted like a flying horse. She swerved. The arching body hit the fender with a final thud and bounced again, hard, into the side of the car. Jancy looked through the rearview mirror and saw the splayed form skidding back along the berm of the road, bouncing twice in slow motion, twirling and stopping.

The road seemed to close like a tunnel. The look of the deer's head, the beginning arch of the body, was all around Jancy. She seemed to see through the image into the tunneling road. She heard, close to her ear, the soft whuff of the large head bent over grass, tearing the long grass with its teeth.

She pulled off the road. I should go back and see what I've done, she thought. She turned the motor off. She felt she was still moving, and the road shifted into three levels. Wet grass of the road banks was lush. The road shimmered; one plane of it tilted and moved sideways into the other. Jancy gripped the vinyl seat of the car. She was sinking. The door wouldn't open and she slid across to get out the other side. She stood up in the cool air and there was total silence. Jancy tried to walk. The earth and the asphalt were spongy. She moved around the car and saw first the moonish curve of the dented fender. The door was crumpled where the deer had bounced back and slammed into her. Jancy imagined its flanks, the hard mounds of its rump. The sheen of it. She staggered and stepped back. The sudden cushion of the grass surprised her and she fell. She saw then the sweep of short hairs glistening along the length of the car. The door handle was packed and smeared with golden feces.

There was really nowhere to go.

Once it was Christmas Day. They were driving from home, from the house her father had built in the country. A deer jumped the road in front of them, clearing the snow, the pavement, the fences of the fields, in two bounds. Beyond its arc the hills rumpled in snow. The narrow road wound through white meadows, across the creek, and on. Her father was driving. Her brothers had shining play pistols with leather holsters. Her mother wore clip-on earrings of tiny wreaths. They were all dressed in new clothes, and they moved down the road through the trees.

The Pastor

Joy Williams

Daniel married Elisabeth one month before he took his first parish. Daniel was nineteen and had great longings. He had always wanted to preach, to have a large family and to know God. His parents are dead. They were Welsh. Daniel knows nothing of the language except for a few childish rhymes.

Daniel does not think about his boyhood much because there is no one to corroborate his remembrances. Elisabeth, too, is an orphan. This seems slightly exceptional to them. The lives they had before they met seem prosaic and without resonance.

They marry in that abstract month of February, that month which everyone agrees must not be dealt with on its own terms. The boredom, the thinness, the immeasurableness of the month! Nothing is of any protection against the immeasurableness except love.

It is important what one does, Daniel writes, *like a lost coin, the human soul can drop into darkness.*

Daniel's church is small. It has twenty-five members. Along with a small salary, the congregation provides the young couple with a huge drafty house. They are always bringing over firewood and cookies. They are kind people and have no troubles about which they really speak.

Daniel writes careful, scholarly sermons in the kitchen which is the warmest room in the house. They have very few possessions and there is almost no furniture. He smiles as he sees Elisabeth moving through the rooms. He skates across the scrubbed floors to her in his socks. Like a Chagall lover.

Elisabeth has dark bobbed hair and large eyes. Daniel is tall and joyful in his faith. Everyone is very fond of them although they sometimes find Daniel's sermons difficult to follow.

Reality is not present around us. It stands only in God. The dreams of reason are intolerable.

Daniel lovingly shapes his words around the absence of event. To be truthful, he is a little disdainful of experience.

They do not have a car yet. For entertainment, they often go to the movies. The theatre in town is free to the clergy and they go there every time the film changes.

They are in the balcony watching Laurel and Hardy move a piano across a narrow suspension bridge. The bridge is slung over a sickening chasm, between a couple of Alps. Midway, the two meet a gorilla.

Elisabeth laughs and laughs.

Daniel says, "Man is never free from his limitations."

Elisabeth makes a slapstick face and pokes him in the ribs.

Later, they are watching Chaplin. THE CIRCUS. Chaplin is surreptitiously eating all of a small child's hot dog. When he's finished, he takes a napkin and thoughtfully wipes the child's lips.

Elisabeth wants a child very much. To see any child makes her thoughtful and increasingly troubled. Years go by.

Elisabeth is very ill. She is in the hospital where the doctors have determined that her womb must be removed. Daniel sits beside her bed just prior to the operation, holding her hand. He does not recognize her face. It is round and frightened, precocious with awe. Daniel tries to say something which can deal with this face, words which carry with them no hint of resignation or acceptance, words which will dissipate the expression of terrible awe and fascination in this stranger's face. Elisabeth's face is beyond and before love, charged and personal for the first time.

It is Daniel's birthday. A package arrives in the afternoon mail. It is a present from Elisabeth. There is a card enclosed and it is addressed to him from Elisabeth and it is signed with her name although the signature is not hers. The signature is round, stern and legible. It seems more a summons than a greeting. The gift is a shirt which Elisabeth has seen in a newspaper advertisement and ordered by mail. It has been wrapped in paper of a vaguely celebratory design and the price tags have been removed. All of this has been arranged by Elisabeth as she recovers in the hospital.

Daniel is shocked. He unbuttons and removes the shirt he wears. He puts on the new one. He does this very hurriedly. He is responsible. It is as though an accident has occurred. He is a witness and he is being pursued. He is a witness and he will be charged.

He rushes to the hospital to see Elisabeth. She is in a pleasant private room that has a colorful bedspread on the bed and plush carpeting on the floor. When Daniel arrives, Elisabeth is kneeling on the carpet, rubbing a spot from it with a washcloth. She has spilled some cologne and there is a small stain. Daniel makes her stop this at once.

"This is not your house," he says to her. His voice seems high-pitched, unnatural. "You must not make everyplace your home!"

Elisabeth loves to travel. They have a good car now. They buy a new Buick every three years. She thinks nothing of driving eighty miles after church on a Sunday afternoon simply for a pound of peaches from a particular candy shop. Many times she and Daniel drive fifty miles for a serving of particularly good Indian pudding, and now they are travelling a good distance for a Christmas wreath that is only ten inches in diameter. Daniel feels, once they have arrived, that they should buy the largest wreath available, but they do not.

The stand where they shop is fragrant with cut trees. Daniel picks up several trees and bounces them on the ground, turning them this way and that, getting white gum on his gloves and coat. Another man is doing the same and is saying to his wife,

"What do you think, what do you think?"

"I don't know!" the woman cries with a good deal of excitement.

The ruts that the cars have made are deep and hard, filled with pine needles and slim wafers of ice. The boy who takes Daniel's money has a great deal of frizzy yellow hair and his hands are mottled with the cold. He touches Daniel's arm.

"What happiness to wake, alive again, into this same grey world of winter rain," he says.

It is not actually raining but Daniel nods because, of course, it is true.

Daniel is in his office. He is thirty-three now. He chews on his lower lip. He types, *the unborn, uncreated, unformed exist. If they did not exist there would be no liberation for that which is born created or formed.* He worries about the words. When he says them aloud, they return, homeless to him. He gazes out the screenless window, through the crispy sick branches of an elm. He wishes they had sycamores here. They seem cheerful, gangling trees, though respected, living well with their faults. He types *substantiality.*   ·

Downstairs, some of the ladies are assembling gift-packages for the children's home. Second-hand picture books. Crepe-paper surprise balls. Hard candy, bubble pipes and underwear. In the pantry, Jenny Mott frosts cupcakes for the ladies' tea. She wears a tennis skirt, a tight black turtleneck sweater and magenta sneakers. Poor Jenny Mott. Her husband is dying, her junipers are dying, her cat had distemper and toppled into the top-loading washer, unbeknownst to Jenny until the final cycle.

Her friends fear she's becoming peculiar although she's never appeared in more disarming health. She sips a little Maker's Mark from a coffee cup and sings while she works.

I GOT THE KEY TO THE HIGHWAY

she shouts over the Seven-Minute Penuche.

Fish, Daniel types.

No, he thinks. He doesn't care for the Lord; no better than a common genie, telling the disciples to cast to the right. They had no imagination. A breeze stirs the papers on his desk. He smells burning sugar, flowering vines, rain on a wind miles away.

Fish, he slowly types again.

He prefers the idea of the fish as the cosmological proof of the existence of God. The world resting on an angel which is eventually supported by a fish. A golden fish in the waters, supporting the world.

Mrs. Mott stands beneath the window, calling his name. She extends a cupcake, holding it gingerly, far away from her body, as though it had died. She uses a sunlamp to protract her skiing tan. Her eyelids glow with nourishment although the eyes themselves are grey.

"Shall I tell the ladies you'll join them?" she calls.

"Thank you, not today," Daniel says. He often sounds as though he is agreeing to something even when he is not.

Mrs. Mott clumps back to the basement, singing

TELL ME BABY WHY YOU BEEN GONE SO LONG

Daniel knocks the bowl of his pipe against the palm of his hand and drops the spent tobacco into an ashtray. A logo on the soda box says *A Miracle Because It Does So Many Things.*

Daniel shakes his head. It's spring. His sermons need levity, bounce. He types, *the goofang, about the size of a trout only much bigger.* This is the fish he will mention on Sunday. His congregation will appreciate a fish like that, *a fish that swims backwards to keep the water out of its eyes.*

Daniel and Elisabeth make love in a shaded room. Her shoulders rise, cast up to him, earnestly, in silence. She brushes a hair off the pillow. It floats to the waxed floor. They watch it disturbed, if even for an instant. It is disturbing. Daniel's hands come off the brass headboard, smelling of polish to hold her breasts. Their lives are so clean—to brush against their lives gathers nothing.

Elisabeth imagines a noise, an interruption. She imagines a child sleeping in a room down the hall, on the sunny side of the house. She imagines this child, their child coming to them in the morning, the rushing footsteps, approaching forever down the hall, taking long moments, taking years, while Elisabeth's and Daniel's embrace unwinds, as the footsteps increase in force, as now, hastily, the child urgently enters the room.

Daniel is just finishing up. Each week, he puts twenty hours of work into his twenty minute sermon.

Only God exists, not the false gods and idols that answer prayers, but the true God. Let us enjoy and delight in Him once more.

Pam Mandelburg bursts into Daniel's office. She has six children, three at home. She is going to have another. She is wed to birthing. She loves it.

"The joy, Daniel!" she has exclaimed previously.

Pam Mandelburg wears large hats and clutches Daniel's hand tightly on Sunday mornings. She has wide teeth and smells of witch hazel. On Palm Sunday, she had bent down at the door to retrieve her frond and had planted her bottom with precision against Daniel's startled knees.

But now she weeps. Her eyes spit tears.

"I'll beat their butts to butter,'"she screams. "I'm at my wit's end. I find jelly in the toilet. How would you like that, Daniel? Can you think of anything more disgusting! Just how would you like *that*! Dumped in the *toilet*! I have to take it out with my *hands*. And who knows what they've done with half the furniture. A large bridge lamp with brass, gone. Vanished! Don't defend them, Daniel. You're defending gangrene. They sneak about drinking coffee. They're three-and-a-half, four-and-a-half and six, for God's sakes. And they are dumb, Daniel, and sly. They have the souls of mice!"

Daniel cannot calm her. Her breast heaves. Her spittle falls in bubbles on his Proust.

"Daniel, stay my hand! They've locked themselves in the car now, out-side. They want to be orphans—that's what they want—but I won't oblige. I think they're poisoning my food. I get dizzy when I bend for shampoo. Where do they get it from! I myself was a mannerly child. An achiever. I was a nice little girl! I played a carrot in the school play. I was innocent. A carrot who could see in the dark. It was my last healthy year. That was before men got familiar with me. I was a sweet girl with my orange hair in a braid and no anger in my heart. I was the carrot who saved all the vita-mins!"

Pam Mandelburg begins to moan. She clutches her large stomach. She rushes from Daniel's office down the dark hall, past the pictures the Sun-day School class displays as their favorites. Daniel dashes after her. On the wall there is a drawing of Shadrach, Meshach and Abednego. They are being shoved into a colorful furnace.

Outside, the woman is scrabbling with a key at the door of her old car. The engine is running. The doors are locked tight. Moisture from the ex-haust has puddled the snow. She flings open the door and the three chil-dren fall out in their red snow-suits. Their complexions are the color of tin.

"The little thugs!" she screams. One of them has thrown up on the seat. There is a messy crayoned line running across the upholstery. It is unbroken and winds through the entire car. It never intercepts its own passage. It is a profane and confident line, accomplishing itself.

Daniel bends toward the children. He feels like a stage performer with no speaking part. He imagines the children scrambling up and sprinting through the gate, into the cemetery. They would leapfrog the stones and the iron urns of evergreens. And Daniel would pursue them. Snow would slide into his shoes as he would seek to catch them and bring them back.

Sometimes Daniel wakes in the middle of the night, feeling quite strange. In these moments, which are very fleeting, he feels that Time has entered him. Time is taking its rest in his heart, a predatory creature nesting innocently in his reconciled heart. It has left the world of those whom he loves, those who depend upon it and has entered him.

Elisabeth is making a cake. She starts to cry.

"Daniel," she says, "I have never made a fuss about my life."

Daniel hurries to her, truly puzzled.

"If I died," she says, "you would continue to pursue your phantoms."

He touches her but she shrugs him off.

She is hostile, unreachable. "Phantoms, Daniel!" she says.

The sterility of men, she thinks bitterly. She swallows with great effort. Her life soars upward, dips, crazily, like a swallow.

"I am a frivolous woman, Daniel," she says. "My mind is always full of the most awful junk. Foolish things always. Frivolous. Do you know what I did today and I'm embarrassed to say it. I was washing a sweater out and the Sak's label on the neckband was coming off and I got a needle and thread and sewed it back on. It shamed me while I was doing it but I did it anyway."

"But Elisabeth," Daniel says, "it's nice to have nice things." He offers her his handkerchief. She looks at it for a moment and then shrugging, accepts it.

"I love you, Elisabeth," he says.

She shrugs again, this time more calmly.

Daniel has dropped in at a youth meeting at the parish house. The children are young teenagers, cheerless, handsome, ill-natured and precocious in their weariness. Daniel survives his encounters with them uncraftily, like a butterfly sailing between a cat's open jaws.

They have just returned from a progressive supper, the sixteenth event on their winter calendar. Four couples from the church have agreed to host them in their homes and provide the various courses. The adults want to be generous but their organization is not very tight. It cannot, Daniel supposes, be considered a success. Each course was a blintze. At the moment, Daniel thinks all the children look a little crazy.

The parish house is full of materials. Styrofoam, scraps of leather and copper, yarn, discarded silverware. The young people are always making something, some impossible construction of junk, some promise of silence to themselves realized.

Daniel works with them for a moment. This night he has made a god's eye on a stick. A cheery confection.

"Umm," he smiles.

"How did it get on a dollar bill is what I want to know," one boy says. He is heavier than the others. He wears thin gold eyeframes which lack glass. "I hate American pragmatism," he says.

"Even a potato eye is more interesting than a god's eye," a girl says. She is pretty and critical. Her friends giggle. "Pink-eye, needle's eye, jeweler's goggling eye," she continues rhythmically, her own eyes almost closed.

Everyone is watching her. Daniel is beset by a blossom. He tenses himself.

"Eye of the orgasm," the girl says sweetly.

"Yes," Daniel says. He has gained the questionable skill of reply. Trapped in his unuseful maturity. "You're right, it is the world which must hold our interest."

Daniel's thought processes are dreamy and associative. This, most when he wants to be purposeful and logical. *Redefine* Daniel says to himself daily. *Reconcile reconcile.* And yet he knows that there is no reconciliation between the thought of life and its actuality.

Daniel has been at a regional meeting in Boston. Now he is going home and he stops at a gas station just before the turnpike. Leaving Boston, he always stops here. The attendants know him. They are large, loud men, fiercely joking. Daniel gets out of the Buick and leans against the fender, laughing with these lively men at their ambiguous, conspiratorial jokes. They fling the hose into the gas tank; they slap their crotches; they wear warm Navy jackets leaking soiled fleece.

Daniel is driving home. It is sleeting and he drives cautiously. It is taking much longer than he anticipated. He turns off the turnpike into a deserted little shopping center where there is a phone booth. He wants to call Elisabeth and tell her that he will be delayed.

He draws on his pipe as he rummages through his pocket for coins. The pipe is made of a "space-age" material and is a rakish red. But it burns hot. He drops some coins into the box.

"Hello, Elisabeth?" he says. At that moment an automobile backs into the phone booth with considerable force. The glass in a lower panel breaks and falls over Daniel's shoes. The light goes out. Over three dollars in change rattles into the return. The bumper that is now Daniel's companion in the booth is painted flat black and has a day-glo sticker on it. The sticker says LET'S BOOGIE.

"My word," Daniel exclaims. Their connection is still good. The car is jammed into forward and squeals out of the booth into the parking lot where it vanishes.

"Well," Elisabeth says and pauses. "Are you all right?" She sounds polite and concerned but at the same time preoccupied as though she were half-listening to a child prattle by her knee.

"Well, yes," Daniel says. His ears burn. He is rather embarrassed. He quickly says good-bye and squeezes out of the broken booth. He does not take the change. He walks stolidly to the Buick, the rain freezing in his hair.

Daniel has been preaching for thirty-five years now and has held six pulpits since he left theological school. Now his robe is becoming a little frayed along the cuffs and hem. It has worn beautifully for a quarter of a decade and Daniel will never get another for they cost $400. It hangs in the closet of his study where a bulb burns continually to prevent mildew. It hangs like folded wings. The door is kept slightly ajar and the robe is forever catching Daniel's eye as he sits at his desk. Several times Daniel has had surprising dreams in which the robe is being used to pad and protect furniture in a moving van, or being used to sop up a spill in a stranger's basement. He sees the robe everywhere in ambiguous situations, lashed to inert objects, warming them.

Daniel's congregations have been remarkably similar. The people are robbed and suffer accidents. They grow sick or better or befuddled. They drink too much and pummel their children on their birthdays. There are abortions and seizures and quarrels and abandonments. Love becomes promiscuity. There are omissions and regrets, complaints and accusations. Concerns fluctuate, obsessions shift. The years pass from them all like smoke through screen.

And Daniel always feels that he stays longer than he should have. Beyond his effectiveness. The God he strives to wrestle with leaves town before Daniel does. He is often depressed about his God who seems inattentive, impulsive and lacking in the zeal both for the battle and His own preservation in daily life. As far as Daniel can see, God has little interest in human experience and is forever wandering off, out of the world with its tedious limitations of mass and time and causality and into the singing void. The truths of the world seem irrelevant to and positively incongruent with the void in which Daniel suspects light and even joy.

It is February. Elisabeth and Daniel are celebrating their anniversary. They have been together for forty years. They go to a lovely old Inn that they remember. In the dining room, the golden floors sag and all the clocks on the linen-papered walls tell different times. A sign over the cashier's desk states that the hotel's kitchen invented apple pie a la mode in the 1800's. The old radiators labor beneath the high slim windows. One of the panes is inexplicably, bewitchingly blue, deadening the view of the snowy street. There are great creaking expanses between the tables. The guests eat dreamily. They push forks across plates without a sound. They speak softly but without inhibition.

Daniel rests his hand loosely on the table. The table is covered with layers and layers of cloth, falling down, past his knees. The mends in the cloth are certainly more wonderful than the cloth itself, tiny flowers, stars, even, perhaps, birds and animals and children. The thread is the same color as the cloth but raised slightly, like a scar. Daniel's hands seem to bounce on the thickness of the cloth. They bounce sideways toward Elisabeth's hands. She is wearing a single, silver bracelet. He can smell the cream she has rubbed into her skin.

They have several glasses of champagne and then they order waffles. Outside, it is snowing. They can see the orange lights of the plows as they move through the streets. They can see the marks the blades have made. Inside, the clocks have painted scenes which move measuredly past, behind the faces. They rise and vanish and reappear again, moons and ships, falling by on an antique, inexhaustible wheel.

Daniel asks Elisabeth if she is tired. They are going to spend the night here and get an early start in the morning. They are taken upstairs to their room. The water is bitter. The bed is an icy iron. They hold each other tightly, warming their flanks. Their mouths sing with the flavor of the complimentary mints.

Man and His World

Clark Blaise

1.

In the season of dust with the sun benign, a man of forty and a boy of twelve appeared at the Tourist Reception Centre, asking for rooms. Failing that, a house, with cook and servant.

The Centre was a modest concrete bunker with thirty rooms and a dining hall, and it was full. This was winter, the time for migrating Siberian songbirds and their Japanese pursuers. For the man and boy the situation was potentially desperate. Udirpur was a walled, medieval town baked on an igneous platter a thousand feet above the desert. To the east, no settlements for two hundred kilometers. To the west lay twenty kilometers of burnt, rusted tanks and stripped, blood-stained Jeeps, a UN outpost manned by a bizarre assortment of ill-equipped troops, then barbed wire, mines, and fifteen kilometers of more trophy tanks and blood-stained Jeeps. In the winter, buses dropped off passengers twice a week, picked up freight, and returned to the capital.

The man—who gave his name as William Logan—really should have booked a room through the central authority. That way, he would have saved the trip and, who knows, maybe his life.

2.

They had been on the road six days from New Delhi. Sleeping on buses, standing on trains, paying truckers. By day, the thin air required a sweater, though the hot sun burned with its mere intention. From March, when summer returned, the town would disappear from tourist maps and the national consciousness and the road become the world's longest clothes-line and camel dung kiln.

Wealth was counted in camels. Camels outnumbered bicycles in the district. Camels pulled the wooden-wheeled carts and plodded around the water-screws, drawing up monsoon rains from the summer before. They yielded their carcasses more graciously than any animal in the world. The first sight of camels grazing in the bush had been a wonder to William Logan. Something half-evolved to mammalhood, comic and terrifying in its brute immensity. It had confirmed him, for the moment, in the right-ness of what he was doing.

In the desert near the Rat Temple, the government maintained a camel-breeding station. The sight of a hobbled cow being mounted by the gar-landed bull, their bellows and the swelling of their reptilian necks, suggest-ed to the Japanese naturalists on their guided tours an echo of the world's creation, a foretaste of its agony and death.

3.

Before the invasion of Aryans, Greeks, Persians and British, the desert people had their own cosmology. The Mother of the World had given birth to identical pairs of camels, tigers, gazelles, elephants and rats. She did not distinguish among her children. She did not have a particular aspect or appearance; whatever their size or ferocity, her children all resembled her, perfectly. The people of Udirpur are still known as rat-worshippers.

When she was nearly too old for child-bearing and the world was already full, she found herself pregnant again. And for the first time, she suffered pain, foreboding, fatigue. She bled, lay down frequently and grew thin. And from her womb came rumbles, lava, fire and flood. When she gave birth, only one cub emerged. His strangled, identical brother fell from the womb and was hastily buried under the great stone mountain in the middle of the desert.

It is said that one brother was evil, but which one? They had struggled in the womb but the secret was kept. The tribes of animals divided. Those giving allegiance to the survivor became his servants. Others retired to the oceans and to the air and to the underworld, growing fins or scales or feathers, or shrinking themselves to become insects. They all kept faith with the one who had died.

It is said the survivor, be he good or bad, is born with sin and with guilt and is condemned to loneliness. Nowhere on the earth will he find his brother or anything else like him. And with his birth, the Mother of the World died and the creative cycle came to an end.

4.

Ten years earlier, over the mountains a thousand kilometers to the north, a woman had arrived in Udirpur: the palest, whitest woman the people had ever seen. She'd been discovered outside the Rat Temple by a lorry-driver who'd been praying to the God for a successful trip. He had offered sweets and lain still while the God's children had swirled over his hands and feet, licking his still-sweet fingers and lips.

Clearly the girl was a hippie—the only English word he knew—one of a tribe he'd heard about but never seen. She carried a new-born baby and nursed him like a village woman by the temple gates. She wore a torn, faded sari, something the lorry-driver's own wife or widowed mother would be ashamed to wear. But she wore it well and seemed comfortable in it.

He spoke to her in his language, offering a ride to Udirpur, where at least there were facilities for foreign women and for babies. To his surprise, she answered in a language he knew. She gathered her sleeping baby and the cotton sack that held her possessions and followed him to his truck, without question. This was the way she had travelled and lived for the past three years. At some point in time lost to her now, she had been a girl in a cold small town on the edge of a forest, near a river frequented by whales, and she had left that town on a bus to work in the city, in the year of a World's Fair. And after that summer she'd not stopped her travelling, until it brought her here.

The lorry-driver knew where to take her. In Udirpur, the city of rats, the Raja had travelled the world. He spoke every language and he welcomed whatever remnant of the world that managed to seek him out.

5.

He lived in a tawny sandstone palace two kilometers from the center of town, at the place where the igneous mesa began to split, where a summer river fed a forest and residual privilege permitted the luxury of a gardener and his family, the appropriation of water, and the maintenance of a very small game sanctuary.

In the British days, the various Nizams and Maharajas had been afforded full military salutes. The British, with their customary punctiliousness over military symbol and social hierarchy, assigned each native potentate a scrupulously-measured number of guns. Thus, powerful rajahs like those of Jaipur and Baroda enjoyed full twenty-one gun salutes, and the no-less-regal but less prepossessing rajahs of Cooch Behar and Gwalior and Dewas Senior and even Dewas Junior (the latter a one-time employer of a reticent young Englishman who introduced Gibbon to the royal reading room) were granted fifteen, or twelve, or eight guns. The Rajah of Udirpur, grandfather of the current resident of the Tawny Palace, had been assigned a mere two guns on the imperial scale. He was therefore called the Pipsqueak Rajah, or Sir Squealer Singh, for the twin effect of his popgun salute and for the only worthy attraction in his district, the notorious Temple of Rats. It is not written how Sir Squealer, a genial and worldly man by all accounts, felt about his name or his general reception.

The grandson, Freddie Singh, occupied two rooms in the sealed-off palace. In those rooms he maintained the relics he'd inherited: swords, carpets, carvings, muskets, tiger-claws, daggers, and the fine silk cords designed for efficient dispatch. Freddie Singh's private Armory was as complete as any Rajah's but no visitor ever saw it. He kept in touch with his subjects, or those few hundred who still acknowledged his rule, and kept out of the way of the State, District and Conservation authorities who actually ran the town.

He had been out of the country once as a young man, then just graduated in business administration from the Faculty of Management in Ahmedabad. The First National City Bank (India, Pvt. Ltd.) had hired him as a stock-analyst, and after two years of the fast life in Bombay, he'd been sent to an office in Rome, then Paris and finally New York, to learn stocks and bonds and how to trade in futures.

Those had been the beautiful years of Freddie Singh, those years on the Strand, in the Bourse, on Wall Street, an exiled princeling, smelling of licorice.

6.

She and the baby—a rugged little chap, half-Pathan by the look of him— opened up a room on the second floor, assisted by the old Royal Groom and keeper of polo ponies (now reduced to cook and gardener and feeder of the royal animals) and his widowed daughter and her very small daughter who became a companion for young Pierre-Rama.

She seemed to bring some order, perhaps some beauty, into Freddie's life. For the majority of people in his ancestral city, the Rajah (though still a youngish man) was either a relic or an embarrassment. When he at last took the unwed foreign mother as a wife, they were prepared to call her Rani if it pleased him. Other names as well, in front of her but never him. The camel, bountiful in all things, provides an anthology of choice insults. The Rani was made to feel as worthy as the slime off a dead camel's tooth. Weeks, then finally years went by, without her ever leaving the compound.

7.

Pierre-Rama was nearly ten when the man and his son appeared in town that cool day in late December. Since the Tourist Centre was filled with bird-watchers, someone asked if the visitor would object to accommodation in the Rajah's palace? No, he would not. Would the visitor mind sharing the floor with the beautiful, exotic, mysterious Rani? No, decidedly, he would not. Would he be patient with the Rajah, who, if he could not marry his guests, would often confer upon them land deeds or Mogul miniatures or dusty carpets that had been his grandfather's privilege to dis-

burse, but which now belonged to the state? Yes, he would be patient
with the old gentleman.

They put the man and his son (a frail lad given to sneezing in the dust
and to whining for the newly-outlawed American soft-drinks) in Youssef's
camel-drawn cart and drove them to the gully-hugging yellow palace. They
made their own way through the garden to the main gate, and pulled on a
rusty chain to alert the *chowkidar*.

It was the Rajah, clad in pajamas and a shawl and smoking an English
cigarette who opened the door. He was younger than the guest, a vigorous
man no more than thirty-five, with a head and mane of glossy curls, a
rounded face and rubbed, rounded body that glowed with a kind of polish
the visitor had never seen. "My wife is upstairs. She is just coming down."
He called up from the stairwell, "Visitors, Solange! Come quickly!" Seeing confusion when a young, familiar-looking woman appeared at the head
of the stairs, bowing shyly and murmuring, "Bonjour," the Rajah winked
and said, "My wife, the Rani. She is from Cue-beck, in Canada. And
where, sir, do you come from?"

"Winnipeg," said William Logan. "In Canada."

8.

That is how, this night in February two months later, under a sky
pierced with stars, with meteorites flaring and bright silent things making
their way across the heavens (not planes, satellites possibly, if indeed so
many had been launched), under a sky that would embarrass a Planetarium,
a sky that thrills the way the ocean or a mountain range can thrill, a sky
that suggests mythologies and seems explicable only in narrative and divine
inspiration, the two are talking, have been talking, for hours. She nurses
the baby, Jacques-Ravinder, the Rajah's son, two months old, honey-col-
ored, plump and good-natured.

How perfect a garment is the sari for nursing babies, thinks the man,
William Logan. They sleep under a lavender or green or yellow gauze, free
of flies and the glare of the sun, the mother sits with her baby anywhere,
nurses him in a crowd with only the little toes peeking from the crook of
her elbow to give him away.

Such is the posture that night. Logan talks. The Rani listens. The
Rajah is almost asleep in his wicker chair, contributing nothing but his benign royal presence. The older boys run through the palace undisturbed,
chasing rats, confining them when possible to the unused rooms.

9.

The stars over the winter desert are mythologically potent tonight, por-
tending stories. The sky is an ocean, thinks William Logan; I could watch it
forever. The Milky Way a luminous smear, the rip and tear of meteorites,
blue-white stars glittering like messages, like interference; he thinks of old

movies, the sputter on a sound system for every break in the film. But here is no sound but the sucking of milk.

Logan is speaking. "Now this is a night for sea-turtles," he says very slowly, because English is the Rani's last language, the one she learned here, with a local accent, from the gardener and his widowed daughter. Sea-turtles she does not understand, but lets Logan go on.

"When sea-turtles are born, they have maybe twenty minutes to memorize the exact location of their birth. Their exact twenty feet of sand, in the world. And these are among the stupidest animals on earth—can you imagine?"

"That is amazing," she says.

"But I've seen them down on the beach at Grand Cayman. Caribbean sea-turtles. The old she-turtle waddles ashore and digs a deep trough about fifty feet up from the water. And she drops in her eggs and pats down the sand and goes back to sea."

"That is beautiful," says the Maharani.

"But they don't make it, see. No, no, the natives hide behind the trees, waiting for the old she-turtles to lay their eggs. They are too tired now to move..."

"Yes, I am knowing that tiredness..."

"And so the natives attack them, turn them all over on their backs. And after a few hours they build fires on the beach and heat iron spikes red hot and then push them under the shell—"

"Oh, Mr. Logan, please. This is terrible. No more, please."

"Please do not be upset, Solange," says the Rajah, snapping awake. "I too have seen this." What we are witnessing, he goes on to suggest, is the death of a species from over-specialization. It had lived two hundred million years in one form or another, an insult to intelligence, without enemies, enjoying near-immortality. It is a model of organization, more like a religion than a living creature.

A long silence ensues. "I have seen skies like this only up north," says Logan.

"I have seen skies like this every night since I left Europe," says the Rani. "The nights on the Black Sea and on the Caspian and in the desert of Kandahar and in the mountains of Kashmir were all like this. I could not live without stars like this. It is a head full of jewels, the people say. And in the monsoons when the stars are covered, the people say the camel has closed her eyes and people get sick."

Mr. Logan had not yet spent a monsoon.

"I was saying, about turtles. Not about the she-turtles—that is sad and barbarian, I grant you. I was thinking of the babies. Just seconds after they hatch and climb up through the sand and they're no larger than fiddler crabs and move just as fast, and there are hundreds of them all on the same night racing from the dunes down across the wet sand of high tide to the water. Thousands of birds have gathered and all the natives who were there for the mothers are there for the babies. They carry baskets and they scoop up turtles with both hands the way we'd pick berries, and that's not the amazing thing. The amazing thing about those baby turtles is this: they have only ten minutes to break out of the egg and get into the water. And they must survive odds that would stop the most intelligent beast on earth. And that's not what they're thinking about. What they must do beyond anything else is plan for their return to this beach, this very beach, for spawning. And they do it by printing the stars indelibly in their brain. A perfect star-chart. It's as though they are born with the most perfect sensitive instrument in the world, they use it once, remember it perfectly, and then when they hit the water, if they get that far, the mind snaps shut and they live on instinct for the next three centuries."

"That is very beautiful," she agrees.

"We are the only animals who can get so lost, Mr. Logan," says Freddie Singh.

Under the sari, the Maharani shifts the baby to the other breast. For several minutes they watch the meteorites and the steadily-moving things that the Rani thinks of as extraterrestrial.

"When our geese are flying south," says Logan, "it is said that they can hear the Gulf waves crashing on the shores of Texas and they can hear the Atlantic surf on Ireland. From Winnipeg, or Montreal."

The Rani says nothing but she feels that she has travelled as unerringly as any turtle or any goose and that even tonight she could hear every voice in every language that had ever been spoken to her. This man Logan, a countryman, was over-impressed with the brains of lower animals.

"You are a restless man, Mr. Logan," says the Rani.

10.

The three-block frontage of William Logan's birth was Stiles to Raglan, between Portage and Wolseley, in the city of Winnipeg. Though life had stretched him, he often returned to that original scene, in his memory, to his house built by his father on land purchased by his grandfather, on the Assiniboine. In his way he had swum the world ever since. He had lost his bearings.

He had been in Montreal in 1967, living in Westmount and working in textiles. He'd just been divorced. He was thirty that year with a two-year-old boy and he remembered Westmount Park, the library, the sandboxes and the slides. He was, then and now, a tall, lean, bald, elegant man—in textiles, after all—walking slowly, fingers clutched by his little boy, eyes alert to the idle young mothers, so rich, so confident and attractive. They shared an idleness those afternoons—he was frequently in and out of Montreal and found himself with half-days to kill—there was a power in being the only man in the park, with a sturdy little child.

In ten years with his mother, the child had grown less sturdy. He was better now.

There was a day when a new adventure began, when he sat a reasonable distance (but on the same bench) from a blond, maturing woman in a lavender sweater. It was late April, perhaps snow still was pushed in ridges but the earth was dry and dusty. A little girl, pursued by an *au pair* girl, ran to the lady and took a good long look at William Logan.

"Mama, that man is *bald,*" said the little girl.

"Damn," said the mother.

Logan, who'd never minded his baldness or the reputation it carried, found it a handy prop in establishing his essential harmlessness with younger women, said, "That's OK. Out of the mouths of babes, etc."

The mother straightened the little girl's jacket and motioned for the *au pair* to take her back to the swings. "Oh, it's not that. It's that now I have to sleep with you to restore your almighty male ego."

"Pardon me?" He'd been out of the country.

She gave her address—a brick house on Lansdowne, just up from the park.

The Rajah stood and poured a final cup of tea.

The baby was sleeping and he took him back to the palace, bidding his guest good night.

11.

"I'll never get back," he said.

"To Montreal?"

"To Winnipeg. Not that I want to. I can't anyway. I'm a fugitive."

The Rani was not disturbed. He had established his essential harmlessness.

"Tell me about the lady on Lansdowne," she said.

He sipped slowly. God forgive me, thought William Logan: she reads minds and her breast excited me though she's my hostess, a Maharani, and nursing an infant.

The lady on Lansdowne was Hungarian. Thirty-five and very beautiful and bold and angry. She was an actress and her husband had left his wife for her. He had much older children, and that obnoxious little girl.

"Her name was Laura," says the Rani.

"Yes, I believe so."

"Now, Mr. Logan, tell me about the *au pair* girl."

Before he can answer, he remembers it all. My God, he thinks. He'd lived long enough, accumulated enough points of reference, for his experiences to start collapsing, growing dense with coincidence.

"You looked familiar the first time I saw you. Solange—of course."

"That day in the park. You called me the *au pair* girl but I noticed you alone in the park and I watched Mrs. K watching you and I could see you were both very experienced in the world. . .I was not, not at all. I wondered how you would get together." She took a long breath, and wrapped the sari-end over her head.

"You speak a lot more when your husband is gone."

"My husband is never gone."

She listened awhile to jackals on the plain, the leathery sway of palms in the desert, the distant clatter of wooden wheels, a cart and camel over cobblestones.

"May I call you Solange?"

She pondered the question longer than he thought necessary. "I cannot stop you."

"Then what are the chances of our getting together? Surely it means something, no? It can't just be (he thought of the stars) just coincidence."

"You are perhaps too restless, Mr. Logan."

"It's just that I don't wait for things anymore."

On his last flight from Egypt to Montreal, Logan had sat next to a pleasant, moon-faced young man bound for Athens, and maybe Montreal. He'd asked Logan shrewd job-hunting questions and Logan had been flattered by his interest. Then he'd asked him what time it was. They were south of Athens. Logan told him and the man jerked into a new posture. He stood and opened one of the Red Cross emergency medical bags that was in the storage area immediately overhead. At the same time, six other young men stood and opened other emergency boxes. *Oh no,* Logan had thought: the boxes were full of grenades.

There is nothing in the modern world quite like eight days of siege to focus a man's attention on final matters. They had landed a few hundred yards from the hillside home of the Delphic Oracle. *Low has fallen the prophet's house,* quoted one passenger. Women and children were released; Logan made his peace. As good a place as any to die; as good a reason as any. His life was a hostage-taking anyway, he was a passenger only, detained by fanatics. He vowed, if he survived, to live his life from that moment on as though the person next to him were a terrorist, that every package contained grenades, that every flight would end on a hillside, surrounded by troops.

12.

Just a few weeks before, but a millenium ago, he had landed in Montreal, flown to Toronto, taken the airport limousine to the door of the expensive school he paid for and asked for Billy Logan, a boy who was a stranger to him and whom he'd come to dislike just a little. He'd taken Billy with him back to the airport and they'd flown to London, bought tropical clothes and Logan had sent telegrams to his boss and ex-wife. *Resign effective immediately. . .I have Billy don't look you'll never find us.* He bought tickets to a dozen destinations, under various names. Not merely restless, he'd become impulsive.

Some nights, sleep is an act of will requiring as sharp a focus as thought itself. Under such heavens there could be no sleep. Listening to the Rani was like listening to an Indian woman—the accent, that is—only better. It's strange but familiar, because behind it is something he can understand. It's erotic, terribly erotic. He cannot control his love, not for her, not for his host, not for his child; he wants to displace the Rajah; he feels he has found his home.

In the second week of residence at the Tawny Palace, Logan had boldly proposed to the attractive lady who did his rooms, the gardener's widowed daughter. Perhaps she had not understood; the daughter, an exquisite child of —what? thirteen?—had appeared. And then to say to her, "No, I meant your mother" when she had presented herself so wondrously to him would have offended his morals as much as taking her. To turn from beauty is a sin, to refuse the daughter would embarrass us all, and be insulting, he feared.

But he had not intended this, any of this, and there could only be one honorable way to act. To enjoy the love of the girl and to try to love the mother. What incredible complications this would lead to, William Logan could not say: only that he was ready to face them. The adjacent space, he had learned, may always be evil, or it may open into the next world, the next level, a higher existence. The girl comes to him after bathing while the mother prepares his lunch. The Rani and Rajah have no suspicions. It is a very private, second-floor affair. The daughter must know—though she has never asked—that in the evenings after the main meal has been cooked and the sweeper has cleaned the rooms and the daughter has washed the dishes that her mother returns, laden with fruits and a small clay pot of sweets, makes tea, then lies beside him.

Is this corruption? At one time he would have known but now he cannot say. He feels at times that he has entered a compact, nothing down, no interest, small monthly payments, but that an unpayable price will be extracted. It is like a nightmare in which he is ice-skating out on the Assiniboine, and he can feel the dark waters oozing from the slashes of his blade; there is still time to skate ashore but a wind is pushing him out to the black open water and he can't turn back.

13.

Freddie Singh sits in his Armory, wondering if this is the night. He has come to like the visitor. The boys have become inseparable; there is hope for the boy. But Freddie Singh is still the Rajah of the Tawny Palace; he knows what happens on his grounds as his grandfather once knew what happened in his larger *durbar*; he knows that an uprooted man is the principle of corruption, will spread it wherever he goes. When you announced yourself from Canada, the Rani said *get rid of him immediately* but I could not. You needed rest, just as the Rani had needed rest. But she has healed, and you have not, my friend.

The people here know of dualities, of coincidence. Every day they see the sand turn to embers. Every night to ice. Ten months of the year, never a drop of water. Two months, walls of mud.

The Rani arrived in India with a friend, another girl from Cue-beck. But the other girl met a handsome Frenchman at the airport and the Rani struggled onward, to the desert. Her friend followed the boy to Bangkok, Hong Kong, Djakarta, Nepal. She loved him, she cooked for him, she helped poison people for him, maybe dozens of young travellers, like her, like the Rani. She may be in jail for the rest of her life. She was not evil, not born evil, but she had become lost.

We have known others, thinks Freddie Singh. A fourteen-year-old girl gives birth in a paddy field in Bangladesh nine months after a week of raping, after her mother's rape and murder, her village's rape and butchery. She slashes the infant's throat and wrists, hacks up the body like a fish's, then throws herself successfully on the knife. But someone came by, picked up the smaller body and took it to the hospital, and the corpse was resurrected. And the baby was adopted by a family in Lévis who named her Marie-Josée and now she's the best student and the best figure-skater in her school.

The people here have seen enough of life to know that coincidence itself is no motive for action. Coincidence on your level, Mr. Logan, is a turtle's coincidence, nothing but instinct.

Coincidence is coincidental, thinks Freddie Singh.

14.

"My husband is back."

Logan, sipping the last of his cold tea, turned in his wicker chair. "Freddie, I—"

In Freddie's hands is stretched taut a valuable artifact from one of the desert tribes. In the old days they had joined caravans across the desert, offering their services as entertainers and animal-handlers. And those caravans never reached their destinations. The people were called *thuggis* and they worshipped the principle of creation no less than other tribes, though their ultimate loyalty was to the brother who had died.

Death moves swiftly across the heavens, obliterating the stars at a point just short of meaning, and across Logan's brain like some long-sought solution made suddenly apparent, only to retreat again. He looks up, about to speak and across to the Rani who now is standing, and turning away. Then he looks down, at himself, sees his head perched crazily on his chest and the widening dribble of tea on his luminous white *kurta,* and the stain spreads to fill his universe.

The Lost Tribe

Jean Thompson

Under the cold black New England trees, a piano is playing jolly songs.
Hunting owls, confused, fly deeper into the forest. Although the piano is
some distance away, beyond 'the sodden muffled turf of a golf course. Beyond the little cove where the ocean laps as mildly as a bathtub. A yellow
moon breaks into spangles on the water. From here you can recognize the
tune: SINGGen in the rain, I'm singen in the rain. The piano jingles, pursued by two dozen voices.

It is Saturday night, Sing-Along Night, in the bar of one of the larger
summer resorts. The piano player is a man in his forties, balding but muscular. There is something athletic in his playing, something of the concen-
tration of the hurdler as he bends over the music, leaping from one song
to another without interlude. One might suspect him of trying to rush the
evening and get home to bed. But these are bright, almost relentlessly upbeat songs—Pennies from Heaven, When You're Smiling, In the Good Old
Summertime—and they don't allow for much of nuance or meditation.

The patrons of the bar are just the sort of people you'd expect to find
here, as if, crossing the Swiss border, you beheld goatherds in lederhosen
and peaked hats. They are middle-aged, Caucasian, sportively and prosper-
ously dressed. But the impression is not quite accurate, for few of them
are wealthy enough to afford this resort, where rooms run from forty to
ninety dollars in season. The tab is being picked up by the Boston-based
packaging firm for which they work. They have assembled here to discuss,
in the daylight hours, certain trends in their industry. At least one man.in

the bar is noting the price of the drinks, which are expensive and not paid for by the company.

Still, a certain prosperity coats these people like scent, or the layer of buttery light in a painting by Rubens. The ladies are drinking White Russians and Daiquiris. The gentlemen specify Canadian Club or Heinekens. The bartender, very young and so tensely polite he verges on formality, is kept hopping in his cramped corner. Business is good, the conventioneers have been told. The company is diversifying. More and more products are being concealed in cardboard tubes and ingenious little styrofoam nests.

The other almost universal quality of this group is happiness. They love the old songs, they love the fizziness of mild inebriation (for no one is drinking enough yet to be mean or messy) which permits them to croon or at least sway along with the music. One little elderly fellow with wistful, feminine features circulates among the tables, beating time with his finger, sprightly as a Walt Disney cricket. A man in an orange and brown acetate shirt waltzes his blushing wife in a corner. The glossy pine walls shine with reflected good humor.

It is true that at one table, a wife glances often towards the piano, where her husband stands next to someone else's wife. This other wife has skin like an overwashed towel, and the wife at the table does not really suspect anything. All the same, she finds it difficult to keep up a conversation with the other wife's homely and voluble husband. It is true that a man in a corner booth is telling a red-haired lady in ample printed chiffon that he is divorced. The divorce was prolonged and wretched. To mention it even this casually makes him gloomy. But the red-haired lady's sympathy is as warming and subtle as the old Scotch in his glass. The divorced man feels his melancholy perfected by such an audience, brought to some satisfying peak. He joins in the chorus of Paper Roses.

The bar is named after a tribe of local Indians which no longer exists. The management has decorated this glossy waxed pine room in an Indian motif, as they say, with tomahawks and arrowheads, with buckskin fringe on the lampshades. Watercolors by local artists show Indian maidens kneeling beside crystal streams, braves silhouetted on ocean cliffs and puzzling over the sunset on the east horizon. If the conventioneers' interest in history did not stop at nostalgia, they might learn that the resort is half a mile from an early English settlement. The Indians did rather well for themselves, destroying the settlement twice and forcing its relocation inland before they themselves were destroyed by smallpox and yellow fever.

All this is preserved in plaques and tourist brochures. The old battlefields are fairways now, and invisible waves crisscross the sky, bringing the citizens their electronic amusements. The shaggy, bloody past is as worn as the moose head in the lobby, its glass eyes loosening and its ears spilling sawdust. So it is fitting that the Indian now advancing on the resort is solitary, unarmed, and a little soiled.

His name is Hector Lame Deer. He is drunk and would like to be drunker. Every so often he stops, considers the cold, pine-scented silence, then plods on, bent and bulky. These pauses are the only thing that indicate his drunkenness. He stops when he feels himself losing his balance. Once a car roars up the hill behind him and he steps into the trees, unwilling to be caught in the headlights. Drinking in town some two miles away, he had a sudden urge to see the ocean. He wishes to perfect his sorrow in the same way the divorced man does his, and the sight of the vast glittering bay will let him float in misery.

Hector is not a lost descendant of the lost tribe, but a mixture of French and the more resilient Iroquois. He is not even from this area, having come here twenty years ago to work in the sawmills. Now he runs a machine which cuts hides in a shoe factory, and his clothes are permeated with the smell of glue and dye. The Gallic portion of his heritage has, if anything, made him look all the more Indian, duskier, leaner. His teeth are bad and he seldom reveals them, so his impassiveness too is exaggerated.

Why is he sorrowful? He is always so. It is his native air. He is forty years old and looks fifty. Rural slums are less obtrusive than urban, but equally efficient at such things. Rural slums are old silver-sided trailers with big metal seams and home-made chimneys, they are shacks built of tarpaper and splinters, front door junkyards and their old car seats, rusting oil drums, boilers, bedsprings, yellow chickens.

All this is sorrowful in a chronic and anti-climactic fashion. As is the image of the Old Days, when the green world was ruled by Bear-People, Otter-People, Deer-People, when trees had voices. It is a grandmother's tale, never quite belonging to him, unable to sustain him through cold nights and colder mornings. Hector's sorrows are blurred around their edges, like a careless woman's lipstick. Walking down the black pine-fragrant road, he thinks not in terms of poverty or injustice, but that it would be nice to sleep on the beach except for all the damned motorboats.

As he approaches the resort he hears the music, a kind of layered sound, each voice claiming its own territory around the beat. He stops in the parking lot where the big cars are lined up like sleek cattle in their stalls. Some have CB antennas sprouting from their trunks, a separate breed. Hector strokes a fender absently, glances at the moon on the puckered water, and walks towards the bar.

He enters in the middle of a song, and while people do not stop singing they turn to look so that they appear to be seranading him: Ma-hargie, you've been my inspiration, dates are never blu-u-u. In fairness, anyone entering the small room would attract attention. But Hector, with his pungent flapping red flannel shirt and old slick jeans, sooty hair falling into his eyes, is something else. The group speculates on him as it heaves into the chorus. Is he likely to insult women or produce firearms? The music wavers for a moment. Then the group regains its confidence and the song ends with a little trill of affirmation for their numerical superiority, the glossy walls and expensive liquor.

As for Hector, planted on the threshold. Yi! he thinks, and Shit! This is no place for a poor man, he knew that anyway, but to find it so crammed with noise and enthusiasm makes him sweat. He regards everything with glazed, somber eyes, feeling little stay-go impulses twitch in him like minnows. One drink, he decides, for the long walk home. These rich loud tourists won't get to laugh behind his back, not right away at least. He edges between the tables, careful not to meet anyone's eye.

Once at the bar he feels better. A draft, he tells the pale chubby bartender, and a shot, he adds out of plain bravado, laying his last five dollar bill on the bar. The bartender hesitates for just a moment, enough to show that he senses the emanations of social incongruity, tannin, and red sugary wine. But after all he is very young, politeness has been heavily stressed, and in case of trouble his lack of responsibility can be defended. Well Mr. Hake, he had the money, he was quiet, it would have caused more of a problem to throw him out. Draft and a shot, says the bartender, once more impassive, obedient.

The music has begun again, or rather, the pianist is walloping out a new song: Up the Lazy River. Hector feels the room regaining its momentum, as if it has absorbed him, accepted him as a minor curiosity. The bartender whisks something before him. A bowl of salted nuts. Hector stares, then, since they seem to belong to no one else, places one between his bad teeth. He takes a whole handful, crunching loudly, and still no one stops him. Eeya! He is pleased! The place begins to look more encouraging.

The room has indeed adjusted to Hector, correctly interpreting that he is a little cowed by it all. Starlight up above, they sing, Everyone's in love, and it is nearly true, everyone bathes in love, in Saturday-night good-fellowship. The husband standing at the piano with the other wife has turned and winked at his own wife, which relieves her. The other wife's homely husband has been talking about architecture. It is his hobby; he knows quite a bit about Sullivan and Frank Lloyd Wright. Now she finds it interesting, and she tells herself that if you only relax about things, life has so much to offer. Even the pale young bartender, juggling cherries, orange slices and little plastic swords, is thinking of his tips, how good they are tonight, the coins fat and the bills cool.

This tide of good feeling sends the little sprightly man to the bar, bobbing and swaying like a small nautical bandleader. Whoa, he commands himself, coming to rest perhaps an inch from Hector's elbow. Please excuse, the little man explains to Hector's large doubtful dirty face. I get carried away with my own musical talent. Three drinks and I'm ready to play the Palace, you know?

Yeah, says Hector, who has just grasped the fact that the man is speaking to him. The piano player is taking a break and the absence of music makes all conversation sound a bit too loud at first. The little man, waiting to catch the bartender's eye, regards Hector with a tentative and unfocussed sympathy. He wishes everyone could be as expansively happy as he is at the moment. Hector does not look happy. (Though for Hector, a recognizably cheerful look would denote absolute hilarity.) The little man feels himself to be fluid, warmly cresting. Even when sober he is a generous, rather impulsive fellow. So he says I bet this Hit Parade stuff isn't your favorite. I bet Indians have their own music. You are an Indian, aren't you?

At the word Indian, sweat blooms freshly in Hector's pores, and he turns, ready to feel whatever is called for, anger or fear or caution. But the little man is so dapper, with his lemon-and-black check shirt and Texas tie, so beaming and tiny, Hector is unsure. So he nods gravely and says yes, he is an Indian.

Ah says the little man, and purses his finely-drawn lips. I could tell. I don't mean to be rude, you know, just curious. You grow up with all the Last Mohican Tonto stuff, what do you really know. But listen to me, I'm being a pain in the ass. I apologize. Bartender, a Seven-Seven and a round for my buddy here.

Hector is gazing at him as if he were an amazing wind-up toy, full of tiny gears and tricks. Thanks, he says when the drinks appear. Thanks very much.

Don't mention it. The little man extends his hand. Charlie Kobel.

Lame Deer, says Hector, gaining strength and craft from the second whiskey.

Lame Deer! That's wonderful. I mean—the little man is suddenly embarrassed, and seems relieved when a woman joins them at the bar. Loretta, he says, how's the girl?

Loretta is a huge old lady with grizzled hair and chapped, bloodless cheeks, dressed in a red pants suit. All her life she has been told Remember dear, God dressed the elephant in gray, and now she's decided the hell with it. Charlie, she says. Her smile contains equal portions of tooth and gum. I see you're still going strong.

Never say die. Loretta, I'd like you to meet Lame Deer.

Loretta, who has bad eyes, inclines her torso across the bar towards Hector. She sees him as if she were looking through a sheet of waxed paper, or a thin smear of milk. How do you do, she says, and smiles again.

Hector sees her huge bony head, the hair beginning to recede like the polar ice cap in warm weather, her long, hollow-looking teeth, and is unnerved. She reminds him of a very old fish. He knows he is getting confused, to think such things. And when Charlie pats his shoulder and says Lame Deer's been telling me all about Indians, and when Loretta says Oh really, in a tone of genuine interest, he knows he's screwed. Too late, too far from home, and crazy people want to talk about Indians. He thinks about trying for the door but there seem to be acres of treacherous chairs in the way now, each having six legs, like spiders.

One thing I've always wondered, Charlie is saying. What it would be like to live the way you people did, off in the woods, hunting, fishing, none of the headaches of civilization. Things must have been better back then, hm?

Hector, who still lives without the headaches of electricity and indoor plumbing, is thinking how strange it is, all he ever asked from whites was to be ignored, all his life they were only too happy to oblige. Now what do they want? He fills his throat with beer. Yes, he agrees, for he always agrees with such people, out of policy, yes things were better back then.

Now these two amiable people are smiling at Hector, even yearning towards him. Their good natures and good intentions are not to be doubted. Like many people of their class and time, guilt comes easily to them. Guilt makes them a little timid as they stand rocking on their heels, and even friendlier. After all, as Loretta will say to Charlie later, how would we feel if the Chinese or somebody took over our homes?

They are believers in the power of individuals, these people, in lighting one little candle, in building bridges of understanding. So Charlie says You do much hunting? I bet this is a good place for deer.

Now Hector does indeed hunt, can dress a deer or rabbit as easily as he cuts the uppers for fancy boots. But all this he does without benefit of hunting license or gun permit, squatting in the snow at dusk with deft, bloody hands. He can only speak noncommittally. It's good hunting. I don't get out much though.

Loretta sighs and her big flame-colored shoulders heave asymmetrically. It's so lovely here. You're lucky to live in a place where it's still so close to wilderness.

Cities are terrible places when you think about it, says Charlie. People aren't meant to live like that, piled up on top of each other and breathing filth.

Hector does not realize they are trying to flatter him. Perhaps they wouldn't recognize it as flattery themselves. The wistfulness they express about nature is habitual; the presence of Hector only makes them articulate it. Indians, they'd say if they had more alcohol or less tact, Indians *know* the wilderness. It has taken three hundred years to develop this wistfulness, this regret. The grim old settlers who pried half-ton boulders out of sucking mud would find this attitude as marvelous as airplanes. The product of all this civilization is being presented to Hector like a porcelain orchid, but he does not acknowledge it.

Well, says Charlie after a moment of silence, plucking at his Texas tie, what we need is more firewater.

Once again the pale young bartender exhibits his dexterity with the bottles. The tumblers are made of amber glass, the ice cubes twinkle, the surface of the bar is cool walnut. Now, says Loretta, her bad eyes making her hoist the glass up to her nose, what shall we drink to?

How about, Here's to wives and sweethearts, may they never meet.

Oh you. Loretta, huge and playful, threatens to pour her drink on Charlie's head.

OK, OK. Charlie hesitates. There is something shy, almost girlish about him at this moment, which is odd without being grotesque. He would like to include Hector in the radiance of his good will, in the tenderness of his guilt. Peace, he says. Peace among all tribes.

Peace, says Loretta.

Peace, says Hector, drinking, and the treaty is sealed.

At that moment the piano player brings both hands down on a chord, pinning it, then breaks into Sidewalks of New York. The crowd turns toward the music affectionately, would embrace it if possible. Only Hector sits unmoving, staring at his hands. They lie before him on the bar like big battered tools.

The evening is nearly over. Before long it will be last call and Good Night, Ladies. Only a few more minutes and exhilaration will start its inevitable leakage. Even the best, dizziest times have that moment of deflation when people realize that everything has already happened. But for now all possibilities are intact. There is so much benevolence here, it streams from the yellow lamps, it covers the music like a husk, it seems about to take some rare and consummate form. It could rise above the crowd like the last gold starburst on Fourth of July, it could transcend anything. Anything! The faces of the singers shine with power.

As for Hector, his sorrow is finally perfecting itself, fluid and rocking like the beer in his glass. Above him the ghost-people, the lost people, drift in and out of his sight like smoke. Silent they are, wrapped in shadowy furs, walking on doeskin. He nods to them gravely. They shimmer above the jaunty music. There are great canoes, and in them war parties, naked as death, gliding up the beach with long knives in their hands. Orange, oily flames curl like hair as the white village burns and the warriors scream with joy.

There is no one else, the ghost-people whisper, to remember them. They are like a star which exhausts its light in black space. Loss must be remembered, and grief preserved. Only the triumphant can afford to be careless. Memory is pale justice, asking only to be acknowledged. A lifetime of loss can be borne if its filaments are held together by memory.

Hector's head is aching with these things, his grandmere's tales and the ghost-whispers swimming together. And he would like to explain all this to someone—the green world, the speaking bones in the earth—and mourn them properly. He struggles to raise himself on one elbow.

Behind him Loretta is saying I don't know what's the matter with me. I saw the whole movie twice, and now I can't think of who played the wife.

Isn't that awful?

Don't be too hard on yourself, says gallant Charlie. I lose track of thirty days hath September, how many kids I have, all sorts of things. Charlie senses Hector stirring behind him and turns. Charlie is getting a little sloppy around the chin. I guess I ain't the flaming youth I used to be, he explains.

They are both smiling at Hector, their faces soft, nearly liquid with tenderness, encouraging. Hector is breathing through his mouth like an exhausted bird. There is only one moment, he feels, when all this can be spoken, right now. The ghosts, he begins. The piano is playing Take Me Out to the Ball Game, chopping at the rhythm. Charlie's ear is cocked towards Hector, the better to understand. Ghosts, Hector repeats heavily. The words are beyond him.

But they are smiling, swaying towards him, just as if everything has been spoken, confessed, pardoned, accounted for. Charlie grips him in the armpit, Loretta round the neck. Sing, they are urging him, and he feels their voices vibrating in his own chest. Now it's root root root for the home. team, if they don't win it's a shame, Charlie wagging a finger, Loretta's bloodless cheeks elongating when she hits the soprano notes. The whole room sways together now. Their love is as massive as their voices, as eager, as overwhelming. Hector is sagging in their generous arms, nearly falling, he is enveloped in harmony, wrapped in song.

War Song

Elizabeth Inness-Brown

Everywhere bands strike up this tune: War is come! War is come! Long live the war!

I told you not to come.

The woman who opens the door wears a bulky robe and a little fist of hair pulled to the top of her head. Her skin has blotched first in hot water then in cold, and she has removed her contact lenses and put them in a small white case.

On the phone, she says. I told you not to come.

She pulls the door open a little wider so that his body can come through full face, no tricks. He's damp from the drizzle. The motorcycle engine hisses as rain falls on it.

Come in. It's raining. I suppose you can't be expected—

He pulls his helmet forward and off. Strands of newly washed hair poke out in various directions from his head, but he draws his hand over it once and makes a sort of order.

All right, she says. But I am not one of those women who don't say what they mean.

She turns and goes from the room. He stands where he is, feeling the rain soak through to his skin, slowly, in the heat. The light coming in is yellow. There are lace curtains, which make a nice design in black against the yellow light. There is a table, four chairs, as if for bridge.

Sit down, she calls.

The murmur of water. There are colorful books, mostly new, on the shelf, their jackets shiny as eyes. There is a Sears catalogue on the coffee table, open to tires.

Do you believe in fate? she asks, coming in again. She holds a brown face towel in her hands and continues to dry herself, her hands, her face, and her neck, as she speaks.

Remember how we all used to worry about cancer? That was the worst thing. What we used to talk about over coffee. That and the shortages. Notice how it doesn't come up anymore.

Outside an empty car speeds by, ripping gauze. It is followed by another, full of men, that turns into the parking lot of the complex camouflaged across the way. Another ripping spray of gravel. A highpitched drumming.

Those Spaniards, she says. Damn it. Keep the lights off.

Something small on the edge of the parking lot is gleaming and teetering back and forth. It gets brighter and brighter.

It's a torch.

An animal, a cat.

A torch. One of them dropped it. Go on.

The gutter over the window has filled with orange pine needles and the water backs up and gushes, backs up and drips, backs up. On the ground everywhere, in the new light, are brown pine needles and pine cones which feel like bombs underfoot. In the back, a tree lies on its side, roots splayed to the open air, an omen, the rusting saw bent across the trunk; when new, the saw cost $15 in gold money. A long time ago.

All right, she says. What is it you think you're after? The milk's on the bottom shelf, juice behind, bread above. That's all of it.

The hot water heater kicks on, the refrigerator, the gas furnace, the central. Humming, buzzing, sighing together. The carpet soft as mice. A narrow voice hits, cracks, plummets.

I don't believe in God anymore, she says. But there might be such a thing as fate.

One poet leaves envelopes lying everywhere, his clues, white footprints blank and rectangular. He wishes for a facility with the new languages, all of them. He wants to understand the new movies, to order the right things in restaurants, in the proper order, soup first and greens last. But it will make them hate him even more, and then one day when he least needs it, a man in the plainest of black raincoats will follow him out of the bright sun and into the park.

People are asking for things they never have before; each has his own request. Mostly, it's the same sort of thing: to make a picture, a movement of perfect dance, a story, a song to be remembered and sung on the front lines, a construction to tower for them where they can't tower and to stand when they lie down, a child to do the weeping, a lasting love. Their

prayers seem unanswered. And then, when the war comes, they all give
their heartbeats to the cause; they are glad to search the cattle cars for their
damaged, to scrabble for an old pit of potato, for a cigarette, for a moment
more of candle. God, how fortunate they are! The war gives them all
they need. It teaches them to sing.

"We must be strong, for the war goes on and on, and the enemy never
runs out of those dive-bombing scorching sky-crazy pilots who love the
blue and dive straight into the black. The gunner in her turret, the spy
with his poison lips. In the streets our constructions crumble, the last
word is found and burned, our young dancers are crippled and our old
painters made blind, we are all made blind; children kiss the pavement for
nourishment, and our loves seize a wild permanence, like a last breath.
This burns us more than interrogation: our loves burning bright and hard
and hot, dying suns."

The first one appears as a small thing gleaming and shifting on the edge
of a road, a universe compressed tight and solid, hesitating to explode—
when it goes, it will scatter stars in the blackout sky and give them away.

She lets the knot out of her hair; it comes free but won't lie flat. A dent
where the rubberband bit. It doesn't matter. The hair is auburn, glinting
coppery red. But he can't see.

How sad. Just once and it's all over. One chance. Does my cigarette
bother you? Did you know that man is below pigs on the list? I don't
know if anything is below man. Pigs. Imagine.

It's late. Rockets going off. Another car, a cat, a torch, and then
streetlights blinking off. Timed, somewhere, wouldn't they be? The one
in front he threw rocks at to get it off so she could sleep. There is a philosophy of sleep. They drag the blanket to the couch, mash the pillows
down, the head finds its rest. This book, its first few words, promotes
drowsiness. It is the best book to be reading at the moment, when the
streetlight across the way blinks off. On. Off. And gauze rips: someone
climbing out through the window catches her blouse on the sill, her earrings jingle. Her shoe slips off into the bushes; a cat has it. Damn. The
jeans are too tight and domestic, high, only good for wiggling it, wiggling
it baby. On the couch the pillows are plumped, sodden. In the window
strips of red gauze dance. This lace has held up well—when d'you get it?
Had it for years, paid a dollar. Where?! And this? 50¢. Good deal—I
know where you can get a side of beef, a hank of lamb, a knot of pork for
less than that. Per pound. Got to get your hands a little bloody these
days. And when we are all at the war, fighting? And when we fall, one by
one, man by man, woman by woman, man by woman, and so on? We
won't remember. It will be a sad day, damn sad. Yes.

Come to the war! Join the war! Come to the war! Join the war! The

children are marching, marching with banners held high, marching with
their small fists black-gloved and wrapped around flag poles, and the words
are spelled out above, as they are sung out below: Come to the war! Join
the war! On their feet sing black boots shining for the day only. The pen-
alty for not returning the boots on time and in prime condition: sixty days
more labor. No one is keeping count. But each child receives the proper
fit; the gloves are borrowed.

My daughter nearly born out of wedlock holy was not. Her parents
were married, and now they are not. Her father had a crewcut. Her mother
was young. The world was nearly peaceful, there were lights everywhere.
Her heart beat a perfect rhythm, 4-4 time, against my ear.
    That is sad.
    Don't you ever worry about the war?
    This is what I have to say about the war: come try and find me. I re-
commend everyone be forty pounds underweight. 4F. And let me go on
record now: the killing of a thing, anything, alive, is more abhorrent to me
than making love to a dog. It is not making love, to fuck a dog. I would
rather die than join the war.
    I believe you. How about you, Judge? Is her case strong enough?
    No.
    What?
    No.
    In the name of God. A woman of such beauty? Look: eyes floating in
steel pools, glints of copper, gold, silver on their surface, the fish of her
eyes flopping over, the liquid, the wonderful tears of her eyes streaming,
pouring, roaring down the lily skin, across the plain small lips, over chin,
into crevice of neck, down collarbone and on! A woman who might well
mother a general, a commander! Whose temple she purifies daily, whose
limbs are as unscarred and smooth as a child's! Perhaps Your Honor misses
the point?
    All right. Put her on night duty.
    Yes, for we know, the war is beginning soon, and our women are being
called. How are they allowed to serve? Front line, night duty, some are
given sick leave, husband's excuse, another has the curse, she lays it on the
war, another starves, water her secret. One runs, can't take anyone with
her. Another stands trial. Did you make it, did you make it, her ancient
mother, seamstress for the natty colonels, begs. The daughter's hands
have gone cold, she has signed some papers, a pool of urine circles her
feet. Yes, yes, she says. Night duty. That's best, says the old mother, her
skin white silk stockings long crumpled in the corner of a drawer. You'll
survive. I don't care, says the daughter. I don't care. Her hands will be
cold, all the weeks, months, centuries into her tomb, a subway tunnel near
Grand Central. Sometimes, she has been told, people do these things be-

cause they want to live a while longer, to see if it won't get better. But the old woman knows her skin is the same as her beautiful daughter's, the same as a babe's, perhaps even the same as that of a baboon who struts his perilous stick up the walls of his cage and down, all for an impervious bitch who sucks her fingers and tries to look uninterested. Nothing makes any difference.

Why don't you get out of here? I don't fall for that twice. The war, the goddamned war, I don't care if it starts tomorrow. I don't care if you die.

Lights. My God, there are lights! And listen—the refrigerator, the water pump, the central. The red one on the radio. The lamps in all the rooms? Even the bedroom!

Who are you. Jesus Christ, sweet mother. You know, I don't think they ought to do this to me anymore. Yes means yes. No means no. Let those damn Spaniards drive their cars, straight in for all I care! The fucking war is over. They've called it off.

You're nuts. It never ends, you know? Can't you get the simplest thing through your head?

Go ahead with your truth. See if I care. It's still *no*.

But here is what happens: A lady. A man. Four dozen notes of music, warbling as if from a flute in jubilee. The lady lifts her hand; a dragonfly lights on it. They are in what was once a garden, and is now ash, all ash. She stands, her back to bricks that retain some sense of order, and, hand up, receives the insect on the outstretched index finger of her right hand, a gesture gentle and touching. And the man: in a black raincoat, plain, without epaulets, without visible buttons; underneath, a suit equally black and plain; and hidden, next to the skin, some gold in odd nuggets, hammered, hangs softly on a chain, warming on his body. He wears shining, gleaming black patent leather shoes. The gun is black, and plastic, the anodized steel barrel dull, short, blunted, the sight glassy. When he holds it, her right eye is the center of a clean black circle. One thing: sometimes the man wishes he were a woman too, as do other men; women seem to like it, the bullet entering, and they just go off into whatever it is that lies beyond, softly; they seem to like it. Sometimes he wishes. But never shows on his face a single wish, of any kind, for meat or shrimp, for rice or noodles, for an easy chair with arms and a small brass lamp over the shoulder. His face is very nearly blank. The woman, wearing nothing black and frankly nothing at all, stands and watches him in her calm, the dragonfly iridescent on her finger, moving his rainbow wings patiently up and down. It anticipates the click of the magazine. It senses what impends. At the right moment it lifts into the air, and carries her away with it, leaving the startled murderer below, wishing, wishing, his startled eyes seeking, knowing suddenly that his gold is no longer warm. On his face, his nose and mouth and eyes come awake, form a last silent wish: that he could undeceive himself of this crime, that he could take back each molten pellet, that he will not be called upon to explain. From behind, shots spit into him, and he is pushed forward without even enough life to put out his hand to soften the fall.

My God, she says. I am already so tired of this idea of war. Hasn't the rain stopped yet?

Lessons: Janie and Ben (June 6, 1964)

Lee Zacharias

It is difficult now, to begin the story of my marriage. Although it has been
fifteen years, I cannot talk about my brother just yet.

I knew a woman. She left her husband. When she told him, he said,
"Okay, but before you take that fat ass out the door make sure I get my
credit cards back." He made a list, and, as she stood in the front hall in a
tattered Mexican sombrero she'd saved from their honeymoon ("Because
how else was I supposed to pack it?" she said), he checked them off: Master Charge, Texaco, Shell Oil, Sears, and Miller and Rhoads. ("That son-of-
a-bitch was always too cheap to join Diners' Club," she said. "Screw him.
I got my own cards now, you know?")

I knew another woman who left her husband. Four days later he shot
her to death. What intrigues me about this is the possibility that both men
felt the same.

Ben bowed his head and wrung his hands in his lap. His bald spot
beamed lamplight; his shoulders shook. If he had looked up, he might have
seen that I was crying too, but he didn't, and so I guess he never knew.
"They guaranteed sickness and health, but I don't remember anything
about everlasting boredom," I said. "This is most unfortunate," he wept.

Of course, he is fifty-five, and I am thirty-three, but I cannot imagine,
even if I live to double my age, that I will be able to say, of whatever hard
knocks the world hits me with then, "This is most unfortunate." I
couldn't say it when my mother died; I couldn't say it when my brother
was killed. Because, though I sometimes suspect that all life is just one of
those unfortunate things, throughout the misfortunes of mine I have been,

intermittently, the man who coolly takes back his credit cards and the man who can take back so little he shoots his ex-wife, or, failing that, himself.

They said Marie said, when the man from Inland Steel asked did mortgage insurance take care of the house, "I don't care about the damn house. Just give me back my husband." They said he said, scuffing first one foot and then the other against the gray rug, "I'm sorry, ma'am. I wish we could do that." They said she said, when he asked was there anything else the company could do, "Get the hell out of my house." I wasn't there; so of course I don't know, but I never heard her swear in my life.

But this story is about Ben, not my brother, whom, after all, I hardly knew.

We lived in Ben's apartment above the square until September that first summer we wed, and I learned to cook (which I'm good at, very good, oh, I'm excellent now), equipped with a teflon-lined frying pan that was warped on the bottom and an aluminum saucepan from the grocery store. His funny little three-burner stove belonged to the apartment; it was just as well—the oven door latched with a padlock that had to be handled with an oven mitt, and its one temperature, 500, was regulated by the degree to which the door was closed. The refrigerator was ours, bought for fifteen dollars from a student couple when Ben's breadbox-shaped General Electric finally broke, and we shot two cans of Raid at the roaches who lived inside the motor when we moved. I remember how they crackled when I swept them up, a cloud of poison like a fist in my lungs, and I sat down and cried until he said, "Well, here's two dollars if it means that much. We can afford to leave a broom behind." Not that it made much difference; the half of a house we had rented on Lincoln Avenue had roaches of its own. Also it had rats, and, when I called the landlady to complain, she said, "Honey, can't your man set a trap?" The rim around my man's mouth went white. "Tell her I'm a professor. I don't set traps for rats." We called an exterminator, and Ben's daughter's dog ate the strychnine and died.

But it doesn't matter, really, about the roaches or the rats, though, if you had asked me any midnight in the bathroom I'd just flushed with light, I don't suppose I would have said it did not. Well, I know, I know, he had warned me, and all through those years I did not forget. I didn't leave him until long after, and, when I did, it was not because of one bit of poor circumstance.

My brother was born in June of 1938. He went to grade school on the south side of Chicago; later he went to Hammond Tech, but he dropped out before he got his diploma to work in the open hearth of a steel mill, which he called the b.o.f., and later the sheetmill where he lost his right index finger on a coil. In his twenty-fifth year he went back to the open hearth as a second helper in number 2. He got married in his eighteenth year, and, when his first wife left him, he married again. He had three children; he owned a house. On his days off he would clean out his mother's

gutters or take down her storm windows or mow her lawn. He paid atten-
tion to his children, was considerate of his wife. He gave her money to
play bingo every Thursday; he taught her to drive. He kept his 1959
Chevrolet Bel-Air in top condition, and, though he never went anywhere in
it, he never complained. In his garage he stacked the insulation he intend-
ed to install in his attic as soon as his next vacation came around. Three
days before his twenty-sixth birthday an overhead crane knocked him off
a catwalk into a vat of molten steel, and a public relations man drove out
from Inland to tell his widow they were sorry—it was most unfortunate.

But I should be more objective, more professional. It is not my intention to blame Ben or make him look bad. A history is of no account if it's
not fair. In 1964, when I met Ben, he was an assistant professor of music,
and I was a freshman on scholarship. Three weeks after I was expelled, we
got married. Three days after we married, my brother died. I went to work
as a typist in the Department of Urban Transportation at the Indiana University Business School. Once I assisted Ben at a recital; we played the
Poulenc *Sonata for Clarinet and Piano.* That was in the fall of 1966. In
1969, when Ben's tenure was turned down, we moved to Richmond, Virginia, where he taught college seven more years and, much against his wishes, I quit typing to audition for the Richmond Symphony. I clerked in a
music store part time; later I toured with the Virginia Symphony and gave
private lessons on the clarinet. Ben taught high school after college, but
that was discouraging. Now he plays accompaniment for a West End Richmond ballet school, and he too gives private lessons. I went to the Eastern
Music Festival in North Carolina to teach and then on to the Aspen Music
Festival as first chair. I've made one recording, have an offer to do two
more. Three months ago I left my job as principal clarinet with the Richmond Symphony; it's possible I will play for the New York Philharmonic as
last chair. ("Oh, Janie," he said when I told him, "how can you even think
about going up there? That city would eat you alive." Which may well be
true, and so I have no idea what I will do.)

My brother was buried as a Catholic; rather, he wasn't buried at all. Be-
cause, when they die like that, there is nothing left, and the corporation
scrapes down the vat to present the family with a billet of the prime steel. So
the casket was closed, with a crucifix on top. "Don't say anything to her," my
mother begged. "They're giving her Librium, poor thing. To lose your hus-
band so young like that." Her voice quivered. "I tell you, it's not easy to
lose your son." She dabbed a balled handkerchief at her eyes. "I don't
know how she got it arranged with the church. They regarded him as a bi-
gamist. You know, Dickie thinks we're going to hell because we don't be-
long."

"Did he say that?" I asked.

She wiped again at her eyes. "No, but you know that's what they teach
them there. Well, Marie's a sweet girl, and I love her, but you just would of

thought she'd ask me how I wanted it done."

I whimpered and put my head in my hands. "Mama, for God's sake, who gives a shit how they bury a hunk of metal?"

Ben was such a wonderful teacher. I don't know why he kept losing his jobs. I don't know why his cars kept breaking down—he had them serviced, he had them washed. When I met him, he drove a Volkswagen, which developed carburetor trouble later that year. Then he had the clutch replaced, and, when the whole transmission went haywire (something to do with a leak in the seal), he traded it in on an Opel, which had to have a valve job the day after the warranty expired. He sold it and bought a Renault, which also had transmission and carburetor troubles, though he kept it until the drive axle broke. Then he got a Datsun, which ran fine until a tow truck failed to yield at the bottom of a ramp to I-95 and mangled the body without putting a scratch on Ben. (I went through the windshield and broke my collarbone.) Now he drives a Toyota. The last I heard it needed a brake job, but, of course, that is to be expected, one of those nuisances considered routine. He had such bad luck, and he didn't deserve it—not with his jobs, with his cars, with his wives, both of whom ditched him, although he was perfectly nice.

Men die in the mills all the time. You can't blame the management. It's hazardous work, no employment for the faint at heart. The floors are slippery with the animal fat used to keep the steel from corroding, and there are great vats of hydrochloric acid used to pickle the steel. Then there are so many cables that might become faulty, all that heavy equipment in operation, and in the tandem mill the rollers are capable of chopping a man right in half. Some men get killed for not being careful; for others it's only bad luck.

It wasn't the best time to begin a marriage. Ben spent most of his days at the Music Building while I looked out at the square through a film of dirt on the window, took hours just to put on my sandals, went out and then remembered I hadn't brushed my teeth, went back in and forgot what I'd gone in for, looked out the window, took naps, and applied for jobs. In the evenings we walked, down Kirkwood Avenue to the campus, past the red tile roofs of the grad and undergrad libraries, the stone tower and gargoyles of Maxwell Hall, down the brick path that went by the Wellhouse, that funny little stone gazebo built from the remains of the first campus gates, into the buzz of tree frogs in Bryan Woods, along the Jordan River, which was in fact only a stream, and back up Kirkwood to gaze into the lighted store windows on the square. Though summer school was in session, the campus seemed empty. All the students seemed to be on the sidewalk in front of Nick's English Hut, where they loitered barefoot and in cut-offs, talking to other students who sat on the hoods of parked cars. The conversation hummed to the steady snare drum beat of business in and out of Nick's latchless screen door. I hated to walk by them. Though they seemed to be in their early twenties, they made me feel old. Still, when my headaches stopped and we tried to go in, I was too young to be served a beer. So we browsed in the Book Nook and admired the house-plants in the window of Ellis Florist while the time and temp flashed on the sign in front of the Monroe County Bank and, when the sunset turned the square rosy, returned to our hot apartment, which was always stale with our sweat and the spray we used to kill bugs. I don't remember if we ever talked on those walks.

We did not go as far as the Music Building. I hadn't been there since Ben played the *Moonlight Sonata* for me and I asked if he wouldn't like to marry me too.

"Why don't you practice anymore?" he would ask, and I would say, "What for?" looking beyond the baggy white boxer shorts that fluttered around his hairless thighs in the breeze from the fan to the line of my reach on the green wall. I had tried to wash it, and there were great light-colored swirls below a greasy headband of gray.

"My poor little girl, come here," he would say, and so I'd crawl into his lap while he sat in an armchair by our one double window and, as he petted my hair and blew kisses across the top, watch the couples straggling past the storefronts toward the brilliant red and white marquees of the Princess Theater and the old Harris-Grand. He was happy. It didn't matter about our apartment or the chicken I served bloody around the bone. He would have drunk his Liebfraumilch just as gladly from a jelly jar as from the Ger-man crystal we'd been given by the Solomons; it didn't matter that, until I found a job, his child-support left us so poor that we didn't light the candles in the silver holders from my old roommate's parents because he wouldn't let me replace them when they burned down. When I was hired by the Business School and celebrated by buying six yards of hopsacking for cur-tains, I had to point them out, and, though he praised my clumsy hem-stitching, I realized he had never noticed that we hadn't had curtains before. Why did I have to care about curtains and crystal? Why couldn't I just care about him? "My dear little Janie-wife," he murmured, and then we made love while the fan blew my juices dry just as fast as they flowed, or, if I was crying too hard, he would listen to Chopin. Sometimes he said, "Why don't you stop torturing yourself? And, by the way, me. It's not as if you and your brother were close."

Which was true, and I can't say that I really missed my brother much. It wasn't as if I would have seen him. What hurt me the most was the way my brother died, with his insulation still stacked in his garage as if it were a great work interrupted by death, that old badly timed luck, a pathetic parody of an unfinished symphony. But, when I tried to tell Ben, he sighed. "I don't think I see the point," he said. "It must be rough, a young woman like that, left with three children to raise." And I would shut up be-cause it made me feel guilty to feel sorrow when I had no such hardships to face, no legitimate claims to be made.

"We're all alone," my mother cried. "Why did God have to take my baby away?"

I cried too. "You don't believe in God," I said. "Why do you always have to say that you do?" I felt dizzy again. (It was because of my concussion. They can't really do anything for that. When your brother dies, you're supposed to know better than to put your hand through a window or to knock your head against a wall. Ben had driven me to the bus station, making me promise that, if I felt dizzy or had headaches, I would see my family doctor. "You don't have to go," he had said. "You're sick. It's not an excuse." "I'm not sick enough," I had said. "My mother called me. I have to go home.") I tried again and took her hand. We were sitting at the kitchen table. "Mama, you're not alone. You have Marie. You have Dickie and the twins." I wanted to add that she had me, but I remembered I'd forgotten to call Ben, and I couldn't. (We hadn't mentioned my marriage since I'd come in the door and she'd said, "Marie's up at the funeral parlor. I think she's in shock, poor thing. She fainted this afternoon, but she won't take a rest. Well, get yourself something to eat, and we'll go on up. There's all kinds of food." "I'm not hungry. Anyway, food makes me throw up. I have a concussion," I added when she gave me an odd, stricken look, as if my brother had died just to raise the moral issue of whether, at funerals, one did or did not waste food. "What happened to your hand?" she asked, and I held out my mitten of gauze. "Oh. It went through a window." She nodded in the same absent way she always had, and it made me so nervous I lifted my other one too, a shaft of light striking my ring through the window like a comic strip gun. "And this one got married." It was such a stupid damn thing to say, but she only nodded again. "Well, get yourself some ham if you want. There's no sweet potatoes or pineapple salad, but the neighbors brought three different pies.")

"You're not alone," I repeated.

She shook her head. "She's a young woman. I can't blame her. She'll want to get married again. And I'll lose my grandchildren." She clutched at my bandaged hand. "I want Dickie back."

I shifted in my chair, feeling very sorry for my mother, who had lost both her husband and her son but had kept her daughter, who wanted to be a comfort but didn't know how. "Mama," I said, "he's dead."

"I want little Dickie." She was kneading my fingers through the gauze. "Janie, we can get him. She's not his natural mother. Don't you remember how we used to take care of him? You and me. He was such a dear little guy, and we raised him like he was our own."

"Sure, of course, I remember," I said, feeling sick because it was as if she were me, asking for the clarinet or the record player I had to tell her I was not able to buy. "We couldn't do that to Marie."

"I want my boy back," she sobbed. "Marie can have the twins."

I put my head on the table and held up a handful of hair. "Mama, you have to stop it."

Now, I'm not saying I didn't like Ben's children. What it was about them, I guess, was this: they were kids, who happened not to be mine. I met them on his regular Monday night the week before we got married. We picked his sons up at home; I waited in the car outside the house while Ben went inside, and then they came out, two dark-haired boys named Edward and Reese, aged twelve and eight, both thin, one already taller than I, the other, in cowboy boots and bermuda shorts, with the humped back Ben had warned me about (he was—we were—liable for their medical bills, but mostly what he'd expressed when he told me was concern) and the palest thin legs, like one of those albino house spiders. Halfway down the side-walk Reese, the younger one, who also had asthma, bolted for the car. "Move," he said to me. "It's my turn to sit up front."

"Oh, okay," I said and got out of the car.

Ben put a hand on his shoulder. "This is Jane. She sits up front from now on."

"I don't mind," I said.

"Well, I do," Edward said, adding, "You're a turd," and I thought he meant me until Reese replied, "Oh yeah? Well, you're a turd-bird." Edward sighed. "You can't ever think up anything by yourself. You always have to call me the same thing I just called you."

"Okay," Ben said, "boys, that's enough. I want you to be nice for Jane. Now we have to get Bridget at camp; so somebody is going to have to sit on somebody else's lap."

"I'll hold Reese," I said, but he said, "Are you kidding?" and scrambled into the back. Ben hadn't told me that he was a claustrophobe, and for what seemed like the rest of my life he screamed whenever anyone even brushed against him in a car. He might have been my favorite since he was the baby, but I swear he got sick on purpose whenever we had plans. I turned my head. "Reese, I have a nephew just a year younger than you. I bet you'd like him."

"I don't like anybody," he said. "And especially I don't like you."

"Oh," I said, and Ben squeezed my knee as he insisted, "Okay, Reese, I said that's all," and we went to get Bridget at cheerleading camp.

She cartwheeled to the car. "How'd I do, huh, Dad?" She was a head taller than I, quite pretty, with dark curly hair and a little pucker of a mouth and an absolutely awful voice, like pink sugar icing squeezed from a tube to make rosettes.

"Just beautiful," Ben said. "Bridget, this is Jane."

"Oh, hi," she said as I got out and she ducked in back, taking Reese, who hollered, on her lap. And that was the last thing she said directly to me until after we had played miniature golf and eaten dinner, and then, as

Ben walked them to the door, she turned around and said, "Bye."

"They're neat," I said when he came back to car. "When are you going to tell them?"

"I already did," he said. "Last night."

"Oh," I said and paused. "Well, I hope they liked me."

"They loved you," he said. "You were great."

"Oh," I said again.

"Mama, you have to get hold of yourself," I pleaded as she sobbed face-down on the kitchen table and I toyed with my uneaten pie. We had just come back from the funeral parlor, where Marie's ghost-white face had looked like a mask clipped to the top of her dress. It was a look that I remembered from my father's funeral nine years before, as if the bodies of the mourners had also departed and what was left was only their clothes. "Now you know Dick wouldn't want us to cry." I was crying myself, and I felt like a fool. Because I hadn't the faintest idea what Dick would want, except that I was quite certain he wouldn't have wanted to die.

She raised her swollen face and sniffled. "I know. You're right."

It was because of Bridget, I found out, that Ben had always assumed I'd end up with him. That first night she had pranced around the miniature golf course while Reese tripped over his club and kicked the plaster pygmy that straddled the hole and Edward scuffed along behind us. At Howard Johnson's she chanted the menu like a fight song, shaking her fingertips like pom-poms and yelling "Ya-a-ay" when the food arrived. She told her father about her new boyfriend in the same sing-song. "She goes through boyfriends," Ben confided, "like Reese goes through shoes." And so, of course, when I had told him I couldn't go to the Kreutzer Sonata because I had a boyfriend, he had bided his time and figured that eventually we would break up. "I didn't take it seriously," he said. "Well, I took it seriously," I huffed. He smiled. "Of course you did. You were only eighteen years old." "I'm *still* eighteen," I said. He kept smiling. "I know, but now you're *my* little girl. Give me a kiss." "Go to hell," I said, and, six weeks into our marriage, we had our first real fight.

It was because of Bridget that, at the end of the summer, we wound up with the dog and so finally moved. We were at Ben's parents' house in Pennsylvania, and, although she had a Cairn terrier in Bloomington, she wanted to take one of their Labrador's puppies home. "Ask your mother," Ben said; so she called, then said, "Mom wants to talk to you," and passed him the phone.

"I know," he said as I curled into the window seat of his parents' bedroom, watching the faint blush of the evening sky turn milky. ("We don't get sunsets," his mother had said that afternoon as we sipped May wine on the patio, letting her hand fly toward the mountain horizon. She had sunk a strawberry in the wine, and the landscape glistened in her glass like seaweed around a brilliant red fish in a bowl. "Not up *here*." She said it as though she wished they lived anywhere else, and I felt guilty because I thought I had never seen anything quite so beautiful as their nineteenth-century farmhouse, its twelve wooded acres, duck pond, and very own swimming pool.) "I *didn't* encourage her. Carla. I *know* you're the one who feeds George. My parents are *not* trying to foist those dogs off on you. I am *not* irresponsible. I never said that. Okay. Carla, I said okay. Well, I'm sorry. Carla—goddamnit." He put the phone down. "She hung up on me."

"Well, honey," I said and rubbed his back, still listening to the pure flute of stream that fed the duck pond, embarrassed to have overheard. But he hadn't asked me to leave, and I had not thought to myself.

"I could make love to you right now," he said and turned to twiddle my top button.

My hand slipped under his and flattened. "Don't you think you ought to report to Bridget? Poor kid, she's going to be so disappointed."

"That's not my fault." He stood to tuck in his shirt tail, and I suppressed a relieved sigh. I couldn't understand it. He did all kinds of nice, licky things Kelly had never thought of. We had been married for three months, and I was trilling to his tongue like strings to bow. It was wonderful, but he made me nervous. I had expected marriage, to him at least, to be a staid old institution. It was quite a shock, all that twitching, all those spasms. It was quite a shock to move into his quarters, where he had, stacked beneath the bed, a year of magazines detailing methods and positions, and in his drawer, not yet removed from their cardboards, were at least a year of juices for my preplanned, mechanized orgasms. "You're going to like this," he had said and cocked the button on a big, black rubber phallus which trembled in his hand like the garden hose Eddie Ziegler had whipped around the legs of cocktail tables in the Lambda Chi house. "No?" He strapped a wedge of stainless steel and plastic to his hand, and his fingers jittered. He kissed my knees. "Honey—little Janie—open." I sat up, and he held his hand out, palm shivering beneath a soiled elastic band. "It's just me." I hugged my knees. "What's the matter?" He snapped the apparatus off. "Sweetheart, we're married. Nothing is weird." "I just thought it would be more personal," I said. So he gave me the personal touch, which was lovely, it was tender and every bit as efficient as his machines. Still, I moaned and thought about rearranging the furniture, I whimpered and thought about making curtains, I came and thought, well, all right, he should have played the clarinet, he was so good at flutter-tonguing. I felt awful. I'd spent my freshman year on my back under Kelly until I got expelled only to find out later I was frigid. I hated sex. I dreaded Ben's touch, and he thought I loved it, and I felt so guilty that I whimpered and moaned and flailed all the more, sucking and stroking our way to his delayed *crise de quarantaine,* which he had the year his tenure was turned down. He was afraid, he finally confessed, that his member would age so that it couldn't keep up our twice-daily union, and I felt like a hypocrite as I reached for his cock and thought, "Jesus, I hope so." And still later, when I had my first (and only) fling (with the second trombone of the Richmond Symphony—it's not necessarily true, by the way, what they say about the brass being better kissers), I knew he would have forgiven me if he found out because I was still young and his drive had dwindled to every other day. If I loved him, then I hated myself.

I gave him a meaningful smile and promised, "Later," and, with his arm around me, we bumped down the back stairs to the library, where his father was watching t.v. with the children.

(It never stopped seeming odd to me that Ben's mother considered me an adult and Bridget one of the children, although, of course, she had reason. She was a very gracious woman, who never once remarked about my age, never once asked about my parents. I suppose Ben had warned her not to. I felt as if they'd found me, full-grown, beneath a cabbage leaf, and any past I had had served no purpose. The proof of Ben's past, his children, slammed doors and shook the stairs, calling, "Grandpa, have you seen my tennis racquet? Grandma, where's my fins?" Mine was a guilty secret, and, as Ben's history was illuminated with information over years, mine grew darker, and, like the shadows on the wall at night, it grew larger too. But I was too old to be afraid of shadows. I took slow walks with Ben and my in-laws while the children tore through the woods; I weeded the flower beds while the children swam; I helped load the dishwasher while the children played Old Maid and watched television. I didn't mind the dishes, only the distinction. Christmas after Christmas I held my finger on the knots while Ben's mother tied bows around Bridget's loud bellbottoms, zippy little mini-skirts, and patchwork vests. Once, when we went shopping, she held up an embroidered Mexican blouse. "Do you suppose something like this would be 'far-out' enough for Bridget?" "I think it's neat," I replied, hoping that just once she would give something far-out to me instead of another beige dacron crepe blouse or white cardigan sweater. She put it down. Most all of my wardrobe came from them or Ben, who always bought me ruffles, and throughout my marriage I felt schizophrenic, on one day a five-year-old princess, on the next a forty-two-year-old matron.)

"Well, what did she say, Dad, huh?" Bridget was knitting a scarf to give her boyfriend next Christmas—she didn't know who that would be, but the thing about scarves is they fit anyone—and she punched Edward to move so that she could retrieve a needle from beneath the cushion of the red leather sofa. I had never been in a house with a library before, certainly not one with leather furniture, Oriental rugs, and bookcases built into the cherry paneling that rose to the ceiling and crossed it as beams. (Ben had such fond memories of the books in that room, from Beatrix Potter to the "trumpets sterne" in *The Fairie Queene,* that he still allowed his mother to call him Benjamin Bunny.) "Can I keep Turnkey?"

Edward scowled. "What do you call him Turnkey for? I don't want to
have a dog named Turnkey."

"Because that's his name," she said and jabbed him with her knitting
needle.

"They're killer dogs," Edward said. "Last year Blackie got all of Grandma's ducks."

"They are not," Bridget said.

"I don't want a killer dog," Reese announced. "I want a parakeet."

I glanced at Ben, sorry that he had to break the news. I felt, at that moment, very tender and protective, irked with Bridget for making Ben humil-
iate himself before her mother and then, as she would, I knew, crying and
carrying on until he felt that he'd failed. He looked unperturbed.
"Well. . . ." He smiled. "Okay."

"Huh?" I said.

"Ya-a-ay." Bridget shimmied her fingertips, and her boyfriend's wine-
colored scarf dropped half a dozen stitches as it slid from the sofa to the
floor.

Ben was still smiling as she hugged him. "I talked her into it. But he has
to live with Jane and me."

Edward kicked her in the shins. "How come she always gets what she
wants?"

I didn't think I could have said it better myself.

*"My daddy died," Dickie told me, wide-eyed with fact. "He went to
heaven to live with Jesus."*

*My mother turned away. "Doesn't that just break your heart? The
poor little guy."*

"And all the saints—they live in heaven too."

*I patted his shoulder. It did break my heart, because I could see that he
made no real connection between Dick and me. The twins were his sisters.
Dick and I had been too old for that sort of relationship. Dick was his
daddy. There was no room in his imagination for me.*

*"You see what I mean?" my mother whispered. "Marie taught him that.
He thinks I'll go to hell."*

*Dickie tugged at my dress. "When I die, I'm going to go live in heaven
with my daddy."*

Bridget was the most interesting of Ben's children. Edward was morose;
Reese's temperament was predictable. He spent so much time in the hospital I could hardly blame him for being spoiled. Ben borrowed the money
for the back operations from his father. Once, in a tight month, I suggested
he borrow his child support too. "It's not my father's responsibility," he
said, and I felt awful and didn't say, "But they have all that money," because I could see that he felt awful too. His back as sleek as a reupholstered
chair, he has just finished his first year of law school. Edward went to grad

school in zoology and now works as a limnologist at a research station in Minnesota. It doesn't surprise me that he hasn't married, although Ben can't understand it at all. He's proud of his sons, two feathers in the cap perched above the twin apples in his eye, Bridget and her young daughter. I've slipped to become the thorn in his side.

In college Bridget traded in her cheerleading sweater for a blue work-shirt and faded jeans. (I was still wearing A-line dresses and stockings to work, where all day I typed and Ko-rec-typed urban transportation re-ports. I hated the dresses as much as I hated the job.) She went to the University of Wisconsin to study elementary education; by the end of the first year she had changed her major to art. "Art?" I said to Ben when she wrote. "Does she paint?" Not that he knew of; so she clarified: she was learning photography, she needed five hundred dollars for a Nikon, she wanted to spend the summer in Arizona with her boyfriend, an anthropol-ogy senior who had a job with a dig, and didn't we think the war was a waste? "Are you sure it was your Bridget who wrote that letter?" I said. The next year, outside the Democratic convention on Michigan Avenue, she got hit on the head with a billy club by the Chicago police. In her jun-ior year she dropped out of school and split for San Francisco to live in the Haight.

We were sitting at the dinner table in Pennsylvania when Ben gave his parents the news. His father put his hand to his heart. He looked as if he were saying the Pledge of Allegiance or having a coronary or both. The watery shadow of his mother's raised glass of Beaujolais trembled on her cheek like an enormous ruby-hued tear.

"Can't you talk to her?" his father asked.

"No," Ben said sadly, "I can't."

His mother dropped her face to her hands as she began repeating, "Oh God, oh God," and I tasted the *carbonnade de boeuf.* "Yum," I said.

"One of those hippies will give her LSD, and she'll jump off the Golden Gate Bridge. Does she know what happened to Art Linkletter's daughter?"

"I don't know," Ben said, and I said, "U-um, that marinade makes this beef just great."

"It'll rearrange her chromosomes and we'll have deformed great-grand-children. She'll wind up on heroin."

"Oh God, oh God," Ben's mother bleated.

"I know," Ben said, and I said, "Honey, try some of this stew."

"What about Jane then?" Ben's father said, and I started, thinking he meant that Ben had better start worrying about me lest I too split for San Francisco, which, in fact, didn't sound like a bad idea.

"What about her?" Ben said.

"Well, she's younger and she's sensible and, if Bridget won't listen to you, maybe she'll listen to her."

"That's a good idea," Ben's mother agreed, and, as they all looked at me, I swallowed a whole chunk of meat.

Ben's mother dialed, and they seated me on a stool at the kitchen counter while they each took a chair at the table beyond.

"Hi, Jane, how are you? How's Virginia?" she said. We had moved to Richmond only last month.

"Oh, great. Hot. We found this terrific apartment in a brownstone right near the campus in this funny old neighborhood called the Fan. We live right across the street from the Little Sisters of the Poor, and we've got a fireplace in every room except none of them work, and we've got a stained glass window in our bedroom, and...." Ben and his parents frowned. "Anyway, we want you to see it." They smiled.

"Yeah, it sounds far out. Well, listen, like Robert and I were on our way out when Grandmother called, but it was good talking to you." Robert was her boyfriend, and we had first met him via her letters when he was just Bob. All spring I had thought she would admit to me that she was living with him, but I supposed she was afraid that I would tell her father, who was no longer Dad but Benjamin.

"Well—" I panned my eyes around the solemn circle of faces—"how's San Francisco?"

"Oh wow." The line crackled. " 'Scuse me. I was just unwrapping a candy bar. San Francisco's far out."

"Great. Well, uh, look. Your grandparents were kind of wondering when you might be coming home."

"Tell her we'll send plane fare." They nodded. "Ask her if she's eating right."

"I mean it is like out of sight. We went to a rally yesterday in Golden Gate Park. At least two thousand beautiful people united against the capitalist war machine."

"Oh. It sounds, uh, far out." I wondered if I was supposed to tell her not to jump off. "Well, look—your dad misses you."

"Tell her not to take any drugs." The nods grew more vigorous. "Ask her if her apartment is safe."

"Oh, and, hey, we went down to Big Sur last week—you wouldn't have believed it."

"It's pretty, huh?"

"Tell her we love her," my mother-in-law mouthed, and I held up my hand.

"Pretty's not the word for it—it's out of sight. And you wouldn't believe—I've heard the Dead, I've heard Joplin—I mean like *Janis Joplin* right in the same room with me—and later on tonight after we get a pizza we're going down to the Fillmore to hear Creedence Clearwater Revival."

"What's she saying?" my mother-in-law asked.

I covered the mouthpiece. "I don't know. Something about hearing the dead and going to a revival."

"Oh my God." She put her face in her hands.

"Well, look," I said, "on the subject of dinner—your grandmother wants to know if you're eating right, and your grandfather says to say he'll send plane fare, and they—I mean we—all send our love."

"Yeah," she said. "Weird."

"They're right here," I pleaded, begging her to imagine the ring of constituents and me, their elected official, just doing my job. "They want you to come home."

"Yeah, I know—it's a bummer. Well, tell them that I love them too—and, oh, I forgot, tell Benjamin thanks for the bread. But this is like my trip, you know? And anyway I'm busy right now. I've got a job."

"Oh yeah? Where do you work?"

"She's working," my father-in-law sighed, and the news buzzed around the table back to me.

"I mean I'm taking pictures, and I think I shot some really groovy stuff at this march, and there's this *alternative* paper that said they'd print some if they're good."

"Oh."

"And I mean like I know Benjamin's really uptight about me quitting school, but it was nowhere, and, if you want to be a photographer—which is like *the* coming art, you know? I mean it's got *commitment*, it's *involved*—what you have to do is go where it's at."

"Yeah," I said.

"So, explain it to them, would you? And take care. It was good talking to you."

"Sure," I said. "Well, peace."

She giggled. "Oh, Jane, you're so funny."

"Well? Is she coming? Where's she working? Did she say she was eating right?"

I shrugged.

Once more Ben's mother dropped her head to her hands. "She's joined one of those kooky religions. You heard what Jane said."

"You should have told her she's ruining her life," Ben's father said.

Ben put his arm around me, a pucker of worry between his eyes. "Anyway," he said, "Jane tried."

Three years later Bridget was back in school. She got a license to teach kindergarten "because, I mean, when they're small it can be a really creative thing," and she taught for a year, then married a banker, gave birth to a daughter "because, I mean, what's more creative than having a kid?" and, when I came home braless last summer and announced I was leaving Ben, she called me long-distance to say, "I don't understand it. Why would you want to do something like that to my dad?"

"I wish I could drive," my mother said as we sat one last time at the kitchen table, which was littered with paper plates neither one of us had

*the heart to clean up. The funeral had been that afternoon. She started to
cry again. "If your brother were here, he could have helped you bring back
your things."*

*"Mama." I touched her hand again. "You want me to stay here for a
while?" It was the second night I'd forgotten to phone Ben, but I was sure
he would understand if I called to explain that I couldn't come back for a
week or so.*

"You know, you can ship boxes by bus."

"I don't need that much," I said.

*She nodded, and for a while she just sat there. "Well, can you manage?"
she asked.*

*I frowned, thinking for a minute that she meant our lives. I had man-
aged mine, I guessed, but I had no idea what to do with hers. "Why don't
you ever go out?" I asked abruptly. "There must be lots of widowers or"–
I looked away–"divorced men your age."*

*"You'll have to remember to use mothballs when you pack your wool
skirts. Well, you didn't have that much when you went down there, but I
suppose you've collected a lot."*

*I sat up straight in my chair and gave her an apprehensive look. Her
face seemed so tired. The round fluorescent light overhead had developed
a faint flicker, and it gave her the appearance of a small nervous tic.
"Mama, I'll be glad to stay for a week or two if you want, but you know I
have to go back."*

*"What for?" Her tone was suspicious, then bitter. "It's not like you're
going back to school." I looked away again. So we would, after all, have
to discuss that. "We respected that when we needed you during the year
–don't call Jane, I said, whatever you do, don't call Jane. Oh, I've had
enough grief–I don't want to talk about this."*

"When did you need me?" I said.

*"When I was in the hospital. I had a hysterectomy. You didn't even
send a card."*

*I rested my forehead on the heel of my hand. "Mama, I didn't know."
I was angry, and I was sorry. I didn't see why I had to be so confused.
"No one told me."*

*"I asked them not to." She sighed and wiped at her face. "I'm sorry.
Of course you wouldn't send a card."*

*"I'm sorry too," I said, wondering if there would ever be a time when
we could stop the endless recitation of the same poor words. "Was it painful? Why didn't you tell me?"*

*"Painful enough." She shrugged. "I had a tumor. It was benign." She
looked up. "Oh, Janie. I couldn't expect that you'd know, but I wanted
you to send a card. Do you understand?"*

*"Yes." In my whole life I never felt closer to my mother, and I wanted
to go around the table to hug her, but instead I just grabbed her hand. "I*

really do." The skin was so unexpectedly loose around that fan of little bones that I was frightened. "Mama, do you have anything to drink?"

But I would have told her I loved her if she hadn't said, "There's milk in the refrigerator. Or you can make coffee."

"No, I mean like whiskey."

She took back her hand. "Are you an alcoholic?"

"Don't be silly," I said, and the moment was lost.

"I suppose that's why you had to leave school."

"No, as a matter of fact, it wasn't."

"Do you know how ashamed I am?"

"I'm sorry," I said.

"I always thought you'd come home and teach at Wilson."

"I told you I wouldn't. I told you I didn't want to direct any grade school band."

"How could you do this to me now of all times?"

"I'm sorry."

"Your brother...." She choked and looked up, her face puffy. "It would have made a difference if...not even to have his body."

"It wouldn't have made a difference." Why did she have to make me angry now of all times? "He's dead."

She shook her head. "Well, just get your things, and I suppose we'll figure out what to do next."

I didn't know her face. I had never seen it before, not even when my father died. Her features were swollen, and her eyes were the color of a new bruise. "Mama, I can't come live with you. Don't you remember? I'm married." She didn't answer. "I married Ben Gabriel, remember? He came to dinner at Marie's." I took a breath. "I have to go back to my husband, but I can stay a little while if you want."

"When I was in the hospital, you never even sent me a card. How could you get married at a time like this?"

"I didn't know it was a time like this. I got married last Saturday."

"You didn't tell me you got married."

"I did. I mean I know I didn't tell you before, but I told you on the phone and I told you again yesterday."

"Don't lie to me, Jane. You've caused enough heartache." I bit my lip and began tearing at the gauze threads that straggled above my bracelet of tape. "Are you pregnant?"

"No. I just got married, that's all. I married my teacher. You met him this spring."

She stacked one paper plate on top of another and then pushed them aside. "Janie, that man must have been twenty years older than you."

"Twenty-two," I admitted, "but...."

"Yes, and look where it got me," she said, though neither of us had mentioned my dad. "How are you going to feel when he dies and leaves you

with children to raise?"

"We're not going to have children."

"And didn't he say that he had children of his own? My God, they must be nearly as old as you."

"Not quite. The youngest one is eight."

"And you want to be a mother to them? Janie, when a woman gets married she wants a family of her own. She doesn't want to be a nursemaid to another woman's children."

"Marie was."

"But Dickie was a baby, and, even so, the circumstances weren't the best. Well, she's done a wonderful job. I certainly give her credit for that." She sighed.

"Anyway, they live with their mother."

"What kind of man would leave his children?"

"He didn't leave them. He sees them twice a week, and he pays their bills."

"So you'll have an interfering ex-wife poking her nose in your marriage too."

"I don't even know her. I met his kids." I looked away. "They're all right." I scraped a paper plate back and forth across the table. "I thought you liked him when he came to Marie's."

"You told me he was your teacher."

"Well, he was."

"What kind of man would sit there and let your family think—what kind of man would take advantage of a girl not half his age and lie like that to her mother? What kind of a man would sneak around and do God-knows-what to her daughter till she's thrown out of school and then?... "

I had begun twisting my wedding ring. It was slightly too big, and it pinged against the table. I inserted my little finger and spun it, watching the gold play with the bluish flicker of light.

"You can't answer, can you?"

I hung my head. "It's not his fault. He wanted me to tell you."

"He wanted you to tell me? He didn't have the guts to do it himself?" I didn't answer. "Why were you kicked out of school? I want to know."

I didn't raise my head. "It wasn't because of him. He's my husband. I can't let you say all those things."

"Oh? And where is he? A man who loved his wife, who cared about her"— her voice caught—"at a time like this. And you come flouncing into your own brother's funeral just to give us the glad news. Well, I wish I could say I was happy for you."

"That's not why I came, and you know it. Anyway, I married him before Dick died." I put my head on the table, and my hair spilled into a smear of mayonnaise on a paper plate. "It was because of this other boy." I began weeping, harder, I think, than I had wept in the last three days. "I loved him. I loved him so much, and I love him now."

My mother regarded me with her chin at a sharp, cold angle below the puffed red blotch of her face. "So you married a man you didn't love," she said flatly. "I suppose you're pregnant with this—this other man's child."

I sat up. "I'm not pregnant, I told you. He—this other boy wanted to get married, and he wanted me to quit school, and I knew—he was Catholic, like Marie, and he was from a great big family, and he wanted to have lots of kids. I mean he didn't say that, but I knew, and I knew I'd never do anything in my life but raise babies."

"What's wrong with that?"

I couldn't answer. What else had she done? What else had my brother done, except get himself killed in the mill and leave a big, fat insurance check for his wife?

"So you got married anyway, and to a man you don't even love."

"That's not true."

"You don't love him. You've never loved anyone."

"I do too. He's very nice." I dropped my eyes. "Anyway, I will in a while."

"What do you want?"

"I loved my brother," I said.

"What is so goddamned important to you that what's good enough for everyone else just isn't good enough for you?"

For a minute I smarted because I had never heard her damn anything before. And then, when I thought of my father and of my brother, as if a cloud of babble had lifted and the truth that was left was so clear I had always known it, I smiled. "I want to be immortal," I said.

Her mouth twisted. "Your brother was so proud of you because you were smart. He always sold himself short. It was my sister this, my sister that. My sister makes good grades. My sister plays a musical instrument. My sister is going to college. I was so ashamed I didn't even show him that letter. And I'm glad he's dead so he doesn't have to see his sister now."

I was still crying, and I'd begun hiccuping. It was the same thing my brother had said about himself when he had to get married after our father died. The dizziness was gone, and for a moment the world was as sharply defined as if it had been designed, black lines printed on white paper like a map. "Mama, I didn't kill him. Don't take it out on me."

I remember my father taking his belt to me once or twice; I remember my mother turning me over her knee. I didn't remember her ever slapping my face, not so hard that the chair I was sitting in toppled and my head hit the wall. The dizziness came rushing back. If it hadn't, perhaps I might have remembered she didn't mean that either, that grief makes people say things and do things, that, while I had lost my only brother, she had lost her only son. My stomach turned over, but I gasped and sat up. "Mama, I'm married, that's how it is. But I can stay for a while if you want."

"I don't want you here." She glanced at the clock and began picking up paper plates. "It's late. I'm going to bed. Not that I'll sleep."

"Please." My elbow had jammed against the floor, and it sent a sharp pain up my arm as I tried to get up. "Please, Mama, I don't know what to do, it was a mistake. I didn't mean to hurt you, I'm sorry, I didn't...." I was crawling, tangling my knees in the hem of my dress.

She threw the last of the paper plates in the garbage and paused at the door. "You've never meant anything but to hurt me."

"That's not so, it's not." I was hiccuping again, and I took a breath. "I love you."

"You've never loved anyone in your life," she said. "I'm going to bed. Turn the light out when you're through."

I cried for a while; then I called Ben. I took a taxi and spent the night in the bus station on State Street. At 6:55 the next morning I left Hammond for the last time. I never saw my mother again.

I left Ben fourteen years later, the day after Marie called to tell me my mother had died.

Land of Goshen

Elizabeth Cox

As a mother, Sara was incapable of feeling anything but pride. In her face
was the expression of one whose wishes for her children would be stronger
than their own wishes, and the misery suffered by them would be in this
woman already suffered. Her hair was a light chestnut color, blond when
the sun hit it, and her pale skin held a silkiness like powder. She had plait-
ed her hair in long braids and rolled them in a crown on top of her head, as
she did on special occasions. The image of her was the way children liked
to remember their mothers, or grandmothers, keeping the face and hair the
same in their minds even after old age had greyed both hair and skin. But
Sara had not had children to remember her in this way. She had one child,
Jesse, and she waited for him now.

She lifted two small shells from the sill, then leaned to pull the covers
of the bed into place. She put the pillows on the folded-back edge and covered them with a clean white-ribbed bedspread, knifing her hand with one
quick thrust in a way that made the fringe hang at the floor as if it had
been trimmed there. She sat, not noticing her expert work, but thinking of
the tornado a few years ago, and how no one mentioned it anymore, except as a reference in time (back before the tornado, they'd say). She
thought of how that day had started out bright and clear, with no hint of
what was to come.

She glanced around the room to see if it looked right. The sheets had
been dried in the sunshine, and she loved the way the room smelled. She
had placed some of Jesse's favorite toys on top of the chest of drawers. He
would be home soon, for the weekend, and Sara would be ready. I've been

ready for a month, she thought. She stood up and wondered how long she would live, sometimes thinking her life would go on forever. She was thirty-three. All her family had lived past eighty. It seemed long enough. The sun came in full across her face, and she looked into it, her heart as open as a blouse.

On the day of the tornado there had been a picnic. The Mt. Calvary Baptist Church had grounds big enough for a town picnic and they offered their space each year, just as long as nobody actually went inside the church. Sara had looked forward to the picnic that year. She climbed the hill to the church, a long, sloping hill she had climbed many times as a child, knowing all its ridges and gullies and the changes that were almost imperceptible. At first she walked slowly and deliberately, but as she climbed she gained speed, until the grain of land ran smooth beneath her and she seemed pulled by strings that would carry her to the top. Jesse was ten, but he had never seen his mother running, and called to her. But she did not hear him. When she reached the top of the hill, she motioned to Jesse and his friends and they ran too, letting the ground move beneath them. And the strings that had pulled Sara, pulled them and they reached the top laughing and shoving each other.

It was the last Saturday in May and the picnic included everyone from the town. The morning was pale and white and people wandered the grounds as if it were a place they had never seen before. They scattered to swim in the pond, and the streams that ran deeper in the woods. The younger children searched for treasures to take home, a rock or a piece of bark, to put on the window sill and during the winter to say this was from the Mt. Calvary Picnic last year, or two years ago. There was no warning of what would happen until the picnic was almost over and Jesse returned with a goat he had brought from a field. People were packing up their blankets and tablecloths. Some were eating pieces of cold chicken or cake that had been left out.

Voices from the lake carried over the water. They were children's voices mostly, laughter and squeals and dramatic calls for help. As the sky developed a greenish cast, the sense of play quickly folded. There was a stillness that made the old people afraid. Sara could see a dark cloud reach straight down to the earth, pointing a finger to where it began and moving toward the Mt. Calvary Baptist Church with a low, bold hum. Songs of birds turned frantic, declaring a territory they sensed was in danger.

Some children broke a window in the basement of the church, pleased at being able to perform a mischief with the permission of their parents, but not finding it as much fun as they had thought. They crawled through and unlocked the back door for the others. The crowd of picnic people surged toward the church like a body of water washing over the land, and Jesse pulled his goat with a steady urging.

"You can't take that goat in there," Bob-Tom said. Robert Thomas was Jesse's best friend and was called Bob-Tom by everyone. They went fishing together and hunting in the fall. Even before Jesse's fever (the fever that would keep him a child), his friend came to play with him. And as they grew older and the other children stopped coming to Jesse's house, Bob-Tom treated him much the same, making allowances for him with a patience that made Sara marvel.

"Yes I can." Jesse pulled away from his friend, pointing toward the church as if the church would speak, then dropped his arm and felt his point was made.

Jesse had wandered off earlier in the day, drawn by the low sound of a bell. He found some goats in a pasture, and when the goats nibbled at his shirt and the pockets of his pants, he took it as a sign of affection. Mary Lil found him chasing the goats. She was exactly Jesse's age and two inches taller. Mary Lil had always paid attention to Jesse, although her attentions were never very kind.

"Coax them, Jesse," she told him. "If you want them to come to you, you'll have to stop chasing them around like that." But Jesse did not trust Mary Lil, so he kept chasing the goats, and the bleating sounds they made, and the sound of the bells bouncing against their necks.

He called to the goats over and over, calling them "kids," even though they were obviously full grown. It was something he remembered from before the fever, Sara had said, because he never went any place that had goats since that train trip through Georgia. He was three, and saw goats being herded onto one of the cars hooked to another train. When they stopped, the animals walked underneath the windows. The smell was so strong that people would not get off the train to get their box lunches, which were in paper sacks but were called box lunches, and which people had already paid for. So the conductor got off himself and brought the lunches onto the train. He had to squeeze past Jesse, who stood on the bottom step of the platform, reaching to touch one of the goats. Jesse answered their bleating with a noise of his own. When he went back to his seat, his mother opened his sack and spread his lunch neatly on his lap. She told him the baby goats were called kids.

"Jesse." His friend called to him again, but Jesse pulled the goat by its collar and bell, continuing to walk with a stubbornness that could outdo any reasoning Bob-Tom might try. "It stinks, Jesse. Don't you smell it?"

"Leave him alone." Mary Lil suddenly defended Jesse. It would be something she could talk about later on: Jesse bringing a goat into the church during a storm. Years from now she could say, "Remember that time Jesse brought a goat into the Mt. Calvary Baptist Church?" and everyone could laugh.

Someone urged them to hurry. It was Jesse's father, Franklin. He gestured with his arms. They ran at dead speed, with Jesse pulling the goat

and Bob-Tom pulling Jesse. Sara had been walking toward the trees, calling, when she saw them coming across the field. She thought they looked
like a scene on her grandfather's Greek coin.

Almost everyone was in the church now and the wind began to lash
against the trees, making them jerk and twist. The goat would not go down
the basement steps, and it was plain that Jesse would not go in without the
animal; so Franklin lifted the back legs and Bob-Tom lifted the front and
they swooped the goat, bleating as hard as he could, into the air, and Jesse
laughing and loving the noise he heard the animal make.

The hum moved closer now, moved into the heads of the people and into the songs of the birds. Both noises seemed to come from invisible
sources, and entered the people, giving them something akin to a sense of
rest, making them want to close their eyes.

The door slammed and the wind hit the church like a hatchet, crashing
and lifting the pews and altar, rattling the stained glass before it broke,
hurling huge pieces of furniture through the walls, picking up the piano
and dropping it through the floor. The steeple of the church broke off like
an icicle in the hand of a child. Mary Lil was badly hurt that day, so that
she never laughed at the idea of a goat in the church basement. Bob-Tom
was killed instantly when a small hunk of metal from a window pane hit
exactly at his left temple and lodged in his brain.

The farmer who had owned the goats was killed. His wife had found
her husband and son in a pile of rubbish that had been their home. The
house was dropped two miles down the road. Sara's house lost half its roof
and all the windows were broken. The tree beside her house, which provided shade for the front porch, had been uprooted. And the crops in one
of Franklin's fields had been destroyed, as if the hook of a primitive plow
had dug one huge furrow.

Sara's leg was broken when a table fell on her, and Franklin had a few
cuts; but Jesse and his goat were unharmed. The tornado had somehow
linked them together so that when the wind died down, Jesse said he
would take the goat home and there was no objection; whereas if there
had not been a tornado and Jesse had suggested that he keep the goat, his
mother would have said no. For that, at least, Jesse was grateful.

Graveside services were held the next day. Jesse went and stood beside
Bob-Tom's casket to watch it lowered. Sara told him that Bob-Tom was
to be buried, but Jesse did not believe his friend was in that box, and he
was not sad. In fact, he searched the crowd for his friend's face and voice.
The people around him kept a cold, hard look of resignation until after the
final prayer when they jerked toward each other and began to scratch their
arms, as if they had just awakened.

It was a few weeks later, when Jesse missed Bob-Tom's visits, that he
locked himself in his room. Sara brought his meals to him, to let him
grieve. After the third day he walked out before breakfast and took the

goat with him. They went to the Mt. Calvary Church which was still strewn over the field and pond, and he watched the people who had been working there every day, his neighbors, rebuilding, gathering what they could. And there was even some laughter and joking among the men as they worked.

Jesse stayed all day to watch.

That was three years ago. Some trees still lay on their sides where they fell. The white maple behind Tinner's Grocery was almost completely soft and rotten, because it fell in the marshy land that led to the lake; but Mason, Tennessee, was filled with white maples and poplars and old sweet gums. The tornado had not taken them all.

Sara leaned with her elbows on the sink and watched the uprooted tree, its torn fact lifted from the ground in a way that made her want to weep. The farmers who had cleared their land for crops, but left one tree or two, to shade the house, felt a personal loss when the tornado took their only screen from the road, exposing the house and yard to passers-by (strangers who could wince or point or look without comment).

At the side of Sara's house, outside the kitchen, branches lay broken and splitting away from the trunk, beginning to have small holes where rain and insects had dug their way in. The roots lay frayed and fierce, turned toward the kitchen window, no longer bent searching for the ground, but dried and curled inward. Sara remembered the wind barely touching its branches when she was a girl and the tree was young. She remembered her father propping it up with stakes and rope to make it grow straight.

When the wind finally had its way, she did not want to have it carted off for firewood. So she let it lie, trying for three years to think of how to prop it up again, to put stakes around it and the rope; and knowing all the time the roots would not catch hold. She came to accept it in the same way she accepted Jesse. The doctors explained how the damage to nerve endings in the brain could not be repaired, and she imagined the tiny fibers curled in and looking as burned and dry as those roots in the yard.

She heard a car drive up and saw Jesse's face framed by the window. Jesse had lived at the Children's Home for six months before returning to spend the weekend with his parents. He had never been away from them, and when Sara saw him coming in the door this morning she thought he looked old, older she thought than herself, older than anyone she knew. Jesse paused inside the doorway before he entered, his mouth beginning to form slow words.

"Nobody came to meet me at the station," he said, his voice almost chiding. But the woman who brought him home corrected him.

"You didn't ride the train, Jesse. I brought you home. I said you could ride the train next time." She turned and pointed to the blue car in the driveway. The woman's name was Miss Harris, and she had orange hair.

Sara held out her arms to Jesse as he crossed the room. She wanted to tell him that she would meet him at the station. His body bent slightly forward and made him look as if he were always leaning. She put her head against his hair and felt his heart beat through her apron.

"He has grown up in the last few months, hasn't he?" Miss Harris did not know what to say at homecomings. She would leave Jesse at home for the weekend, then pick him up Sunday night. She would not linger, but felt the need to say something. "These pants you sent are already too short." She pointed to Jesse's ankles and Sara watched the boy smile at his accomplishment of growth.

"He looks wonderful. Just wonderful," Sara said, and she meant it.

Jesse's hair was brushed away from his face in a way that gave him a fierce look. His eyes darted about like a bird's. He was aware of every noise and movement around him. Sara was not bothered by his nervousness but watched him as if not to miss anything he might do. She saved the memories of this visit, so that she might bring them out on summer days when no one was home and the afternoons were long. She stored his gestures like a squirrel with his nuts for the winter, and feasted on them over the stove, or sitting at the table, or lying in bed.

Franklin came home early for lunch. When Sara heard him, she straightened her dress at the waistline and pointed to Jesse to stand up. He entered manhood this year, at thirteen. There were enough hairs on his upper lip to tease about, and he could wear his father's shoes. Franklin almost shook his hand, but didn't, and hugged him instead. Jesse pointed to his ankles and the length of his pants. He was proud of his growth, although his mind had not developed beyond that of a four-year-old. Franklin assured him of his height.

Jesse sat back down at the table where he was playing with a dump truck filled with logs. He hauled them to different corners, unloading then loading them again. His movements were slow and calculated and appeared to be due to a meticulous personality.

Sara turned the chicken she was frying in an unconscious manner, knowing when it was done by the amount of sizzling she heard. They could hear Franklin outside, washing his hands and face in the spigot.

"Clear that stuff off now, Jesse, and set the table." Sara handed him utensils, three plates and napkins. Jesse stood for a moment gathering his thoughts, then moved to his own place at the table and slid the knife down as if he were putting it into a slot. Sara spent three months teaching Jesse this simple task, and there were times when he did not get it right. Today though he would put each piece in its correct place, and there would be praise from his father.

"All through?" Sara leaned to lift the hot biscuits from the oven. Franklin sat down while Jesse set the places and Sara brought lunch to them in big bowls. She had meant the question for Jesse, but Franklin answered.

"Not yet," he said. "We have some stumps to pull out." He piled Jesse's plate with food and spooned Sara's gravy over most of it. It was what Jesse liked. He looked at the trucks his son had parked beside the table, and suggested to Sara that Jesse go to the field with him in the afternoon. And for the first time this suggestion was met with silence. "He'll be fine," Franklin said. "He needs to work." As he talked, he patted his wife's hand. It was decided.

Jesse was four when he became ill. At first they thought it was the flu, but his fever ran high one night and when they took him to the hospital the doctors told them he had encephalitis, as if they should know what that meant. But they didn't. Not until a week later when an intern explained to them what their life would be like from now on, how Jesse would be regarded as a child, but expected to behave as an adult. And how eventually he should be placed in an institution. Sara asked the doctor questions, but Franklin left the room.

When Sara called him at home later, he told her he was taking a trip. "Where are you going?" Sara asked. Franklin told her that Jesse was his son, and she said she knew that. Then he told her to forgive him, and that he would be back. He suggested that his sister come to stay with her, but Sara refused. She stayed at the hospital until Jesse was able to return home. Franklin left that morning and was gone for three weeks.

It was the end of April and barely light when Sara got home. She took Jesse to the porch and settled him on her lap in the big cushioned rocker. His legs hung over her arm and the arm of the rocker, and his cheek nestled to bosom with a tiredness she had never seen in him, but which she guessed would always be there now. She rocked him and sang songs he had liked before, not knowing if he remembered anything about that time, but singing them anyway until his eyes closed and his mouth lay open. The smell of sickness was still on his breath.

Sara watched the sun go down and darkness creep across the field. She would not think about Franklin or where he might be, instead she chose to fill her mind with the field and the cars going by in some great hurry to be somewhere. She wondered about the families in those cars, wondered if they were leaving or going home, wondered if they had someone like Jesse.

Louise had held Sara on this porch, had played games with her and rocked her in the same chair. Louise was an old black woman Sara had known as a child. She had a lap as soft as pillows from which Sara could see a wide, smooth forehead and eyes that grew bright with thoughts, and a mouth that spoke the truth. "Let's play the marble game," Louise would say, and she would make up rules as she went along. Even then, Sara knew that Louise loved the feel of the cool marbles in her hand more than she loved the games. She placed a marble against her cheek and said, "They're pure glass. All the way through. So you don't have to worry about breaking it. It just chips off; it don't break." She would stare into the marble as if she doubted her own words. "There's nothing you can do to break it." But Sara had broken one one time. Split it down the middle, a clean break that had not shattered either piece. She kept one piece on top of her bureau, and gave the other one to Louise.

When night came Sara could no longer see the families in their cars, but just hear the swishing noise of the tires (it had begun to rain), and not knowing if it were a man or woman at the wheel. She pretended she held her baby, that it was four years ago and Jesse was new, high tight face screwed up like a bud that was now calm and open; his hands that grasped and pulled, but now lay flat and ready to receive whatever was given. He would never experience a burden, but handed that burden in full to his mother, so that now Sara carried more than her share. There was Franklin, she thought, but he wasn't there.

When she woke it was morning and the sun streamed across the porch and hit her in the face like a bucket of water. Jesse still slept. Sara stretched her legs in front of her to get the stiffness out, and thought of how to order her life.

When Franklin returned, he found Sara and the boy in the kitchen. Sara saw him turn in the driveway in the red pick-up she had not seen in three weeks. She did not turn around when he walked in and kissed the back of her head.

"Are you hungry?" she asked.

"No."

"I hired those new field hands you talked to." Her voice was business-like before she turned to look at him. "They're out there now clearing the old Fennel place." Sara saw that the lines around his mouth had deepened and wondered if her own mouth looked as old.

"Fine." He leaned to kiss her cheek. "I'm sorry," he said. His sandy hair and bony face made him appear ethereal, and when Sara turned to him she knew that was all he could say.

"He's a good boy." She led her husband over to where Jesse sat. The boy pushed blocks around the floor, not building anything. He turned to his father without recognizing him, then turned again to his blocks.

Franklin put on his work clothes and his hat and went to the field. It was spring and he would begin planting.

After one of Sara's lunches everyone felt as if he had swallowed an anvil. Jesse took some scraps outside to the goat, who was not kept penned up, but left to roam free in the back yard. The goat's name was Kid, and Jesse had wanted to take him to the Children's Home but pets were not allowed. So his mother kept Kid company while he was gone, and when the goat died four years later, she would replace it. Through the years she replaced goats as they were needed, keeping the same name for each one. Jesse knew when there was a new goat and checked it carefully to find a distinguishing mark so that he would not be fooled when a new one appeared. Each goat connected him to a time before the fever. As he grew older he knew he was different, but that knowledge was sometimes relieved in the familiar sound the goat made. Sara saw him turn to the animal with a quizzical expression, and she wondered if he saw his other life. It lasted only a second: that look of near recognition, but it was enough to make him cling to the animal more than to anyone else.

He enjoyed each goat without mourning too much the loss of the others. Sometimes he would ask his father where they were, and Franklin would say they died of old age, for a goat.

Sara knew Franklin had stopped hoping for miracles. Tonight he would take Jesse frog gigging at sunset, Jesse jabbing at the frogs, then letting them go. It was a time they liked together: the frog gigging, and those times just before dark when they stood beside the lake and watched the sun go down. But tonight there would be a summer rain. The huge drops crackling against the ground and against their shoulders as they ran. Franklin would put his arm around Jesse and tell him not to be afraid. But Jesse never was.

The rain had stopped when Sara saw them coming towards the house. They were soaking wet and she could hear their laughter. As they came closer she saw how rain clung to their faces like drops of oil. They shed their clothes and Sara brought towels to them. It would be late before they stopped talking and playing games Jesse liked to play. Sara could hear the thunder still grumbling in the distance, and the water dripping from the leaves gave an ending effect to the day that eased their minds.

Sara awoke early the next morning. Sometimes she would hear a child's voice call to her, a voice that rang as clear as any child's. She would be up from the bed and halfway across the room before she realized it was not Jesse. This morning Jesse had gone off with his goat. He would work in the field again today with his father, even though it was Sunday. She went to the kitchen window where she saw life coming and going and watched the days begin and end and knew the weather of the day. She leaned against the sink and let the breeze that always blew right there, come against her face and lift the hairs off the back of her neck.

Sara was eighteen when she met Franklin. He was four years older than she and had spent two years in the army at Fort Knox, Kentucky. She had graduated from high school one month before, and worked at Bell's Five and Ten Cent Store. Franklin had come in for some notebook paper (to write to his girl in Kentucky, he said later); but when he saw Sara he wandered the aisles of the store for thirty minutes so it would be lunchtime and he could ask her to go for a hamburger. She did.

They stopped at a drive-in place and Franklin got the hamburgers, making sure she got just what she wanted on hers; then took her to the country for a picnic. As Sara rode past the trees and the houses she had known all her life; she noticed them differently: as if she were in a town she had never seen before and this man had been her husband for eighteen years, rather than the town being her home, and this man a stranger.

He asked her questions, questions she had never thought about, and it occurred to her that this man, Franklin P. Holden, knew her better than anyone.

"You married?" Franklin's head jerked with the question.

"No," she answered. "Nobody ever asked."

Franklin squinted his eyes at her, as if he thought men were asking her to marry every day, as if back at her house lines of men were already gathering at the neck of her driveway to ask this woman's hand in marriage. He looked as if he had never seen a face so soft and thought if he touched her hair it would run through his fingers like the slickest water.

He turned onto a dirt road.

"This is old man McKennon's place," Sara said. "Do you know this place?"

"No. I just turned."

"He's dead now. But there used to be an old bathtub out here." Sara was pointing to the trees as if the bathtub could be in one of them. "Over there, I think." She motioned to a scraggly clump of pines. "It's one of those huge tubs with claw feet and a rim that folds back and under. I got in it once. It was deep inside." They got out and walked in the direction of the pines.

"I saw my grandmother sitting in a tub like that once," he said. "She was a big woman, but she looked small in that tub. It looked as if it had swallowed her."

Sara laughed and showed him the conspicuous white porcelain fixture beside the trees. "There it is. Guess they have to leave it here. Guess it's too heavy to move."

Franklin wiped out the leaves and dirt. "Get in," he said, turning to hold her arm as Sara removed her shoes and stepped barefoot into the deep tub. "Sit down," he coaxed. Franklin climbed over and sat down with her. His arms draped over the fat rim. Sara tucked her skirt underneath her legs.

"I'm going to be buried in one of these things," he said. Sara was staring into the woods. When Franklin took hold of her hands, he began to tremble and the trembling went through them both.

"I have a girl in Kentucky," he said. Sara stared at this man whom she felt she knew, but didn't. "I was going to write to her today. I came to the store to get paper to write to her. And I saw you." There was a finality to this last statement, as if he had made a decision he did not know he had made yet. Sara released her hands from his and stretched her arms to touch both his shoulders. Her touch was so light he had to look to make sure her hands were there. He rubbed her thighs through her skirt and Sara closed her eyes. That's when he kissed her. That's when his hand touched the place she knew she would let him touch as soon as she saw him. He was surprised at the wetness of her pants.

"I'm wet," she said. It was an apology she did not need to make. He stood her up and began to remove her clothes, pulling her skirt down easy. He removed his own pants which was all he had on since he had taken off his shoes and socks before he stepped into the tub, and since he never wore underwear.

"Who is the girl?" Sara asked, as she watched him put her underclothes in a pile beside the tub.

"What girl?" Franklin asked honestly. Sara's body was lean and tan and had a fullness around the calves and hips that Franklin liked. He reached to touch where her hip curved out from her waist.

"Your girl in Kentucky," she said. Sara watched him lean back into the tub.

"A girl I used to know." He pulled her towards him.

Sara smiled and lay beside him in the space he provided. He rolled up his pants and placed them under her head for a pillow.

"I've never gone into anything quite this fast," he said. "I mean not with anyone like you." Sara almost said, "Me neither," but realized he already knew that, and he had begun to probe with his finger in a way that made her hips grind hard against the cold porcelain tub and when he entered her, at first, she thought she would scream, but instead put her mouth on his shoulder, and he took her into a place she had never been. And for years when he entered her, right at the beginning, she felt she would scream; and Franklin said it was because she liked sex, but she said it was because she liked Franklin.

It was late afternoon and Sara sat at the table, facing the corral where a mare and a stallion circled the fence. Franklin had taken Jesse to the field and Sara waited for Pearl to come for pie and coffee. Pearl had been her friend for fifteen years. The pot gurgled its last sounds when Pearl came in without knocking.

"Jesse working in the field?" Pearl asked. She had looked around to the corner where Jesse usually played.

Sara stood up. "Yes. Franklin says we shouldn't treat him like a child." She brought the carton of ice cream to the table. "He's almost grown now, you know."

"*I* know." Pearl said. "I didn't know *you* knew." Pearl had children of her own.

Sara smiled at Pearl's directness. "I guess so."

Pearl looked at her long. "There's a final blow that comes with it," she said, finally.

Sara turned her head away from her friend's gaze. "It's been coming for a long time." As she spoke she leaned forward to give each word a certain weight, the way she did when she wanted a listener to understand fully the gravity of a situation that was too painful to share, one that involved some kind of failing that went back many years. Maybe it involved even her own family as a child, going back to some incident with her own parents that was painful and that was carried into adulthood, even affecting relationships to others for years. Until in old age she would understand that the burden need not have been carried that long, need not have affected her life to such a degree. So it would be tossed off at age seventy or eighty, but not completely.

Sara shook her head and scooped a ball of ice cream on each piece of pie. Pearl brought coffee to the table in large mugs. Both women turned to watch the horses and chewed slowly.

The mare nudged the stallion's nose, moving towards him and away from him alternately. She then backed herself up to him as he climbed onto her haunches. The women did not speak. It was a ritual they had watched before. The stallion moved himself into position until he was no longer awkward; then pushed with a grace that made the women envy the mare. The mare stood still except for her head that rose and fell with small, high cries, and her feet lightly pawing the ground. The hooves of the stallion tightly held her sides and kept him above her as she backed up closer. When finally it was over, the great penis of the stallion sheathed itself, and the women dropped their heads.

"She sure got hers today," Pearl said.

Sara laughed. "She'll foal within the year." She picked at her pie with a fork. "She's a good mare. She's the third generation since we came to this farm. Before we got married, I brought Franklin out here to see this place and decide if he wanted to live in this house where I was born. He said, 'Why, honey, this is the land of Goshen. We can do anything with this land.' And we have, we've done good." She turned toward the horses. "He brought that mare's grandmama out the next day. It was a fine beginning. Fine." The mare was circling the fence again, with the stallion following. In a moment she would hear the mare's small scream of pain or joy. She didn't know which.

When the tractor turned into the driveway, Sara heard Jesse laughing with the men. Franklin told him to go in and clean up because Miss Harris would come by later. Pearl told Sara goodby and went out to speak to Jesse.

Jesse came in holding a ten dollar bill to show his mother.

"Looks like you've earned yourself a full day's pay," she said. Jesse's eyes shone and she knew he was happy. "After your shower, come to the porch. I've fixed a chocolate cake for you."

"Okay."

Sara could hear the shower running for a long time before he finally emerged fresh in the clothes she had laid out and stood before his mother.

Jesse asked if he could sit on her lap, and as she looked at the size of his body she almost said no. But noticing his eyes, how they asked to be held in a childish way, she brushed her lap and patted a place for him. It was almost dark and the orange-haired woman would be there soon. Sara wondered if Jesse were ever held by anyone anymore. She guessed not, but now, tonight, he would be held by her. She remembered the night she returned from the hospital and thought again of the families in their cars.

There would be sixteen years left in Jesse's life, before he died of pneumonia. Sara would be almost fifty. She would walk into the hospital room and hear the gasps Jesse made, and see the nurses holding the oxygen mask a little way from his mouth, like they could not decide whether to hook it back onto his face. She would touch his hands already heavy with death.

"Is he dead?" she would ask, the nurses shaking their heads as the strangles in Jesse's throat pulled at his body, and Sara would know that this last effort was just that.

She would telephone Franklin.

"Franklin?" His silence already knew. "Jesse died. Just now."

"Just now? Were you with him?"

"Yes." Sara tried to think of what he wanted to know. "There wasn't any pain," she said, without any way of knowing if that were true.

"That's good." He said this twice and sounded as if he felt a relief from his own fear of death.

"He went easy," Sara added. "It was easy." Franklin's voice grew stiff and he said he would be right there and would she wait.

She said she would.

Sara hung up the phone and went to the window to see the dogwood blooming. Both nurses had left the room. Her eyes were as dry as sand. Jesse lay behind her, three feet away, underneath the white hospital bedspread.

In a moment the head nurse came in. She did not speak to Sara but walked around the bed and pulled the cover away from the face. Sara saw for the first time the weight of death upon the softest flesh. Jesse's mouth lay open as if he were making some hideous noise which no one could hear, but would be forever heard by Sara. And she thought again of the goat.

Sara held Jesse in her lap, and looked across the field where a hawk circled high, but as she watched it, it came lower. "Hawks circle and circle before they land," Louise had told her. "Why?" Sara had asked. "To be sure. He's got to be sure of what he wants." Louise had smiled at the child's confusion. "Come here." She took Sara's small hand in hers. They walked toward the pasture not far from the house. Three hawks were circling low and diving toward some bushes. Louise pushed away the limbs until Sara saw a clearing and a dog, or what was left of a dog. The hawks had picked his bones almost clean and the clear bright sun beat down and scorched the skin that was left so that it peeled away from the bones, burnt and dry. The dog looked fierce, as if at any moment he might arise and attack them both. Sara jumped backwards and the old woman clasped her hand tighter to make her stay, as if she had something to teach her that might help later on. "It's all right, honey, that dog can't do you no harm." They did not walk any closer but stayed in the protection of the bushes. "Now them hawks. They's the ones you got to fear." They watched the birds with enormous wing spans diving and leaving with bits of dried flesh in their mouths. "They's the ones," she said again, and the tone of her voice made Sara turn. The old woman watched the hawks while Sara had not been able to take her eyes off the dog. "Whose dog is that?" Sara asked. She still had hold of Louise's hand and the old woman moved her thumb in slow circles inside the girl's palm, like if her thumb had been a wing and her body had been smaller, she could have circled with the same kind of ease the hawk had. "They moves like a song," she said. She had not heard Sara's question. "They moves like a song was lifting them and letting them fall, like they had nothing to do with it themselves; but just somebody singing somewhere could keep them in the air and when that person was through somebody else would sing and that song would keep them up just as good, and it don't matter which song, just as long as somebody is singing." Then she sang something Sara had never heard before, and when she was through turned to Sara, and Sara sang the Doxology.

Sara sang the Doxology now, sitting on the porch with Jesse's legs hanging down the side of the rocker, and watching the hawk almost too high to see.

Seven Prophecies of Egypt

Castle Freeman, Jr.

The last oxen in the Town of Ambrose, Vermont, came at the town's hire in the summer of 1940 to haul Nelson's forfeited cabins from Ambrose village to wherever any of their new owners wanted them to sit. They were Murray's team. When Murray brought them to the village he drove them through the woods over Old Egypt. Old Egypt was the name of a road. It had been out of use for a hundred years at the time, and the woods had taken it over almost completely. It was along Old Egypt, fifty or sixty years before, that Nelson's uncle, W. D. Moore, had met with a talking bear one day, in the only wonder, or remarkable providence, to vary the long calm that was the history of Ambrose in the last century. I can see Murray's beasts coming over that useless road, their heads down though they are pulling light, their forequarters swinging easily from side to side; Murray walking on their right, holding a branch which he rests on the near ox's hump.

Old Egypt was hard to find in 1940. People who didn't live near it no longer knew there was a road up there, the ox teamster, Murray, excepted. In Nelson's uncle's time the road was better known but not better used, and it wasn't much less obscure then than it was fifty years later, or than it is today.

Old Egypt was older than the oldest house in the town. It had been cleared out at the time of the first settlements. It went from Ambrose center village up the side and around the top of a minor elevation called Burnt Hill and down the other side to Egypt, a smaller settlement now long since vanished. When Old Egypt was built there were two roads to Egypt village:

Old Egypt itself, which went over Burnt Hill, and another road which took a longer course through bottomlands around the base of the hill. Originally, Old Egypt was the main road, and the road that went below the hill was little used. It has happened that the lower road, over much of its course, has become a considerable highway, while Old Egypt was given up to brush and to the bears one of whose mouths was opened to Wesley Moore.

For a century or a little less Old Egypt was an important thoroughfare. It was on the Brattleboro stage. An historical account of the town mentions goods and ordnance moving over it bound for Lake Champlain in the War of 1812. But better roads were built, going to better places. By the forties or fifties, it must have been, Old Egypt was just a farmer's road, and when the farmers packed up it began to settle back into the forest from which their great-grandfathers had brought it forth.

Murray's drive might be the last time Old Egypt was put to any authentic use. I use it, but not for anything that needs doing. Hunters use it. But it is thirty-five years since Old Egypt has known the weight and pull of a real job of work; since Murray and his oxen hauled Nelson's little cabins out of Ambrose center, for about ten cents on the tax dollar.

                              *   *   *

The cabins came from a tourist camp Nelson started outside Ambrose village. He might have made a success of the place, but the selectmen threatened to close him down because he wasn't insured. Nelson went before the selectmen and stripped them up one side and down the other, but, in the end, he capitulated. He never got the insurance the selectmen required, he never tried to run his place in defiance of the selectmen. He chucked the whole operation, and the selectment sold off the cabins for unpaid taxes. This was in 1938, '39, and '40.

"Selectmen in these little towns," Nelson would say, "take an oath of office to be against anything that's better than what they have always been used to. They just cannot stand for anyone of their own people to do anything in their town except leave, or milk cows all his life, or kill himself working in the woods, like them and everyone else they know. Let anybody try something a little new, that they don't know everything about, and, unless he goes broke pretty quickly, they begin to worry. And if he not only doesn't go broke, but looks like he might be getting by, they fall all over themselves to find a way to bring him down so they can plow whatever he started to do under and plant grass on it and start forgetting it ever happened."

The Board of Selectmen believed Nelson was someone who thought the law didn't mean him, thought his hopes and plans were special, were so much more original than the hopes and plans of others that they had to be exempt from the limits which others' hopes and plans must observe. Ed

MacBean said, "We knew we weren't going to get anywhere with Nelson. All he could think of was how smart he was to get people to pay cash to stay on property that, as long as Nelson or anyone else could remember, wasn't of any use except to grow poor hay. He had them paying him money to stay there. It wasn't much money, but it was easy money: Nelson couldn't see past how easy it was. And that is why we knew we would never get anywhere with him. He didn't want to make money, or get rich, or chisel the tourists. If he had he would have straightened out. But all he wanted was a lazy, easy time, and so, when we read the ordinance to him he just went away. When fellows like Nelson finally figure out that some people don't work as hard as others for their living, they get excited; but when they realize later that, still, almost everybody has to do a few things he doesn't like, they get mad. They feel they have been cheated."

Nelson wanted a better life, only not too much better; a different life, anyway, but not too much different. He wanted to be a proprietor, a taker-in of money, like a merchant. He was one of those country men—children of small farmers, country artisans and woodsmen—whose adult ambition it was to spend his life tending a store. There are not so many with that ambition any more, but there used to be thousands whose experience of the farm or the shop around which they grew up was such that, grown, they wanted nothing better than to move down into a little town and get their living sitting behind a counter. To Nelson it seemed that the tourist trade, in 1938 undreamed of by all but him, would give an easy way into that life. For him no premises to keep up, no inventory to keep track of. His stock in trade would be a few cheap acres beside the highway and his customers tired motorists who, at that time, had no place within thirty miles to go to except his.

His first spring, Nelson bought five acres on the main road at the end of the village. It had been a hayfield, but Nelson ran a drive from the road up the center of the five acres, and then disposed sawhorses, boards, old railroad ties, 55-gallon drums and other junk about the land to mark off ten plots. In each plot he put a circle of fieldstones for a fireplace. Then he put up a signboard down on the road.

WAYSIDE CAMPGROUND
Nightly & Weekly Rates
Cooking Facilities

He charged fifty cents a night and three dollars for a week.

Was Nelson a prophet of Ambrose's destiny, of the whole state's destiny? Did he, even before Ambrose had come out of its hundred years' agrarian enchantment, envision a time when sixty-five cents of every dollar taken in in these parts would come from those very tourists whose fathers he tried to lure to Piss-in-the-Woods Cabins? In however botched and futile a way, was Nelson Ambrose's first modern man? I don't think so, really. If Nelson had a picture of the future it was of him sitting on a camp stool in front of his tent passing the time of day with his tourists, and laughing up his sleeve at his friends and neighbors who still pulled in the old traces—nothing changed from year to year but the date. That is as far as Nelson's vision went, I am sure. Piss-in-the-Woods Cabins was an idea, but it needn't now be a prophecy.

At the end of Nelson's first summer on the campground he closed up and took down his sign, for the season, he said, though he admitted he hadn't made any money. In fact, he was behind. Not so many motorists had stopped, in the end. Not all of the ones who stopped paid up on leaving, so Nelson had begun collecting rent in advance, which cost him some business. The work and expenses involved in running the place, which Nelson had figured for nil, turned out to be, not large, but not nil, either. He found he had to supply firewood, for one thing, and water; otherwise campers would wander into the woods around Nelson's five acres cutting the smaller trees and filling their kettles at the brooks. Those woods weren't part of the property, and Nelson's neighbors immediately complained.

Nelson couldn't understand the complaints at first, he said, but then he began to see the handwriting on the wall. "You ask yourself a minute," he said. "You ask yourself a minute who these people are that, the first time one of my campers' kids puts his foot on their land, start to bawl and raise hell. Well, one of them is Mrs. Hunter. She doesn't like all these people— get that All these people?—taking water out of her brook. Hell, she is eighty-five. She had probably forgotten there was a brook in there until somebody reminded her. The other is Paul Roberts. He doesn't like them in the brook, and he doesn't like them cutting firewood in his woods. He doesn't use firewood. He uses coal. He says the noise bothers him, dogs barking and the rest. But he is half a mile away, and he's got four or five dogs of his own that the whole town can hear any time somebody walks in the road past Roberts' house. But let somebody from my camp go in there and pick up a dead branch, or laugh out loud, and: Oh, God, Oh, Lord, my firewood, my ears, Oh, God! You ask yourself and you see: it isn't the brook and the wood and the noise that they don't like or that is bothering them. It's the idea that somebody is trying something new, and that he is bringing in outsiders. Some of them might decide they like it here. They might decide to stay. They might even spend some money. Wouldn't that be awful? I don't wonder at Old Lady Hunter, but I thought Roberts had more on the ball."

It looked like Nelson was going to have to get in his own water and wood for the campground. When he did, though, and then tried to charge a little money for water and wood, he found some of his campers would pick up and leave. He had supposed anyone who could afford a car and the time to pack his wife and kids all over the countryside would open up easily for anything he really needed. He found he was wrong.

The campground looked like a dead letter, but Nelson had the enterprise to get in a little deeper. The second spring, as soon as the snow was out of Nelson's five acres, he was out there with a helper and a stack of lumber. By May he had put up ten cabins, one in each of his old campsites. The cabins were dark, damp, and, above all, they were small. They were ten by twelve with one window, and they were made up of rough two-by-fours with clapboards tacked over them outside, and, inside, walls of some kind of cheap composition sheet. Each cabin just sat on four little piles of bricks at the corners, and, since the biggest piece in any of them was a two-by-four, they were all more or less rickety: you could take hold of a corner of any of them and move the whole structure. Each cabin had a small oil heater, two cots, a table, a chair, a washstand, a pot. Sanitary arrangements were five or six little shacks backed into the trees on the edge of the property. Piss-in-the-Woods Cabins, they called Nelson's place.

Nelson painted the ten cabins green. He hung up a new sign on the road.

GREEN MOUNTAIN CABINS
Double Accommodations Available
Furnished
Cooking Facilities
Nightly & Weekly Rates

He quadrupled his prices, moved into one of the cabins, and waited for trade.

It was soon clear Nelson had a better thing in the cabins than he had ever had in the campground. For a few days around the Fourth of July all ten cabins were occupied (the campground had never filled up), and Nelson had to make a No Vacancy sign to hang under his Cabins sign. He himself set up in a big Army tent in a corner of the property. He walked about among the cabins, saw that everything was all right, dropped a load of wood, told his guests where they might see a deer, broke up dog fights, accepted a bottle of beer, took in his money.

I can see those tourists who stopped at Nelson's. Hot, sweaty, crabby families from Fall River and Bridgeport, New York or New Jersey—wherever they came from. They rolled into Nelson's old hayfield at the end of a ten- or twelve-hour drive: bored kids, tired wives and sticky seats. These are the pioneers of the Manifest Destiny of American Leisure. And Nelson is there waiting for them. Drive it right over there to Number Four. In the corner. Bumping over the meadow. Engine off. The kids are out, they run into Number Four. Nelson walks up as they unload. Something runs out from under the cabin. Looks like a kitty cat, Nelson says. (Skunk, it was.) Sure, we see deer up here all the time. They come out right behind your cabin. Just at dusk: you'll see them if you're quiet. Saw a good buck right here last deer season, didn't have my gun, though. You don't say.

Two dollars. Say, friend, is there a drugstore in this town?

Ed MacBean looked Nelson up one day. "What exactly are you up to up there, Nelson?" MacBean asked him.

"Up where?"

"Those cabins. What are you doing up there?"

"Doing business, Ed," Nelson said. "Doing pretty well."

"Well, all right, Nelson," MacBean said, "but is that just a temporary thing up there, or do you intend to set up permanently? Because if it's permanent—well, even if it isn't—there are some things we need to get straightened out. The selectmen are a little worried. For instance, what have you got for insurance up there? What if you had a fire?"

"I don't worry about it, Ed," Nelson said. "I don't need insurance."

"You do, Nelson," MacBean said. "You haven't thought it out. All you can think of is how smart you were to throw up those piddling little shacks for next to nothing and call them tourist cabins. If one of them burned down, you say, why, it won't cost you but about five dollars to build another. But what if one of them burned down with someone inside it, for instance? One of your guests. They could sue you, any of them that were left. And if you couldn't compensate, and if they had a good lawyer, they possibly could sue the town. It's happened other places, Nelson. You need liability insurance. I think you'd better look into it."

"What if I decide I don't need liability?" Nelson asked.

"We might have to close you down. We don't want to do that. But if this business you have got up there is a business just like any other business in town, then it has got to act like a business just like any other business in town, and you have to get some things straightened out, including your liability arrangements."

"How could you close me down?" Nelson asked MacBean.

"We think we can close you just for not having the liability insurance," MacBean said. "But anyway we can close you for being a hazard to public health."

"Oh, hell," Nelson said.

"Well, Nelson, Roberts says the brook up there is running a little rank," MacBean said. "Down to Roberts' it's got a head on it like a glass of warm beer, Roberts says."

"Oh, hell, Ed," Nelson said.

"Look into that liability, Nelson," MacBean said.

Nelson called on an insurance company. He described his property, his business, his needs. The agent quoted Nelson a certain figure. At the next meeting of the board of selectmen Nelson stood up.

"Now you can sit here and talk about your duty to the taxpayers and what might happen if something else happened if some other thing happened. But there isn't anyplace where it says the town has a responsibility to taxpayers to make it impossible to conduct an honest business in the town. There isn't any such responsibility. And all I've got to say is if the selectmen or anybody else can say somebody can't conduct an honest business then that's a goddamned hell of a situation. And that's all we have got here. And that's all I have got to say. You have to decide whether you want to force me out of my own business for some insurance you know I don't need, but I don't have to wait on you."

Nelson missed his taxes on the cabins property that summer. MacBean and the selectmen waited. At the time a good quarter of the tax accounts in Ambrose were delinquent. The third spring, Nelson never opened up the cabins. He had a night watchman job in another town. MacBean looked him up again. How would it be if the town took on the property, sold off whatever it could, and cancelled Nelson's taxes?

"Take it away, Ed," Nelson said.

MacBean went to see Murray, the teamster.

"What will you take to bring your team over some time next month and haul those little cabins?" he asked Murray.

"Haul them where?"

"To wherever anyone who bought one wanted you to," MacBean said.

"I could be hauling them until winter that way," Murray said. "I can only work two days for you."

"You will be done in two days."

"Fifteen dollars," Murray said.

* * *

I live in W. D. Moore's house. The house is mostly sound, though the sills on the north side need attention: from beneath the bottom trim outside you can scoop handfuls of rotten sill. The sills have been rotting away for 175 years, so they can rot on for another year or two until I can afford to have them replaced. There is that kind of fool's comfort in a very old house.

Old Egypt passes my dooryard and goes on up the hill into the woods. That road is one of my interests. I have followed it from where it is found above Ambrose village, along beside the villagers' back fields and so up into the woods. Some roads they built in the old days. Old Egypt scarcely doubles back to accommodate the slope; it goes around big ledges, but otherwise it is carried right up the side of the hill, just off the summit. To find the path of the old road in the woods you try to discern a cleared track, and you look for the stone walls that border the old roadway. They cleared the rights of way to be four rods wide, that is sixty-six feet. In some stretches the walls are still standing nearly waist high, elsewhere they have fallen down and disappeared. Where the walls are fallen you can sometimes find them by looking for very large maple trees or oaks. These generally started growing out of the walls at a time when the land the walls enclosed was kept cleared as cropland or pasture. If you can fix on a tree that is much bigger than the trees around it, you can usually find the tumbled stones of the old wall about its base, and so pick up the wall, and the road, once again.

I had easily found Old Egypt from Ambrose village to my house, which is about halfway between the village and the top of the hill. I did my re-connoitering on fair Sunday afternoons as I felt like a walk. In time, I had made out the road pretty well on past my house and clear to the top of its rise. But down the other side of the hill toward Egypt village, where I knew it must go, the road had largely eluded me. I would pick up a segment here and there, but for the longest time I hadn't any sense of the whole road, how it lay. For a while I thought there must be several old roadways down the other side, and I was reminded of the Vermont story of the lost traveler who asks a country man,

Does this road go to East Topsfield?
and is told,

No, but it will get you there.

At any rate, I had lost Old Egypt until one day it was made plain to me by my happening on it out of road-hunting season.

One of Nelson's Piss-in-the-Woods Cabins is my tool shed. Of the ten cabins that Nelson put up in 1939 at least half a dozen are still around the village, including my tool shed and another cabin which Murray and his animals dragged up here over Old Egypt and in which Mariani, my neighbor, now keeps chickens. For cheap and hasty construction Nelson's work has held up pretty well. It would make a piece of archeology to trace in to-day's sheds, camps, coops, privies and shacks components originating in Nelson's premature attempt to cash in on the tourist trade. You would have to do some looking around to find them all: Nelson, MacBean, Murray and anyone else who could direct you are long gone now.

I have never seen a bear in Ambrose. Certainly there were plenty about not so many years ago, but I suppose they are all gone or someone would have seen one, or shot one: for although bears are as wild as any animal they are a wild animal that gets seen, like deer and unlike some others. They have an affinity for men—perhaps it comes from simple resemblance.

In the West I have seen grizzly bears, the greater cousin of our original Ambrose black bears. We flew into the old Blackfoot Reservation up the Cut Bank; that is Montana, almost Canada. We would come in low over the bears at the river bank; I imagine they were fishing or berrying. They would hurry along under us in a kind of awkward, rolling run, splashing across that shallow stream. Seeing the way the bears moved I thought that if I went on all fours I would look just like them. Ninety years ago, if there were an animal that had something to say to Wesley Moore as he went home along Old Egypt, that animal would have been a bear.

*   *   *

Murray brought his team over one day in August. He could take just that day and the next on Nelson's cabins, he said, for he had another job after that time near his own place. Murray worked on jobs that tractors couldn't do, or he worked for people who didn't want tractors. He was glad to have work in the summer, as his team was hired mostly during the winter, for woods work in snow.

He got three boys to help him. They jacked one of Nelson's cabins up off its foundations, cleared the foundations out, and rolled a flatbed underneath. Then they lowered the cabin onto the bed and guyed it down over the roof with ropes. They hitched up the team and started. The oxen pulled up and the whole arrangement bumped off on its way, the cabin lurching from side to side, Murray up front beside the animals, and the boys hanging onto the ropes and the cabin itself, trying to keep it aboard and trying to keep it from falling apart. They hauled several cabins to places around the village, and then on the second afternoon they loaded the last two cabins at once and rolled back up Old Egypt, which was Murray's way home. When Murray spoke to his team he said, "All right, smart." Smart was one of the oxen's names, evidently. The other one did not seem to have a name.

Murray unloaded one cabin at Mariani's, down the hill, and the last one at what has become my house. Then his three helpers walked back down to the village. Murray took his team on over the hill, and his oxen had left Ambrose village for the last time.

*   *   *

I can see Nelson. I knew him slightly when I came back to Ambrose. But I can't see his uncle, W. D., or Wesley, Moore (Nelson's great uncle, in fact), whom the bear unburdened itself to. Wesley was born in 1835. Ambrose's original wilderness settlers—ex-soldiers of Washington's army— were the old men of the town in Wesley's youth. Like their own, Wesley's is a life we can inventory and invoke but never understand: it's too long ago.

He was not one of the town's leading men. He married young, farmed on this property, went to the Civil War, came back, lost his wife, married again, stopped working the farm and took work in one or another of the mills that used to be around the village. Wesley would walk to his mill jobs each morning and then walk home in the evening. One autumn in the 1880's his work was, not in Ambrose, but in Egypt, and he walked three miles each way, along Old Egypt. From the outlying houses of Egypt village three miles over the hill to Wesley's own dooryard there was no house, no opening in the woods.

The bear was to one side of the old roadway, and in the early, October dusk, Wesley thought it was a calf until it came into the path. "Better days are coming," the bear said.

Wesley didn't say anything. The bear kept at a distance of a few yards from him, and occupied itself in searching about near the ground, peering and poking among the low cover. But all the time it was undoubtedly speaking. It spoke in a low clear voice of the period, seventy-five years before, when the hill they stood on was an open pasture; although the bear could hardly have been around in those days. Certainly, no bear that did not have the power of speech has ever lived so long.

Sheep, the bear was saying. "They used to run sheep all over that hill. It was all pasture. There wasn't a tree or a weed higher than a sheep could crop it. There was a woodlot at the top, but the rest was open down to the bottom except for haymows and fields below. Look at it now: no sunlight could get in there—you couldn't see twenty feet into the woods."

"It was as clear as a fairground," the bear said. "They have let it go."

"What are you?" Wesley asked the bear.

"They've let it go," the bear went on, "and they wonder why everybody is working for somebody else and nobody has anything of his own or any pride. Everybody has a boss and nobody is free and they don't have anything, even so. They stopped selling their rightful products and sold their own lives instead, and their health and precious time."

"What do you want?" Wesley asked.

"But it's going to turn around. They will open up the woods again; they will clear them right out. You will be able to see around the country from up here again. There will be houses all over this hillside. No sheep, but gardens, orchards, grass and pasture. Everybody will have his own place and live as equals in the open, and not go sneaking in and out of mills in the dark."

That is all that is supposed to have passed between the bear and Wesley. Supposing their meeting to have been as reported, the bear doesn't show as much of a prophet. Its Jeffersonian order has not come to pass, far from it: Burnt Hill is as wooded and worthless now as it was in Wesley's time— more so, for Egypt village, at its foot, is now part of the same abandonment the bear deplored. They have let it go, too.

* * *

I had some idea of trying out a pair of snowshoes someone had given me. I had forgotten how troublesome they are: they make you carry your own feet. Still, they work. I went up Old Egypt, picking them up and putting them down. By the time I had found a rhythm that suited me, I felt winded, and stopped. Sunday afternoon in the long, long middle of

January. There had been plenty of snow since Christmas: perhaps three feet were on the ground in the woods. I leaned on a stick.

The top of the hill was ahead of me, I saw. Here and there through tree trunks I could just see the hills lying to the south and east, and I thought I could hear the highway in the valley below. It was about here that Old Egypt eluded me in other seasons: past this point, going on down the hill, I had never been able to find it. I hadn't tried to trace Old Egypt in winter. The stone wall fragments, the brushy passages which seemed faintly more open than the surrounding woods, these would be hidden by the snow, I thought.

I went ahead a little, up the last rise and along a level which I knew to be broken ground but which now was made even by the snow. Before me the hill fell away in big steps, steep near the crown, then more gradual. In summer you couldn't see far down there for the foliage, but now the trees were bare. I saw Old Egypt then, plunging right down the hill from beneath my feet, cutting to the left to get around a ledge, then continuing almost straight on down. It might have been the Appian Way. The snow cover, which had indeed hidden Old Egypt, had also revealed it by removing the confusion of undergrowth, lesser trees and shadows amongst which lay its course down to the foot of the hill where Egypt village had given it its name and its terminus.

I stood in my snowshoes and kept watch over Old Egypt for a few minutes. I could never follow it in the snow down to the bottom and hope to get home before dark that day. If I had brought a compass I could have taken the road's bearing from where I stood, but of course I had no compass. It occurred to me that Old Egypt, revealed, might be as lost to me when I turned my back as it had been before I found it: for the fact that I had found it today didn't mean I would be able to next summer, any more than I had been able to in past summers.

Really, though, I didn't think I would have trouble finding Old Egypt in another season. I had separated it out. Fifty times I had been over it in my earlier walks. Old Egypt was one of those queer objects in our experience of perception which we are stuck with if once we come to discern them. The Big Dipper and the Man in the Moon are others: if you see them once, you must see them every time from then on out. Old Egypt, I suspected, was like them, and my seeing it at last was like those acts of seeing that separate out nature's still creatures from their worlds: separate the insect from out of the twig, the partridge from out of the fallen leaf cover, the rabbit from out of the dead brown stalks.

The Crows

Dianne Benedict

Evening was spreading over the long sweep of the land, darkening the prickly-pear cactus into soft, hulking shapes that appeared to be folding slowly towards the ground, like sheep for the night. A man was traveling along the shoulder of the road. He was a tall, gaunt man with a head that jutted forward, and he carried a shotgun swinging easily in one hand, down low, parallel to the ground. He moved lightly on his feet, almost but not quite running. He wore an olive-green jacket and a felt hat, both greased with sweat, and a pair of heavy wool pants that lacked a number of inches in meeting up with his shoes at the ankle.

Suddenly all the long, careless bones of this man drew together, as if someone had tugged on a string at the center of him, and in the space of a few seconds he had melted soundlessly into the ditch at his side, raised his gun to the bead, and, without pause, pulled the trigger. In the deepening, slow-breathing evening air, the sound of this shot breaking barrier after barrier across the countryside was like the end of the world.

The man darted forward a few paces and froze. Then the string at his center fell slack and, pushing his hat back on his head, he rose to his full height, and spit sideways at a cedar post. After that he cracked his gun open and removed the spent shell.

A few yards ahead of him something rustled the weeds in the ditch. A large black fan spread open, then another, and the thing bumped forward, scrabbling along the rocky ground, and then sank on its side.

The man cradled the gun in his arm, went forward and stood looking down at the thing in the weeds.

"Half shot you a crow, have you, Myron?" he said. "Well, shit!"

The old clay-colored truck barrelled noisily through the growing darkness. Beneath the clatter of the stones in the truck-bed, the tires hummed
monotonously on the concrete road, and the tinny music from the radio
drifted in snatches over the darkening range like reflections from a brightly
colored Chinese lantern over a vast black lake.

Everything inside the cab was bathed by the green-white light from the
dash. A small, plastic dancer in a real grass skirt was secured by a suction-
cup to the shelf behind the seat, and a pair of giant foam-rubber dice hung
from the rear-view mirror.

The old concrete road that the truck was moving on passed eventually
in front of a nightspot called The Abandoned Hope, which was a place on
a lake, with live music and a few cabins around it, that was very popular
with the colored folk.

Next door to The Abandoned Hope was a small, run-down, but very
active establishment for buying and selling used cars. This was owned by a
man named Rich Stutts, a wiry, short-legged individual who never wore
anything except Army fatigues with the sleeves ripped off the shirt. When
the clay-colored truck was still about ten miles down the road, Stutts was
standing in front of a fragment of mirror that he had propped up in his
kitchen, combing his carrot-colored hair forward into a shelf over his eyes.
Before long he and a new girl that he had arranged to have for the evening
and the two people in the truck would all join up together.

The young man in the truck, whose name was Jim Wesley White, drove
with his arm resting on the open window. He steered with one thumb
pressed against the bottom of the steering-wheel. He was dressed in a dark
maroon shirt with a white stripe in it and clean khaki pants, and his
straight brown hair, freshly wetted and parted in the middle, still showed
the marks of the comb. He was twenty-one years old. He smelled of
starching and ironing and Old Spice cologne, and there was a look of almost
mystical innocence in his dark blue eyes.

Every few minutes he would glance at his companion, who was a young
woman with heavy dark-brown hair that was pulled back into two tortoise-
shell combs. She wore a flower-print dress with white cuffs and collar, and
she had a handkerchief with pansys on it tucked in her belt. She sat with
her hands in her lap, mile after mile, looking out the open window.

Finally, after they had gone a long while without conversation, Jim
Wesley made a small adjustment to the rear-view mirror. "Have you ever
been out to the lake?" he said.

"Yes," she said.

He looked carefully into the mirror from several angles.

"Do you know a man out there name of Stutts?" he said.

"Yes," she said.

"That's where I work. I work at his place," he said.

"What do you do there?" she said.

"Fix cars."

"He has owned that place a long time," she said.

"Yes," he said. "He said he knew you."

She turned and looked at him for the first time since they had left the city. "What did he say about me?" she asked.

"Oh, I don't know, I guess he said something about how you played the organ in church. I said I knew that, naturally."

"I didn't belong to the church when I knew him," she said.

"Oh," he said, "Well, I guess he knew of it somehow."

Again, they drove in silence for a while. Jim Wesley was thinking about the time, a little more than a week ago, when he and Stutts were sitting on the old split-up car-seat in front of the shop eating freeze-dried salted corn out of the little packages that were sold in the vendor.

"I knew her ten years ago when she was maybe sixteen years old," Stutts had said, and then he had had a great deal to tell about her, most of which was impossible to believe.

"It's not the same one," Jim Wesley had said.

"It is. I know her. It's her." Stutts patted his pockets and brought out his cigarettes. "She was altogether different then," he said. "It was like some kind of voltage always coming out from her. Wasn't any way to understand her. She just started following me around. Just started coming out here to the lake all by herself in her Daddy's car. By God, I still puzzle over her."

"The way I heard it she doesn't go out," Jim Wesley said.

Stutts had laughed at him then and flicked a kernel of corn at him that struck him on the forehead. "Maybe she would with a virgin," he said.

Jim Wesley had reached over and emptied one of the bags of corn into Stutt's breast pocket and then laid his hand on the bulge. "Miss Eugenia," he said, "would it make any difference if I told you I was a virgin?"

"Darling boy, it surely would," said Stutts. "I have to confess a weakness for virgin boys."

"Well, here I am," Jim Wesley said, and he grabbed Stutts by the head, and Stutts had to shove him hard so that he fell off the seat onto the ground. He wrapped his arms around Stutts' legs then, and Stutts fought him off and kicked dirt on him and went, laughing, back into the shop.

Now, as they rode in the truck, he stole glances at her. She was quiet, strong-looking. Her arms were smooth and white, and the curve of her throat moved him, made him feel as if he were sinking, drowning even.

Before the talk with Stutts, he had never thought much of her. When she played the organ in church she had always seemed rather small, sitting up on a level above the congregation. He had always thought of her, when he thought of her at all, as a sort of handmaiden of the Christ among the lilies that looked down on everyone from the stained-glass window over her head. But after Stutts had spoken with him about her, he had come up to her on the lawn in front of the church, and she had said to him in her slow voice, as though it didn't even take any thinking over, that yes she would go with him to the lake or wherever he wanted to go. That had been six days ago. Now it was Friday night and Jim Wesley had everything arranged about going to the lake.

Her father, a large man with pale, shaking hands, had been sitting on the porch-swing when Jim Wesley drove up to the house. The father was drinking wine from a plastic cup and the bottle was on the floor under the swing. The man's handshake was moist and needful. His eyes were bruised, faintly begging. He had been a widower for years. Eugenia had stood at the edge of the porch steps, looking out over the yard while Jim Wesley extricated himself.

He thought about what Stutts had told him about the way she had been. She had got religion, evidently. He pictured pulling the combs from her hair on each side, watching it fall forward.

Her hands with their long, smooth fingers were relaxed in her lap, the palm of one turned upward. It was still with him, from when she got into the truck, the way her legs had swung in together, long and strong under the thin, flowered cloth.

She would at least go walking with him by the lake, he thought. Stutts would have the cabin ready like they had planned, but they wouldn't necessarily have to use it. He didn't know if they would use it. Sometimes, when he looked at her, he wanted to go into the cabin with her like he had thought about; but at other times, especially when he looked over at her hands, at the one so relaxed with the palm turned upward, he would feel a dull cold in his legs and belly, and then it would seem to him that all that business related to the cabin was impossible even to consider.

She couldn't say why she had come with him. Remembering back, she thought perhaps she had come with him because there was something about the way he smelled that reminded her of being in school, and she had momentarily slipped back to that time when, whatever a boy asked you, you said yes.

Then she remembered distinctly that the moment he'd asked her to come with him she'd had a sudden image of the house she lived in with her father, and how dark it was in a certain corner where the stair turned, and up a little higher, on the second landing, a small wire cage that had hung there as long as she could remember, with a few hulls still in the feed-cup and the little wire door standing open.

When he had asked her out, she had been excited to picture sitting on the steps of the porch for the next few evenings thinking about going.

Even though he was too young for her. She had felt a little pull, like the
tension of a spring, under her breastbone.

She had been aware of him a long time at church. She had been very
drawn by him, and it had made her happy to have this feeling for him se-
cretly without him knowing. She was struck by how perfectly propor-
tioned everything was about him—the shape of his head, his brown hands
that she could tell were not hard like a man's usually were, his eyes under
the straight brows looking as though nothing could ever damage him, or
even touch him, like stars glimpsed remotely through a tear in the clouds.

She wasn't able to look at him while they drove. She watched, in a
long sweep of sky, the gold that the sun had left deepen into red. On the
radio, a man was singing about how loving a woman was like being taken
by the ocean farther and farther from shore.

"Look up ahead," Jim Wesley said. He was leaning forward peering
through the windshield, and the truck slowed.

"It's Myron Bless," he said.

"Who is that?" she said, but her voice was covered by the whine of the
gears as they pulled off the road.

They drew up alongside of a man in a felt hat and a jacket that was out
at the elbows. The man squinted against the headlights, and then stepped
closer to the truck and bent down to look inside. He had a cracked-open
gun slung over one arm, and with his other hand he held a crow by its thick
black feet.

"Hey there, Myron," said Jim Wesley. "What are you doing out here?"

"Guess I'm after crow," the man said. He had a voice like a nail coming out of the wood slowly. "Or else they're after me," he said.

Eugenia, watching the crow's head, saw a topaz eye appear, and then
the man stepped back and smacked the head against a cedar post. After
that he gave the crow a hard little shake as if he expected something to fall
down out of it, and the beak and eye widened simultaneously and there
was a great swelling of feathers ending in a shudder.

"I wouldn't keep on with that business," Eugenia said, but then the man
was coming towards them and looking inside again.

"I'm about ready to fold it up," he said. "You going to the lake, I'd appreciate the ride."

"Climb in," said Jim Wesley. He was already shifting gears. The man
tossed the crow carelessly into the ditch behind him and went thumping
up into the truck-bed, and then they were once more on the road.

"Isn't much to look at, is he?" said Jim Wesley.

"Who is he?" she said.

"Myron Bless. Works for Stutts," he said.

She turned around and looked through the dusty back window at the
felt hat that rubbed against the glass.

"What does he do?" she asked. She saw again the defiant topaz eye, the clinched feet.

"Whatever he's told," he said.

Stutts took the girl by the wrist and pressed her hand up into the small of her back. He steered her through all the sweating, slow-moving black people on the dance-floor. He found a little space for them to move around in, and he put his hands on her hips as she began to pick up the beat of the music. She was a new girl, a real dresser. She had on a tight-fitting silver dress with a halter top, and a cluster of rhinestones on a black ribbon around her neck. She had arranged her hair into a twist on top of her head, and under the blunt-cut bangs her eyelids glistened with green and silver dust.

When the musicians stopped for a break, Stutts took the girl over to the bar. After he had ordered the drinks, he put his hand on her back and massaged her neck a little, and she smiled and gave him a long look that said, yes, she was feeling that way, too. He offered her a cigarette and she took it and ran it slowly through her fingers while he lit the match.

The bartender brought the drinks and wiped the beads of water off the bar with his apron. "Jim Wesley White was looking for you a while back," he said.

Stutts swung around on the stool and looked out over the barroom which was so dark and crowded it was hard to recognize anyone, but then he saw Jim Wesley and Eugenia sitting together at a table by the door.

The girl in the silver dress leaned close and said, "Who's looking for you?" and he squeezed her arm, high up where he could feel the warmth of her under-arm, and then he left the bar and made his way across the room towards the other two.

When he leaned down between them and said, "I can get you a better table," Eugenia drew back as if there had been a bright light turned on her and looked up at him with her face tight as though against the glare of it.

Stutts said, "Miss Crawford and I have met before, or do I disremember," and she said, "No, that's right."

White smiled back and forth at the two of them and said, "What do you know about that."

Then the girl from the bar came up and asked to be introduced.

It was well into the evening when Stutts asked Eugenia to dance. He picked a slow number and pulled her to him as soon as they reached the floor. She moved lightly against him, not holding on to him noticeably, but not pulling away, either.

"Been a long time, isn't it?" he said, and she said, "Since what?"

"Since we were dancing together," he said.

She made no reply.

"Hell, since we got this close or anything," he said.

"It was nine years ago," she said.

"I always did remember you," he said. He drew back and looked down at her. She was looking away to the side.

"I knew you only about a month in the summer, I think maybe it was ten years ago," she said.

"But you never did forget me, neither."

"That's right," she said.

He smiled down at her. "You remember all that?" he asked her.

She looked up at him with that look like being under too bright a light again, and said, "Do I remember all what?"

"You and me," he said.

"And the others?" she said.

He thought she meant maybe some other girls that must have been in the picture at the time, but she said, "I mean those others you liked to bring along," and then he remembered. He remembered a night when he had taken her out to the other side of the lake, and they had picked up two other men on the way. He remembered coaxing her to lie with him in the back seat, only somehow nobody remembered that the others were supposed to leave the car. The other men had sat up front, he recalled, drinking their beer slowly and acting like they weren't watching, only they were watching. He recalled that she had lain with him without feeling, not pitching in so as you would notice, but not pulling away either. It had always puzzled him why she went through with it.

"I never did understand about that," he said. She stopped dancing and stood back from him and looked up at him with an expression he couldn't put a name to.

"I mean that whole business there at the end," he said. "That's what we're talking about, isn't it?"

"It was a long time ago," she said.

"Well, sure," he said.

"But I still remember it," she said.

He stared at her. She had taken a handkerchief from her belt and was pressing it where the sweat glinted on her upper lip and under her eyes. A large man behind her bumped against her shoulder so that she dropped the handkerchief, but she was walking away by then and she didn't stop to pick it up.

They walked on a path that was crossed with roots under some live-oak trees on their way to the cabins. The cabins were duplexes, sided with brown asbestos shingles. They stood in a row, with car-ports between them. Beside each door was planted a young cedar tree about the size of a ten-year-old child.

"We can probably sleep in the truck if you're worried about how it looks," Jim Wesley said.

"There's nobody looking at us," said Eugenia.

"Or I could maybe go leap off the pier," he said laughing, "and if I didn't drown I'd probably come up sober." He could barely walk. She had to hold him by the arm.

They reached the step of their cabin, and she took the key from him and opened the door.

"We're lucky to have a place," she said.

"Hell, yes, we have a place," he said. He held onto the door-sill and put his other arm around her shoulders. "Stutts would have given us *any* place. Hell, we could have had *his* place."

"He had this place ready all along," she said.

"Oh, I don't know if you can go so far as that," he said.

"You are too drunk to lie," she said. She had to put an arm around his waist and help him through the door, and then he stood there looking around as though he'd never seen a bedroom before in his life.

The wallpaper in the room was a faded, dull brown with strips of some kind of flowers in it, and a merciless glare fell sharply on everything from a small ceiling fixture with brass arms and four glass tulips. There was a spindly iron bed covered with a quilt, and a dresser with a round mirror in a frame of heavy roses. Thrown down on the cracked linoleum, with its border of ivy-vine, were a half dozen rag rugs.

Eugenia led Jim Wesley to the bed, upon which he fell and immediately lay still and went to sleep. She sat beside him for a while, looking at the dark window across from her where she saw herself reflected. Then she slipped his shoes off his feet, and placed them under the bed, and went into the bathroom.

While she was there she was sure she smelled the smoke from Stutts' cigarettes. He'd been in there, all right, she thought. He'd been in there, picturing how it would be. Well, he could never have in mind the way a thing really was. He could never have any part of it. He would always be thinking one thing, and the way it really was would be another. What did she care what he thought he had? She could let him have it—it was no part of her.

She was washing her face when she saw the two rubbers on a shelf over the sink. She stood with the water dripping from her face, thinking, of course, one for tonight, and one for in the morning. She picked one up and slipped it out of its little paper band and looked closely at it. Then she put the paper band back on and lay the rubber on the shelf exactly where it had been. It was nothing to her.

She came out of the bathroom and walked barefoot over to the door to switch off the light. She took off her dress and slip and hung them in the closet, and then she took off her brassiere and folded it and put it in the single drawer of the stand beside the bed.

She started to undo Jim Wesley's pants, but he came alive suddenly, feverish-looking. "It was those damn mice got under the clutch-plate," he said. He pushed her roughly away and got up and stepped out of his pants. Then he got back in bed, under the covers, and she watched the pinched look ease from around his eyes, and then he was asleep again.

She got in beside him and looked for a long time at his face. There were pale, milky shadows moving over him. The moon was bright in the room, and, in the brightness outside, she could see heavily rocking shadows that were cast down by the live-oak trees.

She lifted back the quilt and then the sheet. He lay on his side with his legs drawn up. His hands were pressed together between his thighs. She opened his shirt and folded it back and lay her hand on his chest. She put her mouth where his neck curved into his shoulder and moved closer to him and pressed her breasts against him. She slipped her hand down over his ribs and around over the curve of his back and after that she took a long time feeling him everywhere, slowly, because there was no reason not to in the quiet room, no reason at all.

Some time later, in the room on the other side, Myron Bless eased himself down into a wicker chair. He had a package of cigarettes in his pocket that he'd taken off of Stutts. When he took the package out, he found that he was down to the last cigarette, so when he took that one out he flattened the package and made a hard twist out of it and dropped it on the floor.

It was dark in the room. Every now and then the blind would billow out at the window and then rest back with a little tapping sound. Myron held the cigarette between his forefinger and thumb and each time he took a draw he would hold the cigarette up and watch the ember.

He was thinking about his first time and the boy it had been with. He hadn't thought of that in a long time. He hardly ever thought on all that anymore, but now he eased back into his memory gingerly, feeling all along if it was wise, and he knew, remembering, that that first one was the only one worth thinking back on. He had always known that. Long, boney, waterfront trash he had been, that first one, name of Kelly from a family of brothers that worked a trawler. Was no place to meet except under the wharf. They hadn't known the first thing about it, hadn't even known enough to bring something to put under them. It had only been just feeling each other, showing each other a little at a time, until the boy had told him one night that some other boy had showed him the way. Behind the unblinking ember, Myron laughed low in his throat. That's what the boy had called it, "the way," as if there was only that one. This is the way, the boy would say, and there in the dark wedge under the wharf, with chinks of light sliding over them as they moved, and now and then a heavy tread on the boards above them from some bloke come out to piss—there they would have what they wanted, and it was all there with that boy, by God, more than it had ever been again. He watched the tiny glow-worms

winding on the ember. You spend a life-time looking, he thought, and all
along it was only just that once, but you could never guess it. Not until
it was all played out from here to hell and back, and it had let go of you,
finally, and you didn't care no more. It was all only brackish water save
for a time going too fast under a wharf, the deep sun-red of the arms
starting at the shoulders and then the long white length of that boy, all hip-
bones and the hollows in the flanks, all that warm, slippery business.

He felt for the ashtray on the stand beside the chair, and ground out the
cigarette.

Stutts would have the girl with him, so there was no going home. Maybe he would walk by the lake until the first light, or maybe he would bed
down by the boat-house. It was the sound of the water under the wharf
made that a good place. Stutts would sleep late with the girl. He would
check in on them around ten, maybe eleven. Start the breakfast. Maybe
today they would go on the shoot. It had been the crow he had got by mistake had put him in mind of it, and he had brought up the idea when Stutts
had come home with the girl, and Stutts had said, hell, why not, if he was
back up on his feet by then.

He opened the door without touching the knob and eased the screen-
door open and stepped out on the porch. He looked down the long, shad-
ow-banded path towards the lake. He felt the moonlight on his face and
shoulders, warm but not warm, blue and bright and quiet. He patted his
pocket for the cigarettes, then he remembered. After a moment he stepped
down onto the path without a sound.

Eugenia knew there was someone in the other room. There had been no
sound, but the smell of smoke had come again strongly, and she knew with
some slow-rising sense that there was someone there, and then she heard a
sound on the path and knew that he was gone.

She got up and took her watch out of the pocket of her dress and
looked at it, and then she went and stood in front of a picture that hung on
the wall between the two rooms. It was a picture of three cowboys around
a fire, with a horse tied up in the background. One man was playing the
harmonica and the two others were smiling at each other across the fire.
One of the smiling men was bent forward passing a plate with a fish on it
across to the other one.

Eugenia went up and took the picture down and stood looking at a hole
in the wall. She put her hand in the hole and felt wood at the back of it.
Then she found the place on the picture where there was a slit in the paper
that could be widened. She put the picture down and went out onto the
porch.

The door to the other room was ajar, and when she went in, the smell of
smoke was strong and also the feeling was very strong that the person had
just left.

She switched on the lights. On the floor, propped up against the wall between the two rooms, was a picture of a Japanese woman holding, on the back of her hand, a small green bird. On the wall, a few feet above the picture, was a length of wood that could be pushed aside, and when Eugenia pushed it aside and looked through, she saw Jim Wesley asleep in the moonlight, uncovered except for one leg wrapped in the sheet.

She turned and looked at the room. The bed looked as though it was made up with only the spread, without any sheets or blankets underneath. There were cigarette butts in an ashtray beside the chair. She bent to pick up a twisted cigarette package that lay on the floor, knowing it was a package of Stutts' Lucky Strikes even before she spread it open.

She moved in front of the long mirror over the dresser. Slowly she raised her arms with the wrists crossed and looked at herself that way. She was the color of plaster in the harsh light. Her dark nipples were stark on her white body and her shoulders were nothing but bone. Her eyes were like live coals far back in a cave.

She leaned over and pushed an ashtray across the glass top of the dresser slowly until it reached the edge and dropped off. There was a vase on the dresser also, half full of water but without any flowers in it, and she pushed that slowly over the edge, too.

Then she crossed the room and sat on the edge of the bed. She sat there looking down at her hands, which were pressed together between her knees. After a while she lay back. She lay stretched out on the bed for a long time, with her eyes open, under the harsh overhead light. It was like being under the eye of the sun in the desert. Some time later, when the dawn came, she was still lying there in the same position, but her eyes were long closed by then and she was asleep.

Later that day Jim Wesley sat beside Eugenia in the back of the truck taking a hard ride. Stutts was up front, driving, with the girl from the night before beside him, and also Myron Bless. They drove over rough terrain, swerving constantly to avoid the pricklebush and low mesquite, heading out for a place Myron knew about that he said was virgin ground.

Jim Wesley would have had no wish to speak, even if he could have been heard over the crack of stones on metal. He rode along with his eyes fixed on the guns. There were five—the three shotguns, and the two rifles for the women. Packed alongside of them was a wooden tool-box, a cooler full of drinks, and a small battery-operated gramaphone that Stutts had wrapped up in a blanket.

It was a long ride. It seemed to Jim Wesley like it would go on forever. They had been driving across open country for over an hour, and now it was well on towards evening, with the sun sinking low enough to be flattening out, and the beginning of a thin pollen-colored haze drifting up from the horizon.

After a while the truck lurched and slowed down as Stutts shifted gears; then they took a sudden turn and picked up speed again. Jim Wesley hauled himself up, bracing against the wind, and saw that they were approaching a great wide-spreading live-oak tree, darkly silhouetted, behind which the sun was going down very deep-colored and swollen.

When they were about a quarter mile from this tree, they came to a table of stones that fell away to the tree and beyond it, and Stutts stopped the truck at the edge of this rubble and got out and came around to open the back-end. Then Myron got out and came around, too, and they hauled out the tool-box and three of the guns and the blanket with the gramaphone wrapped up in it. Then they headed for the tree.

Jim Wesley stood watching them as they made their way over the stones. Behind him, Eugenia sat turned in on herself, with her arms around her knees. She was dressed in a long-tailed khaki shirt and a pair of Army pants of Stutts'. There was no sound except a slow, melancholy country beat coming from a radio inside the truck.

After a few moments the door of the cab opened slowly and Stutts' girl climbed down, her skirt stretching taut over her thighs. She had on the same spike-heeled shoes and silver dress she'd worn the night before, and a small radio hardly bigger than a package of cigarettes hung from a strap on her wrist. Without closing the door of the truck, she began to make her way unsteadily over the stones, following the men.

"Time to decide," Jim Wesley said.

The music drifted back to them from the girl's radio.

"You going to come?" he said. Eugenia didn't answer.

"Whatever happened last night, I'm sorry," he said, and, when still she wouldn't answer, he said loudly, "Only I swear to God if it's anything like I think it is I only wish I could remember it!"

"What do you wish it was?" she said.

"I wish it was just what you think."

"Well," she said, "then that's what it was."

He thought for a moment. "I don't know that for sure," he said.

She began rolling up the cuffs of the Army pants. "I'm tired of the whole business," she said. She crawled to the end of the truck and dropped to the ground. He followed her and dropped down beside her and took hold of her arm. Her face turned hard as if he had hit her, and then she pulled away from him and started after the others.

He hauled out the cooler with the drinks in it and the two remaining guns and hurried to catch up with her. The day was growing unbearably thin for him, yet still he was caught up in an expectation that was without name or reason, and he rushed foolishly after her, stumbling over the stones, with the two guns clutched awkwardly against him, and the cooler getting tangled up with his legs.

When he was even with her, she stopped and put her hands in her pockets and turned halfway towards him. "You were asleep," she said.

"When?" he said.

She lifted the edge of a stone with her foot and turned it over carefully. "You don't even have any idea of it. About all that," she said.

"About all what?" he said, and she glanced up at him, frowning, with her face tight against him and then she turned and walked away.

"Listen," he said.

"I'm tired of the whole business," she said.

"Now, wait a minute," he said, and he began to hurry after her again, but then he stumbled over the cooler and had to set it down, hard, on the ground in front of him. "What the hell's the sense in keeping secrets?" he called, but she had gotten far away by then and had no interest in even turning around to look at him, and so he didn't care to call out to her any longer.

"Bitch," he said softly.

He left the cooler sitting where it was. He went on towards the group of people under the tree. Someone else was going to have to come back for the cooler. It wasn't going to be him. The sun, setting behind the tree, cast long shadows towards him. He stopped and looked back at the truck. The door on the passenger side was still open. The truck looked like it was waiting for him. It was his truck. He didn't like it the way Stutts had driven it over the rough terrain. He was always careful about his truck, treating it as if it had feeling, and it had lasted him a long time. Stutts could ruin a truck in a day. But it was no matter to him, he could always get another one, easy.

Jim Wesley turned and continued on, entering the shadow of the tree. No one in the group of people looked at him. Eugenia was backed up against the trunk, with one shoe off, searching around inside of it for a stone. Myron had his knife out, scraping away at what looked like a length of bamboo. Stutts lay stretched out on the blanket.

The girl in the silver dress was sitting off to one side. She was turning the dial on her radio slowly from station to station, searching for something. Snatches of voices slipped out, now a woman, now a man, now a line from a song, broken off.

The first crow appeared out of nowhere. No one saw it come, but suddenly it was there, moving along one of the high up branches. Myron pointed it out to the others. "Here they come," he said.

Then there was another one, and they all saw that one, and the girl in the silver dress got really excited to shoot at it, but Myron said, "Chrissake, hold onto her, Stutts!" Just then, Jim Wesley called out, "Throw me one of those callers!" and Myron threw him one of the callers he had carved out, and then Myron and Jim Wesley began sending out calls that sounded maybe just a little like crows in a terrible rage.

"By God, they're coming!" said Stutts, and he put a record on the little gramaphone that he'd brought out there. When the record had picked up speed, he set the needle on it and turned up the volume on what sounded like several thousand crows. This sound lifted and filled the space, and Myron and Jim Wesley blew more loudly on the callers, getting really excited over the sound of all the crows on the record.

Then there came the first answer from far away in the dark curtain of dust that the wind had blown up off the land. It sounded like maybe a half-dozen crows answering from different locations. But then it was as if a tidal-wave of crows burst through some smothering barrier with a sound that intensified swiftly until it drowned out the record, and crows began dropping down out of the darkening sky into the tree. In a few seconds, the upper branches were thick with crows, all of them calling, and hundreds more dropping and swooping, until the sky was completely blacked out, and then the men took up the guns and began to shoot.

The crows fell heavily, like stones, and lay on the ground flapping and scrabbling, but still they came as if there was no end to them, flying lower, more brazen, many of them right into the guns. There was no time to count or even take satisfaction in the dead. There was only the rustling mass descending, ever-replenishing, deafening them, and the men loading up and drawing a bead, and blasting off, and doing this over and over, and all the while there were the ones in great number who were moving over the branches, calling and flapping as if there was nothing any different from every other day of their lives.

Then, over the terrible noise of the crows and the guns there came another sound, which was the girl in the silver dress screaming and screaming. Jim Wesley, when finally he heard this, looked over his shoulder and saw the girl with her hands to her face yelling towards Eugenia who lay closeby on the ground with a dark stain of blood on her breast. He gazed without comprehension at this scene and lowered his gun, sensing in that moment that he was the only one shooting. Myron held his gun with the barrel pointed down, and was shaking and white in the face. Stutts had dropped his gun and was waving his hands as if to make everything quiet, and was approaching with careful steps the place where Eugenia lay looking so strange and such a different shape and color from the other dead.

The crows overhead went on calling, but the record had played out, and it was quieter, now, after the guns. No one spoke and the girl had stopped screaming.

Stutts went down beside the body and bent close over it but at first didn't touch it.

"She had the gun on you, Stutts," said Myron.

"She had what?" said Jim Wesley.

"I didn't have no other choice, she had the gun on you," said Myron, this time louder, and then he dropped his gun and sat down on the ground with a low cry.

Half an hour later Jim Wesley sat in the back of the fast-moving truck, along with the gear, which had been thrown in helter-skelter. The guns were vibrating and traveling over the truck-bed, first this way and then that. When one of them got too close to him, he would reach for it and throw it over the side of the truck.

The record player still had the little record on it, and the arm with its needle kept bouncing back and forth across it.

He held the body where they had placed it across his knees, wrapped up in the blanket. Again and again (it seemed to him he'd been doing this for days) he had to keep covering it up. Still, she kept getting exposed.

He gazed steadily at a streak of red trapped between two blacknesses along the horizon, above which there was a sweep of clear, starred, indigo. All he could think of was how much he wished she could take care of the blanket, herself.

For Years without War

Lamar Herrin

Word reached Greg Woolman from the Costa Azul that his mother had died without warning, without pain—a bolt from the heart and it was done. He'd been doing nothing at the time. Some few hours before her death he'd been in bed with Carolyn, but at the moment itself he'd been alone on the Quai d'Orsay overlooking the Seine, perhaps in the presence of a Brandenburg concerto or Levi-Strauss' *Tristes Tropiques*—but doing nothing. The moment he learned of her death he'd been chopping radishes for a salad he would eat and wouldn't taste. She was the last person alive he'd felt obligated to live for. It was as if with her fund of energy she'd beat back the waters and cut a passage for him too in her wake. It wouldn't have done to sink, not while she sailed on ahead.

First, he would see her home. He would see her underground. He would make—an act of homage and final reflection—a tabula rasa of her sea.

The man to speak to in Spain was Antonio Rojo, Tony the Red, who sold land and houses, *her* land and house, and mourned each client's death. They had a perfect connection. Greg could hear every false lift, every faltering note in Antonio Rojo's sales-minded voice.

"She'd come to love it here. There's a cemetery overlooking the sea she admired."

"She'd come to love Acapulco, Waikiki, London and the river Thames even when it was dirty. No, she would want to go home. Have you ever seen Louisville, Kentucky on the map?"

"On the map, no. But she spoke of it." His voice gathered emotion.

"She was a wonderful woman, an—inspiration. Yes, I'll see to it."

"Should I come there?"

"Come here?"

"Yes, to accompany the coffin. I'm not sure of the proper procedure."

"No, it isn't necessary. You should go there to take her down. *Alli*—there!" he heaved. There was incredulity and loss now in the voice, all the distance from blue Mediterranean sky and sea to a benighted point on the mind's map and a cemetery chopped from the wilderness. "The airport there...at Louisville, Kentucky."

He had long known when the way was clear you came through life to death with astonishing ease. And he had long wondered if clearing the way wasn't really all that was meant by the phrase "life's work." Moments from each day he'd taken a seat beside his "life's path" and watched himself jog after "life's pleasures." His mother had sprinted and sailed; she'd shown some style and won admirers, and ever since her husband had died and left them both fortunes, she'd faced no unglamorous alternatives. She knew, as another phrase had it, "how to live." Yet she'd never forgotten her son. He'd been the first to be called from each of the resorts she'd temporarily made home. Over the years they'd made dates to meet in various world capitals—and kept them. What could he possibly complain of? She'd been lovely to look at, contemplate. He would see her once more, and this time he wouldn't jog; he'd want to hurry. Sitting aside, detached, practically freed, he still felt his mouth wizen and tasted bile in his spit. "Rot," he uttered quietly, weightily.

"What, dear?" Carolyn said.

"Rot. I should have taken the plane tonight. The body will rot."

"Stop, please. Try to sleep. You'll get there before she will, anyway."

He turned over and put a hand on her rump. She'd been in and out of his life for years now and as an exercise in faithfulness had managed to stay close. He couldn't conceive of another reason. "You think I'm mourning. You think I'm being morbid, don't you?" he said.

"It's natural," she said.

"But I'm not."

·"You will then. Try to sleep."

"I feel like my life has now changed. I feel like I have survived." He spoke calmly, but with a queer, precise, bottomless resonance. He heard her breathing go suspenseful and shallow. "It's as if a pacemaker's been taken off my heart and I've discovered my own pace."

She didn't reply. They lay with most of the wealth—none of the wretchedness, none of the squalor—of Paris around them as she measured out a silence sufficient to the needs of common sense. "I'm worried about you," she said. "Let me go with you."

"No. Go to Dublin. Go see *your* family."

"Then you'll come back?"

"I'll go to Spain to sell her house."

"I'll come there."

"No."

"Why not?"

"It'll be sold." He sighed. Kindness breathed up through his voice, a relenting, reminiscent taking-of-the-blame. "All right, if you want to," he said. She placed a womanly hand on his forehead which took the blame back, read his temperature, assuaged his brain. He puzzled painlessly. "What is curious is that she bought it in the first place. She's always leased. It's really all that she's left for me to do."

He would fly to Spain and settle accounts for her, but he flew to Louisville, Kentucky for himself. Greg Woolman buried Cynthia Woolman as deeply as the law allowed in the last plot of land a Woolman held title to in the USA. He buried her beside her husband, Greg's father, a casualty at the age of forty-two of immodest fortune-making. Their son, as he stood there before their spacious graves, was forty-five. At the mortuary he'd taken his one look at his mother's body, found her achingly unreal, and had had the casket permanently closed. None of the distinguished mourners had complained. Their memories were of years-gone-by. After her husband's death, Cynthia Woolman had been a spirited force in local politics; then had put money and perpetual beautiful motion behind the founding of an Equity-based theater. Good actors and good politicians would remember her and some of those few who were left in the vicinity attended her funeral. But it amounted to so little. She lay there under deeply polished, soon deeply dirtied wood divided into two camps of imperfectly recalled activity, neither of which entitled her to a life or the ground she lay in. She'd been her energy and the places it had briefly touched down. That wasn't enough. As a mother she'd been a constantly charged force, a commanding if absent presence, but for that to have been enough those who decided such matters would have to look favorably on him: her magnum opus, her leavings, her son. By his example he either justified or condemned her existence. He waited till the coffin hit bottom, then threw in the first clod of dirt.

The dirt was warm and dry. It was mid-summer. Greg remained in Louisville for nearly three weeks, disassociating himself from it, making sure. There'd been a boyhood here, an early marriage and a hasty divorce. He asked himself what he would do if this city of studied southern living and river odors were denied him forever, if it vanished out from under his feet. He would do fine. He would do without.

Was there anything he couldn't do without? Was there anything it would sadden him to give up? He stood there in his slippers, travel-weary, facing the Mediterranean sea. Take slipping a hot, seemingly enlarged, inflamed, and certainly tender foot into cool leather. And take it away.

Would he grieve? Take eating. Take over-eating and coming to capacity;
take under-eating and wanting more. Take love. He'd stood up in love and
like a raging king had watched it blow away. Each time he'd managed to
convince himself he'd been standing in the wrong place. Take the metaphysics of pleasure and quietly take it apart. If pleasure was never enough
perhaps it was never meant to be. Perhaps pleasure made labyrinthine
promises and took labyrinthine liberties in order to guide us finally to the
center of loss, where the beast vanished like a chimera and space staked its
soundless, odorless, vistaless claim.

   He leaned on the railing of his mother's balçony. Immediately below
him arms of volcanic ash reached out to form a cove of sparkling still water.
His mother had gotten the best view, and if not the best, certainly the one
she'd wanted. Her house—white stucco, red tile, and heavily varnished pine
—was built into the side of an arid hill; around her, similar houses, nearly
identical, belonging to Germans, English, Dutch, Scandinavians, a few to
the French. He stood in the midst of an international colony—*Los Viñedos*.

   "Death then becomes the satisfaction of finding the last pleasure and
naming it a cheat."

   He spoke, for all his seriousness, with a self-conscious smile. He felt self-
conscious for the phrasing. It was hard to talk of death without talking of
dread and keep the mouth straight. Yet he believed he'd discovered a genuine disinclination for most things of this life and the idea that tempted
him with its sobriety and logic was that if he cultivated that disinclination
he could come to death prepared. He wouldn't say relaxed and rejoicing, although that's where the idea took him; he stopped before the first hint of
the ecstatic. He viewed death as extinction and his course until then to be
the extinguishing of life's fraudulent pleasures. In exchange, he got his
fear of death and his reluctance to die converted to indifference, or perhaps to another, but strangely attractive, disinclination.

   I know your silences. There are those that would cut me dead, others
that would neglect to notice and permit a certain casual approach. Your
present silence is because you have nothing to say. You've been physically
and emotionally drained. You poor dear, I don't want you to say anything. Your silence asks me to enjoy myself and come closer, slowly, quietly. To do nothing rash. I'm in Nice, at the Belmar. We were here—do
you recall? One of the maids, thinking you were somebody else, asked for
your·autograph; then saw her mistake and asked to be forgiven. I've forgotten exactly how you handled that.
                                                          Carolyn

   What a cacophony of languages, of childish shrieks, of unsynced eating
hours, car motors, musical beats, of half of Europe being their noisy selves
on the side of a hill in Spain—minus the Spanish. Two days after he ar-

rived Greg walked the neighborhood and the only Spaniard he saw was
Antonio Rojo. Mostly he saw wealth put to stale use. The houses resembled glamorous bath-houses; the landscaping—the rock gardens, the lush
patches of lawn, the bauble-shaped pools, the terraces, the raked gravel—
showed an exhaustion of imagination; people looked out of touch with
their property; the hill and its sunny fiefs looked there to be run over, visited fiercely, locked and sold. Antonio Rojo had his headquarters on the
grounds. The two men exchanged somber greetings and expressions of
thanks. It occurred to Greg that what he had here was a fattish and vain
land speculator who had somehow made himself more intimate with Greg's
life than others had in years. He had, between Antonio Rojo and his over-
priced hill, a tasteless denouement to a drama that had never run low on
taste or thrills. Cynthia Woolman had settled here. She'd bought here—
and assured her son of a stay here.

   "I would like to discuss the sale of the house and grounds," Greg said.
   "I am at your disposal." Antonio Rojo performed a courtly nod,
matched with a brief sweep of the hand. He locked his office. "The day is
yours. Shall we walk back to the house?"
   They sat out on the balcony and Antonio Rojo, who knew where things
were, went to make drinks, moving with a soft middle-aged waggle in his
ass. Greg watched the swimmers splashing in the cove. They called themselves Hans, Inge, Ursula, Johan, Jean Pierre, Sarah. Water hung above
their heads in silver skeins, sunlit for the instant and bodied out at the tips
in silver globules. Feeling the sun, feeling the energy spent on the water,
Greg re-entered the house and sat in a wicker easychair before a split-cane
table. Almost immediately he rose and returned to the door he'd just
passed through. He had noticed the bad carpentry from across the room.
The lintel and the jamb met at the point, then opened to a wedge of blackness wide enough to stick a matchbook through. Recrossing the room he
examined a protruding corner beside the flagged fireplace and discovered
the same mismatching of inches, the same flagrant ineptitude. His overall
sense of the room was of haste and impermanence, and at last, within that,
a particularized hurry to be done. He sat back down. Antonio Rojo
served him his gin.
   "Your mother loved this house," he said.
   "Somehow I find that hard to believe," Greg replied, blunting the edge
on his voice, but speaking distinctly. "It's not really her taste, nor is it especially well-made."
   "I refer to all of it—the view, the sea, the people around her. Yes, she
loved it..." For an instant he was gone, fatty and sublime around the eyes,
the cheeks and jowls allowed to fall. Closer by, he added, "The house itself
was secondary."
   "For mother the house was always primary."
   "It was a new outlook, a new experience. She'd begun to feel alive here

..." he continued to reminisce, realizing a moment later the utter impropriety of what he'd just said. With a tiny overstated motion he recoiled in apology.

"Quite all right. Mother felt alive everywhere. That was Mother."

"And now you want to sell."

"I want to discuss it. What do you advise?"

"Advise? I wish I could give you good news *and* good advice." He leaned in, incapable, it seemed, of ruling himself and attending to business. "I must tell you. I believe your mother's death was a bad sign, a portent. Suddenly no one is interested in houses in Spain. Of course there are political troubles, and talk of boycotts and energy shortages, but I am a man of the heart and my heart tells me there are bad days ahead."

"Then you advise waiting?"

"Yes, waiting. At present there is no market, not unless..." Rousing himself, he leaned farther in, but stiff in the back now and firm in his tea-colored eyes. "Do not sell cheap!" he warned. "Do not!"

"No, I intended to get a fair price."

"You do not understand! If one house sells cheap it could start an avalanche. The bottom could fall out. And if this house sells cheap," the tea-colored glare glistened, the voice struggled, "the memory of your blessed mother would be dishonored forever. She loved *Los Viñedos!*"

The man was distraught. The money-maker and the lugubrious mourner changed places, changed back; the roles meshed. Greg felt strangely sympathetic and strangely abused. It hurt to have his mother so grossly misinterpreted and it hurt to have this man mourning a figment of his own sentimental self in the name of his mother; to have his mother made into a pawn in the international dollar-war hurt especially. Yet Antonio Rojo had put himself at Greg's disposal, and Greg wouldn't mourn. How could he mourn the loss of a woman who made loss—the act of losing, of voluntarily giving up—something reproachful, inglorious, and sad? How could he explain—and why should he?—that while his mother lived there'd been a sort of generative force loose in the world that drove blindly on to this, its death, and stopped? He couldn't. So he would sympathize. There were, he understood, a few countries left where professional mourners were still for hire. He would sympathize and, if necessary, pay.

"She lived a full life. It is the only way to view her death."

Yes, it's a charming view—the cove, the children, later that pale scribbled line of the surf. At night you can sit here and watch the lights from the fishing boats bobbing out on the waves. Occasionally you can see the flashing from their catch. And of course there's jasmine in the air, at times an onrush of fig.

Very charming, *de postal,* as the Spanish say. But if you're up to it I'll show you a real view. How are your feet?

They hurt. Greg had climbed to the top of the hill *Los Viñedos* was camped on, only to face a higher hill, un-urbanized, terraced with short twisted trees that he would come to identify as almond, olive, fodder-producing mesquite. He looked for a path that would take him around the terrace walls.

Follow the goat droppings. The goats always find the easiest route. And don't look back till you reach the top. The view will be worth it.

He followed the goat droppings, came to prize them when the way seemed too steep or tangled and they lay out in a sprinkling of hard brown pellets to point him his next step ahead. He didn't look back, but by glancing to the sides where fields of grapes sloped down out of sight he realized he was climbing a huge spur-like promontory. Beyond the grapes he caught a glimpse of the sea. He moved upward through the prickly-fresh odor of mountain herbs, and throat parched, watched the olive trees shiver silver and green in the wind and sun.

Pick an almond—yes, I know they're green. Crack it with a rock. It'll quiet your thirst. And the taste—it's really something quite special. Do you like it?

It was sheath-wet, not yet hard, and yielded the totally unexpected taste of gamy vanilla. He ate half a dozen. He was breathing heavily and for each breath he counted three thudding beats of his heart.

Don't give up now.

What's the point?

The view! I bought the house to have this view to climb up to.

Yes, I know. Your heart...

And yours, but all that's unsearchable, isn't it? Whereas this hill and that sea are there.

He kept on. The hill was terraced to the top, and the labor gone into positioning the rock, the effort it once took to make every inch of land accountable, contributed to his exhaustion. He was vulnerable to the thought that man was an upward-trudging, wall-building, seed-burying, fruit-scavenging animal, and only that. Man was that animal who took his survival to the most unlikely lengths and places, then left it there. Near the top he came across a shepherd's hut. The biggest boulders had been reserved for these walls. Greg stuck his head in, saw dented tin, yellowed specks of paper, disintegrating hemp, bedding straw; smelled urine and the leavings of a lair.

But the coolness is nice.

Minutes later he made the top. He stood before a valley, perhaps twenty kilometers across, where green wheat and red poppies blew and vineyards clung to huge plots of broken ground, and three ocher-walled, red-tiled towns clustered in around their churches. The light was preternaturally clear, yet equable and unsharp. His eyes adjusted to the detail at once. He saw curving black roads sent out among the towns in the name of commerce, courtship, and war, and on those roads he saw tinily-progressing cars and one bus. The farthest they could travel would be the iron-reddened cliffs twenty kilometers across, or the hill on which he stood. Journey's-end.

That's one view. Now turn around.

He was expecting a seascape, placid and blue and restful on the eyes, boats big and small, horizon blur, essentially a fake. But he was three-sides surrounded—the sea swept him up, actually threatened his balance! It was blue, intensely blue, and blank. He was still long seconds away from being able to pick out boats and bathers. The immensity, the loveliness, and the menace held him as if in the grip of a primordial contradiction, and not until the blue became familiar and its shadings found names—storm-blue, aquamarine, the sky's light breath of blue in the shallows—could he regain his wits and look with a discerning eye on anything. The silence was hemispheric—birdsong crossed it, electrically—yet the sea seemed unnervingly near.

Now, slug-a-bed, aren't you glad you came? 360 degrees and there's not much more left, is there? Be truthful. Sit on that rock up there and you can turn like a beacon. Is there?

He sat high on a summit-rock and turned. Church and city, wheat and grape, valley opening out to the sea; the sea; his cosmologer's high perch. He thought: after the shock, after the spectacle, I have nothing to do with this.

It's an outing, a diversion. Or must one treat you now as an invalid?

No. I just wouldn't have bought a house to have this to climb up to.

But then there's that to climb down to. What's the matter? Are you dizzy?

No.... Yes, a bit. It's the heat, the altitude...

And the heart?

Yes, the heart. It wants more.

Lie down.

Later, he followed other goat-droppings down the hill, and came down veering off to his right. Evening brought a long lick of coolness. He got water from a fruit-farmer, then picked up a back-country road twisting on to the sea. Smells of frying sea-food, garlic and olive oil came up the road to greet him and the sound of pooling water led him closer in. Under an arbor of twining fig branches and grape vine he discovered a queer sort of hunger, insatiable but inquisitive, as if he would eat to identify the smells. He ordered by pointing to the contents of ten trays of *apertivos* lined up on the bar. Octopus fried in rings, *a la romana,* squid boiled in its own ink, mussels cooked in lemon, olive oil, and paprika sauce; sardines, three different sausages, snails; he ate what was brought to him and as an act of discipline learned all the names; drank two steins of bitingly cold beer. Then stayed there, under the arbor, close to the basin of a craggy stone fountain,

and watched the light settle on the outer-side of fig and grape leaves. He
sat in aromatic darkness. He felt fully recuperated, as if he'd risen back to
zero and perhaps pushed beyond it.

Now come home.

I'm in Perpignan. I won't enter Spain unless you invite me. I'm surprised anybody enters Spain anymore. Have you been reading the little
general's latest *pronunciamientos*? Foreigners will please keep their ideas
and influence to themselves! They will please spend their money and
leave! Until proven clean all foreigners are suspected of carrying the pest!
Perhaps that's why I haven't heard from you. You've been found unclean,
subversive. But of what? Of what? If I only knew that I might know
what attracts me to you.

But then I think I prefer not to know. I haven't been to confession in
years.

Meanwhile I'm practicing my Spanish, behaving like a Spaniard. Did
you know that Perpignan has more exiled Spaniards for-a-day than Dublin
has midwives? They come in busloads to see all the films banned at home,
and the theaters have Spanish-language versions running from morning to
midnight. As you might have guessed the hit of the town is "Last Tango"
but what you'll be interested to learn is that we've danced in the very spot
the tango scenes were shot in. We really have. I got tipsy on champagne
and ran home. You ran after. I got angry and shot you. You pulled up
the covers and went to sleep.

If I can't insult you I'll drive you mad with jealousy. The town is full
of invitations. Where's yours?

He opened the house to his mother's friends. They came in the evenings, dressed in cool slacks and blouses, the day's sun crisp in their hair,
raw in their solemn and condoling faces. Most came from northern Europe and would never tan. Even those who lived in *Los Viñedos* the year
round and formed the nucleus of the community would remain a baked
and ruddy red. Cynthia Woolman, as everyone knew, had brought her tan
with her from the Caribbean, from Mexico and Hawaii, and had proved to
be not the exception to the rule but the rule that excepted them, then graciously took them in. They'd come back now. She had been lovely. Lovely was the word, and with uncomfortable after-thoughts, youthful. Lovely
and youthful. She'd been a joy to be near. Lively—and again the word set
off a troubling ironic echo. Her death had been a blow felt by all. His
mother had seemed, a Danish lady remarked, like the social hostess for a
cruise. She had planned an eventful and entertaining calendar for her
guests.

Which made Antonio Rojo's hill a boat, his houses first-class passage to
...the Happy Isles.

"If all those countries which give us a bad press could forget politics for a moment and send representatives here to *Los Viñedos* to live, they would see...harmony, understanding—*si, senor*! Look around you. You can see it for yourself. If nothing else Generalissimo Franco has made it possible for us all to live together here. And what will those slanderous countries have accomplished when they finally make it impossible, when they finally manage to drive away all new residents from *Los Viñedos*?

Antonio Rojo came with the visits, was there when they ended. He was part of the whole eulogizing process Greg hosted in the name of his mother.

"No inquiries, then?" Greg asked.

"No, unfortunately, nothing. But it is the same with *urbanizaciones* up and down the coast."

"Sr. Rojo, allow me to ask a strictly business-like question. How many houses do *you* have in *Los Viñedos* for sale?"

"I?"

"Yes. How many houses have been built and remain unsold at this very moment?"

"Few."

"I understand. How many?"

"Perhaps five, six..."

"Sr. Rojo, I can't wait forever. I might have to sell cheap."

Antonio Rojo slumped, wearily misunderstood. "This was your mother's house," he protested, "where she intended to live out her life."

"She did."

"Yes, don't dishonor..."

Greg stopped him with one of the few Spanish words he was utterly sure of. "*Basta!* I appreciate the feelings you had for my mother, but there are some things you should know. Mother was a gadfly, a dilettante, a globetrotter. She was rootless, do you understand? She never stayed in one place long. It was part of her charm."

Antonio Rojo sat shaking his head.

"Yes, I'm sorry, but it's true. She talked of staying in each place forever, but she knew herself well enough to know when she started talking like that she was ready to leave."

"No."

"Yes. It was like a ritual of departure that, unfortunately, other people got caught up in."

The two men exchanged earnest, thoroughly opposed glances. Then, on his feet, Antonio Rojo paced. Greg spoke to the back-side, front-side, of a worried, over-precise waddle.

"I say all this only to explain why I have no qualms about selling the house for the best price I can get. If the times are bad the price will be bad, that's all."

Antonio Rojo came to a quiet, punctuating stop. "Take time to reconsider," he said.

"You're worried about your houses?"

"I'm worried about this house."

"Look at it," Greg said coldly. "It's thrown together and quickly covered up. It will not make a very good shrine."

Antonio Rojo did as he was told—he looked around—but by the time he came back to Greg his face had undergone a change: there was an entranced set to his eyes; along the jawbone and neck were quivers of excitement and risk. "I'll top any other price you can get," he declared resolutely, "and it might do quite nicely as a shrine, quite nicely, if that's what I choose to make of it." Then, stepping in closer, he lowered his voice to a concerned, impertinent bedside murmur. "Do you know, Mr. Woolman, it hurts me to say so, but I'm afraid you failed to understand your mother. There's so much, so very much you've missed."

Years of things he'd missed, he admitted it. But she would not settle for this. Her first rapture aside, this wasn't where she'd choose to stop. He never pretended that one had that choice—for here is where she'd stopped, after all—but there were spots more suitable, more in keeping with character, for bringing one's life to a close, and *Los Viñedos* was a pseudo-spot and Cynthia Woolman had not led a pseudo-life. The spot, he came to understand, suited him, not his mother. The pleasures here, the plusses, were all stale and detachable. They were like gaudy stickers slapped on a man's life. There was sun and sea, hot skin and cool skin; there was the belly and the dull, daily seepage toward the groin. Here, a holiday haven, the mind went on vacation. Why not? he asked himself. For a moment, on a cool freeing shudder, he thought he was home.

The moment ended on a chill. If he made peace with a fictional life he'd win a fictional death. He worked his dialectic to the painful quick. Where would he find an unfictional life to make peace with? When had he lived with such greedy joy that he would be reluctant to part with it even now?

That was the question. But he tabled it. His mother's friends began to ask him to their houses. He went to them all, eventually arrived at a party given by a German financier and his wife. By now he was known and no longer a center of attention. He drank, they all did, he as much as they: Scotch whiskey. At times he seemed part of a night-long conversation, moving in and out of the lives of nations and individuals, keeping a sensible contact with money. Other times he was sinking through a vault-like privacy. Late, quite late, in the garden, the moods, the times, public and private enclosures—all achieved a fit. He heard his hostess, the financier's wife, ask the same question he'd asked himself. "When have you broken your oldest rule and enjoyed yourself?"

She was a handsome and weathered woman, about his age and probably at about his stage of drunkenness. Her English would be better than his.

"I don't know," he said, quite correctly. "Maybe never."

"You are not like your mother," she observed.

"No...no...not at all." He rocked, sloshed. The smell of fig burst in on him. "Not many people are."

"Ahhh..." She smiled, faking a discovery. What was there to discover? Greg wondered. He had loved his mother and resisted her famously irresistible example every step of the way. He was the only one who had.

"Mother practiced over-kill," he said. "Except she over-won."

"But of course," his hostess uttered, stepping back, then stepping in. She studied him. "*You* are the reflective one, the self-reflecting and the self-consuming one. Nothing makes demands on you. No job, no culture. People? No, no people..."

"One, and she died."

"How horrible. You have no weight. *You* are the man who is not sure he is there."

"And she?"

"You and she?"

"Just she."

"Maybe she was the one who got the best out of people, then left them behind."

"Yes," Greg said, without resentment, expecting no relief. The ghost of his mother came out of a Scotch whiskey bottle and stood before him; then stood up in him. He felt how easily, and with what startling calm, she came to take possession of a life. "Who?" he muttered. "For example, who?"

"Antonio, Antonio Rojo, if that's his real name. There's one."

"He's like a fussy old priest."

"They were lovers. They were together when she died."

The woman had bangs, a roughly-skinned but finely-featured face. She wore a loose red dress with a yellow and brown geometrical design at the bust-line and hem. The dress looked Greek. She wore it in an excitingly unencumbered way. She smelled—no, the night did—of fig.

"As a matter of fact," she said, "I was sure you didn't know."

They kissed. "My rules are all broken," she said, "I keep them that way."

They admired the only thing the house had to offer, the view. It was black and silver-trimmed. The fishing boats had already returned. At the horizon summer lightning flashed in the cloud banks like a short in the celestial wiring. A keen, nearly unsalted wind blew in off the sea. They smelled that bit of salt, a trace of tar and fish; heard a curiously removed rumble as the tide sucked the beach stones down into the drink.

At dawn they parted. The water lay quiet and milky-gray. Greg and his ex-hostess—Greg, of course, now served as host—kissed at the door. They both looked haggard. Greg had tried his damnedest and did. His ex-hostess had taken everything she could get away with. It was as if the two of them in their game without rules had gone into every corner of the house and dumped all they'd found of value into an empty pillow case. It hadn't come to much. Still, Greg noticed that the lady's knees wobbled as she made her way down the walk and up the hill. If she could get home with it, fine, he decided. She'd earned it. The house was now empty, ready to be sold. Gulls, routinely patrolling the beach, sang him a ghostly *aubade.*

That evening Antonio Rojo came by with another letter. After glancing at the handwriting on the envelope Greg studied the letter-bearer, as if committing his mother's last lover to memory. He thought at once of puffed wheat: face and body puffed, especially the backside, the kernel of the man lost in his Latin effusions. There were two effusions. This hill of thrill-seekers, this brotherhood of wealth, this *Viñedos,* was one. Greg's mother was the other. Together they took his shape: sybaritic, shrewd, impressionable—a worldly-wise child.

What had she been fishing for in all that?

"The house is yours," Greg told him. "I'll only sell to you, cheap and in private."

Antonio Rojo broke into a blissful smile. At that moment Greg feared he was about to become the subject of a third effusion. "There's no hurry! Stay, do, please! You may decide to stay for good."

"It's unlikely," Greg said.

"Whether you stay or not, I should like to get to know you better. I have my reasons."

"I'm sure."

They stood a yard apart. Goodwill and bestwishes came off the man like a self-replenishing scent.

"Sr. Rojo. . ." Greg began.

"Antonio, *por favor.*"

". . .did she suffer at all?"

"Didn't I tell you? It was quick. She barely frowned."

"Yes, I'd forgotten, you did." Greg turned toward the sea. The boats were going out. Their broad-bellied hulls flattened the rippling waves. "See me tomorrow about the house."

You see, I came after all. An Englishman brought me. Darling, I was alone and gloomy and bored, and you know I'm not exactly partial to the English, but this chap was just divorced from his wife of twenty-one years and he was 'doing the continent' and you know *I am partial* to people who've spent long loving years watching the ground slip out from under them. So I came with him to Barcelona and we comforted each other for a week. He wanted me to go with him to Madrid; I told him I preferred the sea. It was simple, and a bit sad and doomed—just like that. But I know where he is, just as I know where you are. That's not a threat. I'm leaving here the day after tomorrow. I suppose the connections to get to *Los Viñedos* will be rotten.

This city is big and spacious and. . .heavily-sunken. I have the sense of buildings that go as deeply down as they go up. I wonder why? I suppose it's how I feel, nearly immobile, and when I move, getting nowhere. . .Fred was nice, you know. The day we arrived the police ran some students and workers through the streets and bloodied their heads—the fact is, two heads were bashed in and buried—and from then on every corner we turned in the city Fred would lead the way. He was protective. He seemed to be saying, if something twenty years old can break apart so quickly then imagine how fragile something a few days old must be. Unimaginably fragile, we discovered.

I hope you're listening, dear. Because what is truly unimaginable, unimaginably cruel and unjust, is to write off so many years of one's youth and good health as bad luck. Just how many lives of good luck await us? So we sift through the past in hopes of salvaging something to show to the present, something for one's pride, perhaps, or simply something to pay one's way. Something. . .I don't know what. An accomplishment between two people that however little others may think of it hasn't been left to collect dust. Something that involves some upkeep, some maintenance.

Yes, I'm coming. And do you know what? I believe I'm carrying the pest. In some of the neighborhoods here I've seen plaques put up by the residents. They say, "Thank you, dear Generalissimo Francisco Franco, for thirty years of peace and tranquillity, for thirty years without war." Yes, thanks—but no thanks.

A man walked to the beach of sand and gray stones at the end of the cove and took off his robe. He was probably a handsome man; he had a morning tan—he was a morning swimmer—and his stroke showed the strength and restraint of an athlete with years of fitness to come. Up on his balcony, with a view of so much more than the swimmer, with so much early-morning blue and silver splash, Greg couldn't see the man's face. It dipped in and out of the water as the arms reached out and down, as the body glistened and rolled, as the feet paddled noiselessly. The day had barely begun. The Mediterranean air was tingling, cool, lucid, and gold. The blue of the cove was quiet—quivering and poised. The swimmer wrote on it in a silvery script. He swam out to the mouth of the cove in a long lovely arc, then reversing the arc swam back, and Greg read the trail of foam. . .

. . .into motion, the foam carried him into the mysteries of motion, brought him up into the swimming motion and the swimmer, then abstracted the swimmer and left him with the swimming itself, so effortless and clean. And he wondered: once put into motion by bodies, why couldn't certain disembodied motions continue of themselves? Most motions, he knew, had a brutish air of belonging to the body, of being unimaginable without it—motions of strain, chopping, heaving motions, inertly falling motions—but he questioned if there weren't others, some select few, that belonged to the air, the water—to the elements—and were given on loan to bodies, to certain bodies, those who could best appreciate the elemental rhythms and resist to the last all human interpolations. . . .

The questions came with the strokes, with the soundless boiling up of water and the shining out of foam. Greg Woolman sat there on his mother's balcony as a man nearly self-annulled, whose only doubt came in admitting how easy it had been. He'd thought it would take a life's labor and had planned for a sort of siege; but there in the dawn sun, his walls leveled and his sentinels all asleep, he admitted the labor had been over the second it had begun. He had no taste for the lie now. When death comes, he said, it will only mean the shutting of the eyes.

He shut them. He saw the swimmer, every gratifying and quickening muscle in his body; he saw the blue medium in which he swam; he saw the pulsing white glow of the sand beneath and the zones of dark vegetation. The swimmer swam circles now around the cove. Beyond the cove lay the sea. Gusts of wind blew across it, slashing the surface into characters both primitive and brief. He heard phrases: life is not bad luck, lives of good luck don't await us. He saw inelegant, wedge-shaped rushes of wind over water, and felt his mouth fall open and the wind and water rush in. First that filling; then, at once, a vast pouring out.

He opened his eyes. The swimmer was tiring, slowing down. It seemed clear to Greg now that the man was swimming laps, and that he was on his last. When he reached the beach at the end of the cove, Greg stood with him. The man stumbled, shivering, looking for his walking legs, and Greg left him there and waded into the shallows, silent and keenly aroused. The man wished him luck, but the man was quickly gone, and already the water came to Greg's waist, cool but with the standing coolness of the night in it, and the moon's pull. When the water reached his upper chest, he stopped and waited for the constriction. He looked out over the blue mesa, over a body of blue whose skin played tricks with youth and age, and felt the tightening of a final notch there where his heart bled. It was an abrupt pain and like the water, inspiriting, it tipped him over and he began to swim.

He was student and teacher, and he worked on his swimming meticulously, admitting no flaws. It came to coordinating the arm-pull and the leg-kick, the breath-taking and the body-roll. Then it came to further coordinating and refining, and further refining past the point of exactness and into an area of rhythmic abandonment for which no performance records existed. It went on and on. It took amost forever but once he'd gotten it, that was how long it would last. He swam past all doubts, all the cross-questionings of desire, and sometime past that, in a long blue diminishing—stately was how he felt—Greg Woolman passed under.

Paint Job

Debby Mayer

She answered my ad in the paper. Could I give her an estimate? Her voice was low, not too sure of itself. Would change her mind about colors at least three times, I thought, but I'd just gotten back after my year off and I needed money. I had to check in at school that afternoon, so I told her I'd be over the next morning.

"Who is it?" she called down when I rang the bell. "Dan," I told her.

She must have waited on the landing, because when I came around the last corner there she was, one flight up, all legs. She was wearing these little white shorts and some kind of platform sandals. Her legs seemed a mile long, and while I don't claim to be a leg man, there are some things you can't ignore. Lots of girls are fine below the knee, but even her thighs were slim and tight—not skinny, but nothing wiggled when she walked.

But I was still climbing the old stairs. Next I saw the yellow t-shirt—she was wearing a bra, thank God—and her face, pretty, but no match for those legs. Hair a shade of gold leaf. Skin lightly tanned, like quick toast.

"Hi," she said, "I'm Ingrid."

Ingrid's place was a mess. I mean it was clean, and neat as a ship, but most of it hadn't been painted in 25 years. I got out my notebook and went room by room, like George always did.

I think it started when she told me she'd painted the living room and this little alcove off it—"the study," she called it—herself, three years before. Now those rooms looked like they'd been painted maybe a year before. The paint was on even, the spackling smooth. I was impressed.

The bedroom looked like it'd been dynamited. The walls were that buff nobody's used in twenty years, with huge splotches of unpainted plaster all over. She was giving me some story about how she started to paint it, then her landlord tried to evict her, so she stopped. I was thinking about when that hotel, the Broadway Central, collapsed.

She didn't want colors, she wanted white. This in a place where somebody had painted most of the trim chocolate and half the walls olive. In the bathroom, the paint flaked off when I touched it. She had posters and pictures hung all over the place. I knew I should look behind them, but I was afraid.

We wound up in the kitchen, which was as big as my mother's back in Scranton. "What a great room," I said, without thinking. It had a round table in the middle and a huge window that looked out over the tops of some brownstones across the street. We sat down at the table. I had decided to give her a break—not only did I want the job, but there was no sign of a guy around, and nobody with a trust fund would live in a dump like that. It came to $400 though, which seemed high, so I said I'd wash the place down, too, for that price.

"Please buy good paint," I remembered to say as I left. "Please. I can get you a discount on Benjamin Moore."

"I have to get the paint at this store where I can charge it to my landlord," she said. But she promised she would ask for Benjamin Moore.

Maybe it was because she fell asleep the first day I was there. She had agreed so easily to me starting at eight that I tried seven on her, and after a while she said O.K. I arrived on time, glad to have five hours before the sun got high and wondering if she would have the kitchen cleared out. She did. The place was big as a ballroom. Christ, it was big.

"You got that wallpaper off!" There'd been this wallpaper that looked like bricks along one end of the kitchen. I'd thought it was pretty realistic, but she had said she didn't like it and would try to take it off. I ran my hand over the wall. Amazing—she'd gotten all the glue off.

"Took me till four o'clock this morning," she said.

"What!" Her eyes did look a little puffy. "Did you sleep?"

"Couple hours."

With a worker like that as inspiration I rolled out the plastic and started washing. I could hear her moving stuff around in the other rooms. Christ, I thought, a real backbreaker. I'd told her I could do the place in five days, but that kitchen was a monster, and filthy. I don't know why people don't wash their places down once a year. It would have helped me to have something better on the stereo, too, but it seemed early to see about changing the station.

Then suddenly the radio went off altogether and I was reduced to singing to myself. The only song I could think of was "She'll Be Comin' Round The Mountain," so I sang that.

Only when I moved out to wash the hall did I realize she wasn't around.
I'd thought she'd be working in her study (she'd told me by then that she
worked at home, though not on what) but she wasn't there, or anywhere,
until I saw that the curtain had been pulled across the bedroom doorway.
There wasn't a crack in it to look through and I couldn't hear any sound,
but I could see the bed in my mind's eye and I knew the chick had laid
down on it and gone to sleep. I actually stood there and scratched my
head. Either she had balls, so to speak, or she was crazy. Ten days before
she'd gotten my phone number out of the newspaper and today she went
to sleep while we were alone together in her apartment.

She'd told me my references were good, but she didn't say they were
that good. Or bad. Because whenever I have a question about a paint job
I think, what would George do? because he was the one I worked with the
most. And I knew right away old George would be in there now and he
might still have his pants on but he would have thought up some question,
something, to get in there and check out the situation, see how she looked
at him, how she answered.

I stopped singing then because I didn't want to wake her, but I clumped
the ladder—her ladder, she saved me finding one—around because I was
mad. Women. It sounds sexist, but they always throw the decisions back
on you. All I wanted to do was paint the goddamn apartment, get paid, go
home. Instead the job was a multiple choice quiz from the first minute.
Was this an invitation, as George would say? Was I a schmuck, people
were so unafraid of me they fell asleep while I was there?

By lunch time I had washed the bathroom and hall, and just when I was
thinking, O.K., this is it, how do I tell her I'm going out for lunch, does she
want me to come in there, she came out. Her t-shirt was a little wrinkled,
a good sign—at least she had slept in her clothes.

"Well, good morning," I said. "How did you sleep when I was moving
the ladder around?"

She considered this. "Not very well. But if you know what a noise is,
sometimes you can block it out."

True, I thought.

It wasn't that she gave me a lot, or even offered much. No rum Cokes
here—I had to ask for every cup of coffee I drank for five days—that's
about 25 cups. The white shorts never even showed up again—just jeans
and t-shirts, day after day.

But she wasn't stingy. All I had to do was ask, and she'd say "sure."
That was her big word. "Got an extra sponge?" "Sure." "Another cup of
caffeine?" "Sure, Dan." After a while I joked with myself. Could I ask her
for a million dollars? A steak sandwich? This apartment? I heard her
voice in my ears. "Sure," it said, rich and—sure.

The second morning a guy was sitting in the living room when I arrived. Frank. Shorter than me, but with a better build—must have lifted weights. Seemed to know his way around. I didn't expect to become his best friend, but he could have shaken hands, looked me in the eye, something. All he said was, "Let's go," and they moved the bed and bureau into the living room. Then he said, "So long," took a quick kiss off her, and left. I never saw him again.

Ingrid I saw all the time. She went to her office twice and of course to the paint store, but otherwise she was home. A lot of people would drive you crazy, but we didn't get in each other's way.

She spent a lot of time on the phone. Most of it she was interviewing people, about books or something, and she took notes in shorthand. Very impressive. Other times she would sit on the floor, since the chairs were full of books and dishes, and lean up against the wall and talk to friends. Her voice stayed low pitched, so I couldn't hear much of what she said, but I liked listening to the tone, and when she laughed I had to smile.

Some days I think I should just chuck school and be a painter. The fact is, I love to paint. I hate the rest—washing and plastering, moving the drop cloth around—but if you prep the place right the paint goes down clean and smooth as cream.

Not that I'd moved into heaven. I was knocking myself out to stay on schedule, and there was the matter of music. I don't know much about music, but I listen all the time. I like jazz best, but I'll take almost anything—classical, country, rock. But Ingrid listened to the worst goddamn music—that kind of soft rock mellow shit, the one kind of music in the world I can't stand. It got so I thought if I heard Olivia Newton-John or Barry Manilow once more I'd jump out the window, $400 or no $400.

When she worked she didn't listen to the radio at all, but she gave me a small one I could plug in wherever I was. I would search the dial for the best music I could find, hoping to give her a hint, but she never got it, until Saturday when she didn't work and had the radio on all morning, I couldn't stand it any longer. She was sitting on the living room floor, sorting through some papers—people always decide to clean their apartments in the middle of a paint job—and I walked in and said, "Ingrid, can I change the station?"

She looked up, a little surprised, like she'd forgotten I was there. "Sure."

At six she went out, to Frank's, I figured. She left me keys so I could stay until dark and said she would call later to see if I needed anything. When her phone rang around eight I answered it without thinking.

"Is this Benjamin Moore?" came this low voice at me, and my hand on the phone actually twitched.

"Just his advocate," I managed to say.

"I forgot to tell you, I bought a lot of soda—help yourself."

But when I checked out the fridge I noticed a six-pack of beer. George always said beer was better for you than soda. Ingrid had told me to help myself. George is an alcoholic, but beer seemed more like cereal, so I took one back to the ladder.

That beer tasted like a medium rare steak and sweet corn. I made myself sip it slowly because I hadn't eaten anything but coffee for thirteen hours. I still got a rush. That was O.K. because it gave me energy, but it also made me hungry as hell, so I went back to the fridge and eyed the five cans of beer. If I asked her, she'd say "sure." I took another can and went back to work.

Now lights were on in an apartment across the courtyard, and there was a guy, on a ladder, painting. He wore a blue bandanna around his head like a pirate—very sensible, very sexy. I should do that too, to keep the paint out of my hair, but I just look stupid—my nose is too long. From time to time a woman crossed by the window.

They had some wild jazz on, so I flipped the dial until I found it. Then I painted and thought about getting my own place. Mike and I got along, but our apartment was forty minutes from school, and even if it wasn't—I had my bed, the table was mine, and four chairs. I set it up in my head.

Before I knew it I'd put a coat on the bedroom and finished the second beer. I was super-energized by then, and I knew with one more beer I could finish both the bathroom and the hall. What the hell, I figured, and went ahead. I kept an eye on my friends from the window and moved along with the music.

Ingrid was probably fucking Frank that minute. Her business. For me, time to go.

On the way home I stopped in a deli and bought a pack of Kents. I hadn't smoked one cigarette since the night my uncle had called, almost two years before, to tell me my father had lung cancer. But painting and smoking seem to go together. The times I smoked most were working with George. Now I smoked as I walked, lighting a fresh one from each stub. The beer wore off. By the time I got home I was too tired to stand. I went to bed without eating.

On Monday Ingrid had the kitchen all back together again. She'd cleaned the floor and put a print tablecloth on the table. The windows of the cabinet shone and the spices were lined up on the shelf. I like people who take care of their places.

I alternated working on the living room and the bedroom all day, spackling like a madman. Except when Ingrid came in at one and said, "I'm going to have a sandwich in my new kitchen. Take a break—I'll fix you one, too."

"Thanks, but my hands are all paint—"

"So wash them. Come on—"

So I washed my hands and face, sat at the round table looking out at the brownstones across the street, and we ate—I couldn't believe it—roast beef, lettuce and tomato, beer, then blueberries and coffee (I asked for it).

"This is an awfully big job for one person, isn't it?" she asked.

"It's not so bad." I told her about the time George and I did an entire high school in eight days. George had just gotten his new teeth, which made him a double bastard. "You're the one with a job ahead of you," I told her. "You'd better get Frank over here to help you."

She shook her head. "He's working all week."

"Nights too?" Fine timing.

"He's covering the convention."

"The Democratic convention? No kidding—"

She brought out a magazine I'd seen on the stands but never read—too serious. He was covering it for them.

"He draws these sketches, too? They're good," I had to admit. "My father had a talent for drawing. He never used it, but just fooling around he could draw the most lively things."

"What happened to him?"

Had to watch your language with this girl. "He died. Last year. Cancer."

"I'm sorry." Her voice came out gentle but still clear.

"Well, it's hardest on my mother. She married young. And she nursed him."

"So you left school?"

"Just for a year. She's better now. It gave me a chance to work, so I don't have to take any loans for a while."

She nodded. I took a sip of my coffee, but it had gone cold. Later I thought, how stupid, to tell her all that. But she had just sat there, watching and listening, and she had these gray eyes, with a lot of blue in them—almost taupe.

At dark I closed up the paint for the day.

"Could you help me put the bed back?" she asked.

"Sure." I was starting to sound like her.

The mattress went in a wooden frame that sat on the floor. We just had to put it back down in place then put the boards across it that the mattress sat on.

"Watch the paint job!" she warned me, only half joking, when my end hit the wall. Then, "Did you see that man painting across the way there?" pointing to the guy in the bandanna.

"Yeah, I saw him Saturday. He gets good sound from that transistor."

Getting the mattress in from the living room was a little tricky because of the doorways. Finally I picked the thing up and put it into the frame.

"Oh, I didn't even ask you which side you wanted up."

"It's fine."

The agreement was that she'd strip the rooms and I'd paint the apartment. But of course the last day I ended up moving a lot of stuff around. It's the story of my life.

The study would have been cake for me, but she wanted the inside of the closet done. I could see the closet was big—it went to the ceiling—but I still couldn't believe the amount of stuff that came out of it—folders, ski boots, a sleeping bag, about a hundred hats. She kept having to get off the ladder to cart things around, so I told her to hand the stuff down to me, and that way we emptied the closet.

Then she got a phone call. She talked to somebody named Ed and for the first time, her voice changed—got sort of tight and high-pitched. "Ed, I just paid $400 to have this apartment painted!" she said once, and I strained my ears, but I couldn't figure it out.

They talked a long time, and I got a little annoyed. There was still all this junk to move, and if I didn't spackle that ceiling right away I *would* be here all my life. So I started moving the stuff myself. I was almost finished when she hung up.

"What's wrong?" I said.

"That was my lawyer. My landlord's still trying to get me out. He's appealing the last decision."

"Why?"

"It's complicated. Has to do with rent control."

"Wants more money, huh."

"That says it. He probably won't win. But it wears on you."

I should think so. I didn't know what to say. Why would anybody want to evict her? She seemed quiet. And look at all the work she was doing on this place.

"He must be a real bastard."

She just nodded. After we finished clearing out the room she called a couple people and told them what had happened. I noticed she didn't call Frank, but probably she couldn't reach him.

"Ed almost didn't tell me," she said to somebody, and I wished Ed had kept his mouth shut. Here we were—we should have felt as if we had just crossed the Himalayas, and instead it was life as usual, one bummer after another. I stuck to my painting, afraid if I sat down I'd never get up, and suddenly, at five o'clock, just like a normal person, I was finished. I'd remembered all the touching up I wanted to do, closed the paint, and washed up. I kept walking around to make sure I'd really done everything.

Ingrid had a check ready for me. "Thank you. I know it was a hard job."

"It wasn't so bad—you worked as hard as I did, we did it together."

We both laughed at that. I knew I should be hopping down those stairs, thinking about a shower and a steak, but I wanted her eyes on me for just another minute, and then I got taken in my her lips, the top one stretched a little over her teeth, the bottom one full. I bet they tasted good. I bet even her teeth tasted good. We weren't standing close together, but I knew she wasn't that far away, either, and I remember thinking, you can do it now or you can wonder about it for the rest of your life.

I really only meant to kiss her. But her lips were even fresher and softer than I expected, and her cheek smelled tart, like lemon. I wanted to go on breathing it. Then she put her arms up around my neck, resting them on my shoulders, and I could feel the smooth, untanned part of her arm. I moved my shoulders on that smooth skin, put my arms around her waist, then pulled her closer to feel all the skin, smell her neck, like lemon, gather her up and run.

So we went on like you always do, or always think you will and without trying I stopped thinking. That was one of the best things about it—I didn't think. I just did it.

But it was no dream. She was almost as strong as I was, her stomach hard and tasting salty. And I got to see the beautiful legs again, feel them all along mine, firm as a runner's and the thighs sleek with tiny gold hairs.

Afterward I opened my eyes to the ceiling I had painted the day before and thought, what can she be thinking? I turned on my side quickly and she looked over at me in that calm, serious way of hers. And I had the sense to stop thinking again and keep quiet.

"Good luck," she said when I left.

Good luck! I held luck in my hands, in my pockets, I could feel it in the sleeves of my shirt. For the first block, I kept my eyes lowered, or someone would arrest me for having robbed the city of its luck.

But at the corner I had to wait for the light, and standing there I began to feel skinny, like the days when I used to slip through a slatted fence to the baseball games.

That's how it went, all the way across town. One block I'd think, they're mine—the luck, the city, and the girls—the beautiful, tender girls, waiting, asking you to open this can of turpentine or move that carton over there, and smiling back at you.

Then a minute later I'd get a flash of something else—like the time George's old wooden ladder fell apart right under me, and there was nothing I could do except listen to the air go by and watch the floor come up to meet me.

Eclipse

David Long

I came home on borrowed rides, east across the sun-blinded distances of
Nevada and Utah, north into the forests of Montana, slouched on the
cracked seats of pickups, remembering indistinctly what had taken me
away and more vividly what I had found. In the back of my mind was the
idea that being home would put an end to it. The green-painted man was
dead in the bathtub, over-dosed beyond bliss. The shower head had
dripped all night on his startled face, rivulets of poster paint streaking the
porcelain, as if the life inside him had putrified and drained itself. He was
nobody I knew. None of them were. So I had stepped into the early
morning glare, made my way out of San Pedro's dockyards, squinting at
the furious light, fighting off the stink of casualties. The curiosity had
burned off me like a dusting of black powder. It was nothing religious after all, only rumors and attractions, an itch in the bloodstream I had taken
with full seriousness. The Indian dropped me on the corner by the Western-
wear store. "Hey, you take care of yourself," he yelled, pulling away, the
beer cans rattling in the empty bed of his truck.

The wind blew dust in my eyes. I recognized nobody on the streets. I
found that the wave which had carried off so many of us who grew up here
had left only the most stubborn and in my absence they had made families
and leaned into their work as if they were born to it. I felt born to no
work in particular and had long ago been absolved of kin, having no brothers or sisters, a father who had filled his veins with a substance used to eu-
thanize household pets, and a mother who had found religion in an Arizona
retirement community. Though I figured it was as much mine as anyone

else's, I was not carefully remembered in this town and I thought I could use this fact to begin a normal, unobtrusive life for myself. Within a year I married Johanna, a big, pleasant girl whose red curls hung thick and guileless around her shoulders, whose skin smelled of salt and flour, who tended to simple jokes and loose clothes of khaki and checked flannel. If she was on a quest it was for nothing ethereal or terribly hard to locate. I must have seemed like a survivor of distant wickedness, a man in need of good intentions. It was true and I was grateful for the real affection she lavished on me, never understanding it clearly, always fearful she loved the mothering more than its damaged object. I ate her carob cookies, her hardly-risen soybean breads, her breakfast rolls suffocating in honey. I never yelled, I never threatened. After suppers on late summer nights, after the thunderstorms had cleared the air, we would walk along the bank of the low-running river, the swifts darting around our heads, the silence between us comfortable enough. I would watch her sit in the debris of washed-up stones, her soft chin lifted to the light as she studied the familiar pattern of mountains which surrounded us, her eyes unable to hide their satisfaction. Saturday nights we drank Lucky Lager at the Amvets and danced around and round to the soothing tunes of Jan Dell and her band, Johanna's favorite. Home again in the insulated darkness of the trailer's bedroom, she would clutch me, so full and earnest I thought I had succumbed—to her, to every bit of it.

Johanna's father, Darrell, was the district Petrolane distributor, and though he took me with suspicion, he was persuaded to give me a job driving one of his gas trucks. Every day I followed a lazy loop of junctions and wheat towns, contemplating the horizon—stubbled or rich-tasselled, depending on the season. Sometimes the sheer size of the panorama gave me a taste of the planet's curvature, a glimpse of the big picture, but I couldn't hold it. When I stopped I would stand by the truck and listen to the troubles of the ranchers, nodding as if I truly sympathized. Every night I came home and kicked my boots off and stretched out on the recliner by the TV like a thousand other husbands in town.

Johanna had a son the next year and when he had grown past earliest infancy he looked so much like her I saw none of myself in him. She named him Eric after her father's father who had died some months before. He was solid and cheerful, everything I was not. Johanna grew less tolerant. When she wanted to lighten my mood she would come and tell me, "You have a boy you can be proud of." It was not pride but panic I felt. I would often wake and see his round clear-eyed face inches from mine as though he had stood for hours waiting for me to wake. I knew there was something that should flow between us, as unasked for as spring water or moonlight. At night I would lay him in the bottom of the bunkbed he, so far, shared with only the dark room. I would try to make up stories to send him off to a good sleep. Nothing came.

"Tell him what it was like when you were a boy," Johanna said. "He'd like anything from you."

"It's a blur," I told her.

"What is it with you?" she said.

"If I knew I'd fix it," I said.

"Would you?"

I turned away from her and went out and started the pickup and backed it out as far as the mailboxes and couldn't decide which way to turn. I shut off the engine and in a moment lay down on the bench seat and tried to clear my head. I fell asleep hugging myself in the cool November air. When I woke there was a skim of snow on the hood of the truck. I walked back to the trailer. She had left a message on the refrigerator door, spelled out in Eric's magnetic letters. *Give or Go.* I went to the bedroom. A brittle ballad was coming from the clock radio. "Listen," I said, shaking her shoulder, but she was deep asleep.

One Friday afternoon, after the long wasting winter had gone, I came home from my route, later than normal since I'd stopped along the way for two Happy Hours, and found Johanna and Eric gone. In fact, it was all gone, the trailer house and everything. I climbed out of the truck, dumbstruck, a fine rain soaking my hair. Deep tracks curled through the shoots of pale grass I'd finally made grow. The muddy plywood skirts were strewn like a busted poker hand. I was wiped clean. The only thing left on the lot was the empty dog house, canted and streaked after a bad season.

In his office the next morning Darrell handed me my last paycheck in a licked-shut envelope and went back to what he was doing, punching the digits on his pocket calculator as if they were bugs.

"That all you're going to tell me?" I asked him.

"That's about got it," Darrell said.

"What'd I do? Tell me that?"

Darrell's eyes disappeared in a squinty smile. He slid the snoose around inside his mouth.

"Near as I can tell," Darrell said, "you didn't do a goddamn thing."

I took a third story room at the Frontier Hotel and sat on the cold radiator and watched the spavined old horse-breakers limp in and out of the cafe across the street, their straw hats like barnacles stuck to their heads. I quietly considered the loss of my wife and child and felt nothing sharp—except surprise and when I focused on that I realized that the breakup had been a sure thing all along. Her letter came without a return address. Don't worry, she said, she wouldn't be hounding me for money, Darrell had taken care of her. About Eric she said: *He won't remember you. I believe it's just as well.* About her reasons she said only: *I'm sorry, I won't be your rest cure.*

The sun finally took control of the valley. Lilacs flowered outside the dentist's office, road crews patched chuck holes up and down Main Street, the foothills shone in a green mist above the roof of the abandoned Opera House. Strangers nodded *howdy* on the sidewalks. Everything was repairing itself and I was out of time with it. Years before, I had felt myself choking in this town and blamed its narrow imagination and gone off looking for something Bigger Than Life. Now I didn't have the heart to move nor any trace of destination.

I found work at a small outfit south of town which manufactured camper shells for pickups. There I met Clevinger, a scrawny, tiny-eyed man my age, a twice-wounded survivor of Vietnam patrols. He'd worn the others out with his chatter and fixed on me as soon as I arrived. I listened as long as I could. Clevinger's idea of heaven was twenty acres up the North Fork, heavily timbered and remote, a place to disappear. Every afternoon after work he drove out and looked at parcels of land that only a few years earlier he might have afforded, and every morning he jabbered about the bastards who owned the money. As he talked he flexed the muscles in his arms which were white and hard as if they had grown underground. He was a man who'd changed, so certainly I didn't need to know how he'd been before. It showed as visibly as cracks running across his face. Seeing him like that made me know that I was not so different, though I had nothing like jungle warfare to blame it on.

It was a hot rainless summer. The wilderness areas flared with fire time and again, and one afternoon in early September a burn started in a tinderdry draw near town and crept over the close-by foothills. Clevinger and I left the shop and stood in the parking lot watching the black smoke billow above the fireline. A team of helicopters swooped in from all sides, spraying bright reddish streams of fire retardant, through which the sunlight came streaked and bloody. Clevinger said nothing, his arms hugged tight against his skinny chest, the pale skin around his eyes jerking as the smoke drifted over us. It was the next day Clevinger exploded in the shop. All of a sudden he was down in a fiery-eyed crouch, strafing the room with his pneumatic nailing gun. I was caught in the open, carrying a half-built assemblage with a boy named Buster. Clevinger hit us both. The first cleat took Buster above the wrist; he yipped and let go his end, the weight of it falling to me. My back snapped like a pop bead. As I went down a second cleat shot through my mouth, taking with it slivers of jawbone.

I lay flat on the concrete, choking on pain, staring up at the moldering light coming through the quonset's skylight, hearing shouts and grunts and finally the sound of metal striking Clevinger's skull. For weeks afterwards I could see the dark luster of Clevinger's eyes, the look that said it didn't matter who we were. It was nothing personal.

My back was badly torn but would heal if I behaved myself. My jaw had to be wired. When they let me out of the hospital I returned to my room at the Frontier and ate broth and Instant Breakfasts and anything else I could get to seep through my closed teeth. I called Workman's Comp

and discovered I was the victim of a policy called The Coordination of
Benefits. My caseworker, Wayne, treated me like I was both child-like and
dangerous. It was months before I saw a dollar. In the meantime there
wasn't much to do but stay put. My body began to mend itself, but my
imagination had time to dwell on things in earnest.

One night I woke from a late afternoon sleep, got out of bed, took two
or three steps across the room and halted in momentary amnesia. I had no
idea who I was. I stood there in my underwear, becalmed, entranced by
the blue prayer-like light filling my window, and then a few heartbeats later it all came back: the pain in my back, the peculiar tingle of mortality,
shards of waking dreams that added up to nothing but the sense of being
orphaned. I turned back to the bed, half expecting to see a woman's body
curled in the sheets, but there was no one at all.

I wandered across the hall to the bathroom, a narrow slot of a room
with only a lidless commode. When I hit the light switch the bulb flared
and died. I sat on the can with only the last smudge of light in the dusty
glass high over head. When I was done I discovered that my key was
twisted in the lock in such a way that the door would not open. I rattled
the handle. Nothing. A strong cry might've summoned one of the other
tenants of that dim corridor, but their ears were old and tuned a lot out,
and besides that, the hardware in my mouth let me only growl, like a grog-
gy yard dog.

I sat down.

The darkness was complete. Minutes went by and I didn't move, didn't
holler, didn't lift my head. I felt perfectly severed, as though I had waked
into a world I had always known would be there, a silent starless place
where the species began and died in utter solitude, one by one by one. I
thought of Johanna and Eric, saw their faces floating like reflections, the
blackness shining through them. I knew I had not been brave in losing
them, only stiff and sullen. I hadn't understood until now the truth of it:
that I had not loved her, that I wasn't able to. I had wanted a family for
comfort and retreat. All the times I had mumbled love in the dark were
counterfeit. And she had known it first, known it pure and simple.

I had gone on and made a son and covered my lack of father feeling
with an impatient, tin-faced act. Maybe it was true and good he would not
remember me, maybe he would grow toward his own adulthood with only
a strange hulking shadow lurking in the backwaters of his memory. Or
maybe Johanna would turn up a big-hearted man who could believe a small
boy's love was worth the world and Eric would grow into such a man himself.

The sadness oozed around me like a primeval silt. I was stuck in a closet
stinking of mold and old men's urine and didn't care to free myself. I could
blame myself, or not. I could curse the luck of the draw or the God I never
knew. None of it mattered. The world takes it from you, regardless—even

the thrill, even the energy to complain. There was nothing holy and no-thing magical and no point believing it was a quest of any kind.

Shivering, in my Jockey shorts and faded Grateful Dead T-shirt, I started to cry, so hard it was more like a convulsion, every beat of it wincing up and down my backbone. Some time later I became aware of a pounding on the door and then the clicking of a key. It was then, for the first time, I saw Mr. Tornelli, his great head haloed by the red light of the EXIT sign across the hall.

"What's this?" Mr. Tornelli said.

I could say that Mr. Tornelli saved my life, but it wasn't right then, nor did the man seem a likely redeemer.

"Listen, Jack," he said, squinting into the cubicle, "You move your belly-aching out to the hall a minute, OK? I need the shitter."

In a moment I was in the world again, suddenly quieted. I didn't go back to my room but stood on the strip of balding carpet, waiting. Mr. Tornelli emerged after awhile, his eighty-year-old back a little straighter, his suspenders fastened, his collarless white shirt glowing in the weak light. His head seemed too big for the wickery body it rested on, and his moustaches—there were clearly two of them—were folded down over his mouth like wind-ruffled ptarmigan wings. Composed now, he studied me like a puzzle.

"You got pants?" Mr. Tornelli said.

I didn't answer.

He shook his head gravely. "Listen," he said, "you put your pants on and come down to my room. I'll wait right here."

A moment sometimes arrives when you see the different people you are and have been all at once. It happens without warning, the way a sudden shift of light will show depths in water. Before I'd gone into the bathroom I would have shirked the old man's offer, made a note to shun him in the halls. But I stood nodding at him, found myself pulling on my jeans and accompanying him to his room, the last one on the floor, the one next to the fire escape.

"You know this vertigo?" Mr. Tornelli said.

He walked slowly, both hands a little elevated as if holding imaginary canes.

"Afraid of heights?" I said.

He bent to hear my muffled voice. "No, no," he said. "Not afraid of high places. It's. . ." He stopped and swivelled his head toward me and twirled his fingers in the air. "Feels like everything whirls."

"Bad," I said.

Mr. Tornelli smiled. "You get used to it."

Rooms at the Frontier were stark, unremitting. Out of superstition I had refrained from making mine any more attractive. Just passing through, the bare walls said. It was immediately clear that Mr. Tornelli didn't see it that way. His was bright and well-appointed: the bed was neatly made, covered with a star-pattern quilt; succulents and African Violets and Wandering Jews crowded on the desk by the southwest window; the walls obscured by maps and star charts and color blow-ups. A giant photo-illustration of the full moon hung directly over his pillow.

Mr. Tornelli urged me to make myself comfortable. That wasn't possible, of course, but I eased into his straight-backed chair and looked at his little kingdom. He nodded matter-of-factly and sank into his white wicker rocker and folded his hands.

"So," Mr. Tornelli said, widening his great sapphire eyes. "You are a troubled boy and not in a good position to talk about it."

I tried to push the words forward with my tongue, a futile effort. Mr. Tornelli waved me off.

"Don't bother," he said. "You'll just swim around in it." He made an extravagant two-handed pulling motion. "Then you'll want a rope. Forgive me, but I'm not up to it any more." He laughed with a kind of brittle pleasure. "When you get it down to one sentence, then I'll listen. Would that be all right?"

He rousted himself from the chair and went to the dresser.

"But then you won't need me, will you? No, for tonight's trouble there's brandy," he said. "Perhaps I should shoot it into your mouth with a syringe. Would you like that?"

So Mr. Tornelli and I drank the brandy. It worked on me as it does in high timber, back to the wind—I stopped shivering. The cipher of ice in the middle of me began to melt under its heat.

I noticed after awhile that right above the chair where he sat there was a brilliant photograph of a total eclipse: a golden ring shining around a black disk. Mr. Tornelli admitted having taken it.

"Kenya, 1973. Extraordinarily clear, no?"

I nodded.

"It was a good turnout that year, but blistering. Some of these young watchers are very zealous. I spent most of my time under a beach umbrella—and there was some kind of flying ant that laid eggs in your hair." He threw open his hands. "Ah, but I wouldn't have missed it. Over seven minutes dark. I had planned that it would be my last one, but maybe I was wrong." He smiled broadly. "I might live until February and see the one here."

"Too many clouds," I managed to say.

"I know," Mr. Tornelli said. "A bad season for the sun. But I think we might be fortunate that day."

He stood, momentarily fighting the spinning in his head, then began giving me the guided tour: Caroline Islands, 1934; Boise, 1945; Manila, 1955; the Aleutians, 1963. A trajectory of blotted suns progressing across his wall.

"I hope you forgive me my fascinations," he said. "Let me tell you a se-

scret. I was born during the eclipse of 1900. My mother was crossing Louisiana on the train and stopped long enough in New Orleans to have me. Do
you think I am a marked man?"

He laughed again and for the first time in a long while I smiled.

"Do you know," he began again, "*eclipse* means *abandonment*? It does.
Abandonment. Can you imagine what it would be like if you didn't know?
Everything's going along just like always, then *poof,* no sun. *Imagine.*
You'd have some fancy explaining to do.

"The Ojibaways thought the sun was going out so they shot burning ar-
rows at it to get it going again. Another tribe thought all the fire in the
world was going to be sucked up by the darkness so they hid their torches
inside their huts. People have come up with a number of stories...."

In the coming months the local papers would have a bonanza with the
eclipse, playing science off legend. They told about Hsi and Ho, two luck-
less Chinese astronomers so drunk on rice wine they blew their prediction
and were executed, and about coronas and shadow boxes and irreparable
damage to the eye. In all I read I felt a strange longing for an ignorance
that could make it crucial and magical. I thought about Mr. Tornelli's attraction and it seemed that some of the raw amazement survived in him.

"We had a great friendship in those days," Mr. Tornelli said in a while.
"We would meet every few years, take in the spectacle and then go back
where we came from. Never saw each other in between. All unspoken.
Well, many of them are surely dead by now."

"Why are you here?" I asked him finally. It was the only important
question I had.

"Why this fleabag? That's very good," Mr. Tornelli said, stroking the
feathers of his moustache. "Where do you go when you can go anywhere?
You think it matters? I guess. To tell the truth, I knew a woman in this
town once. A married lady, I'm afraid." He drifted for a moment. "Well,
I remember how it was to be here and love somebody. Amazing, isn't it?
Sometimes I ask myself if this was all the same life."

A few minutes past three, Mr. Tornelli finally stood again and insisted
on walking me to my room. A comic, paternal gesture, it seemed to me. He
said goodnight. Neither drunk nor sober, I lay in bed listening to the silence
of the old hotel, the place the old man and I had come to. I imagined what
it was made of: dentures soaking in a water glass, an old woman's dotted
Swiss hanging in a closet with a lavender sachet, dreams beginning and ending in some rooms and in others only the silence that follows the departure
of one of our number. It was a powerful chord. I realized that Mr. Tornelli had done nothing except come between me and myself. Alone again, the
trouble was with me. In the moments before sleep I tried to say its name
in the simple sentence he wanted but I could not.

Autumns here aren't the fiery poignant seasons they have in country

with hardwoods and rolling hills. They are as abrupt here as the terrain.
Indian summer vanishes overnight, clouds pour in from the northwest and
smother the valley like dirty insulation. The rain comes quickly and strips
the few maples and elms in a day, leaving the slick leaves puddled around
their trunks like fool's gold. I woke late that next morning and a single
look at the color of light in my window told the story. My back had seized
up overnight. It took many minutes to get upright, shuffle to the sink and
rinse the scum from my mouth with hydrogen peroxide. Mr. Tornelli
seemed like a figment of last night's gloom.

I dressed and went down carefully to the pay phone and called Wayne
at Workman's Comp. He sounded edgy. The computer in Helena had spit
out my claim again. "Of course," Wayne said, "You know that *personally*
I feel you're qualified. You know that, don't you?" I hung up on him
and walked two blocks to the bank where the story was no better. Coming
out I saw my ex-father-in-law heading toward the cafe. He speeded up to
avoid me, then apparently thought better of it. He stopped and took me
by the shoulders and gave me a good American once-over.

"You look like shit, you know that?" Darrell said.

"That's good news."

A logging truck rumbled past us, downshifting at the intersection, snort-
ing black smoke in a long vibrant blast.

"How's that now?" Darrell said, leaning in a little.

"I'd kick you down to the Feed & Grain," I said.

"No, you wouldn't," Darrell said. "You wouldn't do nothing. Boy, let
me tell you, she had the angle on you all right."

He let go and shook his big pinkish head at me and walked off.

For weeks nothing seemed to change but the tiresome thaw and freeze
in my back. When I could walk any distance I scuffed through the town
park, the sad remains of the founding family's estate, watching the ducks
and Canadian honkers gather in the safety of the brackish pond. Mothers
knelt in the cold grass behind their kids as they tossed wads of stale bread
at the birds. I never had anything to give. Back at the hotel I would sit on
the edge of the mattress and feel the tightening set in.

I saw almost no one, except old Mr. Tornelli. Days he didn't answer his
door I went away undernourished, aimless and vaguely dizzy. But most often he was there and ushered me in with a bright courtesy, as if he'd waited
all day for me. He took my silence for granted. He talked freely, sprinkling
the air with different voices. Sometimes I truly thought there was more
than one of him. He had stared through the giant telescope at Mount Palo-
mar; he had ridden boxcars from San Diego to the Midwest, once delivering
a baby of a homeless woman in the light of a mesquite fire near the tracks;
he had been an optics engineer at Polaroid. He had once been fired from a
teaching position in Wisconsin for being a Communist, which he wasn't,
and later asked to guest-lecture as a blackballed scientist, which he declined.

He had once shaken hands with Neils Bohr, the physicist, outside a hotel in Stockholm. He had taken peyote with Indians in a stone hogan in the mountains of New Mexico. In his vision he had become water, felt himself evaporating from the leaves of the cottonwood and rushing into the upper air and being blown high over the mountains with others like himself, then the great sense of weight and falling at terrific speed through the darkness.

"*Outstanding,*" Mr. Tornelli said. "One of a kind."

I listened patiently. I came to suspect that his talks were something more than reminiscence, that they were aimed at me as if he knew the dimension and velocity of my mood. He always seemed to stop short of conclusions: the stories hung unresolved, in the air.

"Puzzling, isn't it?" he would say with a quick opening of the hands, as if he were releasing a dove, or maybe releasing his grip on all that his mind had tried to bring together. I was entertained, I was diverted, I was moved.

Eight weeks to the day after Clevinger's outburst, the wires were removed from my jaw.

"So," Mr. Tornelli said. "Your tongue is out of its cage. A drink, to celebrate?"

"Thank you."

He handed me a gold-rimmed glass and retired to his chair.

"Now maybe you can tell me about all this gloomy stuff," he said.

"I think you know about it," I said.

Mr. Tornelli leaned forward on his elbows, the light glowing on the waxy skin of his forehead. He looked at me a long time before speaking.

"There was a time," he said finally. "I was at sea, on a freighter in the North Atlantic." He paused, as if squinting the memory into focus. "I couldn't sleep and there wasn't a soul to talk to. I went out and stood at the railing and stared at the ship's wake. My mind was empty except for the picture of my feet disappearing, then my shirt, my head, no brighter in the moonlight than a trace of the ship's foam. Let me tell you, I was right there, a little drunk...."

"What was it?"

"Who knows? A bad time, a bad year. I was sick to death of my failures. I thought the world was a hopeless place. I stayed there all night, and then the horizon lightened a little, the wind came up, and I realized...."

"What?"

He smiled lightly. "I was freezing. Freezing."

Then there were times he just let me in and returned to his chair and said nothing. As winter descended on us these occasions seemed more frequent. The silences weren't painful, but it was those times I could see him without distraction. Surrounded as he was by the battery of eclipses, the piles of spine-cracked books, *Scientific Americans,* flip-top steno pads filled with his faint ciphering, he seemed little and doomed. As he breathed his ribs creaked like a ship's rigging. Sometimes he closed his eyes, battling the vertigo that spun fiercely in his head, fingering the gold medallion he wore around his neck. I finally understood that I had seen a man in his last brilliance. If my affliction was elusive and hard to name, his was as common as birth.

January was a menace. Days of cold froze the ground many feet deep and left anything exposed to the air brittle. Great clouds of exhaust drifted down the rows of pickups idling on the side streets, so thick they would hide a man. Steam rose to the ventricles of the top-floor radiators and we kept warm, the air in our rooms so humid we might have been in a sanitarium. Mr. Tornelli's plants flourished but he seemed more and more unwell. His cheeks were smudged with shadows. I remembered how Johanna bent to the bedroom mirror smearing rouge on her face to invoke the same illusion. Mr. Tornelli was coming by it with a swiftness that prickled the darker chambers of my imagination. He had shown himself to be a man who took care of himself—with grace and dignity—but now I realized there were whole days when he failed to eat.

I began escorting him around the block to a small restaurant which served steamed vegetables with its dinners. It catered to the nearby old folks home crowd, and there, in the midst of his peers, Mr. Tornelli nursed languid bits of Swiss steak and seemed to me for the first time, no eccentric, no quaint loner. Sometimes I would catch him staring at the others and blinking.

"I don't know, Jack," he said softly. "Who are they?"

Midway through February the cold broke and in the space of ten days the temperature rose fifty degrees. We could scarcely look at things for the sheen of the melting everywhere. As the date of the eclipse came nearer I expected Mr. Tornelli's enthusiasm to rekindle. Surely he would muster some sort of celebration. He said nothing. I told him I could get a car and drive up to the National Park, just the two of us. I told him I would help him get his cameras out again. He didn't want to talk about it. He was as short with me as I'd ever heard him. I backed off and waited.

The night of the 25th, Sunday, I went to his door convinced some excitement would show in him. There was no answer to my knocks. He had been sleeping irregularly then, so I swallowed my worry and left the hotel. The sky was streaked, but when I entered the darkness of the alley across the street, I could see a few stars. Months ago he had known the sun would shine. I leaned on a dumpster behind one of the bars and stared up through a film of tears. A police car flashed its spot down the alley and I recovered myself and went in and had a few glasses of beer, though the liveliness of the bar seemed desperate and stupid to me. It was almost midnight when I came out. From the sidewalk I could see the lights blazing in Mr. Tornelli's window.

I ran upstairs and knocked again and this time the silence was terrifying.

I shook the doorknob hard against the deadbolt. I thought I was already
too late. Finally I heard his voice, high and boyish.

"Are you all right?"

"Good enough," Mr. Tornelli said through the locked door.

"Could I come in?"

There was a long silence.

"Mr. Tornelli?"

"Jack."

"Right here."

"Could you let me be alone tonight? Would that be all right?"

"I want to be sure you're OK."

"Goodnight, Jack," Mr. Tornelli said with a queer force. I turned and
went back to my room. I left all the lights on, thinking I'd get up in
a while and check on him. When I woke the sun was up, blasting gold off
the windows of the abandoned Opera House.

It was after eight. The moon was already nearing the face of the sun.
Still in last night's clothes, I ran down the hall and found Mr. Tornelli's
door ajar. I walked in but he wasn't there. The walls and bed and desk
were stripped. A black steamer trunk sat in the middle of the floor, heavy
and padlocked. Even the plants were gone.

I ran down to the desk and asked what was going on with Mr. Tornelli
but nobody'd seen him. I ran to the restaurant and stood at the end of the
counter scanning the old heads bent over their poached eggs, but Mr.
Tornelli's wasn't among them. Back at the Frontier I was desperate. I
went up and down the corridor knocking on doors. He wasn't in the can.
Mrs. Bache hadn't seen him. No one answered at 312. Mr. Karpowicz in
309 offered to break my jaw again. It was just after his door slammed that
I saw what I'd missed.

The door to the fire escape was propped open with one of Mr. Tornelli's
African Violets. The other plants huddled together on the metal slats of
the landing. I turned and saw Mr. Tornelli's little medallion looped through
the bottom rung of the old ladder that led eight steps to the roof. My
heart pounded.

As I poked my head over the edge of the roof, the sunlight was growing
gently dimmer on Mr. Tornelli. He was seated on half a hotel blanket laid
over the moist tar and pea-stones, cross-legged and tiny. This old man who
knew the science of light, who had followed the shadow of the sun around
the world, was at this moment sitting there staring naked-eyed into the
eclipse.

He patted the empty spot next to him.

"Just in time, my boy," Mr. Tornelli said. "Sit please, keep me company."

I joined him on the blanket.

"Keep your eyes down now—don't ruin them," he said.

Darkness came over our part of the world in waves, stronger and faster now. The sparrows fell silent, the sound of tires faded from the streets below. The corona emerged brilliant from the black disk of the moon.

I took Mr. Tornelli's hand and held it in both of mine.

"I didn't know where you were," I said.

"Yes," Mr. Tornelli said. "You had to find me."

"I didn't know."

"So," he said, whispering, though in the stillness his words were bright and clear. "You see how it is with trouble and happiness. There are some good moments, aren't there. Were you asking for more than that?"

All at once the stars were everywhere, pelting their grace down on us.

"This is, ah, what can I say.... We come this far and you and I change places. It's good."

He shut his eyes, smiling still. I leaned over and drew his head down to my shoulder and stroked it as the breath labored in and out of him. The darkness began to ease, the slightest lightening visible at the edge of things.

Vietnam No Big Deal

James Park Sloan

Do you know of any writer who wrote a whole story just to provide the proper setting for a single line? When I was a kid, I used to wonder about that kind of thing. I would read stories through trying to find the single line which had popped into the writer's mind in the middle of a dinner party, or while he was jogging or giving a lecture, and which he had written down on the inside back cover of a notebook in big letters or on a piece of memo paper taped to the wall above his typewriter with a note in parentheses: (PUT INTO STORY!)

I have filled a good many notebooks with lines of my own, but it wasn't until the other night at a dinner party that I knew I had bumped into the real thing. There were about a dozen of us, English professors and writers in various stages of germination, growth, and fruition, and we had gotten onto the subject of the colossal Vietnam films of the last couple of years. Somebody said that films were going to be the primary artistic response to that particular war. Somebody else said that the big Vietnam novel hadn't been written yet. While they were talking, this phrase started pounding away in my head: *Vietnam, No big deal.* Two anapests, just like that. A sort of a chant, or a drumroll. I didn't have the slightest idea where the phrase had come from, and only a vague sense of what it meant. That is, I knew where it fit into the conversation. Everybody had been giving opinions about the Vietnam films, whether they were faithful to reality or not, whether the insignia DeNiro wore were accurate, what they thought of Coppola's cinematography—that sort of thing—and my opinion of the films was that. They were nice, in a way, but they made Vietnam into more than it was. It was just a little war on the border of empires. The same thing had been going on for thousands of years, Roman legions in Gaul and Persia, the Greeks at Syracuse, etc., etc. Men went to places like that, put in a tour, got killed, went back, etc., etc. The films made too big a deal of it. It was really a piece of film criticism: Vietnam. No big deal. Actually I was looking for a way to work it into the conversation. One of the wives noticed I hadn't said anything for a while and took it upon herself to pull me back into the party. "You were there, weren't you?" she said. "What do you think about it?"

To tell the truth I had been drifting a bit, and I couldn't tell for sure if she was asking me about the war in general or some question about one of the movies she assumed I had overheard. I was totally engrossed in trying to find the proper surrounding for my line, and if I had had my way about it I would have preferred to go home that instant and write the line down in the inside back cover of a notebook. In all honesty, I was a little afraid of forgetting it, or of failing to remember it exactly. You wouldn't think a person would be able to forget a little phrase like that—six syllables, with two anapests to prod the memory—but you would be surprised at the little things a person is able to forget. She kept looking at me with a slightly stupid expression on her face and a smile that was beginning to sag a little, and then I remembered that she had spoken last, and according to convention I was obligated to speak next. I noticed that she had pale blonde hair and pale blue pupils and that the white of her eyes was beginning to get bloodshot from the wine and that the fold of her upper eyelid had an almost perfectly Oriental lotus shape. Suddenly I wanted to tell her something terrifically wise about Vietnam, some deep, powerful truth, but the truth is that Vietnam had no effect on me. It didn't affect me a bit. I was able to use it as an excuse afterwards, once when I punched a professor in grad school and again when I got carried away and roughed up a neighbor's kid who had been picking on my boy. At grad school they offered me all kinds of extra help and special indulgences if I had trouble concentrating on my papers, but I concentrated as well as I ever had, maybe a little better, in fact. Once when my wife caught me eating out of the salad bowl with my fingers, she shook her finger at me and said, "What a horror! That must be something you picked up in Vietnam. Now tell me, that's what it is, isn't it, they eat lettuce there with their fingers?" I told her that in Vietnam even the wealthy classes ate rice and meat by wrapping them in lettuce like Moo Shoo Pork. I decided to tell that to the stupid wife with the lotus eyes, but when I opened my mouth I couldn't get it to come out. Instead I said, "Vietnam? No big deal."

For the next few days the line kept going through my head in a low rumble. For a while I wondered if it wasn't meant to be a book title. I had a friend once who could never decide if his Vietnam line was a book title or not. His line was: *I really don't want to talk about it.* He ended up using it for the first line of his book (the whole book was a single line with a two-hundred page parenthesis), and for his title too. After a while my friend dropped out of sight, and since I have never run across a book by that title, I assume that wasn't what the line was meant to be. I decided that my line wasn't meant to be a title either.

I mentioned to a colleague that I was thinking about doing another novel on Vietnam. I had done a Vietnam novel already, but it wasn't really so much about Vietnam as about the inside of one man's head, and for that reason the critics thought it was anti-war. It used to make me nervous when other Vietnam veterans saw the book and thought we had something in common. If there is one thing we don't have in common, it is the inside of my head. My colleague understood all this perfectly.

"What you want to write this time," he said, "is a full-fledged, main-line, head-on war novel about Vietnam. No novel about Vietnam has ever engaged the war head on."

He had it exactly right. I was sick to death of work that had a few scattered and unrelated anecdotes from Vietnam. I went home and wrote notes for a novel on the back page of a scholastic notebook upside down. I write particularly important notes upside down so the first line is at the top of the page and the little unlined section is at the bottom. I wrote out characters' names. The hero was a Captain Royce (or Boyce: Royce is an obscure philosopher, while Boyce was the surname of my first declared love in the ninth grade) who is killed while conducting the futile defense of an obscure outpost. Royce is a philosophical West Point graduate who has read Toynbee and Spengler and Epictetus, and who is constantly telling the bewildered men on his Special Forces "A" Team that Vietnam is just a routine little war in the retreat of empire, a case study in rout and rally, etc., etc. The men have no earthly idea what he is talking about, but one of them, Sergeant Williams (a big amiable black man, the type who is reassuring because you think he might stand up in the black people's meeting and argue against murdering you in your bed; he is based on Sergeant Robinson, whom I knew during my first month in Vietnam) believes that there is something to what Captain Royce/Boyce is saying if he could only understand it. The "A" Team is assigned to defend an indefensible outpost. Here I jotted down the first line of the book, which goes as follows: *It was just a matter of time before the outpost at Cao Lac would have to be abandoned.* The point is that Cao Lac is not worth anything strategically, but the Americans do not want to give the appearance of being chased out. In this sense, of course, Cao Lac is a metaphor for the whole war, for any war on the boundaries of empire. Left to defend the outpost with a handful of native irregulars, Captain Boyce sends all of his men away except for Sergeant Williams/Robinson. Then at the last moment before the attack, he puts Williams/Robinson on a helicopter for Saigon with a phony packet of top-secret documents. I toyed with the idea of having Williams/Robinson punch the captain in the jaw and put *him* on the helicopter with the documents, but decided that wouldn't do. The outpost is wiped out. The "A" Team meets up in Saigon. Nobody knows what to say, but they try, and it sounds silly. They say what a tragedy Vietnam is and the loss of men like Royce; it is Sergeant Williams who says, "Vietnam, no big deal."

As soon as I finished the notes, I knew it would never work. The trouble was that Sergeant Williams could never have said the line. What he would have said when he heard the other men talking bullshit about the wipeout at the outpost (what Sergeant Robinson did say when he killed a Vietnamese civilian on a bicycle with a single shot from his jeep and they gave him an Article 15 and sent him home six months early) was: "It's a normal day." People sometimes say unexpected things, but you can't just make them say anything you want. Sergeant Robinson surprised me more than once. One time I told him I was planning to write a book about Vietnam when I got back, and he said, and I quote, "This motherfucker isn't worth writing a book about. What this motherfucker deserves is a little story." I could never think of a story to get that line into, but if I could think one up, surprising as it is, I don't think there would be any doubt that Sergeant Robinson said it. It wasn't him, but it was, in the same way that Vietnam no big deal was him, but it wasn't. It was the kind of thing he might have said, but it wasn't *the* thing he would have said.

When I catch another writer up in a mistake like that, I say a loud mental "Aha!" I said a big "Aha!," for instance, when Conrad had Mr. Kurtz say "the horror, the horror." Not that it isn't a wonderful line, it is, of course, but the point is that Mr. Kurtz didn't actually say it. He couldn't possibly have. Nobody could have. Brando couldn't say it in the movie. I like to picture Brando standing in front of a mirror for hours trying over and over again to say a line that nobody can possibly say. "The horror, the horror." The trouble with the line is that it is Conrad's line, not Kurtz's, not Brando's. Maybe not even Conrad's, maybe nobody's at all, because it isn't even a line, but an underlying assumption.

I decided it was that way with my line too. It kept drumming away in my head, Vietnam no big deal, but maybe that was the way it was with underlying assumptions. I tried another formulation. It is supposed to take some time, maybe a decade, they say, before a war begins to congeal into material fit for art. My colleagues confirm this, cite Hemingway, cite Heller, etc., etc. You have to acquire a certain distance. You must be able to say (that is, to not say) as an underlying assumption: Vietnam? No big deal.

You have to clear the reality out (search and destroy) to make room for the imagination. Ten years is about the right amount of time. It took approximately ten years for me to get rid of my own Vietnam artifacts.

When I first came back, I had a beret, some medals, and a roll of pictures I posed for in a tiger suit the day before I left for Saigon. The first thing to go was the beret. I used it as a prop for a skit in an Italian language class. The other fellow in the skit had for a prop a towel from the university linen service. I sat at a desk with the beret turned backward (so you didn't notice the 5th Special Forces Group insignia, although of course everyone did notice it; they just noticed it was on backwards) and shouted, "Camerederie camerederie." The other fellow came over with the towel draped over his arm like a waiter and said, "Signore?" and I said, "Un cafe, per favore." At the end of class I left with the girl from the back row who was supposed to notice the Special Forces insignia. I was so busy telling her sad and moving anecdotes about Vietnam that I entirely forgot about the beret. The last time I saw it, it was lying on the radiator in the classroom assigned for Italian 102.

I was sorry to lose the beret, but when I think about it, it strikes me as a fair exchange. From Hemingway, etc., we know that a war owes every man a book and a woman, the difference with Vietnam being that you had to wait and get the woman when you got back. The book took a little longer, and there were more women, and then the woman who was responsible for the disappearance of the medals. I made the mistake of talking about the war in front of her nephews; and being kids, they naturally wanted to see the medals. There was no way of explaining to them that medals aren't things for kids to play with, so after they had looked at them for a while I said, "Go ahead, take them, you can have them," and naturally within a few weeks they were gone. You can't get too mad about that kind of thing. They were just treating the medals with the kind of value medals have for children. I did the same thing with my father's fatigue hat and canteen from the Pacific Theater. My only regret is that the medals couldn't wait for my own kids. Vietnam artifacts disintegrate fast.

The pictures were the last thing to go. Whenever I think of them, it seems just a few weeks ago, months at the most, that I ran across them in a stack of old papers. But the other day when I went to look for them, to show them to the woman from the dinner party, they were gone. I looked thoroughly, too, turning my desk and office and storage boxes inside out. I looked in books and behind drawers and down the back of cabinets where important slips of paper always fall. I looked in my secret places and rats' nests, but the truth which I had to acknowledge was that the pictures had finally been absorbed into the floating pile of everyday junk that is processed in and out of my life. Either that or they had decayed into the air. Vietnam had been cleaned out of my life.

Now I could make a fresh start. The line could pound away all day in my head. I knew exactly what it meant. Vietnam was over, finished for me. No big deal. I had it in perspective. I felt a little sorry for poor obsessed Conrad, sending Marlow through all those irrelevant scenes on the trip upriver just to give Mr. Kurtz a setting for his unspeakable double horror. The war was over for me; it was nothing to me now, so now I could really begin to write about it. The problem was that when I sat down to take notes in my upside down notebook nothing came to my mind. My mind was a total blank. All I could hear was those two anapests pounding away over and over again.

It had been the same way at the dinner party. When the dopey blonde wife asked me to tell a war story, it was the only thing that popped into my head. I had told war stories for years, in my book, at dinner parties, at lectures, in private confidences to people I sit on committees with, apropos of nothing to bores who engage me in tedious conversations, things that happened to me, things that happened to other people, my own fantasies, other people's fantasies, the communal fantasies that get told by every soldier as if they happened to him personally, the story of Sergeant Robinson and the old man on the bicycle, the story of the man who threw his body on the grenade that didn't go off, the story of the Special Forces Team that went over and only one came back, but when she asked me about Vietnam I couldn't think of anything but those anapests. What I finally ended up telling her was the story of Private Ennis J. Scarborough.

It was my last true story from Vietnam and I didn't even know Scarborough while I was there. Where I knew Scarborough was basic training. The whole company knew Scarborough, two hundred and fifty men. He was one of those tall boys with a big Adam's apple from a part of Tennessee where it's hard for a nonprofessional to distinguish where the local speech pattern leaves off and mental retardation begins. I suppose that's how Scarborough made it in in the first place. He did Right Face and Left Face with great difficulty, often in reverse, about About Face, requiring two separate and unrelated motions, was out of the question. He was never able to master manual of arms, couldn't get his rifle back together when it was disassembled for cleaning, and was hampered on the firing range by a crossed left eye. He never fell out in the morning wearing quite the prescribed uniform, and he was good for upwards of a dozen gigs at inspection unless somebody hit a few licks at his area. For some reason he had a knack for rolling socks into the neat little headless ducks the army likes them to be in your footlocker, and he would sit on his bunk for hours patiently making his own socks and anybody else's who asked into meticulous rolls which were compact and identical and without lumps. Because I could never quite get the lumps out myself, I had an exaggerated respect for this skill, which struck me as resembling some obscure, forgotten medieval craft. He also liked to run the big electrical buffer over the floor before Saturday inspection, but after he did it you had to be sure that somebody went over it again.

The other guys pitched in to try to get Scarborough through, but once he got outside the barracks it was hard to cover for him. A couple of times on firing ranges he turned around with a loaded weapon in his hands, and he had an unfortunate habit of smiling a jaw-busting Gomer Pyle smile whenever he was being chewed out. The NCOs gave him holy hell; the smile made it hard to tell when their shouting was getting through, and everybody was completely surprised when Scarborough went back to the barracks after a Saturday inspection and drank a bottle of what he called "wood alky-hol." When the guys found him, his face had turned blue and his eyes were rolled back in his head. I have a memory of Shapiro, the Jewish humanist who was made squad leader because he talked like a New Yorker (to whom Scarborough was a mystery, to whom the name Ennis was as foreign as Cathay) trying to take charge, slapping Scarborough hard in the face and shouting "Anus, anus" at the top of his voice directly into Scarborough's ear. I have a memory of the Tac, arriving a little later, scared out of his wits at the things that might come out if Scarborough died, getting Scarborough to vomit and lie still with a wet towel on his forehead until the ambulance arrived.

They kept him in the hospital for a week, and by the time he got back, training was almost over, the NCOs had begun to loosen up with everybody, and it was be-nice-to-Scarborough week until he shipped out. During that time he told us that everything had been fixed up hunky-dory. "Hunky-dory," he actually said, winked, and made a circle with his thumb and index finger. He had talked to them at the hospital, and they told him the army had made a mistake; he shouldn't have been in the combat arms anyway because of his eyesight. Now that he was in, what they had actually decided was to send him to cooking school. He had an uncle who was an army cook, Sp. 6, and the army had gone to the trouble of looking his uncle up and arranging to put Scarborough under his wing. Everything was going to work out hunky-dory. The big idiot smile was absolutely genuine, and he even seemed to improve a little bit at Left Face and Right Face; and when he broke ranks at graduation exercises the adjutant whispered something to the colonel who nodded and gave what seemed, from the parade field, the closest he had ever come to a benign smile. That afternoon we got on separate buses, and that was the last I thought of Scarborough for more than two years. I went to infantry AIT, airborne school, the Special Warfare Center, Vietnam, etc., etc. Scarborough presumably went to cooking school.

While I was in Vietnam, I fell into the habit of reading THE PACIFIC STARS AND STRIPES, the military newspaper and the last irrelevant and retarding episode of my own journey upriver. I started reading it to follow Sandy Koufax, who was in the middle of his best and last season, but after a while I began to read it like a trade publication the way doctors look at the AMA Journal and literature professors at PMLA. I kept up with technical information on the time in grade needed to make E5, the officers' promotion lists (and passovers, looking eagerly for my superiors), battle reports, etc., etc. With a general professional interest, I fell into the habit of reading the daily casualty lists. It was there, on a day in which nine Americans died, that I read the silent punch line: KIA—Sp. 4 Ennis J. Scarborough.

Don't ask me how. Don't ask me why. Don't ask me where, although it was in one of the units up in III Corps, maybe in the Iron Triangle. The goofy wife with the lotus eyes wanted to know all those things, but I couldn't help her. Maybe he screwed up somewhere, or there was a mistake in his orders, or he moved far enough away from the people who knew about him that he somehow got put back into the infantry. Maybe they got him while he was stirring a big pot of beans, driving a mess truck, serving a chow line under mortar fire. Beats hell out of me. It's a normal day. They just got him.

And suddenly, as I tell this, it comes back to me. It was Scarborough. That's where it comes from. It was in the beginning, when they were on him about not burn-shining his boots, weeks before he drank the alky-hol, the Tac blowing his stinking breath in Scarborough's face while we stood in morning formation, Scarborough smiling back that idiot's smile. The Tac was shouting at point blank range, "You fucking shape up or I'll personally see they ship your ass to Vietnam," and Scarborough answers back politely but firmly, cool as a cucumber, right through the idiot smile, "Vietnam ain't no big deal."

Creating and Destroying

Curtis Harnack

As the street door sighed shut behind her, she saw a vague movement in the darkness between Katz's piano store and the Puerto Rican Catholic church. She did not walk faster, though her blood ran. She never carried more than a few dollars in her purse, intending to hand it over if accosted, for she was seventy-six and knew the perils of living alone in a loft district. Her son Jim warned she'd be murdered if she didn't watch out.

After a hamburger and a cup of tea in a shop near the Chelsea Hotel, she walked back along deserted Twenty-Third Street, and when she neared her door, peered boldly into the shadows beyond the piano store. Perhaps she had only seen a cat trying to raid a garbage can. But when she stepped into the entranceway she smelled the biting, aggressive odor of the intruder. He was old and rumpled, slouched against the inner, locked door. She couldn't get in. "What're you doing here? Get out of this building!"

He was motionless as a sack of coal.

"Are you drunk? Can't you hear me? How'm I to get past you?"

She backed away, wondering if she could find a cop on Seventh, in front of the Veterans Administration building. But she didn't like to involve the police since she was technically outside the law living in her loft. Who would believe if she claimed she'd just come to do night work at her bench —at midnight? Half-way down the block toward Seventh she turned back, deciding she'd have to handle the matter herself.

The bum was gone. Probably a harmless wino. Quickly, she turned her key in the lock and slammed the door shut. Her footsteps creaked ominously as she mounted each step, up into the cavernous darkness. She asked herself: how long have I got?

A night of intermittent sleep, violent dreams. She thought of poor, mad Helen, her son's former wife. After the overdose of Thorazine which almost killed her, Jim consigned her to Central Islip asylum, where she'd remained the past ten years. Everyone said his flagrant womanizing was the cause, but in fact Helen's mental disturbances went way back. Once she slashed her wrists and ran into the street holding up her hands, blood in the white Turkish towel. Since it seemed best for the sake of the girls not to dwell on their mother's tragedy, they seldom spoke of her, rarely visited the hospital—particularly after Jim married the Irish Catholic general nurse, whom he'd hired to look after his daughters. She made no fuss about his philandering—who could know why? She was very devout and converted the girls.

Long ago when Jim was thirteen she'd enrolled him in a Virginia military school for discipline, a seemingly wise move for a widow with a rambunctious boy on her hands. The hard, masculine life down there only made him tougher. Later, in the business world, he drove shrewd bargains and was a ruthless competitor, hustling accounts for a brokerage house. Everyone thought him a great success.

She saw her grand-daughters almost every week, which was the only reason she remained living in New York. Before retirement from her office job at the Christian Council, she dreamt of someday returning to live in her hometown, Toronto. Her father had been a Methodist minister there. She'd never quite liked New York because of its size, the way the immensity seemed to separate one's life from casual connections. To see a tree you had to go to a park; it wasn't just outside the kitchen window. But now Toronto was the same.

Since her apartment was too big to maintain on her modest pension and she was too proud to accept funds from her son, she rented a loft not far from the flower district, an area she knew well. For many years she'd been creating paper flowers to sell at church bazaars and benefits and now had an outlet at Bloomingdale's. She'd studied books on the chemical properties of the famous attar of roses produced in Baghdad. She brewed up only vegetable dyes, some of which came from plants picked by nomad peasants on the tundras of Central Asia. All sorts of petal-like paper had been tested and perfected for her art.

Renovating the loft, particularly installation of plumbing, had cost a packet, but she hadn't spent much on furnishings. Sold all of her old stuff, just keeping a hump-backed trunk with family things the girls might someday want. Only two of her church friends came to see her in her new quarters. The others said the neighborhood frightened them or the stairs were too many—actually, they thought her a bit queer.

Evenings, she would sit at her window and watch the pigeons that congregated on the church roof wheel off into the sky. Light flashed from pane to pane in tall office buildings farther uptown. She waited for the stained glass window directly opposite to light up, as it always did for evening mass: Christ in the moment of His ascension, arms spread wide and face tilted back—floating right up to her in His billowy gown, blue ether all around Him. She had usually spent a satisfying day with her roses at the workbench—she could receive Him.

She awoke in alarm. Somebody was fiddling with the lock. Furtive whispers in the hall, thin moving shadows broke the hairline of light on the doorsill. No, they were at the door of the room next to hers, leased by a Princeton art student who kept his canvases there.

"Have you ever been to Fort Lauderdale?"

"My parents wouldn't let me."

"Why not?"

"You know why."

"Can't guess."

"Hey, not so fast!"

"Ah!"

A radio started up, loud rock music providing the privacy the thin walls didn't. She turned on a bedlamp and tried to read. It was starting to get light, so she rose and dressed. Dawn spread slowly—the glorious fact of one more day for her. What was the point of it? She knew in the sober light of this daybreak that she hadn't worked out her old age so perfectly after all.

Without looking into a mirror she put on her hat, thrusting a long hat pin into it, an auxiliary weapon, and went down to the street for a walk. Near the curb outside the coffee shop where she'd had her meal last night, she spotted the very same tramp who'd leaned against her door. He reached into garbage cans with fingers like claws, finding nothing. Each lid he lifted slowly, like a chef looking into big pots. There was such sadness in the resigned way he settled down the lids. At last he came up with a bit of hamburger roll. She hadn't finished hers last night—it might have been the very one. He stuffed his mouth without even looking at it, like some poor street hound. As she came closer he straightened up. His face was covered with warts and his right eye half hung out. "Don't eat that. It'll make you sick."

"I'se hungry."

"Here's a dollar. Go buy some breakfast."

He looked dumbfounded, then slyly gleeful, as if he'd just played a trick on her.

"Breakfast, I said. Not a bottle at the liquor store."

"No, Ma'am."

"I tell you what. Keep the dollar. You come back to where I live and sit on the steps of the church. Nobody's around this hour. I'll go upstairs and fetch your breakfast. Then you won't have to spend the dollar on it."

He dragged along behind her at a respectful pace, and she laughed at herself for being afraid of this old wretch, who had just been trying to crawl into a burrow last night, any doorway, any opening. She left him on the steps and told him to wait, then fixed scrambled eggs and a cup of coffee, with two slices of bread and butter. "Leave the knife and fork and plate just inside the door. I'll come down later and get it."

"Thank you, Ma'am."

She knew he could get a little change for her plate and cup somewhere —she was testing to see if he'd steal them. This encounter cheered her up considerably because the outcome was uncertain. Later, she retrieved her kitchenware, plate licked dog-clean. When the couple next door stirred alive at nine o'clock—back and forth to the hall toilet—loud music again, she opened her lock and hailed the blond, bearded man, asking if he and his friend cared for coffee and doughnuts. "Guess we're neighbors who haven't met. Come on in." They accepted her offer at once. As they sat at her table, their hands kept touching. They still hadn't gotten enough of each other, and just looking at them rubbing together made her feel good. She resolved never to become a sour old lady, shrink in her soul, turn inward. She'd do anything to avoid it. She would have to keep on giving, doing, creating; it must never stop.

The next day just as she was fixing the odor in the buds, which had to be done at precisely the right temperature, somebody knocked on her door.

"It's me." Nathaniel, the piano student from upstairs, whose face was the color of his ivory keyboard.

"Just a minute."

"A man's here to see you."

"Who?"

"He said you'd feed him."

"Oh, tell him to wait."

"He's right here."

"You let him *in* downstairs?"

"He said—he said you were...his wife."

"He *what*?" She dropped the buds—they were ruined anyhow, and in a rush of anger opened the door. There beside her pale Jewish piano student stood that miserable-looking beggar. "You don't have to make up wicked stories to get a hand-out. You could've pushed the buzzer and I'd've come down. But you can't come in here—I'm working. Nathaniel, I'm surprised at you. You'll believe anything!" In order to get rid of the old man, she handed him half a loaf of Pepperidge bread and a gouda. "Here, now take him out, Nathaniel!" She didn't like the way he was casing the premises.

Lately, her conversations with the piano student had dwelt on grievous social issues, for she'd been astonished to learn he never read a newspaper or looked at news reports on television. He was completely unaware and uninformed about life today. "Look around at the world! It's right here on Twenty-third Street. It'll do you good." He ought to know more than the range of his keyboard. "I started making these flowers and I felt I could take on the world if I had to. You keep playing that piano, and you'll eventually have to live up to the message of your music. Otherwise, forget it!"

Nathaniel reported later that the derelict's name was Hasker. He'd been raised in a Catholic orphanage in Baltimore, was about sixty-seven or sixty-eight, the date of birth uncertain, and until his sister died six years ago he'd been living with her in Brooklyn. No definite occupation. When Nathaniel asked, Hasker replied: "This'n that, over the years."

"Welfare should look into this case. We could refer him," she said, as they sipped tea at her table, "but you can read his character enough to know he would hate that."

"What'll we do, then?"

"Whatever you think."

"He sure needs a bath."

"There's one in the flower market, Twenty-first Street, I think. Take him there, why don't you?"

Finding it shut, Nathaniel traveled with him to a bathhouse on the Lower East Side. While Hasker was getting cleaned up, Nathaniel took the foul clothes to a laundromat. She was a bit surprised Nathaniel was willing to go so far with the old bum this quickly—and disturbed that the boy kept looking to her as mentor. He had almost learned his lesson too well from her and now was acting upon it more literally than *she* ever would have. Though she might regard Hasker as a stinking piece of creation, a compost pile for her rose-making, she had the good sense not to take her metaphors seriously.

Every day that Hasker came to see Nathaniel, the boy would tell her about it later: where they went, what they did. Rode the Staten Island ferry, spent an afternoon in the gardens behind the Brooklyn museum, watched the men playing chess in Central Park. Mostly he was taking Hasker somewhere to eat. "People look at us funny, but I'm getting over it. I guess I like it out in the open—that I'm different."

"All geniuses are different."

"I'm gay, you know."

"Lots of people *are* these days," she said smoothly, without a pause.

"So's Hasker."

"A lot of these old bums, they can be any which way, I guess. It's the liquor they lust after mostly." But she was shocked by the implications, for why was Nathaniel telling her this? What sort of relationship had developed? And to think she'd sent them off to the baths together!

"There's more to him than you ever imagined. He can quote Latin by the yard."

"Oh, his schooling—mine too, in the old days—often included Latin. That's not so much."

"The thing is, he oughtn't to be loafin' around the streets."

"I hope you're not thinking of letting him sleep in your studio."

"Why not?"

"Katz wouldn't stand for it! He'll throw both of you out."

"I've the feeling just a little push for Hasker now—might save him."

"Let me talk to Father Michael at St. Xavier's, since you say Hasker's Catholic."

"Oh, but lapsed."

"Even more interesting to them. You know the reason churches don't pay property taxes? They're supposed to be taking care of the poor. I like to remind these priests of that."

But the day of the appointment with Father Michael, Nathaniel couldn't find Hasker anywhere. He'd fled possible incarceration. "So...we tried," she consoled him.

Nathaniel went back upstairs to his piano, and as if to make up for lost time, spent six straight hours practicing those runs. The whole rickety house filled with his thundering music.

Her son Jim heard the rest of the tale.

For a couple of weeks we didn't see Hasker, and I told Nathaniel he'd gone because he didn't want to be caught. "He hopes to stay free, and we were trying to do too much for him." Then one day in November I took in a matinee at the Winter Garden and there he was in the shadows of the building. "Remember me? How are you, Hasker?"

"Cold 'n hungry. Give me a dollar."

I told him if he'd come by my place in about an hour I'd have an overcoat for him. After giving him car-fare I took a bus downtown to Sal the Tailor, on Fourteenth. I picked out a fairly thick, worn coat, for five dollars—didn't want anything so fancy Hasker wouldn't wear it. Mended a rip in the collar, before he rang the buzzer downstairs. I let him come right up and had him try on the coat. The stink of him drowned out my fine attar of roses, and I complained of the odor, with a smile. He said his dirty body kept him warm in winter, better 'n a clean one would. "Now you got an overcoat—you don't have to worry about not being warm. Wool is better than dirt."

"Ain't you gonna call Nathaniel?"

"He's not in."

He kept looking around my room, gimpy eye going a different direction from his other one. I couldn't tell what he was seeing. Anyhow, I let him put his filthy bundle on my couch and didn't say: "Leave that garbage out in the hall—you can't bring it in here," which is what most would've. His

garbage was better than some people are. It was all he had, see, and you
could only respect it, otherwise you'd be no help to him. I did wonder if
the lice in his hair might travel, or if he had fleas in his clothes. He said he
was holing-up in a condemned building on Eleventh Avenue. "So now
what? You'll have to find a decent room somewhere, and that'll take money. I bet you could still land a job of some sort, if you cleaned up. Messenger man, something like that. What line of work have you been in?"

"Haulin' things. Pickin' things."

"Junk—all your life?"

"Mostly."

That about had me stumped, it was so general. I opened the newspaper
to the want ads, just as footsteps sounded in the hallway. "Nathaniel?" he
asked, brightening.

"Could be." I opened the door. "Nathaniel, look who's here!"

Nathaniel pulled up a chair across the table from Hasker. The sight of
that fresh kid with his great, sad Jewish eyes and neat white hands—he
couldn't keep his eyes off him. Maybe Hasker saw something in life finer
than the ordinary run of things. I still couldn't stomach the other thought:
that he was just itching to paw the boy. In the days following, I watched
Hasker greet Nathaniel affectionately, grab the white, bird-like hand and
place it under his armpit in a funny way, like putting a tiny thing back into
its nest. He'd hold Nathaniel's hand there in his armpit for a minute or so,
and Nathaniel stood patiently, waiting for it to be over. I knew how important it was for Hasker to think we cared about him, for how else would
he get the confidence to find a decent job?

Over the next week or so, Hasker gradually cleaned up and became
more presentable. He even consulted an oculist about his eye, got a prescription lens for the good one and a shaded glass for the other. We helped
him apply for medicare and social security, although his history was so incomplete it would take months for a ruling on his case. From Sal we
bought a second-hand suit, and by the time Hasker went to the New York
State Employment office for a job as messenger man, he didn't look half
bad. I hoped he'd get a sympathetic interviewer but he was assigned to a
hard girl who kept pestering him about his work record and home address.
Finally he fled, went on a gutter-roll, spending every cent Nathaniel and me
had given him. We didn't see the guy for weeks.

Then one morning the old coot was downstairs begging from the folks
going in to church. Like a dog always circling his old home, tail between
his legs, he knew he'd done wrong. Didn't have the nerve to ring my bell.
That shame, I felt, was hopeful. "It's like learning to walk," I said to
Nathaniel. "At first you fall."

We starting building Hasker up for another try, this time to apply from
a want ad directly, for a messenger job. The salary listed wasn't much, but
enough to live on. You see, I took it for granted there would come a point

when he'd no longer need me. That's what people helping others always assume.

When Hasker suddenly failed to show up, I figured maybe his independence had arrived, though in my bones I knew better. Nathaniel said: "Another long drunk, most likely."

"You've given him money?"

"Not much."

Days passed, weeks, finally months. "He's gone for good I guess," I told Nathaniel. "Either dead or on his own somewhere."

Dead was pretty close to it. One morning last month he buzzed me downstairs. Glasses gone, wearing a dirty suit, it was the same old Hasker. "Well now, I thought we'd seen the last of you. Did you go off to California or something?"

"Down to my last cent again," he said, shuffling his feet back and forth in the nervous way you see them do in mental hospitals. "Gettin' hungry, too."

"Where in the world have you been?" I led him upstairs. "What happened?" I yelled up for Nathaniel and prepared a pot of chicken soup out of a package. He was gobbling away when Nathaniel entered—so hungry he could hardly stop long enough to shake hands—but the wayward eye kept feasting on the lad, same as always. When he took off his hat I spotted the great scar across the top of his forehead. He'd been hit by a truck on Eighth Avenue, not two blocks away. The police sent him in an ambulance to St. Vincent's Emergency. Some shyster lawyer saw the thing happen, got together a couple of witnesses, and spoke to Hasker in the hospital when he regained consciousness. Asked to represent him in a lawsuit against the driver of the truck. Seems Hasker wasn't jay walking but just crossing on a green light, paying no attention to traffic making right turns into Eighth. The lawyer got him five thousand dollars in damages, settled out of court. By the time Hasker paid the doctor, hospital, and lawyer, he had only two thousand left. The lawyer hadn't picked him clean yet—he got Hasker a room in a house that must've belonged to a relative or client, and soon Hasker was squandering everything in poker games. "'Fore I knew it, I was wiped out—money all gone." The landlord evicted him when he couldn't pay his weekly bill. "I'll sue—I'll tell my lawyer!" Hasker shouted but he only got the horse-laugh.

So here was Hasker on my hands again, and my heart sank at the prospect. "Why didn't you give half your money to Father Michael or some other priest to keep for you? They do that sometimes, and dole it out when you need it." I guess it never occurred to Hasker you could trust anybody with your cash.

"I'm just an old bum...I never learn." His meekness took me right in. But people who cower really want to hit you.

"*You* old? Why, I got ten years on you, at least!"

I might not have tried to build Hasker up again if the challenge hadn't meant so much to Nathaniel. He said such hopeful, exciting things had never happened to him before. Always, since he'd been a tiny boy out in Cleveland, it had just been the daily hours of practice. Hasker pulled himself into shape for Nathaniel's sake. He wore his prescription glasses, the one lens clouded. He shaved, took baths, and the two of them hung around Foley Square listening to trials or moseyed around Chinatown, I don't know what. They were at the United Nations whenever the world was in the middle of a crisis. Pretty often!

Maybe they'd still be bumming around town if I hadn't put in my two cents, but I said to Nathaniel one day: "What about your practicing? Hasn't your Julliard teacher noticed?" Then he confessed he hadn't been up to school for weeks—he'd simply stopped—and now he wasn't sure he wanted to be a concert pianist after all.

I felt terrible hearing this because I knew Hasker, that old free-loader, had taken Nathaniel too far down the freedom path. Instead of humanizing the kid it had ruined his career. The next time I saw Hasker coming up the stairs I told him to lay off for awhile and let Nathaniel practice his music.

"Mind your own God-damned business!"

"Don't you talk to me like that!"

"You better watch out or you'll get a clout over the head that'll make this scar I got look like a scratch!"

I'd never seen Hasker flare up like that. He was showing gumption—real spunk—but I knew *I* was in trouble. I was afraid of him—and there wasn't any way I could get away.

I warned Nathaniel that the old man was showing a violent, possessive streak—he'd better stay clear of the house for a week or so. Hasker knew I was responsible for keeping Nathaniel away and he'd shout obscenities at me in the street, raising his fists. You see, he didn't know where Nathaniel roomed and didn't have the nerve to try to hunt him up through Julliard. So he stormed and raved at me! I was mostly alone in the building, nights, but once inside I felt safe, with the downstairs buzzer-lock in working order.

It turned out, Nathaniel couldn't bear not practicing. He must have realized he'd already put in too many years ever to turn back. Nobody can spit on his own life that way.

I heard him creeping softly up the stairs—I know his step. "Nathaniel?" I opened the door. "Cup of tea?"

"No, no, don't bother me." He rounded the newel post hurriedly, like a conscientious schoolboy. I closed the door, but maybe ten or fifteen minutes later, after I'd been listening to the Prokofiev upstairs, I heard the stairs creak and knew somehow it was Hasker.

I threw open the door. "What're *you* doing here?"

"Shut up, woman, I don't need you no more."

"Who let you in?"

"I got me own key," and he held it up for me to see.

"Where'd you get it—steal it from Nathaniel?"

"Mind your own business. One day you're going to snoop too far."

"If you try to bother him, I'll—I'll phone the police."

"Where'll *that* get you?" He walked on up the steps. "Hey there boy," he called in a strange, sweet voice. "Hey there baby, it's your old man come to get you. Let me in."

The music stopped. I knew Nathaniel must be rigid over his keyboard. Had he remembered to lock the door?

Hasker rapped louder and louder. "I know you're in there. Now come on, come *on*," fist pounding, the growly voice honey-coated. "Come, baby, what's the matter? Can't we have fun some more? Go out, do something? What're you sittin' in there for? Come on out. I'll give you just ten seconds and then I'm comin' in to get you, and you know what your old man will do to you. You can't give me the slip like this. One. Two. Three... I'm comin' in, Nathaniel. I'll give you such a paddling you won't be able to sit down for a week. Four. Five. Six. Comin' after you, baby boy. You better know it, better believe it. Seven. Eight. I'm *tellin'* you. Coming! Nine. Ten. Here goes!"

A loud crash of splintering wood. I rushed to the foot of the stairs and saw Nathaniel up there on the landing, face white in anger, pushing against Hasker. "Out—out! You filthy bastard. Keep your hands off me!" One mighty shove and Hasker fell backward down the flight of steps, tumbling over and over. I stood there horrified, waiting to see if Hasker would rise again. He didn't—he was out cold. I started up the stairs to soothe Nathaniel.

"Now don't *you* come up. Just haul his ass out of here. Throw him back in the gutter where you found him. I've had enough of *both* of you!" He wheeled around and slammed the broken door behind him.

I was so hurt by his outburst I couldn't move. I retreated finally and stepped over Hasker, who reeked of whiskey. What should I do with him? Nathaniel began the fiery runs of the Prokofiev sonata, hitting the notes with special fervor now that he had made his stand. This was how he'd sound in Carnegie Hall the night of his debut—the notes a veil drawn between himself and the world, chords of anguish laid one upon another. All the balm in Gilead was needed for the world—always *had* been needed. Nothing less would ever ease the universal strife.

I steadied myself on the railing, then searched Hasker's pockets to get the house key away from him. Found it right off. I considered tumbling him down the steps. Surely by the time he reached the bottom the soot-smells and exhaust fumes from the street would revive him. Then before the next squad car made its indifferent round, he'd slip away, maybe this time never to return.

He opened his good eye and stared at me.

I walked quickly toward my room, not so hasty that he'd think I was afraid—but he uncoiled faster than I imagined. I heard him scramble to his feet and ran the last few yards, slamming the door after me. But he was right there pushing and I couldn't throw the bolt. He shoved into the room, then *he* closed the door and locked it. I backed away, trying to reach for the phone behind me, but he noticed what I was after and gripped my arm, pulling me away.

"I want your money. All you got. Where is it?"

I could neither speak nor scream. "Answer me. Where's your purse?" He grabbed my throat, squeezing my windpipe. I nodded toward the door of the inner room and he released me when he saw my bag on the bed.

"Where's the rest of it? Where do you hide it?" Again he lunged toward me. As I backed away, I knocked into the worktable, my hand touching a bottle of rose dye—an acid. The stopper was loose. I waited only a few seconds, then threw the dye into his face. He let out a yell and I sprang away, escaping his fists. His face was wildly red—*that* gave me courage! I picked up the steel shears on my table and jabbed it into him—then I passed out.

When I came to, I saw Hasker lying in a pool of blood and dye and figured he must be dead. I gazed without moving at the roses in the vases on the workbench. How real they looked, how faraway and beautiful. Feeling very old and finished, I got to my feet, thinking: so that's what they're for! I grabbed a bunch and threw them over Hasker. But two dozen weren't near enough. I found more roses in the next room and that about did it.

When she had finished, Jim put his arm around her. "They say he'll recover—only a surface wound."

"I can't go back there. I don't want to live alone anymore."

"You have a home here."

She knew he was just saying that. The apartment was crowded already, and the two girls insisted on separate rooms. His wife was alarmed by the possible change in their fragile domestic situation, which would only add to her problems with a husband who was constantly straying and seldom paying attention to his family. "Only a night or two, till I get my strength back—and make arrangements for the old folks' home."

"They're not called that anymore, Mother."

"That's what they are, though."

"I'll help investigate for you, if you want."

"No, I already know where it is. Out in Huntington—on the Island. Our church has a place there—it's not bad. Only you've got to turn over all your assets and such. I don't have anything to speak of, though."

"You've seen it?"

"Sure—it's just right for me."

She had influential church friends and was able to move right in. Once settled, she decided to get a driver's license, since Jim offered her his old Volkswagen. She studied hard, attended driver's training school, and had her permit the following month. Then she was free to do something she'd been intending for a long time: she drove to the state asylum at Central Islip, where the mother of her grandchildren was a patient.

At first Helen refused to come out to the visitor's room, and the nurse explained that nobody had asked to see Helen in three years. "Not even the girls? How awful!"

"She's not used to having anybody."

When Helen finally shuffled forward, wearing a gray, rumpled smock, her arm held firmly by a fixed-smile nurse, she scarcely resembled the Helen of former years. Her cheeks were oddly sunken and there were dark shadows under her eyes from medication. Her breasts had fallen and her hair was partially gray. She was old.

"Helen! Helen, do you know me? Jim's mother."

"Of course I do," she said feebly.

"Give me your hand—yes, dear Helen!"

"Why did you come?"

"Don't ask that. Nobody has to ask that."

"But why?"

"All right. Now, I'm in an institution, too, not far from here. A home for old people."

"You can come and go whenever you want?"

"Yes."

"Not like here."

"If you want to visit *me,* they'll let you out."

"I suppose I could try."

"You have to."

"I don't know, though...."

"I said you have to."

Critiques

Moral Fiction and Metafiction
Peter Bailey

John Gardner's *On Moral Fiction* argument might carry more conviction were it not for the fact that the writers it dictates that he condemn are precisely those writers into whose company he welcomed himself upon his own emergence into American literary prominence in the early 1970's. "I think anybody who writes the way us guys write is going to be at the mercy of the critics," he told an interviewer in 1973, "—because we're going to be misunderstood." When asked who "us guys" are, Gardner replied, "I think...guys who are storytellers—postsixties writers. I mean Stanley Elkin, Bill Gass, Donald Barthelme...I think they are fundamentally people making sideshows—but good, serious sideshows, because they raise you to your best, *not* philosophically, *not* morally."[1] By 1978, of course, these creators of serious sideshows had been radically re-evaluated by Gardner, who in *On Moral Fiction* finds Elkin concentrating "on language for its own sake, more in love, in principle, with the sound of words —or with newfangledness—than with creative fictional worlds."[2] Gass— toward whose work Gardner clearly feels an ambivalence greater than that inspired in him by the work of any of his other contemporaries[3]—writes stories and novels which demonstrate "what a paltry thing is fiction designed to prove a theory" (p. 68), while Barthelme "cares not about people but about ideas and 'constructs'—in effect, painterly images: the Phantom of the Opera, Snow White more or less realistically conceived..." (p. 80).

That Gardner's literary enthusiasms shifted in the five years between

The New Fiction interview and *On Moral Fiction*[4] is a fact neither to be
doubted nor deplored; literary history abounds with similar instances of
unexpected apostasies occasioned by young writers' sudden ascents to reputation and notice, the abruptness of their rise obliging them to undergo
some of their aesthetic education in public. What is distressing about
Gardner's precipitate conversion is that it is so much a conversion more apparent than real, his current criticism and fiction alike reflecting a sensitive
understanding of, and underlying sympathy for, the very form of writing
(call it metafiction, postsixties writing or whatever) his moral stance compels him to repudiate. He has gone, in short, from being one who recognized that postsixties writers are likely to be misunderstood to being one
who misunderstands them, though even his misreadings are illuminating and
useful in defining precisely what this form of fiction is.

Gardner's description of Barthelme's "Paraguay," for instance, is accurate and useful, even if it does find the story wanting for doing what it sets
out to do. In this story, Gardner argues, Barthelme "simply steps out of
reality to play with literary conventions which once helped us learn about
the real" (p. 80). "Paraguay" asks us, among other things, to accept that
the place we are reading about is not the South American country which
has Asuncion for its capital but some other place,[5] our spatial dislocation
reinforced on the formal level by the presence of a narrative voice whose
rhetorical stance is utterly fluid, relativized so thoroughly that the narrator's
simplest declarative sentences open up vistas of ambiguity and enigma about
the supposedly solid world which is his referent. Barthelme *is* playing with
literary conventions in "Paraguay," then, manipulating them in such a way
as to make them betray their own inherent duplicitousness, forcing literary
precision (of the Hemingway stripe) to mock itself, the syntax reflecting
an assumed stability and certainty that the actual place names, products,
and other features of Paraguay (Deosai Plains, Sari Sanger Pass, bulk art,
a "sea not programmed for echinoderms") ridicule. To some this story
might seem an empty exercise in linguistics, an epigone's Stevensian romp
through the treacheries of language; Gardner, however, knows better. His
insistence that it is not merely literary conventions with which Barthelme
is concerned, but "literary conventions which once helped us learn about
the real" suggests how thoroughly he understands what Barthelme is up to
in this story and elsewhere. "Paraguay" examines not only linguistic forms
of perception but narrative and conceptual forms as well, the story systematically undermining them so as to force us to recognize their fragility, arti-
ficiality, and arbitrariness. ("Barthelme," in Tony Tanner's good phrase,
"fractures the syntax and taxonomies which we hope will keep us sane,"[6]
that kind of sanity bought, in Barthelme's view, at too great a price.) What
Barthelme's fiction—like much of the fiction Gardner appreciates but rejects—presupposes is that forms of perception are a worthy and important
subject for literary works to address themselves to, that the understanding

of understanding is a thoroughly valid objective of poems, stories, and novels.

The central idea behind such literary works is that articulated by Stephen Dedalus in *Ulysses,* he who has spent much of his life attempting to fly by the nets the world sets out to snare him in, coming to realize that the greatest threat comes from within, not from without: " 'But in here it is,' " he tells Bloom and the Nighttown denizens, tapping his brow, " 'I must kill the priest and king.' "[7] For Dedalus as for Barthelme, Barth, Coover, Elkin, Pynchon, and a number of other like-minded contemporary American novelists, the perceptive structures of the mind are, if not the real foe with which we must contend, then at least significantly deterministic elements in our actions and behavior to make their understanding crucial to our comprehension of ourselves and of our circumstances. The "forms that once helped us learn about the real" are precisely the center of interest in much of these writers' best work, then, and an examination of two such stories will not only help to demonstrate how this type of fiction works, but will also suggest the sense in which metafiction is—Gardner's argument to the contrary—moral.

John Barth has proven himself one of metafiction's ablest practitioners as well as—through his 1967 essay, "The Literature of Exhaustion"—one of its more influential theorists, and it is not insignificant that what Gardner responds to most negatively in Barth's work are any reflections in it of that critical argument. Consequently, the story of Barth's which he does praise —"Lost in the Funhouse" Gardner terms "one of Barth's best fictions"—he commends through reading it as an attack upon the kind of art which results from the adherence to the essay's aesthetic stance, as a satire of "the artist who gets so lost in his gimmickry that he forgets the human uses it was invented to serve" (p. 96). The narrator of Barth's story does get lost in the course of the narrative, certainly, but it is not so much gimmickry that betrays him as it is the process of writing fiction—or, more specifically, the conventions necessitated by the transformation of one's personal history into art—which is the source of his dislocation. "Lost in the Funhouse" does, to this extent, reflect Barth's "Literature of Exhaustion" argument: it assumes that the stories we have to tell are necessarily few and familiar, that conventional realist approaches to such stories must by this date fail to bring them to life, and that what stories we have are thoroughly and inalterably mediated by the stories we've read.[8] It is these realities (and their disheartening tendencies to meet, intermingle, and multiply) which make it nearly impossible for the narrator of "Lost in the Funhouse" to get his story written, for his is the hoariest story of them all—that of the sensitive adolescent discovering his artistic vocation.

The typical resolution of this ur-story, of course, consists in the artist-initiate's renunciation of ordinary life and affirmation of his sacred mission, and Barth's story carries out the paradigm meticulously, Ambrose, its

implied narrator and youthful protagonist, accepting his inherent, irrevo-
cable difference from "regular" people and taking upon himself the burden
of 'constructing funhouses for others and being the secret operator'—
"though he would rather be among the lovers for whom funhouses are designed."[9] The problem with all this—what keeps it from fulfilling the Law-
rentian/Wolfean/Andersonian articulations of the myth—is that rather than
withdrawing from life to chart its treacherous and labyrinthine ways for
others, Ambrose can only withdraw from it to create images of his own
confusion, the funhouses he will design and operate for others representing
nothing more than microcosmic images of the place he himself is lost in.
(Gardner's "poet-priest" [pp. 155-7] would not have this problem, a fact
which, as well as any single difference, dramatizes the disparity between his
artistic assumptions and Barth's.) That funhouse has two meanings in the
story (or, more accurately, three: it is also the place in which are revealed
the sexual secrets of life) precludes the possibility of the paradigm's successful resolution here, for the funhouse is at once life and a self-consciously literary image of it, the confusions in the one necessarily transforming
themselves into confusions in the other.[10] This explains why it is possible
for Ambrose to get the ending more or less right (he is perhaps excessively
wistful about not being a lover): he has written the story with no other
point in mind than that he became a writer, a constructor of funhouses. It
explains too why he has such a horrendous time arriving at that conclusion
in the story: because declaring oneself a writer doesn't make one less confused than "regular" people, renders one no less vulnerable to the endlessly
reduplicative perplexities of the funhouse of life and (to use the Dickensian
pun) the life of the funhouse. Ambrose's protracted sufferings in trying to
get his story written (his hesitation, redundancies, clumsy attempts
at symbolism and embarrassed explications of those attempts; his obsessive revisions and fresh starts and mechanically self-conscious rehearsals
of the supposed functions of the literary devices he introduces into his narrative in a futile effort to lend it consonance and coherence) become an expressive analogue of the existential confusions he fails to leave behind in
adolescence, his life (the pun again) remaining fractured, disordered, incomplete. "The climax of the story," he worriedly reminds himself at one
point in the writing, "must be its protagonist's discovery of a way to get
through the funhouse,"[11] and he obviously believes that by narrating his
experiences from the third person point of view, thus distancing himself
from them and objectifying them, he will ultimately stumble upon that
way. But the only climax that the story achieves is the limited resolution
of Ambrose's ascendence to the role of writer, which signifies nothing
more than that he will henceforth dun the "regular" people of the world
with stories dealing with his failure to resolve the story of his life. For
Barth, clearly enough, there is no way through the funhouse, only images
of ways through it.

Left at this, of course, "Lost in the Funhouse" would seem little more than an extravagant courting of the imitative fallacy, a story which proves the failure of fiction by being itself a failure. It is, certainly, more than this. What is a fragmented, unresolved narrative to Ambrose is to Barth a narrative carefully and painstakingly brought to closure; what are errors, missteps, and incompetences to Ambrose are for Barth highly purposeful and expressive evocations of a character's existential condition. The standard by which literary works are judged in the Tlon of Jorge Luis Borges (out of admiration for whom "The Literature of Exhaustion" is primarily written) dictates that "A book that does not contain its counterbook is considered incomplete"[12]; Barth's story, by this criterion, is complete, because it contains its own counterstory, the existence of "Lost in the Funhouse" refuting the point it was written to make. Barth, after all, *does* stand outside of it, the familiar artist-god pulling strings that Ambrose can't see and perceiving as pattern and wholeness all that Ambrose must view as a mere chaos of his own incompetences. What "Lost in the Funhouse" demonstrates, then, are two simultaneous and contradictory notions: the bankruptcy of the aristocratic artist-god idea, of the idea that the artist is able to single-mindedly rise above his past and present selves and transform—transubstantiate, as the Romantics would have it—them into art; and the contrary notion that Barth is able to accomplish this in the course of the story, projecting a self malleable enough to be shaped according to the demands of a fictional design.[13]

The fact that "Lost in the Funhouse" does the opposite of what it says, suspending its meaning in that irresolvable paradox, does not mean it is reducible to a mere philosophical conundrum or aesthetic game. The tension it effectively dramatizes is the real, immediate one of our need to articulate our stories even though the forms (of which the devotee's arrival at his vocation is but one) are threadbare and the devices which we hoped would be expressive and resonant only turn out to call attention to their intended functions. By "confronting the intellectual dead end" of fiction's depleted technical resources—to use Barth's own explanation of one of Borges' stories—and "employing it against itself," Barth is able to "accomplish new human work" and achieve an artistic victory,[14] one dependent—as Gardner's praise of the piece would indicate—on more than intellectual or literary pyrotechnics. For what stays with us of "Lost in the Funhouse" is not so much its surface complications or self-conscious literary technicalities as it is the complex, believable image of a young artist (one humorously similar to the young Barth himself, no doubt) which emerges through them, a young artist whose literary and existential frustrations are both inseparable and eminently recognizable, and whose ambivalence toward the forms which at once express and betray the story of himself he is attempting to tell may also be very much like our own. By turning the tired techniques against themselves, Barth is able to accomplish what Ambrose can't—the successful, coherent, and complete telling of the too-familiar, all important story of Ambrose and his discovery of his artistic calling.

One of Gardner's *On Moral Fiction* arguments which writers like Barth and Coover would find compatible with their publicly-professed aesthetic positions is his assertion that "Real art creates myths a society can live instead of die by, and clearly our society is in need of such myths" (p. 126). A necessary element of that endeavor, they would want to add, however, is that real art has an equal responsibility to examine, criticize, and evaluate the myths we already have, not for the irresponsible or nihilistic purposes of mere iconoclasm, but because our unquestioning acceptance of such myths can allow us to remain psychically bound to patterns of thought from whose implicit content we have believed ourselves long since liberated. We know, for instance, that the elderly are people with lives as real and concerns as individual as our own, and yet a primary image of the aged with which we blithely present our children is that of Santa Claus, an old man who exists solely for the purpose of giving children whatever it is that they want. Although not one of the myths that either one of them has treated in his fiction, the Santa Claus story with its psychic and moral ramifications is just the kind of exemplary narrative their work delights in examining. Barth, of course, prefers to deal with more classical and literary mythic forms, transforming the original stories into—or exploiting their inherent similarity to—contemporary images of confused, self-bedeviled man; the Santa Claus myth would be a more comfortable one for Coover, who has worked with similar popular mythic materials (the stories of Hansel & Gretel; Puff, the Magic Dragon; The Cat in the Hat; Rip Van Winkle; Mighty Casey and—most recently—Sam Slick the Yankee Peddler) and who has also provided a theoretical explanation of his approach to such materials in his Prologue to "Seven Exemplary Fictions" in *Pricksongs & Descants.* Addressing his comments to Cervantes, to whom these "apprentice fictions" are dedicated, Coover affirms that:

> You teach us, Maestro, by example, that great narratives remain meaningful through time as a language medium between generations, as a weapon against the fringe-areas of our consciousness, and as a mythic reinforcement of our tenuous grip on reality. The novelist uses familiar mythic or historical forms to combat the content of those forms and to conduct the reader. . .to the real, away from mystification to clarification, away from mystery to revelation. And it is above all to the need for new modes of perception and fictional forms able to encompass them that I. . .address these stories.[15]

Whether "new modes of perception" is synonymous with what Gardner calls "myths society can live instead of die by" is debatable, of course—in all probability, Gardner would see the stories of "Seven Exemplary Fictions" (and of *Pricksongs & Descants* in general) as products of a writer who, like Barthelme, "cares not about people but about ideas or 'constructs.'"[16] The problem with distinguishing between people, on the one hand, and "ideas or 'constructs' " on the other, is that the distinction ignores how much our thought patterns and behavior are influenced, even shaped, by the stories—the "ideas or 'constructs' "—we have accepted and internalized as explanatory truths. It is the capacity of our stories to dictate our lives and perceptions that most fascinates and dismays Coover, and thus much of his best work, from *The Origin of the Brunists* to *The Public Burning,* takes as its primary subject a central explanatory system or narrative and attempts to illuminate its roots, its meaning, and its worth. Such a story is that of the virgin birth, one which Coover treats in two different works—in his play, "A Theological Position," and in the fiction to be discussed here, "J's Marriage."

At first glance, what "J's Marriage" seems to be is merely a latter day gloss on the Biblical narrative, a Kafkaesque updating of that story not unlike the Faulknerian contemporization of the Noah story in Coover's "The Brother," both fictions viewing their incidents not from Christianity's received, authoritarian perspective but from the perspective of men who are sacrificed to the blessed resolutions which are the Biblical versions' only concerns. And this is part of the story's effect, certainly—we do sympathize with J as a man who suffers on a human plane experiences which can be explained only in spiritual or metaphysical terms, a fact which dictates that he must end his life never knowing what has happened to him or why it has happened. But "J's Marriage" isn't simply a 20th century relativist's approach to the virgin birth, J's perspective presented merely in the service of a facile irony.[17] Rather than inviting us to read his story as a gloss on the Biblical narrative, Coover asks us to read "J's Marriage" as the ground from which the Biblical myth grew. The difference between these two perspectives on the Biblical account is this: viewed as a progression from Bible to fiction, the relationship between the two becomes merely one of source to latter day version, modernization; viewed as a progression moving forward from Coover's literarily realistic account to Biblical version, our attention is held by the process by which fact, over time, becomes transformed into myth. It is exactly that process that Coover, in his Prologue, determined to examine by using "familiar mythic or historical forms to combat the content of those forms."

The numerous references to J's discussions of his situation with those close to him strongly suggest that what we are being presented here is a reconstruction completed by one of his acquaintances some time after his death. The narrator has to be a near-contemporary of J's because he has no inkling of the ultimate consequences of the story he is relating—instead, he insists that there is nothing momentous about it at all, constantly characterizing the events he is recounting as "a common kind of story," one full of details "which need not be enumerated here."[18] He is concerned only with the narration of the events of the marriage, and represents perhaps the last surviving confidante of J's, the last man living to have an account of the marriage, however imperfect, from J's own lips.[19] Consequently, the narrator's tone and attitude throughout the story implicitly reflect and affirm J's judgment, delivered moments before his death, on the meaning of his life: "in spite of everything, there was nothing tragic about it, nothing to get wrought up about, on the contrary" (p. 119). But this judgment, shared by the two of them, is predicated upon J's confusion of the sequence of event and dream which comprised the most important incident in his life. Coover's narrator here—not unlike the narrators who confusedly lead us through a number of Borges' fictions—has told us a story which he only imperfectly understands, but Coover has insured that *his* story will dramatize the truth that his narrator can't see, the truth of the tragedy of J's life and death.

The story of Joseph and Mary, as Coover presents it, is the story of a moment in which two human possibilities, two images of a human future, meet and vie for ascendency, J representing Eros, his wife representing Caritas. To J, his wife is beauty incarnate, "no mere apparition", but the "potentiality of beauty, not previously existent" fleshed out in female form; to her, J is "really nothing more physically substantial than his words, words which at times pierced the heart, true, kindled the blood, powerful words, even at times painful; but their power and their pain did not, could not, pin one helplessly to the earth, could not bring actual blood" (p. 113). He offers her human, purely physical love; she rejects it, her response, "Please, don't," falling between them "like great stone tablets" reminiscent of similarly intended 'Thou shalt nots.' It will be for her son, not her husband, to become the word made flesh; for J remains only the mystic moment of watching that son's birth ("his only indisputable glimpse of the whole of existence"), and the somewhat perfunctory penetration of his wife while she sleeps some months after the baby's birth.

That, at least, is the chronology of events as the narrator has it from J, but even J wasn't sure when the consummation of his marriage happened, if it ever did: "perhaps he dreamt it, he could never deny it, it might have been one of those beautiful dreams from that earlier mystical night, thought forgotten" (p. 118). The magical night in question followed immediately upon J's recognition in his wife of the "potentiality of beauty, not previously existent," the night in which "he buried his face in her breasts and caressed them, and she allowed it. Then, finally overcome with an excess of emotion, he fell into a deep sleep full of wonderful dreams, which unfortunately he could never recall" (p. 115). It was in these unremembered dreams, Coover suggests, that J consummated his marriage, not in dream but in fact, while his wife slept. By the time of the story's narration the correct sequence of events has already become muddled, however, perhaps because handed down, perhaps because J's recounting of them, communicated in the last, senile years of his life, confused their chronology and failed to accurately distinguish the actual from the dream. By the time the New Testament was being written, of course, his wife's idea of love had completely subsumed J's more human version, a fact reflected in the Biblical account's transformation of the dream in which he made love to his wife into the dream in which the angel of God appears to him, urging him on to a sexless union with a woman whose child is conceived of the Holy Ghost and who is to become mankind's redeemer. For J, the "emotional harmony inexpressibly beautiful" that he knew in the early days of his marriage to his wife would have been redemption enough.

One of the traditions which has grown up around Joseph's disappearance from the Bible's pages after Christ's adolescence holds that he died a happy death, and although Coover never refers to this legend or to Joseph's "Saint of the Happy Death" designation, he does depict J's death as something like a happy one. Its happiness, Coover also suggests, however, is founded upon ignorance, ignorance that blinds him to the threefold tragedy of his life. J dies wishing his penetration of his wife had resulted in a son of his own, "a kind of testimonial to leave," when in fact a son had resulted from it, one who became the son of man rather than the son of J; he dies uncertain whether he actually ever did consummate his marriage, a marriage which represented his only self-fulfillment in an otherwise bleak life; and, most importantly in terms of Coover's theme, he dies having unintentionally relinquished his own hopeful vision of human beauty and human happiness, dies having offered it up as a sacrifice to his wife's stone tablets and cult of virginity. What follows upon his death is the New Testament and centuries of Christian history, neither of which Coover chooses to detail in his story, content to let them serve as extratextual glosses on "J's Marriage."

Coover's own attitude toward the Biblical account of Joseph and Mary is clear enough in "J's Marriage," but he is not unwilling to allow hints of another reality to penetrate his story—the possibility, for instance, that the "potentiality of beauty" J sees in his wife is a spiritual rather than purely physical epiphany; the possibility, too, that J's exclamation to his wife in that moment, "Oh my God I love you," represents more accurately the real object of his love. Coover knows, this is to say, that some will insist upon seeing his story as a gloss upon, rather than the ground of, the Biblical story. Myths are far too resilient to be easily shunted aside by counter-myths, Coover would very likely admit, but the tension which results from the juxtaposition of myth and counter-myth against one another may be enough to make us understand the myth for the first time and thus to free ourselves from its tyranny over us. Such, at least, is one method through which Coover's fiction attempts to "kill the priest and king."

For Coover, then, "J's Marriage" doesn't so much "create a myth society can live by" as it dramatizes a moment in imagined history when one such myth gives way to a legalistic, life-denying one. (Significantly enough, the novel of Coover's which Gardner admires most, *The Origin of the Brunists*,[20] contains the same basic antinomies of love and law, human need and cosmic necessity, but there sensuality and secularity—J's ideals—prevail over Christian apocalyptics.) Liberating oneself from the incapacitation of limiting, debilitating forms of thought and explanatory versions of life through the examination of their premises and psychological ramifications is, in Coover's view, a worthy—perhaps even moral—undertaking for fiction, and if he, Barth, and other similarly-minded novelists have, like Barthelme, "stepped out of reality to play with the literary conventions which once helped us learn about the real," they ultimately return to it with interesting and important news about the ways that we put that reality together.

NOTES

1. Joe David Bellamy, *The New Fiction: Interview with Innovative American Writers* (Urbana, Ill.: University of Illinois Press, 1975), p. 182.

2. John Gardner, *On Moral Fiction* (New York: Basic Books, 1978), p. 71.

3. In a dialogue between the two writers at the University of Cincinnati, Gardner accused Gass of "wasting the greatest genius ever given to America by fiddling around when [he] could be doing big, important things." The dialogue is published in *The New Republic,* 10 March 1979, pp. 27-33.

4. In his article dealing with *On Moral Fiction* and the controversy that it sparked, Stephen Singular indicates that the book, originally written in 1965, was revised in 1975, which makes the apparent shift in Gardner's attitude toward these writers an even more sudden one. See "The Sound and Fury over Fiction," *The New York Times Magazine,* 8 July 1979, p. 34.

5. Donald Barthelme, "Paraguay," in *City Life* (New York: Farrar, Straus, Giroux, 1970), p. 19.

6. Tony Tanner, *City of Words* (New York: Harper & Row, 1971), p. 403.

7. James Joyce, *Ulysses* (New York: Modern Library, 1961), p. 589.

8. John Barth, "The Literature of Exhaustion," *Atlantic,* 220 (August 1967), pp. 34-5.

9. John Barth, "Lost in the Funhouse," in *Lost in the Funhouse* (Garden City, New York: Doubleday, 1968), p. 97.

10. Compare Robert Scholes' argument that "Lost in the Funhouse" is "about the difficulty of writing a novel about 'real' experience, as the book is about the difficulty of the writer whose position in existence is distorted by his desire to find fictional equivalents for the condition of being." See "The Range of Metafiction: Barth, Barthelme, Coover, Gass" in *Fabulation and Metafiction* (Urbana, Ill.: University of Illinois Press, 1979), p. 118.

11. Barth, "Lost in the Funhouse," p. 96.

12. Jorge Luis Borges, "Tlon, Uqbar, Orbis Tertius," trans. James E. Irby, in *Labyrinths* (New York: New Directions, 1964), p. 13.

13. Max Schulz discusses the relationship between the third person narrator of "Lost in the Funhouse" and Ambrose, and that between Ambrose and Barth, in "Characters (contra Characterization) in the Contemporary Novel," in *Theory of the Novel,* ed. John Halperin (New York: Oxford University Press, 1974), pp. 149-53.

14. Barth, "The Literature of Exhaustion," p. 34.

15. Robert Coover, *Pricksongs & Descants* (New York: E. P. Dutton, 1969), p. 78.

16. Gardner comments at length in *On Moral Fiction* on one story from *Prick-*

songs & Descants, "A Pedestrian Accident," concluding that no one "would seriously maintain that the world is as Coover says it is" in that story (p. 76). He doesn't, however, refer to any of the fictions based on other fictions ("J's Marriage," "The Gingerbread House," "The Brother") in the collection.

17. In his "Robert Coover and the Hazards of Metafiction" (*Novel: A Forum on Fiction,* Spring 1974, pp. 212-13), Neil Schmitz argues that "J's Marriage" does nothing other than present an unfamiliar perspective on a familiar story.

18. Coover, pp. 117, 118.

19. Compare Borges meditation on the passing of the last man to have seen the living Christ with his own eyes in "The Witness," *Dreamtigers,* trans. Mildred Boyer and Harold Morland (New York: E. P. Dutton, 1970), p. 39.

20. Gardner maintains that Coover's first novel is his "best book," and implies that it is so because it doesn't "illustrate his fictional theory" as outlined in the "Seven Exemplary Fictions" Prologue. See "The Way We Write Now," *The New York Times Book Review,* 7 July 1972, p. 2.

New Fiction, Popular Fiction, and the Middle/Moral Way
Robert A. Morace

> A guy walks along the street and sees this magnificent
> sculpture made out of signs and his day is better for it.
> But what I want the guy to do is continue past the
> signs and go do his job.
> > —John Gardner on the difference between the
> > new fiction of William Gass and the moral fiction
> > of John Gardner.[1]

Towards the end of the novel *October Light,* there is a scene in which
James Page, an old Vermont farmer, wakes up after a crazy night of drinking, driving off the road, wrecking his uninsured truck, and threatening to
shotgun a priest, a minister, and even his own sister. Suddenly, he

> then remembered what he'd done. His heart went out from under
> him. He ached too much to feel, just now, the full shame, or
> shock; what he felt was worse, and duller: simple and absolute
> despair and the farmer's bred-in knowledge that whatever his
> misery, however profound his self-hatred and sense of life's mor-
> tal injustice, he must get up and go milk the cows, feed the pigs
> and horses and, if he could get to it, winter the bees.

In its emphasis on responsibility, this passage is typical of John Gardner's
work: his characters' all-too-human lapses from responsible action, their
subsequent guilt, and finally the sensible, matter-of-fact way in which they
go and do the things that have to be done—angst or no angst, despair or no
despair. This emphasis on responsible behavior runs throughout Gardner's
fiction, from the way *Nickel Mountain* ends with a neat reversal of Rip Van
Winkle's abdication to James Page's milking the cows. It is also present in
his critical writings, most noticeably in his controversial book *On Moral
Fiction.* Here the responsible character is not fat Henry Soames, owner of
a truck stop; or hairless Fred Clumly, Batavia's chief-of-police; or old James
Page, farmer. Rather in *On Moral Fiction* the responsible character is—or
at least should be—the writer, the modern version of the Shaper in *Grendel.*
Although Gardner's theory of moral fiction has already attracted considerable attention, reviewers' polemics have unfortunately tended to obscure
one of Gardner's chief points: the writer's dual obligation to his art and to
his society. In the discussion of this view which follows, three issues are
considered. One is the way in which this dual obligation functions as perhaps the most viable common denominator of elite and popular literature.
Another is the specific American and contemporary contexts of Gardner's

theory of moral fiction. And a third is the relationship between this view and his novel *October Light*.

Admittedly, the author of librettos, of books on Anglo-Saxon poetry, the Wakefield cycle, and Chaucer, and of fiction which has been classified with that of such post-contemporary writers as William Gass and Ronald Sukenick may seem rather suspect as a spokesman for morally responsible popular literature. But Gardner's credentials as a popular writer are impressive. To begin with, all twelve of his books of fiction are in print. Two of his novels—*Sunlight Dialogues* and *October Light*—have had long runs on the best-seller lists. His eight books of adult fiction are available in mass market paperback editions from Ballantine, and three of his five books for children have been republished in paperback by Bantam. Even as a medievalist Gardner has tended towards the larger audience. He has directed his critical studies at non-specialists,[2] and has published two volumes of "modernized versions" of medieval poetry. His popularization of *The Life and Times of Chaucer,* which drew some hostile reviews in the scholarly journals but was widely praised in newspapers and magazines, was reissued as a Vintage paperback just twelve months after its initial publication in April 1977. Of course, Gardner is not the only scholar to achieve popular success: Tolkien proves that.[3] Nor is he the only contemporary writer of experimental fiction to have found a large audience: witness the careers of Barthelme, Kosiński, and especially Vonnegut. What makes Gardner unique, however, is *On Moral Fiction*—that is, his willingness to consider the writer's relationship (or more accurately, his moral responsibilities) to both his art and to his American audience.

I

Let me begin by briefly outlining what Gardner says in the first and more important half of *On Moral Fiction*.[4] "Premises on Art and Morality," as it is called, is "an analysis of what has gone wrong" in the arts, especially fiction, and the criticism of our time. Art is, Gardner claims, "a tragi-comic holding action against entropy," "a conduit between body and soul," and, in a sense, a game, but a game which is serious, beneficial, and "nutritious." Art "gropes" for meaning and is therefore actually a way or "process" of thinking. Since art does affect life and therefore can and should be a civilizing force, Gardner, drawing heavily on Tolstoi, emphasizes art's moral function: to present "valid models for imitation, eternal verities worth keeping in mind, and a benevolent vision of the possible which can inspire and incite human beings toward virtue, toward life affirmation as opposed to destruction and indifference." Looking around himself, Gardner sees very few other artists who are willing to accept this "traditional view." Contemporary critics are "inhumane," concerned almost exclusively with terminology rather than moral "evaluation." And contemporary artists either overemphasize surface texture (Gardner likens such writers as Barthelme to "minor Romantics") or propound "some melodramatic opposition of bad and good" (that is, fiction tailored to a message, such as Doctorow's *Ragtime* or Coover's *Public Burning*). The cynicism, nihilism, and moral relativism engendered by Sartre and the followers of Wittgenstein and Freud have been too readily accepted by today's artists. Lacking "significant belief," our writers fail to take their characters "seriously," and that, Gardner feels, is a sure sign that they don't take people seriously either. Gardner then turns a "Who's Who" of contemporary fiction into a "Who Isn't." Mailer, Updike, and Doctorow are preachy; Vonnegut and Heller are "cold hearted"; Bellow is an essayist; Barth "is tangled helplessly in his own wiring"; Barthelme is merely "clever"; the list goes on. Gardner does approve of Fowles, Cheever, Oates, and Salinger, but the only writers he thinks might survive are Malamud, Davenport, and Welty.

Implicit in all this is Gardner's criticism of the fashionable kind of contemporary writing to which he himself has been linked and that goes by a variety of names: new fiction, metafiction, superfiction, surfiction, fabulation, post-contemporary, and disruptive. Gardner calls it "rarefied" and wonders where the plot and the characters have gone.[5] One of the clearest definitions of the new fiction has been formulated by Raymond Federman, one of its chief advocates and practitioners. Federman draws an uncrossable line between commercial fiction and what he says is

> the only fiction that still means something today...that kind
> of fiction that tries to explore the possibilities of fiction; that
> kind that challenges the tradition that governs it; the kind of
> fiction that constantly renews our faith in man's imagination
> and not in man's distorted view of reality. This I call SUR-
> FICTION. However, not because it imitates reality, but be-
> cause it expresses the fictionality of reality.[6]

It is tempting to see in Federman's remarks a situation analogous to Melville's charging "the dollars damn me" or to Hawthorne's railing against "that damned mob of scribbling women." Unfortunately, there is no new-fiction equivalent of *Moby-Dick* or *The Scarlet Letter,* though it may be a little captious to point this out. Nonetheless, it would be wrong to think of the new fictionists as just one more manifestation of those minor artists who make their complaints against the commercial world that neglects them and then quietly pass away. The new fictionists are not lacking in talent, and they certainly are not going away. Publishing ventures such as Ronald Sukenick and Jonathan Baumbach's Fiction Collective and more established publishers such as Swallow Press are making their works readily and widely available. And, as I noted earlier, there are several new fictionists who have become commercially viable (Gass), even popular (Vonnegut).[7] Perhaps of greater significance, a large and influential academic movement led by Federman, Robert Scholes, and Jerome Klinkowitz[8] has given considerable stature to their writings. So to dismiss Gardner's fears concerning the effect these new fictionists are having on the culture at large because, as Max Apple has claimed in his review of *On Moral Fiction,* "their audience is small enough to fit under Mr. Gardner's fingernail," is to ignore their effect on the way literature is perceived by the general reading public.[9]

Gardner's position is justified for yet another, though related, reason. The writers of the new fiction tend to confuse their aesthetic theory with the practical demands posed by the American writer's relationship to his audience. Federman, for example, claims that in the new fiction, "The writer will no longer be considered a prophet, a philosopher, or even a so-ciologist who predicts, teaches, or reveals absolute truths, nor will he be looked upon (admiringly and romantically) as the omnipresent, omniscient, and omnipotent creator, but he will stand on equal footing with the reader in their efforts *to make sense* out of the language common to both of them, to give sense to the fiction of life."[10] This same kind of elitist egalitarian-ism is also found in Barth's influential essay, "The Literature of Exhaust-ion." Barth rejects the Aristotelian concept of the artist-in-control as "an aristocratic notion...which the democratic west seems to be eager to have done with; not only the 'omniscient' author of older fiction, but the very idea of the controlling artist, has been condemned as politically reaction-ary, even fascist."[11] Against this theoretical commitment to democracy there is the actual practice of the new fictionists: Alain Robbe-Grillet's at-tempts at writing novels whose parts—even sentences—cannot be "recuper-ated" (made into meaningful patterns), or Marc Saporta's novel-in-a-box, whose pages the reader can "order" in any way he chooses, or Ronald Sukenick's writing about a writer writing, or John Barth's work after *The Sot-Weed Factor.* Although the various structuralist strategems such as al-phabetical order and simple arithmetic progression employed by Sukenick, Walter Abish, and others have been regarded as "basic" and *therefore* demo-cratic in that they are capable of being understood by every reader,[12] this kind of clever writing is virtually inaccessible—that is to say, unreadable—to the democratic majority, the composite reader with whom the new fiction-ist purports to "stand on equal footing." At best these works tend to in-crease the distance between elite and popular literature; at worst, as Gard-ner suggests, they make fiction suspect to all but the cognoscente who are either students in or graduates from university writing programs.[13] This separation is also evident in the new fictionists' attacks on cultural clichés, which they feel "deaden the sensibilities when accepted uncritically."[14] Their criticism of popular culture as well as their stylistic innovations are, of course, necessary if fiction is to remain alive and well. But too often the satire degenerates into mere scorn. Robert Coover, for example, has re-fused to write at what he calls "the 'Head Start' cultural vocabulary of the broad audience..."[15] and William Gass has said of popular culture, "This muck cripples consciousness."[16]

II

In addition to the class of writers discussed above—the ones who retreat into what he calls "linguistic sculpture"—Gardner also criticizes those writers who seek the larger audience but mislead it, chiefly by adopting (and thereby more firmly establishing) a fashionably cynical point of view. In effect both groups become, quite unintentionally, threats to their society. This point has been persuasively argued by Howard Mumford Jones in his study of *Jeffersonianism and the American Novel* (1966). Given the drift of modern American fiction, Jones says, it may soon become necessary "...to warn readers that art may conceivably betray the political republic. It may betray the political republic by naively assuming that a primary duty of the political republic is to protect the republic of letters but that it is no primary duty of the republic of letters to protect the health and safety of the political republic."[17] As this passage clearly indicates, there is an American context for Gardner's call to "moral fiction," a context which will become clearer once some mention is made of the vigorous debate over the role of the novelist in America that took place towards the end of the nineteenth century. During that period, a number of factors worked together to focus the public's attention on writers and writing: increased production and circulation of books and other printed materials, the rise of low-priced magazines such as *McClure's, Cosmopolitan,* and *Munsey's,* the lessening of organized religion's opposition to novels, and, especially, widespread literacy. It is important that the significance of this debate not be underestimated, for in a very real sense, what was being decided was the future of the American middle classes—that is to say, the future of the heirs of the then rapidly expanding American reading public. As in the current debate over the role television should play in American life,[18] the chief issue raised was whether the fiction writer should entertain, pander to, exploit, or educate his readers. The two sides in the debate are best represented by Francis Marion Crawford and William Dean Howells. In *The Novel—What It Is* (1893), Crawford, the popular author of historical romances, argued against realism and novels with a purpose and for fiction as pure entertainment. Howells, particularly in the pieces collected under the title *Criticism and Fiction* (1891), was America's most prolific and eloquent spokesman for literary realism and the democratic thrust of the realist novel. To its detractors, realism was a synonym for the sordid; to Howells it meant a fidelity to life *and* a commitment to morally responsible literature. As he noted at the very end of *Criticism and Fiction:* "The art... which disdains the office of the teacher is one of the last refuges of the aristocratic spirit which is disappearing from politics and society, and is now seeking to shelter itself in aesthetics."[19]

The later criticism of Frank Norris is clearly indebted to Howells and, like Gardner, to the Tolstoy of *What Is Art?,* translated into English in 1898. In three essays published in William Hines Page's magazine *World's Work* in 1901 and 1902–"The True Reward of the Novelist," "The Need of a Literary Conscience," and "The Novel with a 'Purpose' "–Norris warned would-be novelists not to "truckle" to literary fashion and advised them to heed their social obligation to seek truth.[20] These essays served to prepare the way for Norris's fullest statement concerning the relation of the author to the popular audience. In "The Responsibilities of the Novelist," he pointed out that because the literary taste of the general public is indiscriminate as to both artistic merit and truthfulness, the ultimate responsibility for whatever good or harm a book causes must rest with the writer. Moreover, he says, the fact that technology has made it possible for the author to reach a *mass* audience means that his responsibility is even greater:

> If the novel were not one of the most important factors in modern life, if it were not the completest expression of our civilization, if its influence were not greater than all the pulpits, than all the newspapers between the oceans, it would not be so important that its message be true....
>
> The man who can address an audience of one hundred and fifty thousand people who—unenlightened—*believe what he says* has a heavy duty to shoulder; and he should address himself to his task not with the flippancy of the catchpenny juggler at the county fair, but with earnestness, with soberness, with a sense of his limitations, and with all the abiding sincerity that by the favor and mercy of the gods may be his.[21]

If the tone of this passage seems overwrought, even evangelical, perhaps we should recall that this same point about tone was raised by most of the reviewers of *On Moral Fiction,* a book in which John Gardner the preacher's son is very much in evidence. However, neither Gardner nor Norris are calling for fiction on the order of Charles Sheldon's *In His Steps,* a novel long on Christian message, lamentably short on art, and incidentally one of the six most popular books of 1896.[22] The far more important similarity involves their shared belief that the author must also accept the role of leader. Norris, for example, whose upper-middle class background made him a bit condescending towards the general readership, distinguished between an audience that could read and one that could critically evaluate what it read. As a result, his best-selling novel *The Pit,* written concurrently with the essays discussed above, includes several scenes dealing with the kinds of fiction that the various characters are reading. In this Norris may have been following the example of Howells, who in *The Rise of Silas Lapham* constructed an elaborate sub-plot dealing with the effects of sentimental fiction on Lapham's daughters and paralleling the moral dilemma faced by the father in the main plot. The effects of literature—usually sentimental ro-

mances, melodrama, and dime novels—is a principal theme in many realist
works: Stephen Crane's *Maggie: A Girl of the Streets* and "The Blue Hotel"
and Henry James's "Greville Fane" and *Washington Square* being just four
of the most obvious instances.

III

A much fuller and more technically complex rendering of this theme is
included in Gardner's Bicentennial novel *October Light*. The fact that nearly forty percent of *October Light* is comprised of a novel-within-the-novel
called *The Smugglers of Lost Souls' Rock* led a number of reviewers to believe that Gardner had actually written two separate and independent novels. Melvin Maddocks, for example, thought that *The Smugglers* came
"dangerously close to upstaging *October Light*."[23] Although Maddocks
was virtually a lone voice in praise of *The Smugglers,* other reviewers made
a similar distinction between it and what they seemed to think was the
"real" novel. Robert Towers, writing in the *New York Times Book Review,* found the "sub-novel" (as he called it) "boring and exasperating."
Perhaps, he suggested, it was self-parody, or maybe Gardner's having written
it in collaboration with his wife made him reluctant "to throw it away." In
any case, Towers concluded, his editor should have insisted upon its being
deleted.[24] More recently, George P. Elliott wrote in *The American Scholar*
that *October Light* is Gardner's "best fiction," "a fine straight novel into
which he inserts a punk anti-novel (now why did he do that?)"[25] There is
a fairly simple answer to Elliott's question, an answer which makes clear
that *The Smugglers* is not the unnecessary appendage to an otherwise good
novel that Towers and others have claimed. As Gardner has explained, the
"inside novel" parodies a "popular form of serious contemporary fiction"[26]
—the parody being what Thomas LeClair has accurately described as "a
Pynchonized *Dog Soldiers* with a sci-fi ending."[27] Taken by itself, *The
Smugglers* is yet another illustration of Gardner's formidable skill as a par-
odist, and as such belongs with the stories collected in *The King's Indian.*[28]
But *The Smugglers* does not exist independent of Sally Abbott's reading of
it. It is the interaction of this parodic novel and its reader—not the parody
itself—that Gardner presents. By making this interaction an integral part
of the larger work in which it appears, Gardner not only parallels his own
readers' situation as they read *October Light;* he also creates an exemplum
in which he dramatizes the major points he was then including in his controversial critical work, *On Moral Fiction,* published a year later.

Before taking a close look at *October Light,* let me make a brief point
about Gardner's use of parody. Ever since the publication in 1966 of
Barth's essay "The Literature of Exhaustion," parody has received far
more praise and abuse than it really deserves. To some, especially those inclined towards structuralism and the new fiction, it seems to have become
the *sine qua non* of contemporary literature, while to others it looms as

the salient mark of fiction's moribund state. Gardner has, I think, avoided both extremes. Parody is, of course, central to his narrative technique, and in his critical studies he has emphasized the parodic elements of such works as *Beowulf,* the Wakefield plays, and Chaucer's poems. But unlike Barth, Gardner uses parody as a means rather than an end in itself; recall Barth's refrain in *Chimera,* "the key to the treasure is the treasure." Moreover, he does not use parody as Robert Coover says he does, to "*combat* the content of [familiar mythic or historical] forms" (my italics),[29] but rather to *test* the contemporary validity of the moral values embedded in older literary works and genres and, in so doing, to establish a sense of moral continuity otherwise very little in evidence in the "disruptive fiction" of the past decade. As Gardner has said in an interview, "...I incline to think out so-called modern problems in terms of archaic forms. I like the way archaic forms provide a pair of spectacles for looking at things."[30] The line between Gardner's use of parody and that of writers such as Barth is brought into even sharper focus in *On Moral Fiction:* "Insofar as literature is a telling of new stories, literature has been 'exhausted' for centuries; but insofar as literature tells archetypal stories in an attempt to understand once more their truth—translate their wisdom for another generation—literature will be exhausted only when we all, in our foolish arrogance, abandon it" (p. 66). It is this search for values that Gardner finds missing from so much of today's fiction and that is, as we shall now see, also conspicuously absent from *The Smugglers of Lost Souls' Rock.*

According to one of the blurbs on its cover, *The Smugglers of Lost Souls' Rock* "blows the lid off marijuana smuggling, fashionable gang-bangs, and the much sentimentalized world of the middle-aged Flower Child. A sick book, as sick and evil as life in America." This is hardly what Gardner would call "moral fiction." Nor does it seem the sort of book that would appeal to a woman like Sally Abbott: eighty years old, a life-long Vermonter, a penniless widow who has recently come to live with her brother, James Page, and who even more recently has been made a prisoner in her own room, locked in by James after he had endured her preaching "a sermon off television about the Equal Rights Amendment." Deprived of her television—James had destroyed it with his shotgun—and her knitting—it's downstairs—Sally Abbott turns to *The Smugglers* for entertainment. Unimpressed by the blurbs and the semi-pornographic illustration on the cover, she opens the novel "indifferently," having no "intention of reading a book that she knew in advance to be not all there." Despite the missing "pages," Sally does begin to read. "'All life...[is] a boring novel,'" says one character; "'Isn't it the truth,'" replies Sally, reading on. More often what Sally reads triggers a memory that she realizes is more real, more true than what she finds in the book. An attempted suicide in *The Smugglers* reminds her of the time five years before when her nephew Richard killed himself. The "loose talk of suicide" in the novel strikes her as "irritating" and the writing "stupid [and] irresponsible," but almost immediately she dismisses her own objections, reasoning that "it wasn't as if the book was in earnest."

At first she reads without commitment. The chief reason she never reads more than a few pages each of the first eight times she picks up the book is her guilt over reading what she knows is "trash." Brought up in the same tradition of hard work as her brother, a farmer, she feels compelled to explain and defend herself. The ghostly presence of her dead husband is especially reproachful. "A reader of serious and worthwhile books," Horace, she knows, would never have read nor have allowed his wife to read *The Smugglers.* Recalling the Shakespearean plays they had seen in New York, Sally realizes how "paltry" her novel really is even in comparison to the simple poems told by her friend Ruth Thomas, one of the last of the country reciters. Then Sally does another about-face. Whatever she may have felt after seeing the plays was the result of her youth, not the plays themselves, and now that her youth, like her husband, is gone, she decides that "Books have no effect at all, no value whatsoever." She's wrong, of course. A few paragraphs later she unconsciously echoes her book when she calls all life "mere dress-up, ridiculous make believe." No longer does she read simply to entertain herself; now it is "to escape the stupidity, the dreariness, the waste of things"—another phrase borrowed from *The Smugglers.* Although she knows that this brooding may be "an unhealthy effect of her novel," she prefers to believe that "She wasn't some child, going to be corrupted by a foolish book." Again Sally is wrong. Rebelling against the tyranny of her brother and later of men, of Vermont Republicans and even of time, Sally becomes, without ever realizing it, the slave of her novel.[31]

Sally's enslavement to the book's tyranny begins after she has read just a few pages:

> ...quite imperceptibly the real world lost weight and the print
> on the page gave way to images, an alternative reality more
> charged than real life, more ghostly yet nearer, suffused with
> a curious importance and manageability. She began to fall in
> with the book's snappy rhythms, becoming herself more wry,
> more wearily disgusted with the world—not only with her
> own but the whole "universe," as the book kept saying—a
> word that hadn't entered Sally's thoughts in years.

The creating of "alternative realities" is, as Gardner points out in *On Moral Fiction,* the novelist's stock-in-trade. Unlike most novels, *October Light* involves two fictional worlds, and unlike the many other post-modern novels which involve a similar juxtaposition, neither of the two "alternative realities" in *October Light* is the creation of a character in the novel. The simpler of the two is the one for Sally in *The Smugglers.* The one for the reader is more complex: it includes both "the real world sections" of

October Light, as Gardner playfully calls them in the "Acknowledge-ments," and also a variant of Sally's "alternative reality"—a variant in that it is inseparable from her reading of *The Smugglers* and so of necessity in-cludes Sally as a participant and in part takes its shape in the reader's mind from the peculiarities of her reading. Her comments, pauses, and so on continually remind the reader that *The Smugglers* is a novel—something that Sally tends to forget. The reader reads Sally reading and as a result learns the difference between fiction that is "moral" and fiction that is not, and learns too what influence fiction can exert and what effects it can have.

Sally's taste in books and television is indiscriminate, and this lack of critical taste makes her especially vulnerable to *The Smugglers'* pernicious influence. As Gardner says in *On Moral Fiction:* "...life's imitation of art is direct and not necessarily intelligent." She is like the characters in her novel who take their heroes from B-grade movies and their visions of hap-piness from advertisements for sportscars and shampoos. It is not surpris-ing then, that after her first night's sporadic reading, she begins to find the novel "improved" and "oddly comforting." She believes she now sees "The delicate way the writer mocked all those foolish things her brother James...set such store by," especially capitalism. Gradually, her real and fictional worlds blur into one. Characters in the book are linked to mem-bers of Sally's family. She gives the novel's hero the features of her dead nephew. Mr. Nit, the monkey-like scientist in *The Smugglers,* at first mere-ly reminds her of her niece's husband, the handyman Lewis Hicks, but soon she forgets Lewis's name entirely and begins to refer to him as Mr. Nit. Her brother James fares even worse; transformed into the evil Captain Fist, he is eventually blamed by Sally for even the misfortunes of her "friends" in the novel. Sally sees herself as the ever-suffering Pearl Wilson, young and black, a rape victim who believes that "the world [is] unspeak-ably dangerous." When Pearl is arrested for a murder that was never com-mitted, thus cutting short her part in *The Smugglers,* Sally tries to fiction-alize a different and happier end for her: a life among "ordinary people." By this point, however, Sally is too much under the sway of her novel's cheap cynicism and romantic glorification of the self, and so rejects the solution suggested by her own healthy imagination: to leave her book, her "friends" in the novel, and her room and to resume her life among "ordi-nary" but "real" people like James.

Sally also rejects the obvious parallels between herself and Pearl's em-ployer, an eighty-three year old paraplegic named Dr. Alkahest. Like Sally, Dr. Alkahest rages against tyranny—even the tyranny of sleep and the ty-ranny of time. His chief obsession is that marijuana "could bring him back WHAMMO his youth." Sally dismisses him as "a gothic cliche, one more version of the old mad scientist," but fails to see that she herself has be-come another stock-type: the madwoman locked in a tower. Gradually, she loses touch with life—so much so that when James's truck goes off the road, she doesn't hear the explosion that sends everyone else out of the house and to the rescue. What does she gain from her reading of *The Smugglers*? Among other things, she gains a vicarious sex-life to compensate her for the one that, as she now believes, she was deprived of in her youth. And there is also the casualness about the use of violence that leads her to plot her brother's murder and that nearly results in the death of her niece—an act for which Sally, like the characters in her book, feels neither responsibility nor remorse.

Gardner's point is that reading does influence beliefs and behavior and that the influence is for the most part subliminal. Nearing the end of *The Smugglers,* Sally "read[s] on...only to find out how far these people would dare go," without ever once considering how far she herself has already gone. Sally never does realize the extent to which she has been transformed by her reading. When a flying-saucer appears at the end of *The Smugglers* to save the hero (appropriately named Wagner) and heroine (the Jane of Dick and Jane), Sally throws the book away in disgust.

> What kind of person would *write* such slop! she'd like to know.
> And not only that, some company had *published it*! Had
> those people no shame? A thought still more terrible came
> to her: there were people out there who read such things....
> She looked out into the evening darkness, trying to imagine
> what debauched, sick people would believe such foolishness
> amusing. "Gracious!" she breathed.

Since art does affect life and because the writer's power to influence his readers is as great as their vulnerability to his power, he must take seriously "the responsibilities of the novelist." This is what Gardner explains—or rather preaches—in *On Moral Fiction.* The true artist, Gardner says, exerts a "civilizing influence." The "maker of trash," on the other hand, is a "barbarian" who extols Nietzschean self-assertion, existential despair, a simplistic opposition between good and evil, and escape from responsibility and commitment. Whether these characteristics are indeed as prevalent in today's fiction as Gardner claims cannot be fully resolved here. What does matter here is that these are the values that are glorified in *The Smugglers of Lost Souls' Rock* and in the book Gardner seems to have parodied, Robert Stone's widely-read novel, *Dog Soldiers,* winner of the National Book Award in 1975. *Dog Soldiers* is typical of the kind of novel Gardner animadverts against for misleading its readers. However, it is not at all an example of the new fiction. *The Smugglers,* on the other hand, though chiefly a parody of Stone's novel, does include a number of elements characteristic of the new fiction, especially its self-conscious (or "exposed") artifice and its "all-life-is-a-boring-novel" theme. The danger of books like *The Smugglers* is that they fail to affirm those values that Gardner feels are basic to (as James Page would say) "man's brief and hopeless struggle against the pull of the earth." In *On Moral Fiction* this danger is explained. In *October Light* it is dramatized in the form of an exemplum which might most appropriately be called "Reading the Reader Reading." By reading about Sally becoming what she reads and about how she becomes lost in an "alternative-reality" funhouse, the reader escapes Sally's fate while at the same time coming under the "moral" influence of one of America's most inventive and affirmative writers.

IV

Simply stated then, the linchpin of Gardner's theory of moral fiction is this: "Art leads, it doesn't follow. Art doesn't imitate life, art makes people do things."[32] As we have seen, Norris and Howells would have agreed about art affecting life, though they would have objected strenuously to the comment about its not imitating life as decadent, something Oscar Wilde would say—in fact, did say. However, this point of difference is not all that great. Gardner and the realists have the same goal—truth in fiction —but go after it each in his own way. The realists reacted against sentimentalism and espoused "real life." Gardner has reacted against the very different kind of realism implicit in, for example, the existentialism of Sartre and has espoused the philosophic idealism that began to go out of fashion in the nineteenth century. What is more important is their agreeing that "Art makes people do things." Several recent studies which have explored what John Cawelti calls the "complex relation" between popular literature and individual behavior[33] have supported both the assumption shared by Gardner and the realists that art does influence life and his contention that art is a major factor contributing to social unity.[34]

The purpose of *The Smugglers* section of *October Light* is to point out, in comic fashion, the serious and harmful consequences for individuals and for society of fiction that is not morally responsible. Clearly, it is not meant as an attack on popular culture. The flattering portrait at the end of *October Light* of Norman Rockwell as a serious and morally affirmative artist who "painted as if his pictures might check the decay" proves that. So does his earlier canonization of Walt Disney as "Saint Walt: The Greatest Living Artist the World Has Ever Known, Except for, Possibly, Apollonius of Rhodes."[35] Today, Gardner has said, "Our best writers are all middlebrow," and he has even made a strong case for the positive *value* of such mass appeal entertainments as John Jakes's novels.[36] Moreover, in *On Moral Fiction* he emphatically rejects both the view that the serious artist can find no audience and its corollary that the mass market writer must pander to popular taste:

> Finally, sane speech is speech to someone. The creative process is vitiated if the writer writes only for himself. This is not to say that all good writing is "popular." In the modern world, with its thousands of colleges and universities, it

is absurd to imagine that any writer exists who is of such
genius that no man of his time can enjoy and understand
him. The wail of the modern poets and novelists—that art
has lost its audience—is a piece of what Hobbes called insignificant speech. . . .

On the other hand, if an intelligent and sensitive writer
would rather communicate with the general public, let him
learn the conventions of popular fiction and turn them to
his purpose. As John le Carre, Isaac Asimov, Peter Beagle,
Curtis Harnack, and many others have shown, one need not
be a fool or a compromiser to write a mystery story, a sci-fi
or fantasy, or a book about growing up in Iowa. The fool is
the man who arrogantly denies the worth and common
sense of the people to whom he pretends to speak.

(pp. 196-197)

As Gardner suggests, the retreat into art and the emphasis on technique
that is so prevalent among the new fictionists is actually their abdication of
the writer's responsibility to society. To Gardner, who views the artist as
Shelley did, as the legislator of all mankind, this is an especially serious
fault.[37] On the other hand, the writer of popular fiction who merely reflects his age—who, as Norris said, "truckles" to fashion rather than seeking
truth—similarly fails. Gardner's solution is "moral fiction," a fiction
which recognizes the demands of art, the needs and limitations of the individual reader as well as the general society, and the author's responsibilities
to both.

Gardner's position is not, I believe, especially startling.[38] But coming as
it does in an age threatened by the further divergence of the highbrow and
the middlebrow and from a writer who enjoys considerable reputation as an
experimental fictionist and as a popular writer, his view is indeed encouraging. *On Moral Fiction* warns that aesthetically and ethically responsible literary works are necessary to the well-being of society; Gardner's fiction,
particularly *October Light,* proves that such works are in fact possible.

NOTES

1. "William Gass and John Gardner: A Debate on Fiction," *New Republic,* 180
(10 March 1979), 29.

2. Gardner has also written "Cliff's Notes" for the works of the Gawain-poet and
for Malory's *Le Morte d'Arthur.*

3. In her review of *The Life & Times of Chaucer* and *The Poetry of Chaucer,*
Victoria Rothschild pointed out that beginning with *Grendel,* Gardner has been trying
"to bring medieval literature out of its Pre-Raphaelite mists into the adolescent world
of the Tolkien reader" ("A Choice of Two Chaucers," *Times Literary Supplement,* 13
January 1978, p. 43).

4. This paragraph is drawn from my review of *On Moral Fiction* (New York: Basic
Books, [1978]), published in *New Mexico Humanities Review,* I, 3 (September 1978),
58-60.

5. "Telling A Story," *Newsweek,* 24 December 1973, p. 84.

6. Raymond Federman, ed., *Surfiction: Fiction Now and Tomorrow* (Chicago:
Swallow Press, 1975), pp. 6-7.

7. Gass once said of his still unfinished novel *The Tunnel:* "Who knows, perhaps it will be such a good book no one will want to publish it. I live on that hope" (*The New Fiction,* ed. Joe David Bellamy [Urbana: University of Illinois Press, 1974], p. 44). Gardner, who admires Gass's talent, if not his theory of fiction, was troubled enough over Gass's view to comment on it several years later: "...the rhetorical *I live on that hope* can only be comic self-mockery, a joke at the expense of exactly that posturing misanthropy which seems to lesser men the proper mark of genius..." ("Big Deals," *New York Review of Books,* 10 June 1976, p. 40).

8. See Federman's *Surfiction;* Scholes' *The Fabulators* (New York: Oxford University Press, 1967), and *Fabulation and Metafiction* (Urbana: University of Illinois Press, [1979]); and Klinkowitz's *Literary Disruptions: The Making of a Post-Contemporary American Fiction* (Urbana: University of Illinois Press, [1975]) and *The Life of Fiction,* illus. Roy R. Behrens (Urbana: University of Illinois Press, [1977]).

9. *Nation,* 22 April 1978, pp. 462-63.

10. Federman, p. 14.

11. *Atlantic,* 220 (August 1967), 30. Federman reprints this essay in *Surfiction* and probably based his own remarks on those of Barth.

12. Jerome Klinkowitz, "Critifiction, American Style," *Novel* (forthcoming).

13. "Telling a Story." Cf. Earl Rovit's directions on "How to Construct a Novel That Will Be Critically Fashionable": don't tell a story, don't have characters, don't be realistic, don't be passionate, don't even hint at approval of middle-class morality ("Some Shapes in Recent American Fiction," *Contemporary Literature,* XV, 4 [Autumn 1974], 542-43. A recent example of the pervasiveness of the opposite view is Richard Poirer's review of Henry Nash Smith's *Democracy and the Novel:* "It is the glory of our classic American writers that they were the first to show the modern world why great literature was to become rewardingly difficult, a part of what might properly be called the resistance in modern art to popularity" (*New York Review of Books,* 22 February 1979, p. 41).

14. Margaret Heckard, "Robert Coover, Metafiction and Freedom," *Twentieth Century Literature,* XXII (1976), 215-16.

15. *First Person: Conversations on Writers and Writing,* ed. Frank Gado (Schenectady, N.Y.: Union College Press, 1973), pp. 158-59.

16. *Fiction & the Figures of Life* (1970; rpt. Boston: Nonpareil Books, [1978]), p. 275.

17. *Jeffersonianism and the American Novel,* Studies in Culture and Communication series, ed. Martin S. Dworkin (New York: Teachers College Press [Columbia University], [1966]), pp. xi-xii.

18. In *October Light,* James Page, who hates television and thinks it belongs in the tractor shed, turns murderous after watching violence on television. For what I take to be a close rendering of Gardner's own view, that the arts and media should act responsibly, see the section of *October Light* called "Ed's Song." Television also plays a part in a much earlier novel, *Nickel Mountain,* where one character, George Loomis, defines love according to what he has seen on television; not surprisingly, he remains a bachelor and lives unhappily ever after.

19. *Criticism and Fiction and Other Essays,* ed. Clara Marburg Kirk and Rudolph Kirk (New York: New York University Press, [1959]), p. 87.

20. Published in *World's Work,* III (October 1901), 1337-39; III (December 1901), 1559-60; IV (May 1902), 2117-19. Rpt. *The Literary Criticism of Frank Norris,* ed. Donald Pizer (Austin: University of Texas Press, [1964]), pp. 85-93.

21. *Critic,* XLI (December 1902), 537-40; rpt. Pizer, pp. 94-98.

22. In "Frank Norris' Letter" (Brooklyn *Daily Eagle,* 1 February 1902; usually known as "The American Public and 'Popular' Fiction" and misdated 2 February 1903), Norris, unlike Gardner, argues that "Better bad books than no books." However, this essay must be understood as an extreme expression of Norris's belief in the evolution of literary taste *and* in terms of the audience for which it was written (the essay was a syndicated newspaper piece). On Norris's writing for particular audiences, see my "The Middle-Class Writer and His Audience: Frank Norris, A Case in Point," *Journal of American Culture,* III, 1 (Spring 1980).

23. "Making Ends Meet," *Time,* 20 December 1976, p. 74.

24. *New York Times Book Review,* 26 December 1976, pp. 1, 16.

25. "Fiction and Anti-Fiction," *American Scholar,* XLVII, 3 (Summer 1978), 406.

26. Don Edwards and Carol Polgrave, "A Conversation with John Gardner," *Atlantic,* 239 (May 1977), 46.

27. "Updike and Gardner: Down from the Heights," *Commonweal,* 104 (4 February 1977), 89-90.

28. The stories collected in *The King's Indian* are best approached as parodies. However all the stories, especially the title piece, concern the role art should play in life and are therefore closely linked to both *October Light* and *On Moral Fiction.* A major difference between the stories and the novel is stylistic. In "The King's Indian," for example, the treatment of the various narrative points of view is either (at best) appropriately and aesthetically complex or (at worst) unnecessarily convoluted. Thus despite all the talk at the end of the story *about* democracy, "The King's Indian" seems less an instance of moral fiction and more an example of the elitist egalitarianism which I earlier associated with the new fiction. Note too that in an interview given at the same time he was writing these stories (*The New Fiction,* pp. 169-93), Gardner speaks approvingly of how contemporary writers like himself enjoy being lost in the fiction-funhouse and then goes on to talk about moral art. Though the two ideas are certainly not mutually exclusive, neither are they exactly bedfellows in *On Moral Fiction.*

29. Robert Coover, *Pricksongs and Descants* (1969; rpt. New York: New American Library, [1970]), p. 79.

30. Edwards and Polgrave, p. 46.

31. To make the reader think of Sally Abbott as the "slave" of her book was, I believe, Gardner's intention. Witness her fondly remembering "Dusky Sally," Thomas Jefferson's slave and mistress.

32. Edwards and Polgrave, p. 44.

33. *Adventure, Mystery, and Romance: Formula Stories as Art and Popular Culture* (Chicago: University of Chicago Press, [1976]), p. 299.

34. For an excellent overview, see Alan R. Havig, "American Historians and the Study of Popular Culture," *Journal of Popular Culture,* XI, 1 (Summer 1977), 180-92. See also Robert Jewett and John Shelton Lawrence, *The American Monomyth* (Garden City, N.Y.: Doubleday, 1977).

35. *New York Magazine,* VI (12 November 1973), 64-66, 68-71. Gardner attributes Disney's "greatness and appeal" to his having been "a man who wanted to please, a man who had a downright awesome faith in the ordinary. He was a celebrator of man-as-he-is. He had no grand programs for improving man's character, only programs for making man's life more enjoyable, more healthy."

36. Edmund Fuller, "A Novelist Calls for Morality in Our Art," *Wall Street Journal,* 21 April 1978, p. 17; interview with C. E. Frazier Clark, Jr., *Conversations with Writers,* vol. 1 (Detroit: Gale Research, [1977]), p. 90.

37. *The New Fiction,* p. 178.

38. Reviewers were quick to point out other modern critics who have espoused moral fiction: D. H. Lawrence, F. R. Leavis, Lionel Trilling. Perhaps the most widely known call to moral criticism is Leo Marx's "Mr. Eliot, Mr. Trilling and *Huckleberry Finn*" (*American Scholar,* XXII, 4 [Autumn 1953], 423-40). The only study that I know of to compare with Gardner's in comprehensiveness and emotional commitment is Erich Kahler's *The Disintegration of Form in the Arts* (New York: George Braziller, [1968]). Although Gardner is, as he says, virtually alone among the new fictionists in calling for moral fiction, other, more conservative writers, have expressed their disdain for much of contemporary American fiction. Saul Bellow, for example, has pointed out how the contemporary writer's "romantic separation or estrangement from the common world" has "enfeebled literature" ("The Thinking Man's Wasteland" [an excerpt from Bellow's NBA acceptance speech], *Saturday Review,* 3 April 1965, p. 20). And Isaac Bashevis Singer has lamented that "Literature has fallen into the hands of people who are indifferent to literature" (quoted in David W. McCullough, "Eye on Books," *Book-of-the Month Club News,* February 1979, p. 12).

LETTERS and Ethics: The Moral Fiction of John Barth
John Domini

"Letters?" one of the characters here writes to John Barth, one of the other characters here, "A novel-in-letters, you say? Six several stories intertwining to make a seventh? A *capital* notion, sir!" Capital: the word in either spelling connotes great size, firm and classic structure, the forums where decisions affecting nations are made, and of course letters themselves. And this "old-time epistolary novel," as the subtitle has it, contains all four senses of the word. Spanning seven increasingly more complicated months in 1969, it manages to recapitulate all American history, rising in the end to a drama of the conflict between those who make events happen and those who stand back to see their effect:

> But tho savagery was savagery, the Baron maintained
> that all were not tarr'd with the same brush... Neither
> [side in the American Revolution] were yet routinely
> dismembering & flaying alive, or... impaling children
> on pointed stakes—had not done so, routinely, since
> the Middle Ages. Differences in degree were impor-
> tant: this was the 18th century, not the 12th; the
> fragile flower of humanism, of civilization—

Comprising 88 letters from two fairly limited general areas along our eastern coast, the novel brings into its near-900 pages enough extravagant physical detail as to suggest the entire range of sensibility, ascending finally to a grandiose allegory of the struggle between the human spirit and unconscious nature:

> Nature bloody in fang and claw! Under me, over me,
> round about me, everything killing everything! I had
> dined that evening on crabs boiled alive and picked
> from their exoskeletons; as I ate I heard the day's news
> ... Horrific nature; horrific world: out, out!

At the same time, *LETTERS* is belle-lettres, rife with allusions, multilingual puns, and other "literal" games. Its author's seventh book, it contains seven characters, and the title seven letters:

> Left to right... like files of troops the little heroes
> march: lead-footed *L*; twin top-heavy *T*'s flanked by
> eager *E*'s, arms ever-ready; rear-facing *R*; sinuous *S*—
> valiant fellows, so few and so many, with which we
> can say the unseeable!

Codes, especially, abound. According to one, each letter must begin with some symbol or letter of the alphabet, in order eventually to spell out the book's subtitle. According to another, the date of each letter is finally seen to be part of a still larger code.

This novel, then, is an enormous, multiple undertaking. Indeed Barth has always been one of those rare authors who labor to meet the greatest demands of aesthetic achievement. As he himself put it in his much-anthologized 1967 essay on Jorge Luis Borges, "The Literature of Exhaustion,"

> What makes... [Borges an artist] of the first rank, like
> Kafka, is the combination of that intellectually pro-
> found vision with great human insight, poetic power,
> and consummate mastery of his means, a definition
> which would have gone without saying, I suppose, in
> any century but our own.

But as it happens, that essay has been badly misunderstood. It is not about exhaustion; on the contrary, it argues that the great artist, and the capital work, are forever *in*exhaustible. Nonetheless, unequivocal as the passage quoted seems, John Barth continually has to explain and re-explain his point—most recently to a member of the audience at an excellent colloquy between himself and John Hawkes, published in the New York *Times.* Likewise, although common sense would argue that any author who aims so high should be honored for the attempt, if anything Barth's ideals have got him into trouble.

Over the last ten or a dozen years, his name has become something of a battle cry among critics and writers. On the one hand, William Gass effused, in a recent *Paris Review* interview, "Several of his books, in particular *The Sot-Weed Factor* (1960), are the works which stand to my generation as *Ulysses* did to its." On the other hand, John Gardner, reiterating an earlier argument of Gore Vidal's, dismissed Barth as "ambitious and fake" —though unfortunately *On Moral Fiction,* where Gardner made this argument, also reiterates the hastiness and illogic of Vidal's earlier "American Plastic: The Matter of Fiction." Barth's *Chimera* wins the National Book Award for fiction in 1972; yet Robert Scholes, long one of his staunchest supporters, expresses his disappointment with the book in *fiction international.* These examples are by no means definitive, granted, but I believe the impression they convey is correct. The great bone of contention, generally, is Barth's penchant for what he calls "self-reflexive literature." "Metafiction" is the more common name for it, and in the Borges essay Barth describes the mode as literature in which the story is "a paradigm or metaphor for itself." Now, this self-concern—this yen to describe the theory behind what he's doing *as* he's doing it—is undeniably integral to his art; the approach is most pronounced in his book of short stories, *Lost in the Funhouse* (1968), and in the three linked novellas which make up *Chimera.* Yet those books are already sinking into the past, their brighter bits sticking to our better anthologies, and thus before addressing them, I will consider the new work. There will be time to circle back later, to reflect upon Barth's career, and, ideally, to reconcile some in those opposing critical camps.

LETTERS immediately makes clear that it is a departure. The setting is not the timeless era of Scheherazade and the Greek gods, as in *Chimera,* but the Eastern Shore of Maryland and the Canadian border in and around Niagara Falls, lushly evoked, with an attention to natural detail such as this author hasn't demonstrated since *The Sot-Weed Factor.* Moreover, the political colors are painted into the picture as well:

> . . . a seven-year battle between the most conservative
> elements in the state—principally local, for as you know,
> Mason and Dixon's line may be said to run north and
> south in Maryland, and the Eastern Shore is more
> Southern than Virginia—and the most "liberal". . .who
> in higher latitudes would be adjudged cautious moder-
> ates at best.

Politics in Barth! But within the first twenty-five pages we have also Indian tribal rites, within the first thirty-five some madness about abducting Napoleon from St. Helena, within the first hundred a fevered love affair and a sprawling, tension-ridden scene in which some radicals attempt to blow up a bridge. Any reader with patience to go that far should be, thereafter, firmly hooked. For this is Barth at his most rollicking, his most energetic, the Barth who has been praised, by Hawkes, as "a comic Melville." While comparisons to *Moby Dick* generally do more harm than good, it can be said that *LETTERS* is less an unmoving funhouse mirror than a riotous Nantucket sleigh ride, booming over the waves after the biggest game.

And—thinking again of *Sot-Weed,* that book's parody of 17th-century prose, otherworldly as it might have seemed in 1960, should not keep us now from the perception that the novel's strengths are largely, and laudably, conventional. Few books can match *Sot-Weed's* headlong dramatic pace, for instance, or, above all, its way of following through on philosophic speculations until a satisfying wholeness is reached. Similarly, in some of its essential workings *LETTERS* is unabashedly plain. The conceit is that six characters are corresponding with "Mr. John Barth, Esq., Author" —that is, with another character, only slightly like the 49-year-old, twice-married father of three, John Barth. Some write directly to him; others have their mail forwarded by lawyers, lovers, surviving relatives. Therein lies the book's plainness: the characters must carry it.

None of them are young. All soon reveal themselves nearly hamstrung, furthermore, by unnerving hints that their experience is recycling as they age. Indeed—most dangerous, so far as their carrying the story is concerned —with one exception, all are drawn from Barth's earlier fiction. But that exception, importantly, is Lady Amherst, the book's greatest creation. Erstwhile lover of James Joyce and several other of this century's literary eminences, still heartsick over those love affairs and, especially, over the mysterious disappearance, thirty years previously, of her American husband and the child she bore him, nevertheless she is still full of delicious, nasty asides about her adopted country, spunkily hopeful of rediscovering her lost family, and genuinely a connoisseur of all that sensual experience has to offer, from a well-broiled trout to the heft of her lover's slack genitals. It is Lady Amherst who initiates the action, during the first week of March. By mid-month, it is she who has that fevered love affair, with one Ambrose Mensch, a reincarnation from the more ordinary episodes of *Lost in the Funhouse.* Mr. Mensch, though an avant-garde writer, is most profoundly concerned with things very much *rear*-guard: his family. His thirty-page story of their struggle up from German immigrant beginnings— humble domestic realism, for the most part—is the novel's first tour de force.

Thus these circlings intersect: juicily. Their route in previous novels is always clearly described at once, so that newcomers to the game may easily join in. Now, no summary can possibly convey the whole septagonal plot, and in fact the principal narrative throughout the first half is the heating up —as spring, naturally, heats up into summer—of the Amherst-Mensch affair. Be that as it may, the four remaining characters demand some attention, and two of them in particular.

As for Todd Andrews and Jacob Horner, they are more or less the same as in *The Floating Opera* (1956, Barth's first novel) and *The End of the Road* (1958), respectively. Andrews finds himself falling in love, at age 69, while getting deeply involved in a probate case very similar to the one that nearly led him to kill himself in 1937; Horner has his near-catatonic fifteen-year retreat in a Canadian asylum disrupted utterly by the reappearance of the man whose wife he, Jacob, killed. Andrews is, after Lady Amherst, the book's most sympathetic character: coolly intelligent about the law, his profession, he is nonetheless fiercely humane where it matters, and soon comes to function as something akin to the novel's conscience. Horner on the other hand is the story's weakest link, well and humorously handled, but not particularly interesting.

With Andrew Burlingame Cook IV, however, descended from the protagonists of *Sot-Weed,* and with Jerome Bray, a relative to the Henry Bray of *Giles Goat-Boy* (1966), we enter a more troubling, more deceitful world. The letters of Andrew B. C. IV are, ostensibly, written in 1812, and they purport to explain how the author himself was responsible for the war with England which began that year. Yet in the present, 1969, we again and again encounter an unsettling character named Andrew Burlingame Cook *VI.* This man proves by turns fatuously rednecked and disturbingly well-informed on everyone's movements and motives; he's a shadowy power in those conservative Maryland politics, and in the university where Lady Amherst works, a university that has grown no less than

350-fold in seven short years. Then has he in fact got Something Going? And if so, is his plot on behalf of the rednecks, or on behalf of the radicals, and the angry blacks in nearby Cambridge? During the novel's first half we get no straight answers, but we do have the four letters from the contemporary Andrew's namesake ancestor, and they are replete with plot and counter-plot. Apparently Andrew IV was a master player of "the Game of Governments," a spy and diplomat and much more as well, who strove to bring down his hated "U. States" by means of something that was as much on the national mind in 1812 as in 1969: a second American Revolution. His best gambit, always, was pretending to work *for* the enemy, in this case the conservative elements in the young country, the rednecks of 1812 you might say... though his work keeps him away from home for long stretches at a time, so long that from that distance it's not always clear just which side he's on....

But the most astonishing character of *LETTERS,* both in itself and as an example of making piecework from older material serve admirably, is the bizarre flying insect-man who generally goes by the name Jerome Bray. In Bray's letters, Barth gives his affection for all the playful aspects of literature its head. This insect-man "writes" on a bewildering computer, which among other problems cannot restrain itself from flashing RESET every time it spots a pattern developing; the results are simply uproarious, the funniest writing Barth has ever done. More interestingly, Bray's letters soon reveal themselves to be a parody of the self-reflexive impulse. For if one writes a novel by computer, as Bray is trying to, one does in fact get the references and the proper echoes at the flick of a switch, yet the upshot is nothing more than ream after ream of paper covered with *numbers*—devoid of human inspiration, and therefore absolutely useless. But at the same time, this computer-novelist excercises strange powers, particularly over women he happens to fancy, and he does keep promising that all those who betrayed him will pay, will RESET.

The point of the summary is this: not only that each character lives in this satisfyingly as in any earlier one, but also that he or she or it comes soon to signify some grander idea. My intention here is not to explicate each of the symbolic items held by each of the seven figures in this frieze, but to consider *LETTERS* more generally as part of Barth's whole oeuvre. But I will point out that in the letters from "John Barth, Esq." the Authorial figure intrudes, as all such figures have done since Cervantes, and so makes clear, for example, that Lady Amherst is intended "to represent letters in the belletristic sense," or that the Burlingame-Cooks speak with the voice of History itself. The explanations are always brought off with a light touch, and are addressed to other characters rather than, overbearingly, to the reader. Nonetheless soon the structure's size is given the additional support—additional to vividness, to emotional involvement, to the plots within plots—of allegory.

With all that, *LETTERS* cannot long remain primarily the love story of
Ambrose and the Lady. Their tale is, indeed, poignant and rambunctious—
Ambrose has one child, a retarded teenage daughter, and though Lady
Amherst is pushing fifty, both by mid-summer are committed to having a
baby. Yet any map of tranquil Chesapeake Bay, after all, soon "turns into
a catalogue of horrors—*204.36: Shore bombardment... area. U.S. Navy.
204.40: long-range and aerial machine-gun firing....*" And as Todd
Andrews reminds us, it was in Cambridge, Maryland, in 1967, that H. Rap
Brown made his famous pronouncement, "Violence is American as apple
pie." In the fourth section of the seven total, then, the second *T* of the
novel's larger code, we find a series of letters making reference to either
Lake Chattauqua, in upstate New York, or the small town of Chattaugua,
Maryland. We learn that the word—again, in either spelling—is an Algonkin Indian place-name, meaning "a bag tied in the middle." An emblem,
characteristically erudite and apropos, for what's going on in the novel's
structure: here in the middle the grab-bag narrative is tied. Here too, as the
emphasis shifts to the unfinished business of American history, let us consider briefly John Barth's career.

His own artistic "combination," recalling what he said about Borges, is
clear enough. His belletristic leanings have much in common with the art
of Vladimir Nabokov—in fact, Barth was one of the very few contemporary
Americans Nabokov singled out for praise in his essay, "On Inspiration."
On the other hand, this author's prolixity, and his way of developing each
character to represent a philosophical issue, recalls the methods of the later
Thomas Mann. Both of those novelists, too, are notoriously cool, and
Barth likewise gives us fiction more dispassionate than that of most Americans, preferring to wring his best effects from irony, or the manipulation
of hard decision-making and unlikely coincidence. Yet unlike the two older authors he has a grinning glee about sexual matters—sometimes unfortunately juvenile, as in the "Frig we must" joshing that undermined parts
of *Chimera.* And his most pervasive, most illuminating quality, while at
the same time his least appreciated, is the penchant he has for the big
scene.
When Todd Andrews first tried to kill himself, it was not merely by
poison or razor, but by blowing up a showboat on which he and nearly the
entire population of his home town were attending a performance. Ever
since, with the exception of the most inward-looking tales from *Lost in the
Funhouse,* Barth's fiction has seethed with battle action, high-wire litiga-
tion, or sex at the point of a knife. It is significant, for instance, that in
the ten years since *The Sot-Weed Factor* first went into paperback, the
book has enjoyed nine reprintings. From that fact, readily available on
Sot-Weed's title page, certain common-sense conclusions can be drawn,
conclusions essential to understanding this author, yet if any previous crit-

ic has made the point it has escaped my attention. Clearly, only a well-nigh incredible amount of classroom assignment would create a demand for a new printing of a 600-page novel nearly every year, even at the lower level of the standard reprint rate—roughly 25,000 copies. And while a horserace between Barth and his contemporaries, up and down the bookstore shelves, would serve no purpose here, it is worth noting that the shorter books (naturally, the ones more often assigned) have up to twice as many printings, and that the most closely comparable reprint rate I found was for Thomas Pynchon. Therefore Barth must have won a modest but stable general readership, on his own merits. Since not even Gore Vidal accused Barth of churning out potboilers, of titillating the reader with gratuitous sex or obvious gossip, then the most popularly appealing of his qualities would be, simply, providing good stories that hinge on big scenes.

The rest follows. Since he will abide no small-bore initiations and climaxes, likewise he won't sit still for those inarticulate boys and girls who generally stumble into them, and so we have that phenomenal array of human mercury, his characters. Even the naive ones can be light on their feet as Chaplin, conniving as W. C. Fields—though the family of Ambrose Mensch, here, is in general an exception to that rule. Since their minds are so quick, the problem for these people is repeatedly the same: *How make a decision?* His characters are Hamlets, brilliantly capable but too brainy for their own good, and thus Barth's voice adapts from book to book like that of the Player King. He has no one instantly identifiable tone, like Faulkner or Lawrence; his rhetoric, his metaphors, are made subservient to the dramatic situation. He can rise to poetry when it's called for, as he does with conspicuous success during the burning-of-Washington episodes in *LETTERS,* and all his voices demonstrate a remarkable flexibility, rather Jamesian, which allows him to contain several ideas in one sentence without losing syntactical force. But thus finally, as the problem of deciding what to do next and the problem of finding a voice drew ever closer, he was brought to metafiction.

Therein lies the best defense of Barth's self-reflexive explorations: that he was brought to them, by the honest, rigorous pursuit of his creative obsessions. Certainly, with the publication of *LETTERS* it becomes clear that his earlier theoretical excesses were something of a one-shot deal, and so we can appreciate better how genuinely *strange* these stories are. A piece like "Title," for example, from *Funhouse,* is far stranger than most of Walter Abish's work for New Directions, or than Raymond Federman's for the Fiction Collective. Stranger, because it is more austere: almost devoid of sensual detail, "Title" poses the Author as a numb interlocutor between the vaudevillian Tambo and Mr. Bones who bedevil any artist, one arguing that the effort is worthless, the other wishing to struggle on. In its dozen pages, "Title" doesn't merely upset one or two of the reader's expectations; it challenges the whole notion of meaning existing behind words.

Moreover, the half-dozen or so pieces from *Chimera* and *Funhouse* which do succeed (and despite its idiosyncrasy, I would not number "Title" among them) are exemplary: rippling mirrors that show us, by their very form, the formlessness that may underlie our most thoughtful decision. *"Drolls & Dreamers that we are,"* Andrew Burlingame Cook IV meditates, *"we fancy we can undo what we fancy we have done."*

This latest novel therefore is Barth's undoing of the fancy, his return to the world of social conscience and physical pain. For if our imagination can turn a mirror into a monster, it is only in part because we perceive then that we are nothing more than reflected light; we also see monsters because the tortuous history of mankind has proven time and again what rough beast confronts us in the glass. Take, for example, this reprisal for Iroquois atrocities committed under the leadership of an early Burlingame-Cook:

> Colonel Bouquet's counter-expedition that year was
> Senecan in its ferocity. The English scalpt, raped, tor-
> tured, took few prisoners, disemboweled the pregnant
> —even lifted *two* scalps from each woman, and im-
> paled the nether one on their saddle horns...

Who is Andrew Burlingame Cook IV? Using a bizarre family gift for transforming his voice and his features, he can lead Indian massacres in—ostensible—revenge against the whites, and yet also insinuate himself among the highest levels of government and society, supping with Aaron Burr or Madame De Stael, indulging in parlor talk about Romanticism and Realism with Lord Byron, all in—ostensible—attempts to undermine the American leadership. He claims to be proud of his Ahatchwhoop Indian blood, and has sworn vengeance on the entire white race. Yet the one act of revenge he carries out flawlessly is that of killing the harmless, aging poet who may be his long-absent father. Andrew slips the old man—the diplomat and sometime-poet Joel Barlow—a blanket infected with pneumonia, as they flee from Russia with Napoleon's decimated army. But this one certainty only leads to still-greater uncertainties: who is Andrew Burlingame Cook *VI*? From the first, one doubts the authenticity of those letters supposedly written in 1812. They could easily be another disguise, forged in 1969, in a last-ditch attempt to win back the current male heir to the dreadful family business, who now despises *his* father and nurses, no doubt, dreams of patricide.

In a letter sent, mid-summer, from ABC VI's home in Chattaugua, Md., to "John Barth's" home in Chattauqua, N.Y., we have tied together for us the history of the Burlingame-Cooks: from Andrew IV's middle age, in 1812 or so, to Andrew VI's, currently. Thereafter we hear no more from the ancestor; Andrew VI writes directly to his son, claiming to summarize later letters from his namesake, letters that were originally set down in a code of numbers (suggesting, to be sure, Jerome Bray's mad ambition to

have a computer do the work only the human heart and mind could accomplish). Then is it *true* that Andrew IV did all his amanuensis claims for
him, causing Washington to be burnt in 1814, and abducting Napoleon
from St. Helena in 1821? True? False? Whatever: "it is an age," as Lord
Byron is reported to have said, here, "in which the Real and Romantic are,
so to speak, fraternal twins." Bonaparte himself was "that man... who
play'd as none before him the Game of Governments, & convinced a
whole century, for good or ill, that one man can turn the tide of history."
The Burlingame-Cooks, all their lives, have—for good or ill—spun a similar
Romance out of *their* reality. Precisely which tides of recent history
Andrew VI is responsible for, we never do learn, but between his long yet
swift-moving paragraphs of history, we perceive enough to make us shudder. His deeds are not quite so monstrous as his ancestor's—differences of
degree are important; this is the 20th century, not the 18th. Still, bad
enough: Andrew VI's own father was "vaporized," oh quite accidentally,
at Alamagordo, New Mexico, in July of 1945. And before that, some thirty
years ago now, while wearing another face and another name, our Andrew
married good Lady Amherst in order later to drive her insane with his ab-
sences; then once she was helpless he could more easily throw her out,
leave her to chase pathetically after her literary men, while he of course
kept their infant son.... All for the cause, he claims, the cause. But
which cause? This very summer he may have forced the woman to suffer
a kind of drugged rape at the hands of that Caliban, Bray; how could such
an act do The Movement any good? And more than once he has proven
coolly efficient at quelling student riots and keeping the blacks pacified.
Who *are* these people?

   The best answer is the simplest: both Burlingame-Cooks are growing
old. Indeed, the reader can stomach the outrages their letters portray
largely because the sensibility we see through is, to choose a reference both
men make good use of, past *mezzo cammin*. Yes they've always been well-
educated; they know their history, their Indian languages, their personal an-
niversaries; but now these minutiae have become precious to them, as precious as all their high-minded ideals. Andrew VI may claim that he has

> ...turned (to cite the motto of this border state) from
> *parole femine* to *fatti maschii:* from "womanly words"
> to "manly deeds," or from the registration of our
> times to their turning.

Yet the statement, like most of his, is the opposite of the truth. He has
reached "the border state" in a sense other than merely settling by the
Chesapeake: deed and word, Romantic and Real, this cause and that one
have blurred. Yes, "the battle is joined," as he wanted it to, outside Washington or outside Moscow—but what is the upshot? "Men begin to die,"
nothing more. The Burlingame-Cooks begin to note that there are better
ways to serve humanity than conspiracy and murder:

> Their way takes them through the Piazza di Spagna.
> One wants to call across the fifteen decades: "Stay!
> Put by a moment these vague intrigues, this nonsense
> of Napoleon: young John Keats has just died here!"

Who is ABC IV? Well who are the ABC's for? Letters are fickle, are they not, changing to suit any need, any passion? Thus after breakneck cross-country runs and wild sea-chases, after battle action so vivid, so detailed, and so grandly orchestrated as to recall Tolstoy's Borodino, these two men have been stunned finally by the same simple emptiness that Ambrose Mensch once spotted, alone, in a certain dark funhouse mirror. The Burlingames' boiling game, one might say, has at last blinded them with its steam. And so stunned, so blinded, they can't decide what next. They have murderous offspring of their own after them by now, but they lumber on, struggling to repeat, redo, make amends. . . .

LETTERS makes ample mention of Freud's "compulsion to repeat," and of Marx's famous observation that history repeats itself first as tragedy, then as farce. Yet the novel implies, in the end, a deeper reason for our recapitulation. The implication grows as the B's here—Barth, Bray, Bonaparte, Burlingame, Barlow and many others—gather and hum; "mother of letters," Ambrose Mensch says of B, "birth, bones, blood & breast: the Feeder." And the point is underscored by means that have little to do with literature: Todd Andrews, for example, noses his skipjack *Osborn Jones* into a ferny, isolated cove off the Chesapeake and there makes love with the woman who may be his grown, illegitimate daughter, a woman who urges him: "No obligations. No problems. Feel." We recycle, in other words, because we are part of that pervasive, unconscious embodiment of pure feeling, Nature. In our makeup we carry the remembrance of the mollusk we were billions of years ago, and no metaphor crops up so often in Barth's fiction as that of the mollusk shell, which excretes an entire circle in reverse in order to grow. In *LETTERS,* as the furious plot unwinds—as that probate case draws everyone inexorably into the Burlingame-Cook web, and towards an epical re-enactment of the bombardment of Fort McHenry—the character that looms largest is the "bug," the "nut," the "disturbed, unearthly boy, more like a bird or bat or bumblebee," Jerome Bray.

"We did not know that slang expression," his computer writes, "nothing foreign is human to us." So his letters run, insane and murky as a strobe-lit disco floor, and to describe what Bray does in direct language would do no justice to the novel's effect, because a large portion of his menace is in its scattershot presentation. Horrid things are done, but we glimpse them only round the corner of a punning phrase, or in an offhand reference using some code-name of his own devising. Thus it is only after several hundred pages of this book's interdependent correspondences that he comes to terrify. At first, reading that he refers to all women as "females" is ludicrous, and the name he's chosen for his farm, "Comalot," well...but as we see these women being reduced to a blinking, drooling, animal state, as slowly we understand that even Lady Amherst may have suffered the sting of his come, then the laughter turns hideous. Surely, the jokes here are grim as any to be found in the entire current generation of so-called Black Humorists: grim as Vonnegut digging up Dresden, grim as Pynchon in "the Zone," grim as the most scabrous conversation in William Gaddis's *JR*. We learn that Bray's grandmother, for instance, was a Tuscarora princess named Kyuahaha, yes ha-ha, but we discover later that in Algonkin her name meant "unfinished business."

When at last his continually RESET-ing computer, significantly named LILYVAC, is glimpsed, humor dissolves into sinister strangeness:

> ...at least some of what you'd taken for metal or plastic was a scaly, waxy stuff, unidentifiable but vaguely repulsive; some of those wires were more like heavy beeswaxed cord, or dried tendons.

Then deliberately, inescapable as the autumn, which now comes to the Eastern Shore, Bray carries out his early comical threats. He "seeds" one or two of his "females" gruesomely, drops on other enemies like a buzz-bomb. When he surprises even the Burlingame-Cooks, since that family has so dominated the second half of the novel, it would seem nothing could ever stand up against his mad 7-Year Plans, his revenge, his final, braying triumph. And yet, and yet... Lady Amherst has remained with us all along, and the child she carries these days may not be Bray's after all, but rather the one she and her new husband Ambrose had so longed for; it may be, in fact, the fulfillment of their middle-aged hopes. Similarly, though there is unfinished business in the courts, unfinished business in Baltimore, in Washington, that in itself means there's time enough, still, to turn the enemy's strength against him. Bray and the Burlingames have been so busy they've forgotten someone, and Ambrose Mensch could show up with time enough, still, to prove himself a man, a brave man. He says boldly: "Entropy may be where it's all headed, but it isn't where it is." He knows there's a certain weakly-constructed but tightly-locked tower on a certain overgrown Maryland university campus... and we cannot forget, also, that Todd Andrews has a history of bad luck when it comes to expecting large explosions....

Large explosions; big scenes in which capital notions contend: letters and the fickle, fragile spirit of humankind; repeating numbers and the heartless hum of nature. But it should not be inferred that because *LETTERS* ends with such bold headlines (it does, literally: "*On this date in history:* ... 1814: Fort McHenry bombardment ceases; F.S. Key reports flag still there"), it resolves with a simple big bang. No; *Giles Goat-Boy,* regrettably, was in the final analysis that sort of one-noted book, a stale layer-cake of allegories. *LETTERS* however is weighty in quite another way. Setting aside what it has to say about those shameful chapters of American history that haunt us still, setting aside its powerful feminist argument, setting aside even its investigation of "natural" reality and "artificial"–life seen versus life imagined–nonetheless the attentive reader will discover more: a profound ethical question. The resolutions of its final, sinuous *S* are ambiguous as the snake itself: offering wisdom, threatening a Fall. John Gardner's broadsides notwithstanding, the decision to taste the fruit of Good and Evil is never simple, for an end, a cause, may seem clearly to justify any means until we have *already* bitten the apple–that is, until we have grown older and experienced a more painful, second education. Thus these six several stories intertwine to make a grander seventh, an American allegory of the Fall. Within their apple, its peel scarred by a thousand codes, these characters have discovered an enraged bee, bringing home to them more forcefully than ever before in their lives that accidents of nature can undo in a moment our most intricately thought-out decisions.

Yet that summary, too, seems over-simple in retrospect. Much else crowds the mind, much. For example: what the novel shows us concerning love (another experience fraught with the compulsion to repeat) suggests no *Pilgrim's Progress,* nor any computer manual, but rather the seven intertwining novels of Marcel Proust. Which suggests further: to even bother bringing such subtlety into print, these days, when most of us, buzz-happy with the media, can't take time for letters, lower-case, let alone in capitals–well it seems quixotic, and therefore of course noble, in the best, paradoxical sense. Which suggests... which suggests, further... but let those three dots by themselves make, so to speak, my final point. In order to write a mighty book, Melville tells us, you must choose a mighty theme, and with this novel John Barth establishes more clearly than ever before that his themes are *not* literary or academic, as has been too often and too hastily assumed, but rather ethical, philosophical, historical. It is tempting, on the basis of such vast issues rendered in so striking and multifaceted an idiom, to place him with the great myth-destroyers and -remakers of the present international generation: Gabriel Garcia Marquez, Gunter Grass, Italo Calvino, and Pynchon and Gaddis in this country. But whatever the eventual standing of his stock, it rests on a corpus of work which demonstrates, gaily, that the world is indeed a university. For what is lifeless, what dry-as-dust, about seeking Truth? His characters continue... continue as these three dots continue while ending... gamely they sift through the documents of their lives, getting stung whenever they bang up against the hard facts of nature, and so with their bruises multiplying and changing color, with their cumpled heap of discarded lies growing ever larger around them, they produce unknowing a new image for the face of God.

A TRESTLE of LETTERS
Brian Stonehill

> ...he put his lines together not word
> by word but letter by letter.
>
> —*Stephen Hero*

At a recent symposium of the Modern Language Association, Benjamin DeMott launched a vigorous attack on what he portrayed as the increasing toleration of incest in our society.[1] DeMott's invective was implicitly directed at John Barth's novel *LETTERS* (1979), as Barth was one of the panel's featured speakers. We may briefly consider the question raised by DeMott's polemic: is the generous presence of seemingly unpunished incest in *LETTERS* immoral?

First of all, let us correct that "seemingly": DeMott and other reviewers, misled by the novel's crafty concealment of its own climax, are mistaken in believing that the incest goes unpunished. In fact, the explosive finale in which the multiple plot-lines of *LETTERS* culminate is not even dramatized in the novel, but is only *about* to take place at the end of the novel's latest (but not its last) letter. The climax may thus be said to be hidden between two of the novel's eighty-eight epistles. Here is what actually happens.

Marshyhope State University College is about to dedicate "the Morgan Memorial Tower, variously and popularly known as the Schott Tower, the Shit Tower, and the Tower of Truth."[2] But a young revolutionary (the year is 1969) has planted dynamite charges around the tower's base, and is resolved to blow it up at the precise instant of sunrise. In the tower (as can only be gleaned from small details scattered across several letters) lurk three characters, each there for reasons unknown to the others. Jerome Bray, an evil maniac who, during the course of the novel, has drugged and raped five women and murdered, among others, a filmmaker and a poet, has mounted the doomed tower, "his business finished," in order to "ascend" to his mythical grandmother. Ambrose Mensch, apparently unaware of the dynamite, has pursued Bray into the tower so as to bring him to justice for the rape of Ambrose's angelic, mad, 14-year-old niece. Finally, 69-year-old Todd Andrews has barricaded himself in the belfry, fully cognizant of the terrorists' plans, determined to rectify the suicide attempt he botched in Barth's earlier novel *The Floating Opera*. This time, Andrews has been driven to despair and self-disgust by his own sexual abuse of his probable daughter Jeannine and by his concomitant cruelty to his ex-secretary and lover Polly Lake.

The "codicil to the last will and testament of Todd Andrews," which Andrews drafts in the belfry and sets his initials to an instant before sun-

rise at 6:54 on 26 September 1969, is the last-dated epistle in *LETTERS,*
although the novel's principle of organization requires that eight other letters ostensibly written before Andrews' sign-off appear *after* it in the book.
Ambrose, in a letter to "the Author," has warned us that

> the narrative, like an icebreaker, like spawning salmon,
> incoming tide, or wandering hero, springs forward,
> falls back, gathers strength, springs farther forward,
> falls less far back, and at length arrives—but does not
> remain at—its high-water mark.... (p. 767)

Thus, although the novel, like Ambrose's own fiction, recedes from its climax without actually dramatizing it, the explosion about to topple the
Shit Tower/Tower of Truth and kill at least three characters does indeed
mark, as "the Author" belatedly announces thirty-four pages after the fact,
"the end" (p. 772). (A similarly undramatized climax, we should note, con-
cludes Pynchon's *Gravity's Rainbow,* where a falling rocket-bomb is *about*
to explode over our heads in the novel's final line, but does not do so
within the book's pages.) Along with a self-conscious writer and a homi-
cidal rapist, whose depradations seem not to offend Barth's "moral" critic, the father whose incest does incense DeMott is thus just as certainly if
surreptitiously punished for his sins.

So much for answering the limited accusation that Barth's novel is immoral because it contains generous scenes of unpunished incest: it does
not. But surely there is a deeper issue here, and one more deeply troubling: the notion that works of art are to be condemned as immoral if they
contain representations of vice unpunished or virtue unrewarded, or fail to
hold up a model of moral behavior worthy of emulation. "Any [...] more
or less artistic medium," John Gardner asserted in his book *On Moral Fiction* (1978),

> is good (as opposed to pernicious or vacuous) only
> when it has a clear positive moral effect, presenting
> valid models for imitation, eternal verities worth
> keeping in mind, and a benevolent vision of the pos-
> sible [...]

> Moral art in its highest form holds up models of
> virtue [...] [3]

Now clearly it is natural and right for us to consider our reading of fiction as an integral, rather than an isolated, part of our lives, and it is neither philistine or naive of us, when reading the best literature, to hope to
learn something of, in Joseph Conrad's phrase, "how to be." But just as
clearly, what is objectionable in Gardner's proscriptive and prosaic call for
"valid models for imitation" is that it ignores, overlooks, or deprecates
those of fiction's inestimable resources—irony, obliquity, and above all
metaphor—that "by indirections find directions out."

Confronted by Barth's new novel, DeMott, as if he were intercepting letters passed between his own mother Gertrude and his uncle Claudius, condemns as wicked the posting of such incestuous sheets. This is the same sort of excessively literal mentality that leads Barth's character, Jerome Bray, in his efforts to "get the bugs out" of an experimental computer, to program the machine to delete all references to insects of any sort. Barth is no more recommending, in *LETTERS,* that fathers sleep with their daughters, than Nabokov, in *Lolita,* endorses the seduction of 12-year-olds, or in *Ada* advocates that brothers and sisters should become lovers like Van and Ada. "Valid models for imitation" have nothing to do with it, for fiction is not, despite Gardner's efforts to portray it as such, a form of blunt weapon. The image of a father committing incest with his grown child, for example, is appropriate to *LETTERS* in specifically metaphorical, thematic terms, because the novel is not only centrally concerned with, but is itself the result of, an author's endeavor to beget new fictional life upon his imagination's previous offspring.

For, in order to cast his seventh work of fiction, Barth has gone back to his previous efforts and drawn one character from each book, and has thereby endeavored to make of *LETTERS* not only a sequel to each of them but also a critique that extends as it interweaves all of their themes. (Barth's efforts in this direction are paralleled by those of two *new* characters, one of whom, Lady Amherst, is reading her way through all of Barth's previous books as this one progresses, while another, Reg Prinz, is busy making a movie based upon Barth's prior opus that claims to "anticipate" Barth's current work-in-progress—requiring *LETTERS,* in effect, to try to keep up with the film that is being made of it in its own pages.) From *The Floating Opera* (1956) comes Todd Andrews; from *The End of the Road* (1958), Jacob Horner; descendants of Ebenezer Cooke, hero of *The Sot-Weed Factor* (1960), abound in *LETTERS,* and from "Grand Tutor Harold Bray" of *Giles Goat-Boy* (1966) Jerome Bray traces his descent; Ambrose Mensch, now grown into an avant-garde writer, is taken from three of the stories in *Lost in the Funhouse* (1968); and from the three novellas called *Chimera* (1972) comes the dramatized version of "the Author" who in the new novel is credited with writing letters to the other six characters as well as to the reader.

This recurrence of characters across a number of discrete fictional texts creates a strange and paradoxical effect. On the one hand, characters seem more like real people when they cannot be contained between the covers of a single book. This is the principal effect in Balzac, where, for example, the identities of Vautrin and Lucien de Rubempré acquire an almost palpable independence from the individual novels in which they figure, by dint of their repeated appearance throughout the *Comédie humaine.* In *Ulysses,* too, when Stephen Dedalus reminds us that he is "A child Conmee saved from pandies,"[4] he is asserting that he is the same Stephen as that of

A Portrait of the Artist as a Young Man, and therefore somehow less of a
fictional property and more of a human being living a continuous existence.

On the other hand, however, the recycling of characters from previous
fictions ineluctably reminds us that they are, after all, fictional. The apparent ease with which Barth transplants his characters from one book to
another underscores the fact that these figments can be at home nowhere
but *in* books—an effect paradoxically opposed to the enhancement of
plausibility just described. Recurrence earns characters a bonus of "apparent reality," but at the same time it brands them as bogus. The result-
ant tension—peculiar to art that displays its own art—invites us to believe
in a self-evident fiction.

This paradoxical twinning of narrative illusion and disillusion is nowhere more evident in *LETTERS* than in the dramatized presence of "the
Author." According to the novel's subtitle, "the Author" is to be regarded
as one of the "seven fictitious drolls & dreamers" whose correspondence
comprises the text. "The Author" as he appears in the book is therefore
not to be confused with the actual John Barth, presently living in Baltimore and occasionally to be seen (dramatizing himself in other ways) at
conventions of the Modern Language Association, although the novel invites that confusion on every page. By reducing the representation of
"John Barth" inside the novel to a level of fictional reality and *vraisem-
blance* equal to that of the other characters, the Barth who wrote *LET-
TERS* thereby seems to boost the implied reality of those characters to
equivalence with his own. By blurring the line between Fiction and Fact,
that is, he bolsters the believability of what happens in his pages.

And yet—here is that paradox—each time "the Author" appears, supposedly (but not actually) *in propria persona,* it is infallibly brought to our
attention that all the creatures in the book are "his" creation, and that the
dramatized "Author" himself is a fictional creation of the actual John
Barth. One of the novel's letters itself refers to "the 'Author' character in
LETTERS" (p. 48), suggesting the image of a concentric series of masks
stacked one behind another. It is not the same nor so simple a matter as
the author's enhancing his characters' plausibility as real people by treating
them as equals, for Barth's fictional "Author" overtly addresses them as
"Characters from the Author's Earlier Fictions" (p. 190). The correspon-
dents of *LETTERS* are thus rendered both more and less human by the
same paradoxical gesture. When "the Author" writes to Ambrose,

> never mind that in a sense this "dialogue" is a mono-
> logue; that we capital-*A* Authors are ultimately, ineluc-
> tably, and forever talking to ourselves   (p. 655),

we acknowledge the statement's truth at the same time that we take its advice to put it out of our minds. To update Coleridge's view of this phenomenon, we suspend our disbelief wittingly as well as willingly.

So that when Barth shows us Todd Andrews coupling with the grown woman whom he, Andrews, engendered in Barth's first novel, what we are to see, besides a true-to-character confirmation of both Andrews' inability to resist seduction and Jeannine's immunity to taboo, is one of a dozen or more metaphors by which *LETTERS* dramatizes the conceptual principles of its own composition. This is the sense in which the novel is most clearly "postmodern": it is both "about" the lives of its characters and the ways in which those lives intertwine with each other and with History; *and* it is "about" the very question of what it means to be "about" something. Like Joyce—the instigator of the current cycle of self-conscious fiction but by no means the first in a line that includes Cervantes, Marivaux, Fielding, and Sterne—like Nabokov, and like Pynchon, Barth uses fiction to probe and divulge fiction's own presuppositions. The stories of the characters' lives, as they are rendered in *LETTERS,* manage both to be engaging, engrossing, suspenseful, funny, and rewarding on their own, *and* to function as fully realized parables of their own problematic ontology. As befits the tradition in which he is working, Barth's goals are ambitious, and his achievement of them in *LETTERS* is extremely impressive.

Ambrose Mensch mentions to "the Author" of *LETTERS* that its "theme seems to me to want to be not 'revolution'—what do you and I know about such things?—but (per our telephone talk) *reenactment*" (p. 562). Without wishing to define the notion of "theme" too narrowly, we can agree with this reading. Germaine Pitt (Lady Amherst), although she is the "new" character, nonetheless re-enacts the letter-writing of her namesake and forebear Germaine de Staël; Todd Andrews draws diagrams to document what *LETTERS* dramatizes, "his life's recycling"; Jacob Horner spends the novel trying to "Rewrite History"; A. B. Cook IV and VI rehearse the "action-historiography" of their forebears in vain hopes of avoiding those forebears' fates; Jerome Bray's quest is the computer-generation of *NUMBERS,* a digital rehash of that other J. B.'s *LETTERS*; Ambrose Mensch is careful to repeat each of his previous affairs within his present involvement with Germaine; while, like the filmmaker Reg Prinz, "the Author" (and *his* author) recycles Barth's previous characters and fictions. There is no immediate way of knowing which, in I. A. Richards' terminology, is vehicle, and which tenor; no way of knowing, that is, whether Barth has written a multi-leveled novel about reenactment because he sees reenactment as central to the lives we lead outside of books, or whether he has invented fictional images of reenactment in order to dramatize the conceptually prior strategy of his novel. In any case, the motto of Marshyhope State University College, *"Praeteritas futuras fecundant"*—the past fertilizes the future—may be taken as the motto of the novel as a whole. It accounts not only for the curious importance to the plot of preserved excrement (for "the past manures the future," too), but also for the efforts of all the characters to give direction to their futures by reenacting their pasts.

The motto applies as well to the analogous attempts by fictional fathers
and actual authors to enrich the future by embracing in the present what
they have engendered in the past.

In fashioning his novel from the stuff of previous fictions, Barth might
be charged with turning his back on the real world; with framing a fashionably hermetic response to Flaubert's famous call for "a novel about nothing."[5] It is *here*, rather than on the spurious issues of sexual metaphor or
the lack of models of virtue, that the claims of morality upon fiction must
be taken most seriously. For to deny that one's words engage the values
of the world—to assert, as the title of Barth's novel seems to do, that one's
book *signifies* no more than what, on the most material level, it *is*, a more
or less artful arrangement of letters printed on paper—this is surely to de-
prive fiction of the *spiritual* value which, from our greatest writers, we
know to be among its most honored resources and justifications. Our readings, as a Biblical epistle urges, should be "Not of the letter, but of the
spirit; for the letter killeth, but the spirit giveth life" (2 Corinthians iii.6).
The morally serious question to be asked of John Barth's novel, therefore,
is to what extent does its self-referential introversion prevent it from fulfilling fiction's ultimate responsibility to address the concerns of living men
and women?

For a start, certainly, *LETTERS* must be recognized as prodigiously self-
referential. If the initial (alphabetic) letters of each of the novel's eighty-
eight epistles are strung together, they form a coherent phrase: AN OLD-
TIME EPISTOLARY NOVEL BY SEVEN FICTITIOUS DROLLS & DREAMERS
EACH OF WHICH BELIEVES HIMSELF ACTUAL. The novel is thus a huge
(772-page) acrostic that spells out its own self-descriptive subtitle. Furthermore, if the dates to which the novel ascribes its letters are x'ed-out on
a calendar for 1969, the x'es will spell out a word: LETTERS. Not only,
then, is the novel, *inter alia*, an acrostic of its own self-description, but it
also mimics the physical shape of the word that is its title. *LETTERS* begins, in the first words of its first letter, "At the end," and ends at "the
end," that is to say, back where it started; so that the form of the whole
book is that of the closed ring or Ouroboros (the serpent-with-its-tail-in-its-
mouth), familiar from *Finnegans Wake* or Nabokov's story "The Circle" as
the structure that proclaims an artwork's autonomy, purity, and inviolabil-
ity from the messy claims of the chaotic world outside. Clearly, "art" is at
the center of Barth's strategy as it is of his name. The book's whole intricate baroque patterning, in fact, produced (as in *Ulysses*) by the characters'
unwitting conformity to the author's scheme, suggests that its concern is
less with the world than with the playing of its own neat games.[6] And
when every page reminds us of "the Author" responsible for the novel we
are reading—and reminds us that it *is* a novel, and that we *are* reading—it becomes impossible seriously to believe that any of the narrated occurrences

did ever occur or *might* ever occur in the world in which we live.

LETTERS thus denies its literal validity to transcribe the World; all it claims to do, literally, is to transcribe the Word—or its letters, rather, as alphebetic units, as epistles, and as the domain of literature (*belles-lettres*) in general. However: Barth's novel retains its claim to moral seriousness by offering, in place of the literal validity it disowns, a *metaphoric* validity to render the World. This metaphoric validity is strongly felt by anyone who reads the novel; and it is obviously nonsense to maintain that Barth, for whatever esthetic purposes, has excluded felt life from his book, when clearly the claims of the real world to enter this fiction are heeded with such encyclopedic generosity. Whether it be sequential, as in A. B. Cook's vivid reports of key battles in the War of 1812, or sliced up and restacked according to Jacob Horner's "Anniversary View," there is (as in *Ulysses* and *Gravity's Rainbow*) an enormous amount of History present inside this fiction. The wedding of a seemingly chaotic welter of fictional matter to a highly organized, ornate structure is a ceremony that Dante and Joyce, among others, have previously invited us to attend, although we still have not understood all its mysteries. It's the Grecian urn filled with an ideal gas. It's the heroic imposition of order upon chaos, the resistance against entropy, the analogue of whirling, bouncing atoms of carbon and hydrogen assuming the stunningly shapely forms of life. We may learn from *LET-TERS,* if we choose to, a prodigious amount about the world outside books: not only about American history, but also how to sail a skipjack, how to crack a code, what it's like to love at seventy, how it feels to lose a brother to cancer. Of all of Barth's work, surely *LETTERS* is imbued with the most convincing and genuine of human feelings: love of parents for their children, of sons for their fathers, of siblings for each other. Nor are the darker sides laughed away.

The novel thus *does* achieve what one of its characters calls "the transcension of paralyzing self-consciousness to productive self-awareness" (p. 652).[7] It succeeds in "transcending" its self-consciousness by renouncing its claims to "truth" on a literal level, while restating those claims on a metaphoric plane that is perhaps ultimately more tenable. William H. Gass has warned, with Wildean perversity, that "The appeal to literature as a source of truth is pernicious. Truth suffers, but more than that, literature suffers."[8] Barth, however, acknowledges the relation between fiction and fact to be considerably more complex. As the narrator of one of the stories in *Lost in the Funhouse* puts it,

> inasmuch as the old analogy between Author and God, novel and world can no longer be employed unless deliberately as a false analogy, certain things follow: 1) fiction must acknowledge its fictitiousness and metaphoric invalidity or 2) choose to ignore the question or deny its relevance or 3) establish some other, accept-

able relation between itself, its author, its reader.

In *LETTERS,* Barth has established that "other, acceptable relation." The epistolary form, as recovered by Barth from the literary past, achieves "a détente with the realistic tradition" (p. 52), by ostensibly refining the author out of existence to the point of allowing the characters to speak exclusively in their own voices, while at the same time permitting those apparently authentic voices to acknowledge the ventriloquist who produces them. Hence the characters' stories are plausible as fictions and yet do not overstate the author's claim to have a handle on reality. All the implied author of *LETTERS* claims, as far as realism goes, is that "This is what such a character would write were he or she to indite a letter about the situation in which I have chosen to place him or her." That is, "epistolarism" weds authentically moving stories to a conspicuously inauthentic text.

This yoking of seemingly opposite tendencies is analogous to that paradoxical rendition of character as simultaneously "real" and "fictional." The novel embodies an invisible but dramatic struggle between the characters' seeming independence from authorial constraint (no, they *won't* cooperate with him, yes, they *will* lead their own lives) and their equally apparent subordination to the (geometric, alphabetic, chronologic) demands of the novel's organizing principles. Lady Amherst, for example, resists "the Author" 's expressed wish to allegorize her—"I am *not* Literature! I am *not* the Great Tradition! I am *not* the aging Muse of the Realistic Novel! I am not / Yours," (p. 57)—and yet in her last letter to "the Author" she acknowledges herself to be "Your / Germaine" (p. 692). Her efforts recall Molly Bloom's plea to the author of *Ulysses,* "O Jamesy let me up out of this" (*Ulysses,* p. 769). Like Nabokov's Van and Ada, Barth's marionettes steal our hearts even as they deny the existence of the strings that we all can see. In fact we feel for and pity self-conscious characters more, not less, for their being visibly trapped inside the fiction. Their situation, moreover, as subversively acknowledged fictional characters, is ultimately not subversive after all, in that Barth makes their situation into a metaphor for our own contingent relation to life itself. The characters allude to their Author much as, were we in their shoes, we should call upon our own. Thinks Todd Mensch of the daughter he has abused and lost track of, "Jeannine, Jeannine: what has our Author done with you? And if your little cruise with me furthered His plot, can you forgive me? We've little time" (p. 735).

The error of self-proclaimed moralists such as Gardner and DeMott is that they wrongly assume that fiction must be *either* mimetic *or* self-referential. When confronted by a work that is clearly concerned with the autonomous nature of language, they condemn it for immorally neglecting the serious concerns of real life. But the wonderful and inadequately understood fact is that all fiction, and most explicitly self-conscious fiction, may *both* "render the highest kind of justice to the visible universe" and at the same time "not mean but be."[9] Ambrose Mensch describes the calendrical organization of the novel in which he appears as

> a form that spells itself while spelling out much more
> and (one hopes) spellbinding along the way, as lan-
> guage is always also but seldom simply about itself.
>   (p. 767)

LETTERS thus offers a TRESTLE (in the sense of a bridge) between "postmodern" sophistication and the "old-fashioned" springs of narrative; between the World as the writer's only legitimate subject and the Word as his or her only available medium; between the word as exploratory tool and the word as reflexive toy; a TRESTLE between History and Fiction, between believable characters who stand on their own and an acknowledged "Author" who just as clearly pulls their strings; a TRESTLE between tradition and experiment, as between earnest and game. This farrago of ambition and obsessions, this macédoine of Modernist Formalism and "Historical Fiction" is, like *Ulysses,* an inquiry into History that endeavors to roll all time and space into one neat, compact ball. An atomization of language conjoined to a conflation of the entire tradition of the Novel in English, a narrative in which character and fate cooperate with alphabetical priority and postmodernist generative devices in establishing the novel's texture and form, *LETTERS* takes a bold step forward with eyes fixed firmly behind. The past fecundates the future, in our lettered lives as in these lively letters.

NOTES

1. "The Self in Writing: A Forum arranged by Norman N. Holland and Murray M. Schwartz, Center for the Psychological Study of the Arts, State Univ. of New York, Buffalo, and sponsored by the Divisions on Literary Criticism and Prose Fiction," at the 94th Annual Convention of the Modern Language Association of America, San Francisco, California, 28 December 1979.

2. John Barth, *LETTERS* (New York: G. P. Putnam's Sons, 1979), p. 734. Future references are in the text.

3. John Gardner, *On Moral Fiction* (New York: Basic Books, 1978), pp. 18, 82.

4. James Joyce, *Ulysses* (New York: Random House, 1961), p. 190.

5. Gustave Flaubert, letter of 16 janvier 1852 to Louise Colet (No. 398), *Oeuvres completes* (Paris: Club de l'Honnete Homme, 1974), XIII, 157-60.

6. For example: Lady Amherst lives at "24 L Street," an anagram for "LetterS" plus the number of letters she is credited with writing; Jerome Bray, who calls his mother's mother "Granama," is thus descended from an anagram of "anagram."

7. This "transcension" is best dramatized in the growth of the character who introduced himself in *The End of the Road,* "In a sense, I am Jacob Horner," and who starts out in *LETTERS* by writing to himself, "In a sense, you remain Jacob Horner." By the end of *LETTERS,* however, he has remobilized himself,\and is able to conclude affirmatively (no longer "in a sense"), "I am, sir, / Jacob Horner" (p. 745).

8. "William H. Gass" (an interview), Carole Spearin McCauley, int., in *The New Fiction: Interviews with Innovative American Writers,* ed. Joe David Bellamy (Ur-

bana: University of Illinois Press, 1974), p. 34.

    9. The former quote is from Joseph Conrad, Preface to *The Nigger of the 'Narcissus,'* rpt. in *The Theory of the Novel,* ed. Philip Stevick (New York: The Free Press, 1967), p. 399. The latter quote is from Archibald MacLeish, "Ars Poetica":

        A poem should not mean
        But be.

Reviews

William Kittredge, The Van Gogh Field
(University of Missouri Press)

Just now setting down the eight stunning stories that are *The Van Gogh Field* (co-winner of the 1979 St. Lawrence Award for Fiction), I realize how tempting it is to simply call William Kittredge one of our finest "western" writers. He is that, of course. His evocations of life and loss of it are situated in the "Big Sky" country, that breadth of place running down from the buttes of eastern Oregon into the various wilds of Idaho, Montana, Wyoming, the murderous backwaters and vacant crossroads, the awesome mountains and roadside graves of busted combines and pick-up trucks, the barroom brawls and hopeless nights sustained only by the pitch and whine of country music, the bloodied revelations of men and women ever at odds with themselves and the overwhelming landscapes they suffer and glorify. All this is common yet unforgettable fare for a Kittredge story.

But Kittredge is more. For one, he is an articulate, masterful prose stylist, no less a talent in this regard than Thomas McGuane and Stanley Elkin. Indeed, it seems possible to open to any page and run head-on into a knock-out passage. Here, for example, is a description of an old man dying: "Everything was the same, and he was imprisoned to await cessation like a living rodent within the darkness of a snake's digesting length, already engrossed in useless panic and wanting back his freedom to be always old and cold and alone."

Kittredge also displays the unique and considerable ability to create character in league with environment: "Clyman Teal: swaying and resting his back against the clean-grain hopper, holding the header wheel of the

Caterpillar-drawn John Deere 36 combine, a twenty-nine-year-old brazed and wired-together machine moving along its path around the seven-hundred-acre and perfectly rectangular field of barley and seemingly infinite slowness, traveling no more than two miles in an hour, harvest dust rising from the separating fans within the machine and hanging around him as he silently contemplates the acreage being reduced swath by swath. . . ."

What, finally, Kittredge achieves—within and without his familiar western settings—is a fiction that renders beautifully the shifting, subtle relationships between what is real and what is perceived as real. Succeeding in this, Kittredge has now moved forward as one of our finest story writers, boots and saddles aside.

In this far country, in the parade of mangled lives, cindered hopes and missed connections, Kittredge provides massive doses of sympathy ("The Van Gogh Field"), the ravages of history ("The Stone Canal"), second-hand love ("The Man Who Loved Buzzards"), and gut-clenching terror ("The Soap Bear"). But with Kittredge it is misleading to label by themes or trends. Instead, his stories are ultimately textures, unique fields of experience, given to touch, vision, reflections, complexities unto themselves. Further, the people of these stories are neither so exaggerated as to be caricatures nor so predictable as to be stereotypes. They are, in all their diversity, quite believably human. I can wish for you nothing better than a few evenings to enhance your mind by allowing William Kittredge to become an important and permanent part of it.

G. E. Murray

Jean Thompson, The Gasoline Wars
(University of Illinois Press)

"Worldly Goods," the third story here, might have made a more apt title for this first collection, since this book shows the marvelous range of Jean Thompson's fiction—quite enough worldly goods for any reader, and satisfactions that only begin with fine sentences. The ten stories are excellent: clear, honest, paced, fair. In the fashion of Eudora Welty's fiction, they cast a wide net for the truth.

The truth is a black woman beaten by her husband, in "The People of Color," and her white neighbor learning this and more: that not all women's wounds are visible as black eyes, treatable as broken bones. It's that bleak Midwestern longing caught so beautifully in "Worldly Goods" and "Driving to Oregon," when even the answers fade to a pinpoint in a flat landscape that never stops. In "The Lost Tribe," it's an Indian getting drunk in a bar at a white convention for a Boston-based packaging firm—

the Indian perfecting his sorrow, drowning his ghosts. In this big story, we sentimental, inappropriate whites are the real lost tribe, and Hector the Indian goes under the tide of our misdirected and naive love like a bloated fish. The truth is the stylized game of a love affair in the finely-executed "Paper Covers Rock." And it is the meagre limits of the fictional eye, in "Bess the Landlord's Daughter": "I am a tourist of the emotions, visiting only the most well-worn spots. It is romantic, that is, a distortion, to imagine whole lives from the barest observation." And the limits of fiction itself. "Applause, Applause," a story about a writer, catches all the self-consciousness, the bitterness, the preening, the despair, but ends (believe it) with a blessing on language and the work with words.

What a pleasure to read a writer who depends not on fancy tricks and literary sleight-of-hand for her work, but instead on the foundations of the best fiction: characterization, situation, tension, release. And what pleasure to read stories that don't rest on their wisdom (which would only make it precious) but instead pass it along as they go. Consider this casual observation about a moony 15-year-old girl: "At her age sometimes you only had to look at a man to have all of him that you needed." Or this, about the writer in "Applause, Applause": "He even admitted to himself that beneath everything he'd wanted his success acknowledged. Like the high school loser who dreams of driving to the class reunion in a custom-made sports car. As if only those who knew your earlier weakness could verify your success."

These stories mean to tell us how we are. Such information is not usually to be found in the crafty O. Henry ending, nor in the spangled somersault of the self-conscious writer who delivers you a hot image in the last line. But instead it is usually located half-way between here and there—we don't get all that we want, but we get something. The longing and dreaming have a use—they count—and so does the failure. We get old mortality, sometimes sweet compromise, the choice of whether to laugh or cry, and always the choice to endure. If we're talking about moral fiction, Jean Thompson is a writer to celebrate.

Mary Peterson

John Casey, Testimony and Demeanor
(Knopf)

The narrators of the four stories by John Casey in *Testimony and Demeanor* are all men of a singularly isolated turn of character; and their solitude seems to me poignantly American.

There are, in fact, rather few heroes in European fiction whose essence and trademark is their inability to get along with their fellow men: the only one who comes immediately to mind is Martin Chuzzlewit, and, neatly enough for my thesis, *he* ends up working out his problems in the New World.

American literature, to the contrary, breeds a species of protagonist whose main attribute is discomfort with his own humanity. One branch of the tradition of isolation is noticeably Calvinistic and implies solitude by divine fiat, or at least by physical fact: birthmark, brand, impotence, idiocy, whale-mutilation, something which is unchangeable, stamped on indelibly, a mark of innocence or guilt not to be outgrown.

Casey adheres to the other branch; the aloneness of his heroes is not predestined, or fated, or, on the face of it, even terribly serious. It derives from a feeling of shame brought on by a sense of intellectual and moral superiority. In European fiction, a sense of his own power tends to lead a man straight to classic excess or Romantic damnation: to becoming Don Juan or Faust. In American thought, which appears to be controlled by rigid laws of modesty, perhaps because they are necessary to support a democratic ideal, a sense of superiority more often leads merely to deep discomfort; to the strange paralysis epidemic in Wharton and James, or, as in Casey, an inability simply to identify oneself as a member of the human race.

Each of John Casey's narrators is central to the story he narrates, and the isolation of each is the central fact of his being. They are four characters in a single mode, observers who recognize the distortion implicit in their aloofness but who struggle against being drawn into passions they intend only to observe.

In "A More Complete Cross-section," for instance, the narrator is delighted to go on active duty in the Army because he feels he will "see a more complete cross-section of my fellow man." What he sees is little more than their shadow reflected against his own insistent coolness, until at last the power of their indifference breaks through even his ironic armor. In "Mandarin in a Farther Field," another aloof young man is called into a sort of inadvertent espionage. In his "opposite number," a Russian clerk called Pavel, he sees the positive reflection of himself, the charm, spontaneity and warmth which he has already begun to stifle under encroaching cautions. In the title story, the last in the book, a young lawyer, cautious, callow, hardworking, is persuaded towards life by his older *Döppelgänger,* a partner in the firm, who is, clearly, the younger man as he will be when his mechanical and soulless youth has been wounded and disappointed into a feeling, searching, and garrulous old age.

In "Connaissance des Arts," the longest and most complex of the four stories, a graduate teaching assistant at a state university avoids, then succumbs to, the crush of one of his students. The piece, which is certainly more about the relationship of life to art and art to life than about anything so simple as love, is full of delicious moments. A favorite is that in which the love-struck Miss Hogentogler is practising the part of Viola in *Twelfth Night,* and our hero, the teaching assistant, is forced into reading the Duke. Painfully embarrassed by the awareness that they are re-enacting in their reading the roles they play in each other's actual lives, he is totally at the mercy of the part he has been given: he can no more change his character, knowing himself a self-conscious fool, than he can change the Duke's comically pontifical insensitivity.

These are marvelous stories, brilliant evocations of the loneliness of an ironic disposition and the self-deception of self-reliance. Much more than that, they are also portraits, exquisitely felt, of the relationship of growth to mortality. Caught in a paralysis of self-awareness, the heroes of these stories seem under an evil enchantment, male carriers of the Lady of Shalott's disease, forever spectators of their own lives rather than participants. They cannot engage with themselves as aging, changing, feeling beings, but see their aging, changing and feeling selves externalized as someone else: as Pavel, the vital analogue of the narrator's fading enthusiasms; as Mr. Pelham, the vulnerable, tired old lawyer, urging experience on his reluctant, youthful *alter ego.*

The characters of these stories are extraordinarily well-drawn; Pavel, Miss Hogentogler, and Mr. Pelham are particularly admirable portraits. The writing is splendidly entertaining. And if there is something rather adolescent in Casey's division between his protagonists and the life which flows by around them, it is adolescent with witty, self-knowing, self-mocking genius, the tragi-comedy of American malaise at its finest.

Edith Milton

T. Coraghessan Boyle, Descent of Man (Atlantic-Little, Brown)

It occurs to me that T. Boyle is in danger of being packaged in a wrong wrapper, that such hype as is possible with a new writer's first story collection—and remember, when his novel is ready the hype can be as considerable as a publisher thinks the traffic will bear—is unfortunately conceived. Glitterature. *Descent of Man* presents Boyle as a kind of bookpage Mel Brooks; we get a heavy fix of his cranky facility with the language, his gift for parody, his mad-scientist skew on character and situation. The result is a breathlessly artsy book, hard to read except in small doses, remembered finally for its inventions, its perversities, its general unpleasantness. Boyle is one hell of a writer—imaginative, energetic, bright, with an ear for dialogue and eye for detail few of his contemporaries can match; I think what gripes me is that this collection sells him short. He is not just clever; he is not some berserk Scrabble player; he is not a movie freak volunteering for an experiment in automatic writing. Poor T. I so much like some of his stories that aren't collected here, I sound as if I'm writing a negative notice.

Only partly. Here are some stories worth savoring, long after you've laid the book aside: "The Champ," about a battle between two heavyweight gluttons; "A Second Swimming," in which Chairman Mao becomes a new Jesus; "De Rerum Natura," the one story in which all of Boyle's talents, facilities, and eccentricities mesh to create The Inventor—in as satisfactory a biography of God as you could wish for—and "Drowning," which is not a particularly pleasant piece, but which haunts in spite of itself.

For the rest, there are nice moments and dull, realized ideas and failed. A lot of ersatz Kafka—"The Champ" and "The Big Garage" owe a debt to "A Hunger Artist" and *The Trial,* respectively; a bit of formula-upside-down, as in the Lassie story, "Heart of a Champion"; some movie-buff tropicana, as in "Green Hell" and "Quetzalcóatl Lite" (which play off the jungle plane crash and white goddess genres), and "De Rerum Natura" (which manages to break free of the weird scientist paradigm); and just a touch of the literary-mythological—"Earth, Moon," with its allusion to Icarus, and "Bloodfall," whose bow seems to be toward the Old Testament. It all adds up to a fast shuffle through the work of a writer whose publishers don't yet realize what a good man they've got.

Robley Wilson, Jr.

Stanley Elkin, The Living End (Dutton)

Murdered during a holdup of the liquor store he owns in Minneapolis-St. Paul, Ellerbee, one of the protagonists of Stanley Elkin's fictional triptych, *The Living End,* ascends to Heaven. Not only does he find the Streets of Gold and Pearly Gates and Heavenly Choir of the Celestial City to be exactly as the conventional wisdom has always pictured them; he realizes, too, that his translation into the next world has significantly improved his vocabulary and thus heightened his perceptivity to the little ecstasies of paradise. No sooner does he realize this, however, than he finds himself cast down into Hell—because he took His name in vain, God will subsequently explain to him, because he coveted his neighbor's wife and stayed open on Sundays. Expanded lexicon and exaggerated sensibilities intact, Ellerbee spends his time among the damned, dodging pitchforks hurled at him by cloven-footed demons and suffering all the familiarly terrible torments of the netherworld, aware now that heightened perception can sometimes be a mixed blessing.

Mixed or otherwise, heightened perception is the blessing that Elkin's fiction has consistently attempted to bestow upon his readers. Each of his stories and novels are dedicated to examining the images we carry in our heads and to altering the ways in which we think about things. In *The Dick Gibson Show,* for instance, he used the projected reality of American broadcast radio as a medium through which to explore our assumptions about the ordinariness, the everydayness, the routineness of existence; in his most recent novel, *The Franchiser,* he gave imaginative substance to the American energy crisis by metaphorizing it, in harrowingly visceral terms, into the disintegrating nervous system of a protagonist succumbing to multiple sclerosis. In *The Living End* he takes on the received Christian vision of the afterlife and, among other things, has a rousing good time with it, pointing up its absurdities, deflecting its moral import, humanizing and ultimately transforming it from the authoritative Western myth into a lively and delightfully suggestive fiction.

In recasting Christian eschatology in highly idiosyncratic terms, Elkin's small book runs two large risks: that his imaginative recreations of Biblical narrative will be dwarfed by the magnitude of the material he is attempting to transform, or that his book will seem nothing more than a Bronx cheer aimed at the West's major symbol system, a cynical gesture lacking utterly in the resonance of the stories it tries, half-seriously, to replace.

Elkin skirts the first objection through pure power of imagination, his inventive reinvigoration of Christianity's conventional wisdom captivating enough to muscle the original temporarily out of mind. What prevents the book from degenerating into mere anti-Christian raillery is the extent to which Elkin cares about his mortal and celestial characters alike, the all-suffusing sympathy which, in *The Living End,* as in much of his fiction, distinguishes dark comedy from black humor. The man who attempts to subvert God's eternity by having his fellow Hell-dwellers count it out in human seconds, the Christ who holds His crucifixion against the Father and spites Him by parading His unhealed wounds and crippled limbs through the streets of Paradise, the boy precipitously snatched from the Earth to play Suzuki violin for the Queen of Heaven—all are caricatures, but caricatures with a life of their own who refuse to be reduced to the allegorical point they were introduced to make. Even God, the unmistakable bully of the piece, is not left without some of the author's sympathy, for He understands, as Elkin does, how bitter a thing it is never to have found a large or appreciative enough audience for One's work.

Perhaps more responsible for the book's success in overcoming the gravity of its source material and establishing itself as something beyond scriptural parody is Elkin's highly precise, endlessly evocative language. We are shown, for instance, sufferers in Hell whose "nerves like hideous body hair grew long enough to trip over and lay raw and exposed as live wires or shoelaces that had come undone." We meet Jay Ladlehaus, kicked out of Hell and back into the grave by God for heresy, who thus becomes the first truly dead man in history, lying six feet under, "his consciousness locked into his remains like a cry in a doll." Or we have Mary's bitter meditations upon the Father's amatory techniques: "He was the Creator and He'd been around the block a few times. With Leda, with Semele, with Alcmene, with Ino and Europa and Danae. In all His kinky avatars and golden bough Being and beginnings. He was a resourceful lover and came at you as holy livestock or moved in like a front of gilded weather."

It is with descriptions, images and similes like these that Elkin transforms his blasphemous cartoon into something like poetry, into a compelling fantasy which has as its method as well as its object the heightening of perception through language, through story. In making us think about the stories we have, *The Living End* does what all good fiction should do—it makes us think about the stories we need.

Peter Bailey

Robie Macauley, A Secret History of Time to Come (Knopf)

It is a recondite premise: in dreams frontiers dissolve. Somewhere beyond the boundaries of space and time, the dreamer presages the dreamed and, once awake, forges a certain continuum, a written link, between himself and others to come. As long as one passes on the fact of his existence to another, civilization survives.

The dreamer in this haunting, intelligent novel is a black Defoe, a Chicago newspaperman recording the events of his own plague year at the end of the twentieth century. The reporter bears witness in his secret diary to the holocaust caused by civil war, black man against white, an "agony and excess of sorrow" (Defoe's words) that will lead at last to the devastation of America.

The dreamed man is Kinkaid, whom the black recorder senses is searching for him, a successor who appears to symbolize the continuity the black man establishes by his act of writing.

Skillfully weaving the reporter's record of his final days with the beginning account of Kinkaid's odyssey—decades, perhaps centuries, hence—Robie Macauley mounts a stunning tale as suspenseful as it is ingenious. Once immersed in Kinkaid's travels through the dis-united states of the future, the reader willingly suspends disbelief and joins Kinkaid as he struggles westward from Pennsylvania, following a relic document of the forefathers, an Esso roadmap of the North Central states, toward the fated objective, Chicago: "the endless streets of the forefather place...the many-towered city by the great lake—drawn toward his dream rendezvous...." It is a journey through tangled forests and urban ruins, a land of slave trad-ers and victimized survivors and, instead of the *Argonaut,* Kinkaid leads two horses through the wasteland.

This is unwieldy material, but never does Macauley let it get out of hand. The fact that characters rise and fall—village merchant Greenberg, who turns back; young Berk, who swims away; Mary, loved and lost when enemies ravage her village; fellow adventurer Haven and his daughter, who are torn away by the raging river—all serves to highlight Kinkaid's isolation and courage. What we have here is a classic hero, and the author's compas-sion for Kinkaid is infectious.

In his 1964 analysis of fiction skills, *Techniques In Fiction* (with George Lanning), Macauley wrote of place, setting, milieu: "The country and the weather of a story are always those of the writer, too. He has so seized in his imagination upon a particular place that it has been transformed into something which, although it may retain a recognizable geography, depends for its 'truth' upon the consistency and passion of his vision."

Having decided that most science fiction is my own personal plague, I haven't a clue if *A Secret History of Time to Come* conforms to genre pro-totypes. I only know that in the silence of forest and fields and man-erected broken canyons of steel, there is terror, overwhelming sadness, and beauty. The professor has practiced gorgeously what he preached.

Laurie Levy

Fred Urquhart and Giles Gordon (Editors) Modern Scottish Short Stories (Hamish Hamilton)

> *Knedneuch land*
> *And a loppert sea*
> *And a lift like a blue-douped*
> *Mawkin-flee.*
> —Hugh MacDiarmid

I quote MacDiarmid only as a reminder of how aggressively Scottish it is possible to be in the interests of a national literature. The editors of this collection of stories attempt a more modest settling of scores. MacDiar-mid's fabricated dialect deliberately defies cooption by the foreign cultur-al tradition which so easily absorbed as its own the works of Scott and Stevenson. Fred Urquhart and Giles Gordon claim only to demonstrate that "what is being written in Scotland today" displays at least as much "gusto, passion, rumbustiousness and vigour" as the work of contemporary English short story writers. There is nothing here to suggest that the interests of a narrow nationalism are being served. The correction here attempted, therefore, is unlikely to draw fire upon itself, and as unlikely to promote the book's wide circulation. And yet I am uneasy with the editors' claims, not because they are excessive (except, perhaps, where they take the form of glib assumptions about the influence of Scottish "vigour" on the literature of other countries), but because they are at odds with the actual strengths of the anthology. What emerges as one reads is less an awareness of the competence of the writers—there are no noticeably weak contributions—than a sense of the rich possibilities of Scottish experience as a source of effective fiction. Thus, when the editors justify the inclusion of a particular story on the grounds that it "depicts a side of Scottish life that [they] wanted to show," they strike a more convincing note than is achieved elsewhere in the introduction.

The broad range of Scottish life is amply represented here. Eona Macnicol's "The Man in the Lochan" and Naomi Mitchison's "The Sea Horse" reveal the persistence of the old legends of Gaelic tradition and render the soft cadences of the Highlands and the islands with convincing skill. The grim humor and harsh realities of ship-yard and coal mine appear in Margaret Hamilton's "Bung" and George Friel's "A Couple of Old Bigots," which also reproduce the dialectal forms of a still vital Scots language. Fred Urquhart's "Maggie Logie and the National Health" employs a uniquely Scottish idiom to sustain its broad comedy. Such stories evoke a history and a folklore filled with energy and sensitivity and a contemporary national life that is as varied and as complex as one could imagine. It is in the inclusion of these stories, which clearly spring from deep-seated affections, that the worth of this collection is most fully demonstrated.

To say this is not to slight those pieces which are really Scottish only by virtue of the parentage of their authors. Douglas Dunn's "The Blue Gallery," for example, is innovative and effective, revealing affinities with the work of Donald Barthelme which would be worth pursuing. This piece, and others like it, serve the stated purpose of the editors, confirming the range and originality of the Scottish imagination without necessarily drawing for their inspiration on identifiably Scottish motifs or settings. The cosmopolitan character of these pieces is no bad thing in itself, but it seems a drawback here, where we are attracted most strongly to those stories which serve to confirm the vitality of a national experience.

Kerry Grant

Jim Harrison, Legends of the Fall
(Delacorte/Seymour Lawrence)

First of all, because there will be some niggling criticism later, let us get this much straight. "Legends of the Fall," the novella, is an item I regard with clear and nearly boundless enthusiasm. Maybe it has something to do with the fact that we both, the story and I, live in Montana.

I say this because "The Man Who Gave Up His Name" is also a quite remarkable and precisely evocative piece of business, and yet I am less drawn to it. A friend, quite an accomplished fellow, recently nominated for the National Book Award in fiction, rather urban in his tastes to my notion, thinks "The Man Who Gave Up His Name" is the clear masterwork in this collection of short novels. All I can say is that I do not agree, and that my reasons are emotional. Sometimes you like one good horse more than you like another good horse. Sometimes you make bets on such a basis.

About "Revenge," the third of these stories, well, darn, like the others it is wonderfully imagined and specific for the most part, and yet at the end it is embarrassing. The romantic technique which succeeds so wonderfully in "Legends of the Fall" stumbles and goes face down in the mud of sentimentality.

Schoolboy lesson to be learned again: Sentimentality is unearned emotion, the story asking the reader for an emotion it has not generated. It is a technical fault. There are no inherently sentimental human situations. But there are sentimental people, as we know too well, who blather on and on in soap-opera fashion about emotions they cannot in their telling bring us to share. Stories are like that. They must generate in us the emotions they seek to evoke, by dramatic actions we have seen and/or imagined in enough specific detail to believe in and care about. The ending of "Revenge" is overblown, that is, puffed-up and out of proportion to the willingness to care it has generated.

Enough niggling. Let's deal with rumor. On the grapevine of reward and jealousy we have all heard the movie stories about this collection, tales of Big Money. Jack Nicholson is supposed to have financed the writing. And, you know, with his blessings, somebody down there in Hollywood bought "Revenge" for A Lot Of Bucks. Well, God Bless. High Time. Jim Harrison was a fine poet before most of us discovered typing. *Farmer* is just a dandy novel. Rumor has it he is going to build a kitchen on his house with some of the money. Good cooking to you, James Harrison.

On this subject of writing and making money, I am moved to quote a poem by Brecht I recently found in the *New York Times Book Review* and pinned up above my typewriter.

> Teaching without pupils
> Writing without fame

> Are difficult
> It is good to go out in the morning
> With your newly written pages
> To the waiting printer, across the buzzing market
> Where they sell meat and workman's tools:
> You sell sentences.

Of course, those of us who have stayed Sadly Pure can bask in the irony that Hollywood bought "Revenge," the least successful of these novellas. It remains true, we are Too Pure.

Or not. In the first place movies are another breed of cat, as we all should know by now, proving themselves in visual ways which are sometimes quite distinct from the methods of writers. Without getting further into this thicket, let me say it is quite possible "Revenge" could be a terrific movie.

As could be, it seems to me, "Legends of the Fall." Back in 1971 or so, when I first read *One Hundred Years of Solitude,* I was moved to all sorts of bombastic diatribe heralding Romance as the coming thing in narrative. A way of storytelling which could be both serious and popular. We all know how Northrup Frye defined Romance: Stories about characters who are somewhat larger than life. If I could lay my hands on my copy of *The Anatomy of Criticism* I might be more precise. Anyway, let that do for these purposes.

The characters are larger than life, and the world is a heightened version of our own. Precisely the case with "Legends of the Fall." While the world here is not inhabited by magic, as it is at times in *One Hundred Years of Solitude,* the people are as possessed and obsessional, committed to actions which move the world in extreme ways most of us never contemplate. They are active in a world in which actions count. The life of the mind is revealed in its embodiment in those actions. In Romance we find narrative freed from the closet of interior life, the so-called trap of the mind so prevalent in realistic fiction—the notion of point of view being centrally operative here, as is the idea of perspective in realistic painting. The psychology of seeing in the case of painting, the psychology of experiencing in the case of fiction. In any event, psychology. Romance steps out from psychology, and focuses its attention upon actions which reveal. Film, being primarily visual, is much the same. Ideally, in film, you don't get much introspection, since the ways of presenting it tend to be so awkward and forced, soliloquy and voice-over and what have you. Again, the life of the mind has to be revealed by its embodiment in action.

Which is why a superior Romance such as "Legends of the Fall" should be a straight road, if there ever was such a thing for film-makers, into a crackerjack movie. A world of places whose names we know is encountered, embraced, fought against, lived in at times with ease and at other times with enormous difficulty by men and women whose vitality demands we care about them. Perhaps they are not larger than life; could be they are just large as we ought to be.

> They sat still and fireless through the night and then at
> dawn in the fine sifting snow they crept forward in the snow
> and wiped it from the faces of a dozen or so dead until Tristan
> found Samuel, kissed him and bathed his icy face with his own
> tears: Samuel's face gray and unmarked but his belly rended
> from its cage of ribs. Tristan detached the heart with a skin-
> ning knife and they rode back to camp where Noel melted
> down candles and they encased Samuel's heart in paraffin in
> a small ammunition cannister for burial back in Montana.

Well, maybe my choice of that quotation says something about me, but God Dammit. I want to say that maybe the most central thing we take from this book is a sense of possibility, that it is, despite rumors, possible to live on this planet. I have gone and said it.

Legends of the Fall is an accomplishment of enormous energy and grace, niggling aside, cause for celebration among those who love fine stories and the craft of revealing them. Money in the bank for all of us, storytelling taking a step back toward its ancient role of making the world sensible and worth bothering about.

William Kittredge

Mary Robison, Days (Knopf)

Mary Robison's stories recall those '70s superrealistic airbrush paintings of Chevy convertibles, gas stations, hamburger stands, and other pop Americana: they dwell on the common, making art of it, with that same unrelenting blown-up detail. As a result they're bigger than life, both magnetically attractive and awfully plain, and sometimes frightening, as in this description from "Care": "He took out a thin green cigar and set fire to it." The greenness of that cigar, the violence of its lighting—this is the kind of brightness Robison plays with, the kind of image-making that makes her stories intensely satisfying to read, but unmemorable, much like the paintings.

Each of the *Days* is a moment excerpted from someone's longer story, beginning in the middle and ending in the middle, standing like an acronym for the whole. More often than not, the characters are family, the scene domestic, the events mundane but with implied importance. It's also implied that nothing much different happened before or will happen after the story. The rendering is clean, flat, accurate, full of dialogue, and nearly emotionless, and the total effect is what Barth calls a "hard-edged, fine-tooled, enigmatic super-realism."

Though nothing much happens, the incipient draws the reader on. In "Kite and Paint," two men in their sixties await a coastal storm in their beach house; when the storm is imminent, they decide to fly some exquisite handmade kites, sure to be destroyed in the rising winds. The story's ending is typically Robison, typically incisive:

> The fan quit by itself, in mid-swing, and the noise from the refrigerator stopped.
> "Uh-oh," Charlie said. "That means the hot water, too."
> He got off the rug and went to the window and stood holding back the curtain. "It looks like a good one," he said. "How about flying your kites from the porch roof, if I rip up an old bedsheet? For the tails, I mean. You want to climb out there and try it?"
> "I do," said Don.

End. Finito. Robison shows us everything we need to see, tells us nothing, and we get the point. A beautiful precision.

Sometimes an event of some drama is allowed to intrude, as in "May Queen." A seventeen-year-old girl's dress catches fire from a candle during a religious ceremony vaguely medieval and barbaric. Irony enough in the girl's being "May queen," in the fact that she was about to place a wreath on the head of a statue of the Virgin, object of worship on the day—irony enough, and Robison recognizes the sufficiency, leaves it alone. Waiting for the ambulance, the burned girl's father tries to sooth her:

> "When this thing is over," Mickey said, "and you're taken care of—listen to me, now—we'll go up to Lake Erie, okay? You hear me? How about that? Some good friends of mine, Tad Austin and his wife—you never met them, Riva—have an A-frame on the water there. We can lie around and bake in the sun all day. There's an amusement park, and you'll be eighteen then. You'll be able to drink, if you want to."

There's sympathy here, but also humor—cutting, sad, understated, but humor nonetheless. And even more at the end of the story, when Riva, fed up with her father, simply says: "Will you shut up?" The impeccable ear of a master dialogist.

Always the ruthless surgeon, Robison, when she writes in the omniscient voice, seems almost evil, so cold is the result. But sometimes she risks a warmer point of view, and these stories—"Pretty Ice," "Camilla," and "Widower" among them—are the most successful. "Widower" is told from the point of view of a child reminiscing from the distance of adulthood, and the story shares its poignancy, lets us feel more:

> Nicky got out of bed and came across the room and performed what I thought was a startling and eerily correct

> impersonation of Katherine Hepburn. He said, "Oh, kiss me, Stewart."

Characteristically, relationships and emotions are foggy, sensed rather than known. We're not sure, for instance, if the two men in "Kite and Paint" are lovers; Robison carefully omits the irrelevant, no matter how tantalizing. It's as if we're invisible guests in so many strange homes, visitors to whom nothing can be clear, even with all the evidence of observation. Sometimes we're not even sure a "story" is being told; fortunately, the end is always superbly clinching.

Eight of these stories first appeared in *The New Yorker,* where—short and sweet—they read like bolts of lightning revealing ravages of a storm that the rest of the magazine, with its slick ads and cute cartoons, steadfastly denied. This collection of twenty was much anticipated by readers hoping for confirmation of that slicing talent. The stories flatten and give an odd, myopic view of things when they appear side by side, so that it's difficult to read more than one or two in a sitting, but this could well be a good thing. One by one, they quietly attest to the consistency of Mary Robison's ability, and to the design of her art, its clarity and potential.

Elizabeth Inness-Brown

Rudolfo A. Anaya, Tortuga (Editorial Justa Publications)

The title of Rudolfo Anaya's new novel refers, first, to the "magic mountain" (with a nod here to Thomas Mann) that towers over the hospital for paralytic children, the setting for this *Bildungsroman*; and second, to the nickname of the hero, whose upper torso through half the novel is encased in the hard cast of the "turtle." It also provides the novel with its central metaphor: the movement from dependence to autonomy, and all that entails.

Anaya builds his story with recurring patterns of imagery: water, sun, fire; desert, mountain, sky; the cycle of seasons. The imagery is developed in complex and unexpected ways. For example, early on the water is associated with a maternal healing power; but gradually the metaphor deepens, presents the more ominous possibility of a suffocating reliance. The resolution of this conflict is certainly one of the novel's high points, as the character Tortuga, dumped into the water by accomplices in his suicide attempt, "sheds his shell" and achieves a spiritual rebirth.

Like the Latin American "magic realists," Anaya works at the level of myth, dreams, and fantasy. Indeed, the principal strategy of the novel is to infuse every incident with myth; to expand and combine and deepen the elements of the myths until they become palpable and living.

The strategy is admirable and many times it works. It seems, however, that Anaya tries to include too much, and some of his motifs aren't developed. Also, he sometimes loses control of his narrative voice. Chapter three opens: "The daughter of the sun awoke to weave her blanket with pastel threads. Her soft, coral fingers worked swiftly...." The Homeric rumblings here are confusing; but what is more troubling is the voice of the author entering so obtrusively in the narration.

At bottom, Anaya seems reluctant to let his remarkable images guide the reader, and so he tries to explain precisely what can't be explained, what doesn't *need* explaining. Stylistically, there are a few rough spots in the novel, but the reader who stays with it will find there are many rewards.

Angelo Restivo

Richard Grayson, With Hitler in New York (Taplinger)

"If you have any complaints about *With Hitler in New York,*" the author declares in his dust jacket copy, "address them to the anarchist whose bomb snuffed out the life of the Czar. I take no responsibility for this." This incident, according to Richard Grayson, "led to the Russian pogroms and to the anti-Semitic May laws of 1882." To these latter events, Grayson claims that we owe the myriad contributions of Jewish people to American culture: from Woody Allen and Lenny Bruce to Al Jolson and the Ziegfeld follies; from Nathanael West and Philip Roth to Father Coughlin; and from Mark Spitz to the condominium culture of southern Florida. And last, but presumably not least, to that sequence of events we can attribute this book of stories by Richard Grayson.

Perhaps Grayson should have included the Marx Brothers in his list, for it is their brand of zany humor which this collection frequently—though often unsuccessfully—endeavors to achieve. In the title story, a German character named Hitler visits friends in New York. Together, they do the ordinary things Americans routinely do, such as watch television, swim, and go out to dinner. In this anomaly lies the humor but also the failure of the story. It is amusing, certainly, to see Hitler as an ordinary tourist. Yet it is also disappointing, especially to the reader of Ishmael Reed, E. L. Doctorow, and other contemporary writers who have given us such memorable and outrageously hilarious treatments of historical figures in fictional settings. The mere title "With Hitler in New York" creates expectations which the story itself fails to satisfy.

It is worth noting that despite its title, this book does not belong to the growing list of works which have recently taken a serious interest in the personalities and/or victims of the Third Reich. (Aside from the countless popular novels on Third Reich themes, there have been such works by a number of highly regarded writers: *Sophie's Choice* by William Styron, *The Führer Bunker* by W. D. Snodgrass, and several poems from Ai's recent book, *The Killing Floor,* just to name a few.) It is certainly appropriate that serious writers are becoming concerned with the consequences of fascist thought and practice. This being the case, Grayson's deadpan treatment of Hitler comes across as, at best, cute.

Cuteness is frequently a shortcoming among these stories. Often, clever ideas are not adequately developed. Consequently, some stories such as "Chief Justice Burger, Teen Idol," "Classified Personal," and "The Finest Joe Colletti Story Ever Written (So Far)" seem facile.

Yet some of these pieces are successful. "Lincoln On The Couch" is a skillful portrait of the sixteenth President; and while it may be implausible as history, the story effectively presents an unexpected view of Lincoln as something other than epoch-making paragon. "But In a Thousand Other Worlds" is perhaps the most successful of the humorous pieces. It is the story of a mediocre story that strives to be published. In the course of its odyssey, "But In a Thousand Other Worlds" is condemned as immoral by John Gardner. It retaliates by biting Gardner on the leg.

Despite his preoccupation with nihilist humor, Grayson is at his best in his serious pieces. "Wednesday Night At Our House," "The Princess from the Land of Porcelain," and "Kirchbachstrasse 121, 2800 Bremen" are the strongest stories in the book. All of them sensitively probe the dynamics of personalities and relationships.

David Lionel Smith

Ishmael Reed, Shrovetide in Old New Orleans (Avon)

Reed's latest collection of essays, reviews, and interviews is aptly titled, especially if one considers that Mardi Gras in that charming, poetic city just might be an index to the total environment from which "literature" is produced in the twentieth century. Anyone who has followed Reed's work from *catechism of d neoamerican hoodoo church* through *A Secretary to the Spirits,* has watched the deadly free-lance pallbearers mumbo jumbo on their flight to Canada, heard the yellow back radio break-down over the last days of Louisiana Red, and caught Reed as pugilist in the mass media—anyone who has been that much into Reed's efforts to explore spatial and temporal possibilities of the word, to discover the repressed humanity of writing, will certainly not be disappointed with *Shrovetide.*

Reed calls the thirty-odd pieces in the book an "installment of an autobiography of my mind." While it is dangerous to take Reed at face value (his ironies will clobber you), in this case it is safe to read the book as the mental autobiography of an engaging, brilliant, provocative writer. It is the life of a mind dedicated to bringing the enigmas of America, and selected cultural crimes, into court for cross-examination. We may not agree with the verdicts. We may scream for a retrial. But we leave *Shrovetide* cleansed of illusions. Reed's deft handling of satire and comedy as strategies for projecting the seriousness of issues is effective. In the post-Kantian world of modern literature, seriousness must be masked as triviality. The pieces collected in *Shrovetide* demonstrate how skillfully Reed walks the tightrope.

Reed's fiction always has revealed an obsession with the problematic relationships that exist between the self and the narrowly defined space the self is asked to inhabit. As instruments of revolutionary discovery and readjustment, his novels reaffirm the power of the intuitive over the rational. The same applies with his poetry, rituals of demystification. His preoccupations fit well with the themes of hedonism, responsibility, confession, absolution, and penance developed in this "autobiography of mind." Whether he is giving his version of carnival in the Crescent City, providing overdue attention to the work of David Henderson and Chester Himes, defining the problems of the literary establishment, or conducting self-analysis by way of self-interview, Reed brings remarkable control to his writing. Readers are cajoled into righteous indignation.

Shrovetide explains something about Ishmael Reed that was predicted in Genesis: "And he will be a wild man; his hand will be against every man, and every man's hand against him; and he shall dwell in the presence of all his brethren." Knowing that, one can enjoy *Shrovetide* as affirming celebration and a sagacious tonic.

Jerry W. Ward

David Porush, Rope Dances
(Fiction Collective)

Imagine yourself slumped in a thread-bare chair, positioned before a darkened movie screen, isolated and anxious. This cinematic tableau, far more appropriate than its literary counterpart, will prepare you for *Rope Dances,*

David Porush's first collection of short stories. These disturbing tales
shadow the inevitable disintegration of our fantasies into the petty and
barbarous rituals that daily demonstrate our need for one another. But "la
vie quotidienne" is not what fashions this author's universe. Instead, as if
in the throes of a Hitchcock or Corman nightmare, the reader becomes a
captive voyeur to a series of grotesque events that sicken and titillate simultaneously. Porush's special talent becomes evident as he plunders and ex-
pertly dramatizes our deepest desires.

Porush's is a laconic style, his careful juxtapositions providing rich irony
at every turn. His prose is always flowing and precise though never predictable. The quality of his language evokes the prose poem, where every
word counts. Yet Porush's chief power lies in his talent as an imaginative
story-teller.

The collection is divided into three sections—"Frayed Threads," "Dream
Strings," and "Rope Dances"—that trace Porush's subtle attitudinal shifts
towards the human condition. A favorite piece, "The Somnambulists," explores one level of Hell:

> Beauty is a vehicle for nightmare, a point of disarming cyclop's
> vision that drives through unnamed barriers and then looks
> out when you're not looking through your horrified eyes.

Here is the living contradiction of the dream that does not dream. The protagonist finds himself tormented by dreams of his twin's destruction. Such
drama foils the commonplace nature of his sadistic relationship with his
girlfriend. His inescapable role in their "rope dances," executed with violent sexual tension, mocks him unrelentingly. Finally, he must choose between culpability and eternal sleep.

The other stories range from "Imperial Place," a disquieting account of
a Western diplomat stationed in a chaotic, third-world country who relives
his past as "a series of discontinuous horrors," to "Venetian Blind," a humorous chronicle of one man's obsessive compulsion to project both his
wife's infidelity and his subsequent voyeurism. "King Kong Dismembered"
dishes out a do-it-yourself recipe for debunking the myths behind the Great
Ape's appeal, while "Rope Dances"—the most conceptual and unfortunately, also the most belabored piece—examines the minute cruelties intimates
inflict upon each other.

When we choose to surrender our sensibilities to a master filmmaker, it
is in anticipation of a rare pleasure. David Porush's *Rope Dances* calls for
the same surrender.

Julie Siegel

Paul Bowles, Collected Stories, 1939-1976
(Black Sparrow Press)

There is little doubt that Paul Bowles is one of the most important—if largely unrecognized—influences on contemporary American literature. His novels and stories are startling, violent, and disturbing enough not to be easily forgotten. For over thirty years, Bowles has been exploring themes involving the contrasts between the primitive and civilized, the impossibility of love, and of nature that is typified by chaotic violence—breakthrough themes in the non-realistic tradition of contemporary literature. As with other neglected American writers such as B. Traven, Bowles has spent most of his life in Latin America and Morocco, where he continues to live. His first story appeared in the late thirties, a branching out from his studies as a composer. *Collected Stories 1939-1976* covers over thirty years of his writing. Chronologically arranged, it marks the re-appearance of many out-of-print stories.

A strange transformation in character and setting takes place when we enter the world of the Bowles story. A "civilized" outsider finds himself or herself surrounded by the sounds and smells of the rain forests of Latin America or the harsh desert of North Africa. Something takes hold of this character immersed in this foreign setting as he or she moves among the strange sounds and colors of this world. The rattling sound of a jungle insect, the persistent growth of vegetation as it chokes out human activity, puts this character face to face with a violent topography—the booming silent sounds of the abyss. Contact with the primitive world seems to strike a corresponding chaotic chord which easily undermines the identity of the character—and of the reader.

The results are startling. In stories such as "At Paso Rojo" or "Pastor Dowe at Tacate," a character becomes suddenly violent or sadistic, erratic and unpredictable as his or her civilized notions are shaken to their very roots. Bowles utterly rejects the traditional notion that nature equals serenity and order but instead sees, as many very recent writers do, nature as a violent exercise in disorder.

Human nobility is absent in these stories. In "The Delicate Prey" a young boy is raped and mutilated by a traveling companion, and this man is in turn methodically tortured when found out by neighboring villagers. A reader can never forget the transformation that takes place in a character called the Professor in "A Distant Episode" as his curiosity about primitive North African tribes is ended by violent capture and the slitting out of his tongue so that he will better serve his "new" purpose as valuable object and trained animal for the tribe. These pre-Kosinski stories clearly illustrate the disturbing results of an intersection between primitive and civilized mentalities, and most importantly reflect the violent act as central to the natural world.

The chronological arrangement of his collection demonstrates Bowles' development as a writer of stories containing vague undefined characters who are subservient to the horrors of a natural setting that develops a strangely character-like presence. "The Circular Valley" presents the setting in the form of unusual deities invading the insides of animals, including humans, who enter a primitive valley, causing violent and unexplainable results. Surely the concept of character is not sacred in Bowles. His stories move from the identity of a character invaded by the jungle setting to a character controlled and finally overpowered by a re-occurring dream—"A Thousand Days for Mokhtar" in high Borgesian fashion.

This Bowles retrospective, *Collected Stories,* represents the work of an innovator in American literature who seeks to debunk apparent order residing deep within nature and to dismiss man's reasoning power over the world as irrelevant hallucination. As with the finest of contemporary works, the thrust of the Bowles story rests in the disjointed ambiguity of human activity rather than the germ of order in a world, as Kosinski put it, where identity cannot exist, only situations. Paul Bowles mixes disharmonious elements of reality, the jungles working within the imaginative framework of human-like impulses and actions, to create a character of chaotic situation, rather than a stable identity. This personification of the setting, in the end, meshes with the violent jungle of human situation— posing as human identity.

Thus, Bowles' *Collected Stories* take the arguable position that rationality and pragmatism, the hallmarks of contemporary Western Civilization— our "rage for order"—appear to be hollow gestures in the face of the jungles that appear before us or within us.

Michael Krekorian

David Ray, The Mulberries of Mingo (Cold Mountain Press)

In the space of only six brief stories David Ray goes a long way toward refuting the negative old saws that often accompany the idea of "a Poet's fiction." It's true that Ray's literary reputation has developed from his stature as a distinguished poet and adventuresome editor, but clearly these capabilities only enrich his verbal senses and insights as a storyteller.

Throughout this tightly woven set of short fictions, Ray addresses the physical and emotional hungers of growing up in rural Oklahoma, circa World War II—the sad, desolate barnyard lives of ordinary people scratching out a limited existence in a dust-bowl landscape. Here, for instance, is a recollection of the homefront from the fine story "Grampa's Wagon":

"It was a soggy farm settled into a net of muddy roads and rodlines, those steel connecting rods that slide along little supportive poles set in the fields, rods endlessly pulling and pumping the oil wells, rods radiating uphill and down from a central powerhouse with great wheels always chugging away."

Against this barren backdrop Ray unfurls generous, heartfelt stories of the pursuits of love and emotional survival, told largely from the point of view of a foster child, drifting from the Children's Home to Pops Bowen's tumbledown farm and back again. Yet for all the advanced pains of growing up alone and dislocated, Ray ultimately leaves us with an abiding spirit of faith in self, acknowledging "This is the way of it," and proceeding from there. However bleak in outlook, Ray injects a deep river of sensitivity into his prose, a refreshing clearwater way of talking about memories that matter. This is David Ray's first book of fictions. It serves to beg for others.

G. E. Murray

James Schevill, The Arena of Ants (Copper Beech Press)

James Schevill has taken leave of his senses, which in the case of an author of inventive and meaningful fiction is to say he deserves the very highest praise.

Schevill is an awkward case for critics, and impossible for a casual reader, not only because he leaves the visible world but precisely because he comes back with an elegant summation of possibilities beyond the grasp of our ordinary senses. In the world of Casey Stengel, you can look it up. In the world of James Schevill, you must make a voyage.

The Arena of Ants is about a handful of American soldier-guards and their many German prisoners in an internment camp in Colorado during World War II. One of the captors has killed two Germans in a senseless shooting, and the camp is on the verge of revolt. Thousands of battle-seasoned German troops murmur plots among themselves while ill-trained Americans, assigned to the prison because they are physically unfit for combat, bungle and fidget away control of their captives.

The story unfolds through a shared narrative that flips back and forth between a young American lieutenant with orders to cool the prison heat and a young German with orders to keep his mouth shut and stop thwarting the spreading of terror. The American and the German each tries to save himself by imposing order on the other.

Let us say at once that American literature reverberates with the now tiresome theme of a hero's efforts to pull order from chaos, to confront a mindless world and in it discover the means to say something interesting about himself.

And *The Arena of Ants* would be one more tiresome playback were it not for the sheer depths the story reaches. In plain English, the American and the German reach a plausible understanding of what compels their fellows to rush toward self-destruction on this desolate strip of home front/ enemy territory.

The American and the German each recalls the things he has experienced but finds no pride or relief and, more important, nothing of much use. There also seem to be some efforts on their parts to contrive things they have never before known, as though they were following their author away from the world of experience to some reservoir of the imagination. And here they stumble into a bizarre world that is unaided by reason or experience, real or contrived. It is a virtual state of unconsciousness, of mere motor-reflexes, where hate is the most persuasive force.

The discovery is neither sudden nor explicit. Rather it is like a composite drawing of a criminal put together by various eyewitnesses. None holds a complete picture—neither saw the culprit completely—but a picture of the culprit nonetheless emerges.

On the surface of things, the American becomes suspect among his officers. The German, diagnosed as a victim of "barbed wire fever" is written off as insane. The German war machine collapses in Europe, averting what was starting to look like an inevitable German victory in Colorado. And, so to speak, everyone goes home. Even the German and the American go home, though they will never again trust the mere look and feel of history.

In a singularly old-fashioned way, Schevill has invented the story—not merely the plot, snatches of which may well be autobiographical—but the bold and delicate story itself which reaches beneath the world of explanations. *The Arena of Ants,* once read, feels as though it will dwell with the reader for a long while to come.

Tim Murray

Tom Clark, Who is Sylvia?
(Blue Wind Press)

For a poet/graduate instructor in American Lit at a British university, American Bob Dark has a depressing amount of free time to roam London reveling in amphetamines and skipping his classes. But, for the six-odd months of 1966 in which Tom Clark's first novel takes place, there is Sylvia, a scarred, enigmatic nymph whose attraction for Bob Dark seems to reside solely in her body and her constant supply of black beetle pills.

Who is Sylvia? is a novel of drugs, action, and atomized human relationships. Dark has spent four years in England, and "dipped his wick with abandon." He is lured from a London poetry reading by Sylvia Pender while her sadist lover Brian McDeath is reading at the podium. Temporarily rescuing her from McDeath's penchant for drawing purple swastikas all over her body during sex, Dark is then dragged into the breakneck pace of Sylvia's pill-popping, and her psychopathic response to anything resembling a sustained relationship.

Her six-month marriage is the first bit of autobiography Sylvia reveals after they get to her apartment and make love. At nineteen, a week into nuptial bliss, Sylvia ran off with a Boston jazz musician, turned onto heroin, and was institutionalized in a catatonic depression after her young, rich American husband found her and carted her home. A suicide attempt and several months of confinement later in London, and Sylvia was released, diagnosed as having an "arrhythmic brain."

Incipient catatonia is a haunting presence throughout the book, forever evaded by drug-induced euphoria. When Bob meets her, Sylvia had been "out dancing five or six nights a week. She saw a number of men. She developed an interest in poetry and started going to readings around London. She heard Brian McDeath read his poems. The poems made no particular impression on her, but when McDeath asked her out, she went. And she slept with him, naturally." Dark and Sylvia spend their time together on great sleepless rampages of sex, sight-seeing tours, and visiting with Sylvia's cousin, Caroline.

Isolation and the degeneration of relationships infect every character in this book. Sylvia's cousin is in the process of divorcing her husband Paul, and at the artist's colony in Vence, France, where she accompanies Dark for the summer, monotony and nonproductivity are rapidly eroding the marriage of Susan and David. Even the bilious Madame O. of the colony strikes out from a festering solitude.

"Bob had latched onto Sylvia out of loneliness, and likewise she to him. Together they'd been able to drown their separate alonenesses in a sympathetic bond neither of them had understood. Now in isolation they began to grow back into those old lonelinesses."

It is almost as if these characters can't help themselves to dissolve the barriers to intimacy. The despondency and malaise from which they are fleeing (and by fleeing, defining as their prisons) is too strong to combat. Bob and Sylvia never really talk to each other. For all he knows of her past, Dark keeps Sylvia at a distinct distance from any contact with the substance of his own being, his poetry. After weeks of nothing more than an ancient stack of *Life* magazines to divert her in Vence while Dark writes, it is not surprising that Sylvia enters another depression. "Still," Dark reflects, "it surprised him that he knew so little about what made her tick, even now. Was she really 'crazy'?"

The poignant loneliness that pervades this book surfaces most clearly when Dark is alone in his seaside cottage. For all that has not been said, or shared, he wonders if perhaps he doesn't love her.

Who is Sylvia? has been compared to the expatriate novels of the 20s and 30s, and in its portrayal of ennui, faulty human connections, and escapism, it is a worthy analogue. The journalistically lean prose recalls Hemingway's gritty realism. People meet in loneliness, and fall away for the same reasons. Their hold on a locale is casual at best. But the difference is that these characters don't talk about hope or despair as their literary grandparents did. They are terser, if that is possible. They act and react on a surface of language transparent as glass.

Kathleen Hirsch

Kelly Cherry, Augusta Played
(Houghton-Mifflin)

Imagine for a moment something quite different in the way of a new novel. Assume that the author has managed to blend two wildly-different strains—the stylized comedy of Sheridan and Congreve, and the sweet-astringent sense of modern life felt in such movies as *Manhattan*—and has produced a brilliant hybrid. Broad farce somehow combined with an elegant style of epigram. And further imagine that there are two chief characters, lover-antagonists, named Augusta (Gus) and Norman and that both are wonderfully drawn, nicely articulated in every action and emotion, completely appealing. "Margaret Drabble has given us a masterpiece of wit," says the *New York Times*. Or—"Joan Didion shows a simply dazzling talent," says the *Chicago Sun-Times.*

It's all true except for the part about Drabble or Didion. Neither is capable of the novel I've described—but, if she were, the reviews would read something like my quotes. Instead, the book was written by a relatively unknown writer named Kelly Cherry, as yet unranked in the celebrity list. The result was that most of the reviews ranged from bored incomprehension to displays of malice by Alice Adams in the *Sun-Times* and Nora Johnson in the *New York Times.*

But that—the ineptitude of most newspaper reviewers—is an old subject and non-famous novelists will have to continue to suffer from it. One of the commonplaces of literary small-talk is the notion that fashion, no matter how ignorant it may be, cannot obscure a good book forever. We all know the famous examples of course—*Leaves of Grass, The Charterhouse of Parma, Moby-Dick.* It will be interesting to see if the old rule of survival and revival works in the case of *Augusta Played* or if the debased currency of popular fiction drives out the one genuine gold piece of wit circulated in 1979.

Pamela Painter

Jonathan Baumbach, The Return of Service (University of Illinois Press)

Jonathan Baumbach's fiction takes place somewhere in a buoyant region of the intellect, where what is real is only the process of writing itself, those moments of invention, fantasy, play. So, *if it ain't nailed down, it's up for grabs, and if it kin be pried up, it ain't nailed down*—Baumbach steals, mimics, parodies, puns, slapsticks, jokes, and puts the fictive back in fiction. Here, among other things, we find a parody of *The Maltese Falcon* ("Another Look at the Blackbird"), another of *King Kong* ("King Dong"), and a third on the werewolf theme ("The Curse"). Punny titles: "A Moving Story," a story literally about moving, and "The Return of Service," which is about—you guessed it—tennis. And in the satirical vein: "The Traditional Story Returns," in which the traditional story does not, and "Neglected Masterpieces IV," in which, in a way, it does.

My favorites—I enjoyed all twelve—are two whose protagonist is referred to only as "the baby." Remember that old TV series in which a baby was given the voice, sophistication, and wit to comment on the strange behavior of his elders? Looks like Baumbach does. In "Crossed by the Love in Her Eyes," the baby falls in love with his babysitter, Marie. Skirting the edge of cuteness quite successfully, the baby enters his father's study for serious man-to-man talk:

> "When you're married," he asks after a point, "does that mean you have to sleep in the same bed as the other person?" He asks the question with both hands over his face, one eye peering through the slats of his fingers.
> "Only if both people want to," I say.
> "Well, both people do want to," he says, "and that's final." He does a parody of his father storming furiously out of a room.
> He returns. "What about love?" he asks.

The rise and fall of the baby's romance with Marie is not a children's story, believe me, though it may well be the story of a child.

A bit more serious in tone, "Disguises" is a story of early initiation with Freudian undertones, in which the baby's identity as *the* baby is threatened by the birth of an imposter, his new brother. Off he goes to reclaim his rights as progenitor, even fabricating a mask so that he can impersonate his former self—but nothing is the same anymore, now that his parents have betrayed him. But what if it's his parents who are imposters? He forms an alliance with his brother against them, but even this solves nothing, as he knows in his heart—

> One day he will wake up from a different dream no longer himself, transformed in his sleep as his parents had been, as others will be, into a perfect imitation of the real thing. It is his fortune, he supposes. It is the way things are.

This ironic voice, coming from some unshared inside knowledge of "things," owes an allegiance to Kafka, or to that which is Kafkaesque. In "Birthday Gifts," there is a recognition of the dreaminess of waking existence, of the unsolvability of the mystery of our lives, that reminds of Kafka's *The Trial.* But an edge of self-parody in Baumbach's style lifts this recognition from despair to humor; where Kafka may have been almost alone in viewing his work as funny, I doubt that'll happen to Baumbach. In "Birthday Gifts," the narrator's father brings a roomful of strangers to help celebrate "a former birthday uncommemorated in its time," giving his son a box of birds as a gift; there is a character called "K"; a sniper, bizarrely unnoticed, shoots up the street below his window; and a presidential candidate and his entourage are trapped in a Twilight Zone traffic jam.

Like Kafka, Baumbach explores the possibility of *time* as a character, referring to its presence often and strangely. In "Birthday Gifts," the statement *The time of the man who waits will come* nearly becomes a refrain, reverberating in this passage near the end:

> "Just take your time," says the candidate. "They can't do anything until we get there."
> "What's the latest?" I ask the interpreter.
> "They've stopped voting," she says. "Everything's at a standstill."

In another Kafkaesque tale, a baseball story called "The Fields of Obscurity," time, the ordering of events, takes on an oddly familiar fluidity:

> One day he was on the bench watching a game and he daydreamed that he was in the clubhouse watching a movie of a game played the day before. It might even have been an old game, the cinematic representation of former glories. When you weren't playing, and even sometimes when you were, one game could seem very much like another.

In one way, these stories are about nothing so much as they are about storytelling itself, the ordering of events, the losing and finding of the

Publisher addresses: Editorial Justa Publications, P.O. Box 9128, Berkeley, CA 94709; Cold Mountain Press, P.O. Box 5765, Austin, TX 78763; Copper Beech Press, P.O. Box 1852/Brown University, Providence, RI 02912; Blue Wind Press, P.O. Box 7175, Berkeley, CA 94707.

thread of narrative. What makes them very fine—aside from the quality of the imagining and rendering—is Baumbach's willingness to embrace and acknowledge his sources, and to give up the ghost of probability to chase the specter (a shady lady, no doubt) of possibility.

Elizabeth Inness-Brown

ing at Skidmore College in Saratoga Springs.

T. CORAGHESSAN BOYLE's novel, *Water Music,* will be published by Atlantic-Little, Brown in the fall of 1981. Excerpts appear in current and upcoming issues of *Antaeus* and *Paris Review.* His story collection, *Descent of Man,* has just been released in paperback from McGraw-Hill.

ELIZABETH COX lives in Durham, North Carolina, with her husband and two children. Her poems have appeared in *Southern Poetry Review, Greensboro Review, Hyperion,* and others. A chapbook of poetry, entitled *White Sugar Candy,* was recently published by Coraddi Press.

JOHN DOMINI has published both fiction and nonfiction in many magazines, including *Sports Illustrated* and *Paris Review.* He has won a grant from the National Endowment for the Arts, teaches writing part-time at Harvard, and is working on a novel.

CASTLE FREEMAN, JR. lives near Brattleboro, Vermont. "Seven Prophecies of Egypt" is his first published story.

CURTIS HARNACK's most recent book is the novel *Limits of the Land,* published in 1979 by Doubleday. *Under My Wings Everything Prospers,* a collection of short fiction, was published in 1977.

LAMAR HERRIN teaches at Cornell. His first novel, *The Rio Loja Ringmaster,* was published by Viking in 1977, and his second novel, *American Baroque,* will appear in the fall of 1980 as an original paperback from Avon. He has published stories in *Paris Review, Epoch,* and *Bennington Review,* and he won the Aga Kahn prize for fiction in 1974.

ELIZABETH INNESS-BROWN teaches at the Center for Writers at the University of Southern Mississippi in Hattiesburg. Her work has been published in the *North American Review* and elsewhere.

HAROLD JAFFE's novel, *Mole's Pity,* was published in 1979 by the Fiction Collective, and his latest, *Dos Indios,* is scheduled for release in Canada in 1980. He has published fiction, verse, articles, and reviews in *Aspect, Confrontation, Poetry Northwest, Beloit Poetry Journal, The Nation, The New York Times, Commonweal, The Windsor Review, American Book Review,* and elsewhere.

DAVID LONG's book of poems, *Early Returns,* is due out from Jawbone Press in Seattle. His fiction has been published in *North American Review, Northwest Review, Confrontation,* and *Canto,* among others.

DEBBY MAYER won a Creative Artists Public Service (CAPS) grant in fiction writing in 1979. She has published stories in *Redbook* and *Gallimaufry* and is editor of *Coda: Poets & Writers Newsletter.*

ROBERT A. MORACE has published criticism in *Studies in the Novel, Markham Review, Journal of American Culture,* and *American Literary Realism.* He is at work on a collection of essays on John Gardner (with Kathryn VanSpanckeren) and a John Gardner bibliography.

JOYCE CAROL OATES is currently teaching at Princeton. Her forthcoming novel is entitled *Bellefleur.*

JAYNE ANNE PHILLIPS recently received the $1000 Sue Kaufman Prize from the American Academy and Institute of Arts and Letters for her book *Black Tickets* published by Seymour Lawrence/Delacorte. This year she will be a Fellow of the Bunting Institute at Radcliffe College.

JAMES PARK SLOAN lives in Chicago and teaches at the University of Illinois at Chicago Circle. His books include *War Games* and *The Case History of Comrade V.*

BRIAN STONEHILL is Assistant Professor of English at Pomona College, where he teaches courses on James Joyce and Contemporary Fiction. He is currently completing a study of self-conscious fiction entitled *Art Displaying Art.*

JEAN THOMPSON is the author of *The Gasoline Wars* published by the University of Illinois Press. Her fiction has appeared widely in magazines such as *Carolina Quarterly, Mississippi Review,* and *Ploughshares* and in *The Best American Short Stories 1979.*

JOY WILLIAMS won the 1980 National Magazine Award in the fiction category for her story, "The Farm," which appeared in *Antaeus.* Her novel *The Changeling* was published in 1978, and *State of Grace* was nominated for the National Book Award in 1973. Her stories have appeared in *Esquire* and *Paris Review.* She lives on Siesta Key, Florida.

ROBLEY WILSON, JR. is the well-known author of *The Pleasures of Manhood* (University of Illinois Press) and *Living Alone* (fiction international). His story "Living Alone" appeared in *The Best American Short Stories 1979,* and he is currently at work on a novel.

RAMSAY WOOD is an American who lives in Scotland and England. He attended schools in Europe, the Philippines, and the United States, including Harvard, where he majored in English.

LEE ZACHARIAS is the coordinator of the writing program at the University of North Carolina at Greensboro, editor of *Greensboro Review,* and a National Endowment for the Arts grant recipient. Her first volume of short fiction, *Helping Muriel Make It Through the Night,* was published by Louisiana State University Press in 1976.

Four new collections
in the program
William Peden has called
**"one of the most significant
undertakings in contemporary
university publishing."**

ILLINOIS SHORT FICTION 1979

Jonathan Baumbach **THE RETURN OF SERVICE**

This is the first short story collection of Baumbach, one of the founders of the Fiction Collective and co-director of the MFA program in creative writing at Brooklyn College. His novels include *A Man to Conjure With* and *Reruns*, and he has had stories included in both of the annual anthologies of best American stories. ". . . an exceptional writer, one of the best I know—inventive, controlled, witty, sensitive . . . I can think of few authors who could deliver an entire set of stories of such class as these." —Robert Coover.

Gladys Swan **ON THE EDGE OF THE DESERT**

"Each of these fine short stories reveals ghosts from the past. Misfits, loners and wanderers in the desolate Southwest—people living at the edges of society—recall the searches and escapes that have brought them to the present." —*Publishers Weekly*. Swan's stories have appeared in *Virginia Quarterly Review, Colorado Quarterly, Maine Review, Great Lakes Review,* and *Cumberlands*. This collection was a semifinalist in the award series in short fiction of the Associated Writing Programs. Swan teaches at Franklin College in Indiana.

Barry Targan **SURVIVING ADVERSE SEASONS**

Targan's first published collection won the Iowa Award for short fiction in 1975. The title story of this second collection appeared in *Best American Short Stories, 1976*. His work has also appeared in *Sewanee Review, Esquire,* and other journals. He teaches creative writing at the State University of New York at Binghamton. "Barry Targan is, quite simply, one of the best short story writers we have. And here he is writing at the top of his form." —Robert Boyers, editor of *Salmagundi*.

Jean Thompson **THE GASOLINE WARS**

"Four talented enough stories, surrounded by six absolutely wonderful ones that are aglint with a naturalness, a humor, and an off-centered instinct for what really matters to people. . . . A sterling debut." —*Kirkus Reviews*. "With apparent facility, Thompson captures a wonderful range of characters and lifestyles. This is her first collection of stories; one hopes there are many more to come." —*Publishers Weekly*. Thompson teaches creative writing at the University of Illinois at Urbana-Champaign.

UNIVERSITY OF ILLINOIS PRESS
Box 5081, Station A   Champaign, IL 61820

Cloth—$10.00 each
Paper—$3.95 each

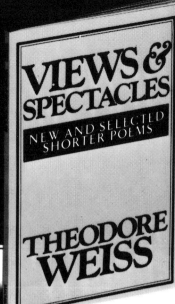

ANNOUNCING...

The Drue Heinz Literature Prize

The University of Pittsburgh Press and the Howard Heinz Endowment announce the Drue Heinz Literature Prize for a collection of short fiction. The prize consists of a cash award of $5,000 and publication by the University of Pittsburgh Press.

The contest is open to writers who have published book-length collections of fiction or a minimum of three short stories in commercial magazines or literary journals of national distribution. Submissions should consist of a manuscript of short stories or novellas, and should be of no fewer than 150 and no more than 300 typescript pages; work previously published in book form may not be included. Manuscripts will be judged anonymously by a screening panel consisting of three writers and editors, and by a final judge who is a nationally known author of fiction. The winner will be announced during December 1980.

The prize has been established to support the writer of short fiction at a time when the economics of commercial publishing make it more and more difficult for serious literary artists working in the short story and novella to find publication.

The Howard Heinz Endowment has long supported a variety of projects in the arts and education. The University of Pittsburgh Press for fourteen years has published the Pitt Poetry Series, one of the best-known publishing ventures of its kind. In 1979 one of its poets, Odysseus Elytis, received the Nobel Prize for Literature.

Writers should request the complete rules governing the competition from: Drue Heinz Literature Prize, University of Pittsburgh Press, Pittsburgh, PA 15260.

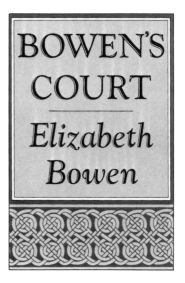

BOUNDARY/2: a journal of postmodern literature

announces two forthcoming special issues

Revisions of the Anglo-American Tradition

Winter 1979 (VII/2): Part I

PAUL BOVÉ, Nietzsche's *Use and Abuse of History* and the Problems of Revision

EUGENE VANCE, Chaucer's *House of Fame* and the Poetics of Inflation

MEREDITH SKURA, New Interpretations for Interpretation in *Measure for Measure*

MARGARET FERGUSON, Sidney's *A Defence of Poetry*: A Retrial

MICHAEL HAYS, *King Lear* and the Social Uses of Irony

GERALD GILLESPIE, Scientific Discourse and Postmodernity: Francis Bacon and "Revision"

JAMES BUNN, The Tory View of Geography

WILLIAM WARNER, Temporality and Authority in a Scene of Richardson's *Clarissa*

HOMER BROWN, *Tom Jones*: The "Bastard" of History

C. H. KNOBLAUCH, Samuel Johnson and the "Prose of the World"

JERROLD HOGLE, The Self in Godwin's *Things As They Are*

THOMAS McFARLAND, Beyond the Heavens: Being, Transcendence, and Symbolic Wholeness

Spring 1979 (VII/3): Part II

CYRUS HAMLIN, The Hermeneutics of Form: Reading the Romantic Ode

JONATHAN ARAC, Bounding Lines: The *Prelude* and Criticism

CAROL JACOBS, *Wuthering Heights*: At the Threshold of Interpretation

KARL KROEBER, Deconstructionist Criticism and American Indian Literature

JOHN CARLOS ROWE, The Language of Being in *A Week on the Concord and Merrimack Rivers*

JOSEPH RIDDEL, The "Crypt" of Edgar Poe

EDGAR DRYDEN, Melville's *Pierre* and the Problem of Reading

DANIEL O'HARA, "The Designated Light": Irony in Emily Dickinson

NATHAN A. SCOTT, JR., Santayana's Poetics of Belief

WILLIAM SPANOS, Repetition in *The Waste Land*: A Phenomenological De-struction

boundary 2, SUNY-Binghamton, Binghamton, NY 13901

Subscriptions (three issues): $10 individuals, $7 students, $15 institutions; $4 single issues; add $1 overseas postage

ASPEN ANTHOLOGY

Featuring the best in contemporary fiction, poetry, essays, interviews and book reviews

Published twice annually in Aspen, Colorado, by Aspen Leaves, Inc., a Colorado nonprofit corporation and public educational foundation, with a press run of 1000 copies. Subscriptions, advertising, submissions and correspondence: Box 3185, Aspen, CO 81611; telephone: 303/925-8750. Submissions will not be returned without a stamped, self-addressed envelope of appropriate size, and no photocopies will be considered.

The Georgia Review

Winter 1979

Focus on Women Writers

❧Eudora Welty's "Later Thoughts" on her first published story (1936): *Death of a Traveling Salesman*, here reprinted in its original form.

❧Flannery O'Connor and Caroline Gordon's Correspondence—a preview selection by Sally Fitzgerald

❧Harriette Simpson Arnow—a newly discovered story and an essay on her work by Glenda Hobbs

❧Other essays on Eudora Welty, Gertrude Stein, Flannery O'Connor, and Mercy Warren (America's first dramatist)

❧*GRAPHIC FEATURES:* The Folk Art of Mattie Lou O'Kelley. Also some previously unpublished photos of Flannery O'Connor.

❧*NEW FICTION AND POETRY* by Joyce Carol Oates, Mary Hood, Marilyn Waniek, Ellen Bryant Voigt, Kelly Cherry, Susan Ludvigson, Linda Pastan, Siv Cedring Fox, Debora Greger, Rita Dove, Katherine Soniat, Paula Rankin, Betty Adcock, Mary Oliver, and many others.

❧*BOOK REVIEWS* by such critics as Peter Stitt, Christine Lahey-Dolega, Brina Caplan, Stephen Tapscott, Iris Tillman Hill, Diane Cole, and more.

"A quantity of quality" . . . "the best bargain in American publishing today."

Please enter my subscription to *The Georgia Review* (4 issues per year):

___ 1 yr/$6   ___ 2 yrs/$10   (outside U.S. add $1/yr—U.S. funds only)

Name: _____

Address: _____

City _____ State _____ Zip _____

The Georgia Review is published by the University of Georgia, Athens, Georgia 30602

MR 25/26

MISSISSIPPI REVIEW / $4.50

MISSISSIPPI REVIEW IS PUBLISHED THREE TIMES A YEAR BY THE CENTER FOR WRITERS, SOUTHERN STATION, BOX 5144, HATTIESBURG, MISSISSIPPI 39401. SUBSCRIPTION RATES: ONE YEAR $8.00; TWO YEARS $14.00; THREE YEARS $20.00. FOREIGN SUBSCRIPTIONS $2.00 PER YEAR ADDITIONAL.

fiction international

Reviews of Gail Godwin, Margaret Atwood, Ishmael Reed, Vance Bourjaily, Bernard Kaplan, Rosellen Brown, Raymond Carver, Andre Dubus, Alice Walker, Mark J. Mirsky, Iris Murdoch, and others.

8/9   *Living Alone*—Fictions by Robley Wilson, Jr.

Sixteen fictions ranging in subject matter from the commonplaces of domestic and illicit togetherness, to the mythologies of love and death in America. Here are gangs of adolescent girls who systematically "violate" innocent men, a middle-aged accountant enslaved by the fattest woman in the world, a father who perceives his children as animals, a poet who volunteers for the U.S. astronaut program.

Title story selected for inclusion in *Best American Short Stories 1979.*

10/11   *Tranquillity Base and Other Stories* by Asa Baber.

Twelve short stories whose citizens abide in Chicago, in the Orient, in Greece, in Twain's Hannibal, but most often in the twitching center of paranoia, on the razor edge of unreality. Delightful, horrifying tales filled with the sad irony of modern isolation, informed by a surreal vision and by precise, convincing knowledge of an eccentric world.

Title story chosen for inclusion in *The Pushcart Prize V: Best of the Small Presses.*

YES! I WOULD LIKE TO SUBSCRIBE !
(Individuals only. Institutional rates on request.)

Please enter my subscription to **fiction international** for:

□ one year (#12) — $5.00
□ two years (#12, 13) — $8.00
□ three years (#12, 13, 14) — $11.00

_____
(Name)

_____
(Street Address)

_____
(City, State, Zip Code)

fiction international
St. Lawrence University
Canton, N.Y. 13617

Send the following back issues:

SAVE — *take 30% off order of any two or more back issues!*

Quantity	Issue	Price
( )	2/3	$3.50
( )	4/5	$3.50
( )	6/7	$3.50
( )	8/9	$5.00
( )	10/11	$5.00
( )	SPECIAL PRICE! Complete set (5 issues) —$15	

(Issue #1 available on microfilm)

I enclose $ _____ (subscription)
             $ _____ (back issues)
             $ _____ Total